日本生物武器作战调查资料

〔日〕近藤昭二　王　选／主编

第六册

社会科学文献出版社
SOCIAL SCIENCES ACADEMIC PRESS (CHINA)

目　录

8　美国海军情报局技术情报中心报告

9　指控——盟军总司令部法务局调查

8　美国海军情报局技术情报中心报告

8.1 5 Aug. 1947: Naval Aspects of Biological Warfare, From: Chief of Naval Intelligence

资料出处： National Archives of the United States, R330, E199, B103.

内容点评： 本资料为 1947 年 8 月 5 日美国海军情报部部长 T.B.Inglis 海军上校提交的有关细菌战报告，又称 Inglis 报告，由美海军情报部技术情报中心制作，题目：海军角度的细菌战。

4 June 1948

REAR ADMIRAL INGLIS
CHIEF OF NAVAL INTELLIGENCE

A copy of the report named on the attached ~~list~~ slip is desired for the use of this office.

A copy for retention is preferred, or if such is not available, we would like to borrow a copy for about two weeks.

Could we get this today?

Respectfully,

CAB
C.A.Buchanan

CAB:sdh

NAVY DEPARTMENT
OFFICE OF THE CHIEF OF NAVAL OPERATIONS
Washington 25, D. C.

Op-32-F24/ms
(SC)P2-2
~~TOP SECRET~~
Serial 0003217P32

5 AUG 1947

From: Chief of Naval Intelligence.
To: Distribution List.

Subject: Naval Aspects of Biological Warfare.

1. This report has been prepared by the Technical Intelligence Center of the Office of Naval Intelligence as the result of a study of all available information on this subject. In order to present as accurate a picture as possible, the information in this report has been correlated with that information available in the Biological Warfare Section of the Scientific Branch, Intelligence Division, War Department General Staff, and reviewed by the naval members of the Biological Warfare Committee.

/s/ THOS. B. INGLIS

THOS. B. INGLIS
Rear Admiral, U. S. Navy
Chief of Naval Intelligence

DISTRIBUTION LIST

Admiral Leahy
SecNav
Op-00
Op-09
Op-001
Op-03
Op-30
Op-34
Op-36
Op-04
Op-05
Op-50
Op-52
Op-57
BuMed (3)
BuShips
BuOrd
BuAer
BuY&D
CIG (4)
G-2 (7)
AID (via 32V)
ONR
CinCPac (2)
CinLant (2)
Op-20-Z
JRDB (Committee X)

JAPAN

In both Germany and Japan, the heads of government forbade the use of B.W. as a weapon of offense; this, however, did not prevent the carrying on of research. In the case of Japan, moreover, research extended to the use of human beings as subjects—the only admitted occurrence of this kind. Further, the KWANTUNG ARMY launched actual B.W. attacks against the Chinese. Briefly, the tactics were as follows: After the Chinese had been driven back from certain defensive positions along a railroad, the Japanese would then spread the desired B.W. material over the area. A "strategic retreat" would follow. Of the 12 attacks of this kind, nine gave positive results; i.e., plague, cholera, or typhoid developed. In one area where 96 cases of plague broke out, 90 percent proved fatal.

According to the Chinese, in 1940 and 1941 the Japs dropped cereal grains mixed with infected fleas over CHUSIEN,NINGPO, and CHANGTEH. Bubonic plague broke out in those areas, where there had never been plague before. Chinese claims have been verified by the admissions of Japanese B.W. personnel and by American investigators.

BOEKI KYUSUI BU (Organization for B.W.) engaged in research on the instigation and prevention of anthrax, typhoid, plague, cholera, "Songo" fever, and other diseases. The work on vaccines was extensive, 20 million dosages being produced annually. The life-span of numerous strains of microorganisms was investigated, as were bacterial clouds, plant pathogens, and animal diseases. Ground-contaminating and wound-infecting bombs were developed and given field trials, in some instances against humans. Experiments with cholera, plague, and anthrax on MANCHURIAN criminals who had been sentenced to death were conducted.

In spite of the enthusiasm with which the research program was invested, Japanese B.W. had but a limited success. One reason is that close cooperation between the munitions designers and the biologists was lacking; hence the weapons were not truly efficient. Another deterring factor was the failure to increase appreciably the viability of B.W. agents except that of anthrax spores; still another, the personal objections of the Emperor.

Had they been able to provoke one or more full-scale epidemics, as

contrasted with the isolated outbreaks that were started, the Japanese would have had a powerful weapon for use in their theatre of war where sanitation is at a low level.

As for the future, should vigilant supervision over scientific research be relaxed, Japan could continue its pursuit of B.W. knowledge; and, if so desired, could probably wage effective biological warfare within five years after the removal of Allied control.

ITALY

The Italians were unable to realize a successful B.W. program although they engaged in research and field trials from 1934 to 1940. Italy did not benefit from the extensive knowledge possessed by the other Axis partners in this field. Italian researchers, however, have said that they feel the development of methods of biological warfare are well within their capabilities.

If Allied control of Italy were to be withdrawn, it is thought that this country could, with intensive effort and the correction of past mistakes, be ready to wage biological warfare in about five years.

SWEDEN, SWITZERLAND, BELGIUM, AND THE NETHERLANDS

While these countries cannot be said to have biological warfare programs as such, research in defensive measures is being carried on to some extent by all of them. Work is being carried on in the university and industrial laboratories under the supervision of military authority. Such projects as there are, are still in a blue-print stage. It is not believed that any of these countries intends to use biological warfare as an offensive weapon.

CHINA

At least five, and probably ten years of intensive research would be required by China before any successful, large-scale use of biological warfare would be possible. Even then, this would only be possible if such a program were organized efficiently in the near future and had the complete backing of governmental authorities. It is believed that at the present time the Chinese Government is not contemplating any such research and development.

INDEX OF APPENDICES

APPENDIX XIII

BIOLOGICAL WARFARE IN JAPAN

INTRODUCTION

Interest in the wartime use of bacterial agents became active in Japan largely through the insistence of General Shiro ISHII. In 1932 General ISHII (then a Major) while visiting in Europe became imbued with the idea that biological warfare must possess distinct possibilities, otherwise, it would not have been outlawed by the League of Nations. The apprehension of a number of Russian spies in 1935 carrying bottles filled with bacteria was capitalized upon by General ISHII in obtaining recognition for his proposed project.

Research directed towards the development of biological weapons was started at the HARBIN MILITARY HOSPITAL in 1935. By 1937 the work had reached the stage where it impressed the highest military authorities, the Japanese War Ministry giving it active support. The project, however, not only failed to receive the approval of the Emperor but was actually forbidden by him.

Failing to obtain the approval of the Emperor, General ISHII proceeded to set up an extensive organization for the investigation of biological warfare as a special sub-division of the WATER PURIFICATION DEPARTMENT of the KWANTUNG ARMY. The sub-division was given the misleading name of "ANTI-EPIDEMIC WATER SUPPLY UNIT". Since General ISHII was in charge of this Department for the Army, he was responsible only to the Commanding General. The fact that the biological warfare project had to be carried on from beginning to end without the knowledge of the Emperor was a most important factor contributing to the weakness in the organizational structure and eventually proved fatal to the complete success of the mission.

THE PINGFAN INSTITUTE

The Pingfan Institute set up by General ISHII south of HARBIN was of considerable size and was largely self-supporting. It comprised about 50 buildings ranging from laboratories and barracks to warehouses and animal sheds.

The personnel under General ISHII, engaged in various phases of the work, amounted to as many as 5000 in 1939. Of these probably 3000 were located at Pingfan, the remainder being scattered about CHINA for the purpose of investigating water supplies.

ACTIVITIES OF THE BOEKI KYUSUIBU AT PINGFAN

Ostensibly the activities of the Institute were divided among four sections:

Section I - Immunology Research (typhoid, dysentery, anthrax, erysipelas, viruses, and rickettsia)

Section II - Epidemiological Research

Section III - Water Supply and Purification

Section IV - Vaccine Production

The biological warfare activities of the Institute were carried on in secret. These had the two-fold purpose of determining:

(1) Methods of culture of biological warfare agents.

(2) Methods of dissemination.

DEFENSIVE RESEARCH

(1) Immunization Research

The spectrum of vaccines produced embraced the following:

(a) Anthrax
(b) Glanders
(c) Typhoid
(d) Paratyphoid A
(e) Paratyphoid B
(f) Cholera
(g) Plague
(h) Epidemic cerebro-spinal meningitis
(i) Typhus
(j) Dysentery
(k) Tuberculosis
(l) Smallpox
(m) Tularemia
(n) Infectious jaundice
(o) Tetanus
(p) Gas gangrene
(q) Undulant fever
(r) "Songo" or epidemic hemorrhagic fever

The magnitude of the project is indicated by the fact that 20,000,000 doses were produced annually.

In preparing typhus vaccine, as many as 50,000 hens and roosters were used to produce fertilized eggs. Two types were produced:

(a) R. M. Vaccine (Rickettsia Mooseri) from the lungs of rats.

(b) R. P. Vaccine (Rickettsia Provasecki) from chicken embryo.

Both vaccines were prepared in the liquid and dry forms.

The dose necessary to prevent the outbreak of an epidemic is believed to be:

R. M. - 1 cc. in the first and 2 cc. in the second injection.
R. P. - 0.5 cc. in the first and 1 cc. in the second injection.

Sufficient R. M. vaccine for six persons can be obtained from one rat. R. P. vaccine for 30 persons can be produced from one egg.

Vaccines for plague, typhoid, dysentery, cholera, and glanders were also developed, the details of which are given later in this report.

(2) Epidemiological Research

The work consisted of a study of methods of epidemic prevention. This involved the disinfection of trucks, equipment, and personnel; mosquito extermination; the use of prophylactics, etc.

(3) Water Supplies

The work of this section embraced the following:

(a) Epidemic Prevention - This includes looking for water sources and water analysis; the purification of water; and the examination of sanitary conditions in the area.

(b) Field Water Purification - This section was attached to the Army. Its duties were to supply water to the armed forces, to provide serums and vaccines in case of epidemics, and to have charge of quarantines.

(c) Fixed Water Purification - The section supplied water to lines of communication, prepared Army vaccines and serums, did research on vaccines, serums, and sanitary procedures, and provided training in epidemic prevention and sanitation.

OFFENSIVE RESEARCH

(1) Organisms Considered

The following organisms were considered at PINGFAN as of potential biological warfare value:

(a) B. Typhi
(b) Paratyphoid A and B
(c) B dysenteriae
(d) V Cholera
(e) P pestis
(f) B anthracis
(g) M malleomyces
(h) Anerobes
1. B welchii
2. B vovgii
3. B Hystolyticus
4. B tetani

Experimental research embraced only a few of the above. The S-form for all organisms was used except for anthrax bacillus where the R-form was studied.

(2) Method of Culture

Bacteria cultivators designed by General ISHII appear to have been used exclusively. These consisted of an oven 14 x 9.85 x 21 inches,

TOP SECRET

holding 15 trays in which the bacteria were grown. The cultivator was made of duralumin and weighed 24¾ lbs. It held 6.78 qts. of agar medium. Nine-hundred cultivators were required to produce sufficient bacteria for one shell, each cultivator yielding 40 gms. of B typhii per harvest.

The culture medium used had the following formula:

Peptone	15 gms.
Agar	30
NaCl	5
H_2O (dist)	1000 cc.

The pH was 7.45 after sterilization.

A few modifications of the above formula were used. In the case of anthrax the peptone was 7.5 gms. and the NaCl 10 gms. For plague 0.01 gentian violet was added as an anti-contaminant; for glanders 0.01 percent of organic iron was added. The culture temperature was 37°C.

The harvest consisted of taking scrapings at regular intervals. For the enteric organisms it was 24 hours; for plague, anthrax and glanders, 48 hours; and for the anerobes, one week.

(3) Viability Investigations

The ability of the biological warfare agents to remain alive at room temperature (18 to 25°C) was tested by sealing a bacterial suspension in flasks with rubber stoppers covered with paraffin. The suspension was then tested periodically.

The following results were obtained:

Organism	Life Span
(a) Dysentery	5-7 days
(b) V Cholerae	3-5 days
(c) P Pestis	5-7 days
(d) M malliomyces	Not studied.
(e) Anthrax spores	Stable for more than 10 years in 0.5 percent phenol, dried egg albumin, soil, chocolate, bread, and face powder, and for at least three years in tooth powder and dairy products.

As a result of the shortness of most of the above life spans it was at first decided to confine field tests to the simulant, B prodigiosus and to anthrax spores. Later, tests were expanded to include plague, cholera, and others.

Field tests on wells and water supplies showed that enteric organisms in general die within two to four days although there appeared to be a great variation between areas. A correlation of the possible factors influencing the viability of bacteria in wells led Colonel MASUDA to conclude that in areas where there had been a recent outbreak of cholera, typhoid, or dysentery the life of the organism was shorter than in areas where no epidemics had been reported.

(4) Methods of Dissemination

Four general methods of bacterial dispersion were considered by the Japanese: (a) artillery shells, (b) bombs, (c) dispersion from planes, (d) saboteurs.

(a) Artillery Shells

Two types of shells were studied, an ordinary gas shell and a 75 mm. HE shell with the bacterial suspension replacing a portion of the bursting charge. Both were soon discarded due to their impracticability.

(b) Bombs

The principal offensive effort was directed towards obtaining an effective dissemination bomb. The two bomb types receiving major attention were the Uji and the HA.

The Uji was an all-purpose bomb. It consisted of a porcelain container 27½" long and 7" in diameter. It held 10½ quarts of fluid. The bomb was provided with celluloid fins; they were of inferior quality and resulted in a faulty trajectory.

The HA bomb was designed specially for use with anthrax spores. It was of the thin wall steel detonation type, containing 1500 cylindrical particles immersed in 500 cc. of anthrax emulsion.

The RO bomb was of the same general type as the HA, only larger. It held a pay load of 2 liters of bacteria fluid.

A special B.W. bomb called the "mother and daughter" was designed and one was built. It consisted of a mother bomb containing a radio sending apparatus and a cluster of daughter bombs containing the pay load. The mother bomb was dropped first, followed by the daughters. The daughter bombs were designed to explode when the mother bomb struck the ground due to the cessation of the radio signal. The bomb was believed to be promising but was expensive to build.

The intent of the Uji and the "mother and daughter" bombs was primarily ground contamination; the infliction of infected wounds was secondary. The HA bomb, on the other hand, was designed primarily for

the purpose of inflicting anthrax-infected wounds.

Field tests were conducted on animals, some 100 horses and 500 sheep being used over a period of two years. Tests were also made using the simulant B prodigiosus for studying ground contamination.

(c) Bacterial Clouds

Preliminary tests were made using the vivid colored dye, rodamine, and a 2-5 percent dextron broth. The scattering was detected by spots on white paper placed at intervals over a radius of 1000 meters. It was claimed that the particle size down to 50 microns could be analyzed. Both static bombs and bombs dropped from airplanes were tested. The results showed the large particles to drop near the center of charge and the smallest particles near the periphery.

Limited studies were made on the direct dispersion of mists and dusts. In one test 920 liters of simulant were dispersed per second. A mixture of 50 percent glycerine and 10 percent gelatine was found satisfactory for dispersion. Tests were carried out at altitudes of 4000, 2000, 1000, and 200 meters. At 4000 meters one hour elapsed before all the particles reached the ground. The lower levels gave better results.

(d) Saboteurs

The spreading of biological warfare agents by saboteurs was not attempted to any appreciable degree. All studies of this means for spreading pestilence were claimed to be for purposes of defense against the Russians and Chinese who, it was contended, were using saboteurs. (The Russians and Chinese maintain that the Japs poisoned their wells and springs.)

INFORMATION ON HUMAN EXPERIMENTS

THE MOST RECENT INFORMATION ON JAP B.W. REVEALS DATA ON THE USE OF HUMANS FOR TEST SUBJECTS, AND CONFIRMS THE CHINESE CLAIMS THAT THE ENEMY EMPLOYED PLAGUE, CHOLERA, AND TYPHOID AGAINST THEM. THE DATA, SUBSTANTIATED BY NUMEROUS SCIENTIFIC DETAILS, ARE PRESENTED IN THE FOLLOWING PARAGRAPHS.

An interesting report has been received on the theoretical and mathematical considerations involved in particle-size determinations, and on droplet distribution of B.W. materials disposed by bombs or aircraft sprays.

Twelve field trials were conducted against Chinese civilians and soldiers. A summary of the results and a map of the villages and towns involved have been submitted. A brief description of this summary and the tactics employed will be given below.

A short report has been received from one individual who had been connected with the free balloon project. In this report it was admitted that considerable attention had been given to using the balloons for dissemination of B.W. agents, but it was concluded that they were unsatisfactory for this purpose.

It was found that an organization completely separate from PINGFAN had carried on a considerable amount of research in the veterinary B.W. field.

The human subjects used at the laboratory and field experiments were said to be Manchurian coolies who had been condemned to death for various crimes. It was stated positively that no American or Russian prisoners of war had been used at any time (except that the blood of some American POW's had been checked for antibody content), and there is no evidence to indicate that this statement is untrue. The human subjects were used in exactly the same manner as other experimental animals, i.e., the minimum infectious and lethal dosage of various organisms was determined on them, they were immunized with various vaccines and then challenged with living organisms; and they were used as subjects during field trials of bacteria disseminated by bombs and sprays. These subjects also were used almost exclusively in the extensive work that was carried out with plague. The results obtained with human beings were somewhat fragmentary because a sufficiently large number of subjects to permit statistically valid conclusions was not used in any of the experiments; however, in the case of the diseases which had the most emphasis such as anthrax, it is probable that several hundred subjects were employed during a period of several years.

A brief summary of the many details given in the 60-page report on

B.W. activities directed against man is as follows. Unless otherwise mentioned all of the data given refer to experiments on humans.

(1) Anthrax

(a) Infectious or Lethal Dose

The MID_{50} (minimum infectious dose for 50 percent of the animals employed) was determined to be 10 milligrams subcutaneously for both man and horse, and orally it was 50 milligrams for man (the Japanese workers seldom did plate counts, but expressed all concentrations in terms of milligrams of moist organisms derived from saline suspensions obtained from cultures grown on solid medium; however, they did give a conversion factor for anthrax, i.e. 1 mgm = 10^8 organisms). The MID_{50} for other usual laboratory animals was about the same as that determined in this country. It seems probable, however, that the strain used by the Japanese was considerably more virulent orally, although little work on the oral route has been done here. The mortality rate in infected humans was 66 percent when infection occurred subcutaneously, 90 percent orally, and 100 percent through open wounds and by inhalation. An interesting finding was that horses immunized with an attenuated spore vaccine were highly resistant to subcutaneous infection, but only slightly resistant to infection by the oral route.

(b) Direct Infection

Data are given for the preparation of suspensions used, the incubation period and the clinical course of the disease. The post-mortem findings are also covered in considerable detail.

(c) Immunization Experiments

The methods of preparation of vaccines employed are given in detail. It was found that a heat-killed vaccine gave no protection, while an attenuated spore vaccine gave complete protection against four MID orally; however, the living spore vaccine in humans was followed by such violent reactions that it was concluded it could not be employed except in emergencies.

(d) Bomb Trials

Full details and diagrams of the field trials are given. In most cases the human subjects were tied to stakes and protected with helmets and body armor. The bombs of various types were exploded either statically, or with time fuzes after being dropped from aircraft. No

determinations were made of cloud concentration, nor of particle size, and the meteorological data are rather crude. The Japanese were not satisfied with the field trials with anthrax. However, in one trial with 15 subjects, six were killed as a result of wounds from the bombs, and four were infected by bomb fragments (three of these four subjects died). In another trial with a more efficient bomb ("Uji") six of 10 subjects developed a definite bacteremia, and four of these were considered to have been infected by the respiratory route; all four of these latter subjects died. However, these four subjects were only 25 meters from the nearest of the nine bombs that were exploded in a volley.

(e) Pollution of Pastures

The usual experiment was to explode five bombs statically five meters from the ground in a straight line across a field, and then have various animals graze along lines at different distances from the bomb burst. It was found that all types of animals grazing within 25 meters of the explosion sites and within an hour after the explosion, contracted the disease, and 60 to 100 percent of those grazing 50 meters away became infected. The contaminated grass was infective for at least four days, and after one month about 33 percent of the spores was still found on the grass. During the observation of animals after trials of this type, it was found that usually 25 percent of normal animals kept in the same barns with the infected animals developed secondary infections.

(f) Spraying Experiments

In a typical experiment four human subjects were placed in a glass room 10 m^3 in size, and 300 cc. of a 1 mgm/cc. suspension were introduced using an ordinary disinfectant sprayer. No particle size determinations were made, but two of the four subjects developed skin lesions which eventually resulted in generalized anthrax.

(g) Stability

Extensive data are given on the stability of anthrax spores. The Japanese found that adding 0.5 percent phenol was one of the best methods of insuring stability. Their data show that spore suspensions are stable for more than 10 years in 0.5 percent phenol, dried egg white, soil, chocolate, bread, and face powder, and for at least three years in tooth powder, butter, cheese, milk and cream.

(h) Accidental and Laboratory Infections

After one field trial for pollution of pasture land, three laborers entered the area without wearing protective clothing. All three developed skin lesions but were cured with serum. However, two other laborers living with these three also contracted the disease and one of these died. Several laboratory workers contracted the disease presumably by the respiratory route even though they were protected with masks.

(2) Plague

(a) Infectious or Lethal Dose

The MID_{50} was found to be 10^{-6} mgm subcutaneously and 0.1 mgm orally. Respiration for 10 seconds of air containing five mgm/m^3 was infectious to 80 percent.

(b) Direct Infection

The incubation period was normally three to five days and death occurred within three to seven days after onset of fever. In most cases of artifically induced plague which terminated fatally the usual bubonic form became pneumonic three days before death and was then highly infectious.

(c) Immunization Experiments

Three avirulent strains were used for vaccines and gave about 50 percent protection against a challenge subcutaneously with 1000 MID. An acetone extract of a virulent strain gave considerably less protection.

(d) Bomb Trials

A summary of three or four of the best trials is given below (in these trials the concentration of bacilli on the ground around the subjects was measured with plates).

Concentration on the Ground mgm/m^2	Infected (approx.)		Type of Infection
over 10 over 5	5/5) 7/10)	--	Eye-plague, tonsil-plague
over 1 under 1	3/20) 1/30)	--	Generalized plague

The conclusions from all the bomb trials was that plague bacilli were not a satisfactory B.W. weapon due to their instability but that it was much more practical to spread plague by means of fleas.

(e) Spraying Experiments

The results indicated that this method was highly effective, both with subjects held within a room and also exposed to bacilli spread from aircraft at low altitudes. Thirty to 100 percent of the subjects used in various trials became infected and the mortality was at least 60 percent.

(f) Stability

No success was attained in stabilizing plague bacilli either in suspensions or by drying.

(g) Infected Fleas

A great deal of work was done on methods of breeding fleas and infecting them through rats. Methods were developed for producing many kilograms of normal fleas (one gram = 3,000 fleas), and for infecting them on a production basis. This flea work is described in great detail and represents an excellent study.

It was found that infected fleas survived for about 30 days under the best conditions and were infective for that length of time. It was also found that one flea bite per person usually caused infection. It was also found that if subjects moved freely around a room containing a concentration of 20 fleas per square meter six of 10 subjects became infected and of these four died.

Bomb trials were carried out using the "Uji" porcelain bomb with primacord explosive. The fleas were mixed with sand before being filled into the bomb. About 80 percent of the fleas survived the explosion which was carried out in a 10-meter square chamber with 10 subjects. Eight of the 10 subjects received flea bites and became infected and six of the eight died.

(3) Typhoid, Paratyphoid A and B, and Dysentery (Bacillary)

Very little work was done on these diseases in humans except to determine the MID and to test various types of vaccines.

(a) Typhoid

The MID_{50} orally was four mgm and this produced only mild and typical cases with no deaths. The best vaccine protected only eight of 13 subjects challenged with 150 mgm of freshly isolated organisms (in the control group 12 of 13 became infected).

The stability of typhoid bacilli in soil was tested and it was found that these organisms survived 27 days without a significant decrease and then gradually diminished in number. A laborer collecting soil samples 17 days after the start of this experiment contracted typhoid fever.

Typhoid organisms were coated successfully with gelatin and would then withstand several times the amount of chlorine that would kill the normal bacilli.

(b) Paratyphoid A and B

The MID_{50} orally for man was one mgm with both of these organisms. No immunization experiments were performed with human subjects.

(c) Dysentery

The MID_{50} orally for the Shiga organism was 10 mgm, and for two Flexner strains it varied from 10 to more than 200 mgm. Results with heat-killed vaccines of all these strains were almost completely negative; any effectiveness attributed to the vaccines was probably more the result of the natural acquired immunity of the subjects tested.

(4) Cholera

(a) Infectious Dose

The MID_{50} orally was 10^{-4} mgm of moist organisms and 10^{-6} cc. of a mixture of freshly isolated organisms and feces. About half of the cases so induced terminated fatally within five days.

(b) Immunization Experiments

The results with heat-killed and formaldehyde-killed vaccines were negative, but a vaccine produced by the ultra-sonic method using 6500 kc. for 30 minutes gave complete protection in a small group of three subjects; the challenge dose was approximately 10,000 MID.

(c) Spray Trials

In one trial in which the organisms were sprayed at low altitude from aircraft, eight of 24 subjects became infected but there were no deaths.

(d) Stability

Suspensions of the organism were very unstable and the Japanese had no success in drying them, even with the lyophil process.

(5) Glanders

The Japanese did not do very much work with this organism because they definitely were afraid of it. They had seven cases of laboratory infections, of which two died, two were cured by amputation and three received effective serum therapy.

(a) Infectious Dose

The MID_{50} subcutaneously for man was 0.2 mgm and this produced a mortality of 20 percent. Fairly good details are given about the clinical course of the disease and post-mortem findings.

(b) Immunization Experiments

Heat-killed vaccines had no protective effects with guinea pigs and no experiments were done on man.

(c) Bomb Trials

Only one trial was conducted using 10 human subjects and 10 horses. Three of the horses and one of the men became infected, but there are no data on cloud concentration or density of the organisms on the ground.

(d) Spraying Experiments

These experiments carried out in chambers were highly effective. In one trial one gram of dried bacilli was placed in a small glass box and stirred with a fan; a rubber tube attached to the box was inserted into the noses of three human subjects and all three became infected after inspiration of an estimated 0.1 mgm.

(6) Epidemic Hemorrhagic Fever ("Songo")

This is a so-called "new" disease which appeared in Manchuria in 1938-1939. (It probably was endemic for certain sections of Manchuria at that time.) The B.W. group conducted extensive research on this disease and isolated a virus that proved to be mite-borne. Full details are given about the epidemiology of the disease, the clinical course, pathology, and causative agents.

(7) Conclusions (given at end of the 60-page report)

Various diseases, other than those described above, were investigated in the earlier stages of the B.W. program. These included tuberculosis, tetanus, gas gangrene, tularemia, influenza, and undulant fever. It was found that the intravenous infection of tuberculosis bacilli

[redacted]

caused rapid development of general miliary infections but that it was not easy to infect man by the respiratory route. In general it was concluded that the only two effective B.W. agents they had studied were anthrax (and this agent was considered mainly useful against livestock) and the plague-infected flea. The Japanese were not even satisfied with these agents because they thought it would be fairly easy to immunize against them.

- - - - -

In the field trials with B.W. the usual tactic was to direct one or more batallions against the Chinese at two points about a mile apart on a railroad. When the Chinese were driven back the Japs would then tear up the mile of track, and spray or spread in some other manner the desired B.W. agent, and then stage a "strategic retreat". The Chinese would come rushing back into the area within 24 hours, and then within a few days plague or cholera would develop among the Chinese troops. In all these cases the Japanese tried to leave spies behind in the contaminated area to report on the results, but they admitted that this frequently was not successful and results were not clear. However, of the 12 trials that were reported all but three were said to have given positive results. In two trials with plague-infected fleas scattered from aircraft at about 200 meters altitude, definite localized epidemics resulted. In one of these, 96 cases were known to have been produced of which 90 percent died. In three other trials with plague-infected fleas scattered by hand along railroads, small epidemics were produced in every case, but no figures are available. In two trials with cholera and two with typhoid in which the organisms were hand-sprayed on the ground and into water supplies around the railroad area, positive results were obtained in all cases.

EVALUATION OF THE JAPANESE BIOLOGICAL WARFARE PROGRAM

The purpose behind the Japanese offensive biological warfare program is not well defined.

A survey of the work would suggest that the Japanese were primarily interested in directing their attack against armies. The HA bomb, designed to produce wounds infected with anthrax, could have no other purpose. The scatter bombs and bacterial clouds may also have been intended for use against civilian populations and feeding herds.

Although the use of saboteurs was disclaimed, enteric diseases were investigated and were kept on the list of possible biological warfare agents. These diseases do not lend themselves to dissemination by shells and bombs of the types investigated, but would be preferred for saboteur activities. The only evidence suggesting that the Japanese contemplated the use of saboteurs is the study of the viability of various organisms in springs and wells.

Assuming that the intent of the biological warfare program was to render a limited locality or installation uninhabitable by the scattering of anthrax spores and other disease-producing bacteria, or to enhance the fatality of wounds by infection with anthrax, then the conclusion is inescapable that the results to be gained failed to compensate for effort expended.

General ISHII and Colonel MASUDA attributed the failure of the B.W. program to the fact that they were unable to obtain the necessary supplies and cooperation with other branches of the military service since the project was forbidden by the Emperor. This is undoubtedly true as far as the development of special bombs was concerned. There was, however, a more important defect in the program in that the method of culture invented by General ISHII was not adaptable to the method of dissemination by bombs planned by Colonel MASUDA. Considering the fact that 900 cultivators were required to fill one bomb, it must be recognized that at the best the use of B.W. bombs could be justified only at a few selected points where there is a high concentration of enemy personnel.

The method of culture employed is cumbersome and not conducive to mass production. It certainly is not adequate to provide sufficient material for widespread scattering of biological warfare agents by either bombs or clouds. However, it will yield a concentrated product without too much effort. The method, therefore, while not suitable for saboteurs operating individually, could be used to good advantage for a centrally organized and supplied saboteur program.

The Japanese failed in developing means for enhancing the viability of epidemic forming organisms. This is probably the reason for the feeble effort placed on these diseases. This failure is most important since epidemics would have been a very potent weapon in their war theatre, where sanitation is poor and means for fighting epidemics are limited.

To sum up, the Japanese biological warfare program failed because:

(1) It lacked the support of the Emperor.

(2) It lacked practical coordination between scientific and ordnance personnel.

(3) It lacked good meteorological data.

(4) It did not adapt its procedures to the field of operation.

It is believed that, should the surveillance of the Occupation Forces be terminated, Japan could make herself ready for B.W. activity within five years.

PERSONALITIES

Lt. Gen. Shiro ISHII, M.C. - Director of the B.W. program, with title of Chief of Water Purification Department.

Lt. Gen. Masaji KITANO - Commander of Pingfan Institute from 1942.

Col. Tomosada MASUDA - Associated with B.W. for many years.

Maj. Jun-Ichi KANEKO, M.C. - At Pingfan for 3½ years.

Lt. Col. Enryo HOJO, M.C. - Army Medical College; author of "About Bacteriological Warfare".

INSTALLATIONS

PINGFAN B.W. INSTITUTE, HARBIN - 3,000 employees at peak production.

ARMY MEDICAL COLLEGE, TOKYO - Defensive B.W.

MANCHURIA STATE COLLEGE OF SCIENCE - B.W. research.
(Branch in HSINKIN - B.W. research)

9　指控
——盟军总司令部法务局调查

9.1 14 Dec. 1945: OCCIO Opns, MEMORANDUM FOR THE OFFICER IN CHARGE, Memorandum from Japanese Communist Party

资料出处：National Archives of the United States, R331, B1434.

内容点评：1945 年 12 月 8 日，远东国际军事法庭国际检察局设立后，与侵略战争相关的具有国际性质的问题转由其主管，盟军司令部法务局的职能限定为对一般性战时违反国际法的战犯的搜查和起诉，履行犯罪嫌疑人的登记等手续，下设部门有起诉科、调查科、战争犯罪人登记科、法律科。盟军占领日本后，日本人告发细菌战战争犯罪人的信函都转到法务局，由法务局调查科逐案调查。本资料为 1945 年 12 月 14 日法务局调查科备忘录，题目：来自日本共产党的备忘录。内容为“石井防疫给水部队的活动”。

CONFIDENTIAL

4808

OCCIO Ops
APO 500
14 Dec 45

MEMORANDUM FOR THE OFFICER IN CHARGE:

Subject: Memorandum from Japanese Communist Party.

The following memorandum was received by the Research & Analysis Section from the Japanese Communist Party. It is copied below without change in language. The report is in two sections, the second part relating to General (Rtd.) ISHIHARA Kanji. A quick check of the names mentioned in the first part of the report, relating to Japanese bacteriological warfare, revealed no record in CIS.

"ACTIVITY OF ISHII B.K.A. CORPS

"Ishii B.K.A. (Bacterial War Army) was established in Harbin under commandership of Lieutenant-General Shiro Ishii. A large bacterial laboratory built in Harbin, succeeded in cultivating pest in 1944, December. Pest was applied to Manchurians, in Moukden was applied to several American citizens captured during war. For experiment sake, rats implanted with pest were dispersed in and around Moukden, as a result of which it was proved successfull. When Ishii after these experiments was about to start actual manufacturing in large scale war termination was declared. Japanese army bombarded the laboratory wherein most precious documents, equipments were destroyed together with hundreds of laboratory members engaged in study. The research works were conducted in cooperation with Tokyo and Kioto Imperial Universities medical laboratories.

"Most leading personel engaged in this research were Rinnosuke Shoji and Hisato Yoshimura in the Laboratory and Kiyu Ogata of Chiba Medical University assisted from outside. In 1944 spring Ryoichi Naito succeeded to Ishii. Most of medical institutes, universities were mobilised for the purpose, which are:

"Densenbyo Kenkyusho: Saburo Kojima
Shogo Hosoya
Hidetake Yahagi
"Kioto Imperial University: Kozo Kunimoto
Shiro Kasahara
"Medical Bureau of War Ministry: Lieut.-General Hiroshi Kanbayashi
Lieut.-Colonel Hiraga
Asaoka
Kaji
Maj.-Colonel Otaguro
Akuzuki

CONFIDENTIAL

CONFIDENTIAL

"Rinnosuke Shoji is Professor of Kioto University concurrently Prof. of Shamasu University (Manchuria) under whose guidance Dr. Kyugo Sasakawa, Professor Ko Inouye, Iyemori worked as assistants.

"There is a Medical Doctor in Kioto City by name of Minowada Masuzo who also participated in the research.

"Kioto Imperial University: Teiji Hoshino
Shun Mashita (dead)
Shogo Funaoka
Senri Araki

"Osaka University: Ryojun Kinoshita
Eiji Taniguchi

"Chief of General Affairs Department of Ishii Corps was Lieut.-General Tanabe."

"Kanji Ishihara

"One of leading supporters of his movement is Miyazaki, former Managing Director of S.M.R. Research Buro. Ishihara is connected with Katsuzo Nishi who hold peculiar influence among Imperial family for instance Prince Higashikuni, Prince Chichibu. Nishi was once Director of Electric Buro of Tokyo Municipal Government, later retired and started famous 'Nishi's Health Engineering Method' and won a great popularity. His method was prohibited by Government in accusation that his method has no medical basis."

CONFIDENTIAL

9.2 21 Dec. 1945: 2025, TRANSLATION IN FULL, letter, TO: CIS, FROM: IMAJI, Setsu（今地節）: The following notes are for your reference concerning the activities at the Secret Laboratories of the former Army Medical School

资料出处：National Archives of the United States, R331, B1434.

内容点评：本资料为 1945 年 12 月 21 日美军太平洋部队司令部反谍报长官办公室文件：12 月 15 日东京今地节（IMAJI，Setsu）投寄盟军最高司令部民间情报部（CIS）的告发信函及其译文，题目：有关原陆军军医学校秘密实验室。

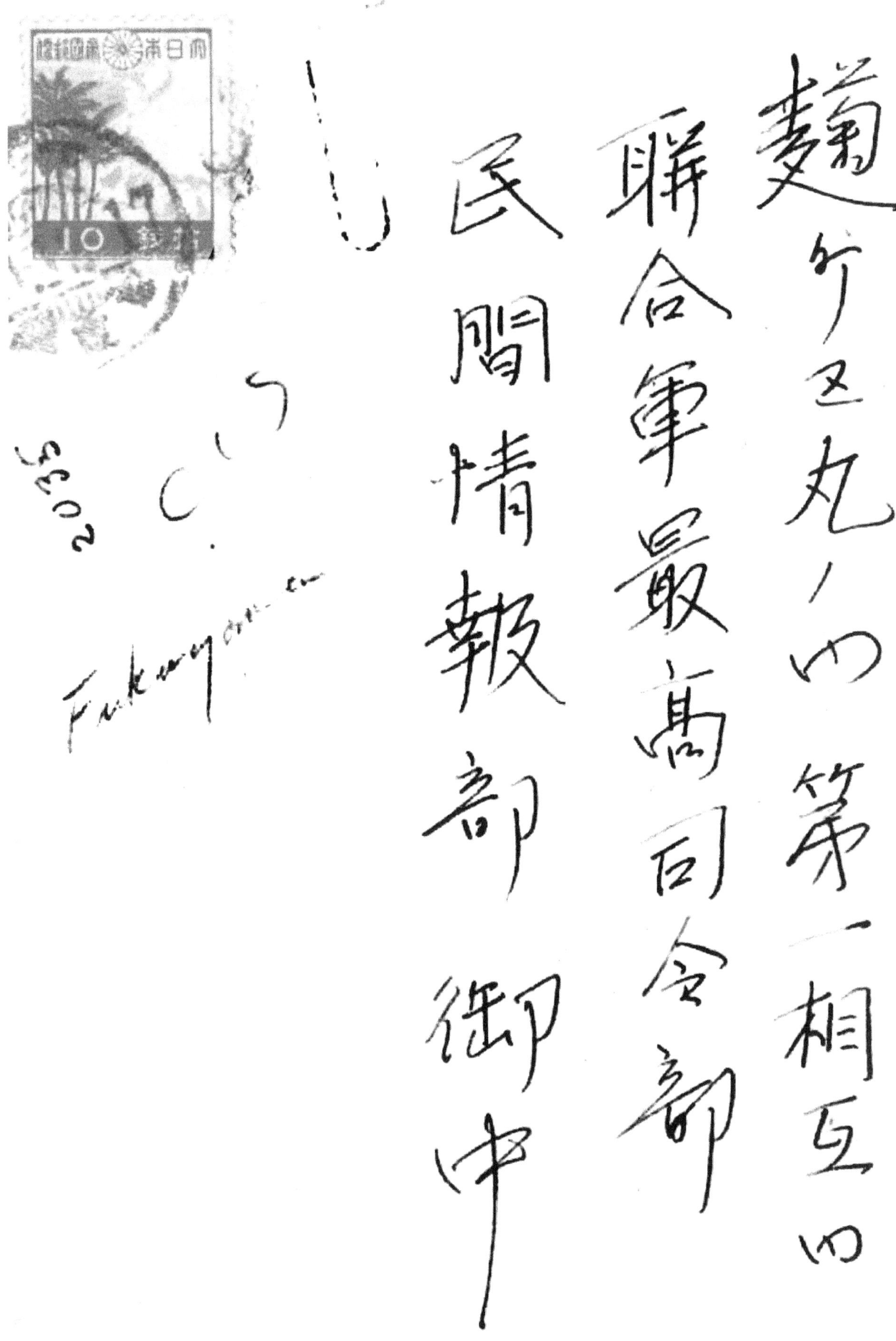
大日本帝國郵便
10 錢
麹町区丸ノ内第一相互四
聯合軍最高司令部
民間情報部御中
Fukuyama

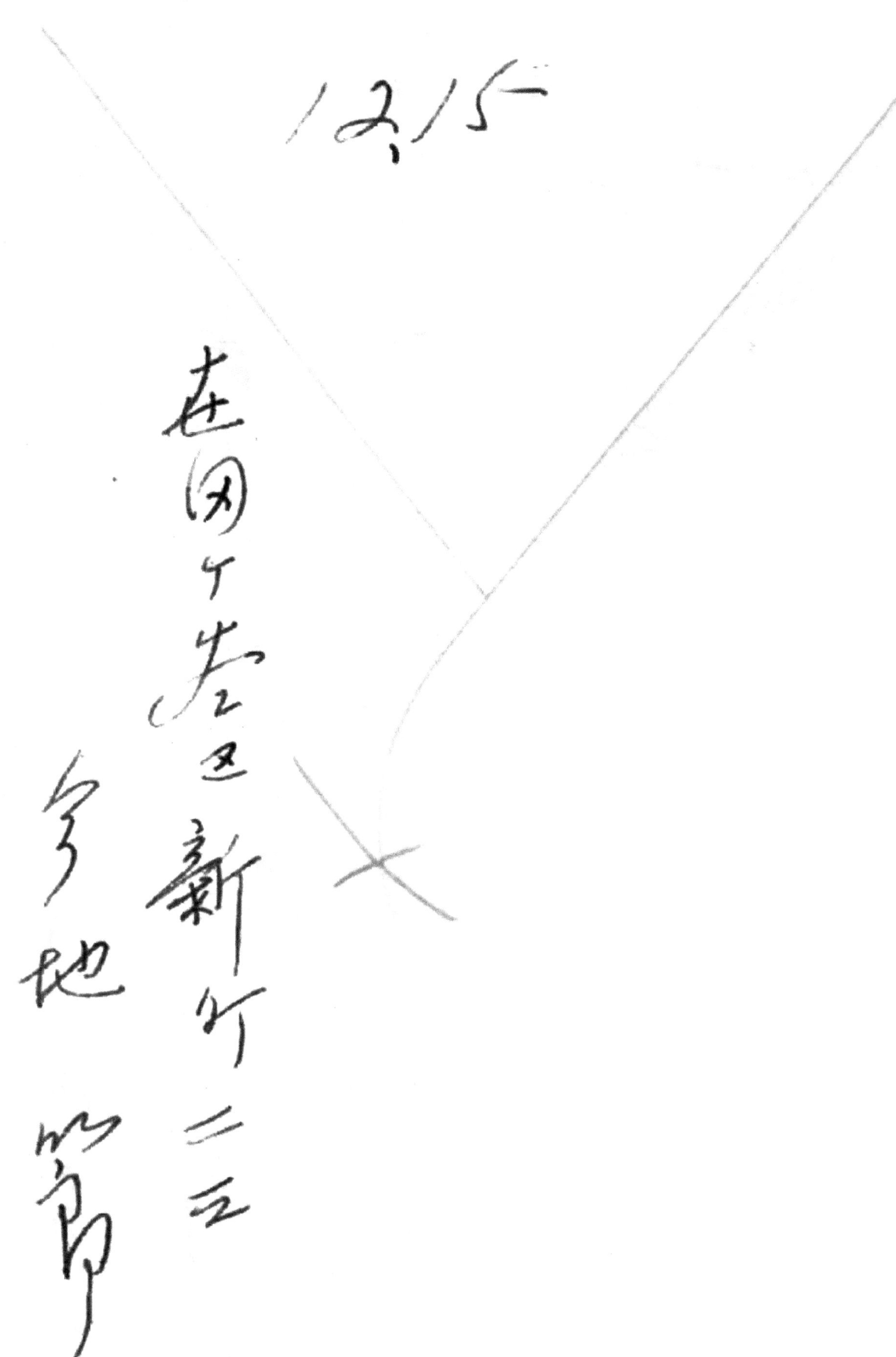
12.15
新竹

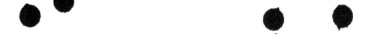

GENERAL HEADQUARTERS
UNITED STATES ARMY FORCES, PACIFIC
Office of the Chief of Counter-Intelligence

2035 21 December 1945

TRANSLATION IN FULL
letter

TO : CIS

FROM: IMAJI, Setsu, Shinmachi, Setagaya-ku, TOKYO
15 December 1945

SUBJECT: The following notes are for your reference concerning the activities at the Secret Labaratories of the former Army Medical School.

1. This laboratory headed by Medics Lieutenant General ISHII, Shiro was outwardly conducting researches on bacteria and water purification. While secretly they had employed technicians covering a very wide field for military purposes. This secret laboratories was first established near the HAIIN( ) River Railway Station of the Manchurian HAIRARU( ) line. ISHII, Shiro then a Major General, had assumed the alias of TOGO, Hajime and all other officers also went under aliases. Later they moved to the plaine on the outskirts of HARBIN and continued their activities.

2. Their most atrocious act was to use humans instead of animals for their research on bacteria. Although the majorities of the victims were convicted criminals there were also innocent farmers, Russian interpreter, officers of the Communist Army, womenand children. At HAIIN River alone there were over a thousand victims of experiments conducted on horse glanders bacteria, Hidatsu Sakin( ), Tansokin( ), pestilence bacteria and other strong poisons, also as a result of experiments on contagious diseases, starmation reaction, reactions to electricityand certain medicine many were victimized. Moreover, General HISHIO, Yoshizo, who has been colled a war cremineal onve investigayed this laboratory when the was the Chief of Staff of the KWANTUNG Army (1935).

3. There was no change in the positon of ISHII, Shiro, as virtual dictator of this plant, and along with the Laboratory Staff members he even controlled the following economic actions.

4. Machinery such as the water filter machine and mircoscopes were purchased under the name of The Japan Special Factory Inc. (KURITSU, Mitsuichi, Wakamatsu cho, Ushigome-ku, TOKYO-to acted as representatives). Altho this factory was mangged alone by KURITSU,

at the start, it was later incorporated and ISHII, Shiro and his condorts reaped huge profits by receiving dividends under the names of dummy stockholders (their wives and relatives).

The entire fortune of ISHII, Shiro and his Larboratory Staff members was accumilated from the illegal profits gained from the by-products of their atrocious deeds. Moreover, because of the fact that ISHII's wife was the daughter of ARAKI, Torasaburo , President of the Peers School, ISSII was very intimate with the Former War Minister ARAKI, Tadao and received unlimited help from him.

5. Persons responsible for the Atrocious Acts:

1. Medics Lieutenant General ISHII, Shiro, President of the Army Medical School from 1932 to 1945.
2. Medics Colonel NISHIMURA, Eiji
3. " Lieutenant Colonel SAKAKURA, Jun
4. " " " ONODERA, Yoshio
5. Civilian not on the reglar staff, A certain Professor at the Nagasaki Medical College
6. Civilian not on the regular staff ISHIYAMA, Kinzo
7. Medics Colonel, HOHO, Enryo
8. Civilian, KURITSU, Matsuichi
9. Civilian not on the regular staff, SUZUKI, -----
10. " " " " , SAKURAI, Kanichi
11. " " " " , IIDA, ------
12. " " " " , YAKIZAWA, Yukinara
13. Techinician, SHINBO, SHINICHI
14. " TAKAHASHI, Yoshiichi

The aboves statements are a rough outline of the actions of ISHII Shiro and his group. According to investigation, new facts and developments can be expected.

Translator: S/Sgt Fukuyama
TM

9.3 26 Jun. 1946: Translation of Transcription of the Interrogation of TAKESHI KINO (紀野猛), JOHN R. EGLSAER, 2nd Lt., Inf., Investigating Officer, Legal Section, GHQ., SCAP

资料出处： National Archives of the United States, R331, B1434.

内容点评： 本资料为 1946 年 6 月 26 日盟军总司令部法务局调查科 John R. Eglsaer 少尉于日本九州福冈对纪野猛（KINO，Takeshi）的讯问记录。纪野猛为原日军驻长春 100 部队（关东军军马防疫厂）队员。

CONFIDENTIAL

ALLIED OCCUPATION FORCES)
CITY OF Fukuoka)

I, TAKESHI KINO, being duly sworn on oath, state that I had read to me and understood the translation of the foregoing transcription of my interrogation and all answers contained therein, consisting of 2 pages are true to the best of my knowledge and belief.

Takeshi Kino
(Signature of Witness)

Subscribed and sworn to before me this 26th day of June 1946

John R. Eglsaer
John R. Eglsaer 2nd Lt, Inf.
Investigating Officer
Legal Section, GHQ., SCAP

ALLIED OCCUPATION FORCES)
CITY OF Fukuoka)

I, TARO SHIMOMURA T/4, being duly sworn on oath, state that I truly translated the questions and answers given from English to Japanese, and from Japanese to English respectively, and that after being transcribed, I truly translated the foregoing deposition containing 2 pages, to the witness; that the witness thereupon in my presence affixed his signature thereto.

Taro Shimomura
(name) (Rank) (Arm)

Subscribed and sworn to before me this 26th day of June 1946

John R. Eglsaer
John R. Eglsaer 2nd Lt, Inf.
Investigating Officer
Legal Section, GHQ., SCAP

ALLIED OCCUPATION FORCES)
CITY OF Fukuoka)

I, JOHN R. EGLSAER 2nd Lt, Inf, certify that on the 26th day of June, 1946, personally appeared before us TAKESHI KINO and according to TARO SHIMOMURA, gave the foregoing answers to the several questions set forth therein; that after his testimony had been transcribed the said TAKESHI KINO, had read to him by the said interpreter the same and affixed his signature thereto in my presence.

John R. Eglsaer
John R. Eglsaer 2nd Lt, Inf
Investigating Officer,
Legal Section, GHQ., SCAP

FUKUOKA, KYUSHU, JAPAN

26 June 1946.

CONFIDENTIAL

RESTRICTED

TAKESHI KINO, after having been duly sworn, testified at the 6th Marine Headquarters, Fukuoka, Kyushu, Japan, on 26 June, 1946, as follows:

Q. Please state your full name, age, and address.
A. TAKESHI KINO, age 29, address Miyazaki-ken, Koger-gun, Takanabe-machi, Inari-machi.

Q. What is your present occupation?
A. I am unemployed at the present time.

Q. When did you serve in the Army?
A. February 10, 1940 -- called into the army, at Kumamoto, 6th Cav. Regt.
February 28, 1940 -- Haeraru, Manchuria, 836 Unit (Regt)
November 1940 -- Harbin to study Russian Language.
June 6, 1941 -- back to the 836 Unit. (The 836 unit were scouts for mechanized units)
April 6, 1943 -- Deschargrd
I was working as a civilian employee at the Kwantung Army Quarantine Stables from June 6, 1938 to February 1940 when I went into the army. I received my discharge in Manchuria in April 1943 and went back to the Kwantung Army Quarantime Stables located at Mokaton which is close to Hsin King.

Q. Did you hear of POW's being infected with glanders disease and then dissected for an experment?
A. I heard a rumor that something like that but I don't know if I heard it as POW's or coolies. (Chinese labor)

Q. Exactly what was the rumor that you heard?
A. I think I overheard someone saying that a person had been injected with the disease. But I didn't hear about their being dissected. It may have been about Jan 1945 that I heard about this.
The "Ishi" unit in Harbin was making experiments on the disease of man so they may have done it.

Q. Who was commanding officer of the stables?
A. Major General WAKAMATSU, YUJIRO. His home address is Yamaguchi-ken, Otsu-gun Hagishi, Tsuchihara 172. % Fujita, Nabbo.

Q. Who was in charge of the experiment section?
A. Major HOSAKA.

Q. Who else do you remember that was in the Experiment Section?
A. Major YAMAGUCHI — 1st Lt. NAKAJIMA
Capt. OHKI — " TAKIZAWA
" NAKAJIMA — " SASAKI
" YAMASHITA — 2nd Lt. GOTO
" TOBA — " TOYOKI
" NISHIYAMA
There were about 300 personnel in the experiment section and about 30 officers and I wasn't in that section so this is all I can think of.

Q. Do you know the address of Major YAMAGUCHI?
A. No I do not.

Q. Do you know Lt. Col. YASUZAKA?
A. I'me been at this stable close to 10 years but I've never heard of YASUZAKA.

Q. Do you know Capt MATSUSHITA, SHIRO?
A. I haven't heard of him either.

T. K.

RESTRICTED

Q. Do you think Major HOSAKA knows about persons being injected with glanders and then dissected?
A. In the first place, I don't know if a thing like that actually happened but if it did, he should know and Major General WAKAMATSU should know.
There was a part of the experiment section where they carried out secret experiments and the only ones allowed was the C.O. and person directly connected with the experiment. So they may have made such an experiment.

Q. Do you have anything further to add to this statement?
A. No.

Kino, Takeshi
TAKESHI KINO

9.4 28 Jun. 1946: Translation of Transcription of the Interrogation of YAMAGUCHI MOTOJI, JOSEPH F. SARTIANO, ASN 01321253, Captain, Inf., Investigating Officer, Legal Section, GHQ, SCAP

资料出处: National Archives of the United States, R331, B1434.

内容点评: 本资料为1946年6月28日盟军总司令部法务局调查科Joseph F. Sartiano上尉对山口本治（YAMAGUCHI，Motoji）的讯问记录。山口本治为原日军驻长春100部队（关东军军马防疫厂）队员。

~~RESTRICTED~~

ALLIED OCCUPATION FORCES)

CITY OF FUKUSHIMA)

I, YAMAGUCHI MOTOJI, being duly sworn on oath, state that I had read to me and understood the translation of the foregoing transcription of my interrogation and all answers contained therein, consisting of two (2) pages, are true to the best of my knowledge.

Yamaguchi, Motoji

s/ YAMAGUCHI MOTOJI (Japanese)

Subscribed and sworn to before me this 28 day of June 1946.

Joseph F. Sartiano
JOSEPH F. SARTIANO
ASN 01321253
Captain, Inf.
Investigating Officer
Legal Section, GHQ,SCAP

ALLIED OCCUPATION FORCES)

CITY OF FUKUSHIMA)

I, Tec. 5 HIDEO TACHIBANA, 37364987, AUS, being duly sworn on oath, state that I truly translated the questions and answers given from English to Japanese and from Japanese to English respectively, and that after being transcribed, I duly translated the foregoing disposition, containing two (2) pages, to the witness; that the witness thereupon in my presence affixed his signature thereto.

Hideo Tachibana
Hideo Tachibana, T/5, AUS

Subscribed and sworn to before me this 28th day of June 1946.

Joseph F. Sartiano
JOSEPH F. SARTIANO
ASN 01321253
Captain, Inf.
Investigating Officer,
Legal Section, GHQ,SCAP

C E R T I F I C A T E

I, JOSEPH F. SARTIANO, Captain, Inf., O-1321253, certify that on the 28th day of June 1946, personally appeared before me YAMAGUCHI MOTOJI, and according to Tec 5 Hideo TACHIBANA, 37364987, AUS, gave forth the foregoing answers to the several questions set forth therein; and that after his testimony had been translated and transcribed, the said Yamaguchi MOTOJI, had read to him by the daid interpreter the same and affixed his signature thereto in my presence.

Joseph F. Sartiano
JOSEPH F. SARTIANO
ASN 01321253
Captain, Inf.
Investigating Officer,
Legal Section, GHQ,SCAP

FUKUSHIMA, HONSHU

28 June 1946

GENERAL HEADQUARTERS
LEGAL SECTION
INVESTIGATION DIVISION
APO 500

Yamaguchi Motoji after being duly sworn to speak the truth at room 10, 88th Military Government Co. at Fukushima testified as follows.

Q. State your name/age and address and religion?

A. ~~Major~~ JK Yamaguchi Motoji - Murata Machi- Otsuki-shita, 61. Age 32. Buddist, married, 2 children.

Q. What is your present occupation?

A. Veterinarian, principally treat horses and cows.

Q. How long have you been doing this kind of work?

A. Since 1938.

Q. When were you inducted into the Army?

A. April 20, 1938, as a p"Probational Officer," at Chiba Ken- "Narashino-16th Cavalry Regt."

Q. What were your duties there?

A. A Veterinarian.

Q. How long did you stay at Chiba Ken?

A. From the middle of April until 30 June 1938.

Q. Where did you go from there?

A. Tokyo Military Veterinarian School; as a 1st Lt. and took a course in horse diseases, until about the 20th of December 1938. From there I went to the 10th Cav Regt in Hemiji, until Aug 10, 1940, as the Unit Veterinarian. From there the Unit moved to Jamusu, Manchuria, after which I was promoted to the rank of Captain. I stayed in Jamusu until March 1942, as the Unit Veterinarian. From there I went back to the Tokyo Military Veterinarian School for an advanced course in Veterinary; majoring in Pathology. I finished this course in March 1944; then immediately was sent to Hsinking, China with the Kwantung Army, Horse Disease Prevention Unit, as the Veterinarian.

Q. How long were you there?

A. Until August 12, 1945. From there the Unit retreated to Seoul, Korea.

Q. Were there any Prisoners of War in your area?

A. They were in the area, but I never saw them.

Q. Did you ever have anything to do with any Prisoners of War?

A. No.

Q. What kind of experimentation work did you do at Hsinking?

A. I experimented on the treatment of glanders by using "Sulphur pyridin," "Sepharantin" and Cyan Copper. These are Horse Serums.

Q. Are any of these serums either contagious or destructive?

A. All these serums are supposed to be beneficial and were tried on horses only.

Y. M

se serums tried on other animals?

A. Yes, on Guinea Pigs and Rabbits.

Q. What would happen to a man if you used any of these serums on him?

A. I wouldn't know as I have never tried or have heard of anyone ever trying tehm on men.

Q. Did any of the other officers ever discuss about experiments other then the ones you knew about?

A. Gen'l Wakamatsu Yujiro, 57 yrs old, Yamaguchi Ken, Hagi-Shi c/o Naohito Fugita, was the commander. Never discussed anything like that. I worked at the experimental Laboratory until Lt. Col. Yasutaro Hosaka, Tokyo Setagawaku-Tomagawa, Okusawa-Machi 3 Chome 45 took charge of the experimental station, but I never heard of any Prisoners or men being infected with contagious or destructive diseases of any kind.

Q. Who is Yamashita Shiro?

A. He was assistant to Gen'l Wakamatsu and had charge and the administration. He lives in Fukushima Ken Shirakawa Gun at the Gumba Hojubu. He would not know too much about any experiments that went on.

Q. Do you know Nishimura?

A. Yes, he lives in Nagano Ken. He is about 33 and is also a veterinarian. He used to make the Serums at No. 3 station. The 1st station was some kind of an inspection and prevention staff; the 2nd station was the experimental station; and the 3rd station was where they make the Serums. He is a very moody person; he was a civilian and worked under me when I transferred to No. 3. We have had words but that was when Nishimura stole a few bottles of Glucose and another time stole some food and I as his superior had to reprimand him.

Q. While you were in the experimental station did you at any time have Prisoners of War brought in for treatment, or dead men to be experimented on?

A. Never.

Q. You are going to sign under oath that no contagious serums were ever given to any men by either you or other officers in your area.

A. No contagious serums was ever given other than to animals.

Q. Have you anything further to add to your statement.

A. Nothing.

Y.M

9.5 22 Jul. 1946: PMR 141, TO: Japanese Liaison: G-2, GHQ, SCAP, Records of WAKAMATSU Yujiro, T. KAGOSHIMA, Military Section, Political Division, Central Liaison Office

资料出处： National Archives of the United States, R331, B1434.

内容点评： 本资料为 1946 年 7 月 22 日日本战后联络中央事务局政治部军事课向盟军总司令部 G-2 提交的若松有次郎（WAKAMATSU，Yujiro）履历，若松有次郎为兽医少将，曾任日军 100 部队部队长。

IMPERIAL JAPANESE GOVERNMENT

CENTRAL LIAISON OFFICE

PMR 141 22 July 1946

TO : Japanese Liaison: G-2, GHQ, SCAP.

SUBJECT : Records of WAKAMATSU Yujiro.

1. Reference: a. Check Sheet LNO 2274 dated 9 July 1946, subject: "Records."

b. PMR Letter No. 134 dated 20 July 1946, subject: "Records of WAKAMATSU Yujiro."

2. The military and biographical history and the present location of WAKAMATSU Yujiro is as follows:

Date of Birth: 1 Feb. 1897.

Military and Biographical History:

1922:	Graduated the Agricultural Department of the Tokyo Imperial University.
(Date unknown):	Served at the Epidemic Research Institute.
("):	Stationed in Germany.
("):	Appointed to a staff of the Military Service Bureau of the War Ministry.
("):	Appointed to a teacher of the Army Veterinary School.
("):	Appointed to the Chief of the Veterinary Branch of the 13th Army.
1 July 1942:	Appointed to the chief of Quarantine Stables of the Kwantung Army.

Present Location: 173 Tsuchihara, Hagi-Shi, Yamaguchi Prefecture.

T. Kagoshima

T. KAGOSHIMA,
Military Section,
Political Division,
Central Liaison Office.

#330

9.6 22 Jul. 1946: PMR 144, TO: Japanese Liaison: G-2, GHQ, SCAP, Records of HOSAKA Yasutaro, T. KAGOSHIMA, Military Section, Political Division, Central Liaison Office

资料出处： National Archives of the United States, R331, B1434.

内容点评： 本资料为 1946 年 7 月 22 日日本战后联络中央事务局政治部军事课向盟军总司令部 G-2 提交的 HOSAKA，Yasutaro 履历。

IMPERIAL JAPANESE GOVERNMENT

CENTRAL LIAISON OFFICE

PMR 144 22 July 1946

TO : Japanese Liaison: G-2, GHQ, SCAP.

SUBJECT : Records of HOSAKA Yasutaro.

1. Reference: a. Check Sheet LNO 2278 dated 9 July 1946, subject: "Records."

b. PMR Letter No. 137 dated 20 July 1946, subject: "Records of YASUZAKA."

2. The name YASUZAKA described in the Check Sheet of the Legal Section may presumably be HOSAKA Yasutaro. His military and biographical history is as follows:

Domicile : 41 Yoka-Machi, Kofu-Shi, Yamanashi Prefecture.

Date of Birth : 29 Sept. 1908.

Military and Biographical History:

9 Apr. 1931:	Entered the Agricultural Department of the Tokyo Imperial University as Commissioned Student of the Veterinary Affairs Department.
Mar. 1933:	Graduated the Agricultural Department of the Tokyo Imperial University.
4 Apr. 1933:	Appointed to Veterinary Cadet.
30 Jun. 1933:	Commissioned ~~Veterinary~~ 2nd Rank Veterinary.
1 Aug. 1935:	Attached to the 25th Field Artillery Regiment. (Note. The Regiment afterwards changed the name to the 25th Mountain Artillery Regt
28 Apr. 1936:	Attached to the Artillery Regiment stationed in China.
15 Feb. 1937:	Commissioned to Veterinary 1st Lt.
1 Mar. 1937:	Commissioned to Veterinary Capt.
19 Feb. 1938:	Attached to the Hq. of the North China Region Army.
10 Mar. 1938:	Attached to the Hq. of the 5th Independent Mixed Brigade.

MIR# 330

10 Dec. 1938: Appointed the staff of the Military Sanitary Material Depot.

1 Aug. 1941: Commissioned to Veterinary Maj.

31 Mar. 1942: Appointed to the staff of the Research Division of the Army Veterinary School.

20 Aug. 1942: Appointed to the staff of the Veterinary Branch of the Kwantung Defence Army.

22 Jun. 1944: Appointed to the staff of the Quarantine Stables of the Kwantung Army.

1 Mar. 1945: Commissioned to Veterinary Lt. Col.

T. Kagoshima

T. KAGOSHIMA,
Military Section,
Political Division,
Central Liaison Office.

MIR 330

9.7　22 Jul. 1946: PMR 147, 164, TO: Japanese Liaison: G-2, GHQ, SCAP, Records of YAMASHITA Shiro; 30 July 1946: PMR 164 TO: Japanese Liaison: G-2, GHQ, SCAP, Records of YAMASHITA Shiro; 13 Aug. 1946, PMR 195, TO: GENERAL HEADQUARTERS OF THE SUPREME COMMANDER FOR THE ALLIED POWERS, Educational History of YAMASHITA Shiro

资料出处： National Archives of the United States, R331, B1434.

内容点评： 本资料为1946年7月22日、30日日本战后联络中央事务局政治部军事课向盟军总司令部G-2提交的山下四郎（YAMASHITA Shiro）个人资料、军职、履历；8月13日提交的山下四郎教育履历。

LEGAL SECTION

ROUTING SLIP

DATE:____________

FROM:______________TIME:____________

TO:

CHIEF SEC. _____ DOC.ANAL._______
EX. O.__________ SUPPLY _________
ADM.O.__________ BRITISH_________
PROS.DIV._______ AUSTRALIAN______
INVES.DIV.______ CANADIAN________
APPREHENSION____ NEW ZEALAND_____
LAW DIV.________ DUTCH___________
LIAISON ________ CHINESE_________
P.R.O.__________ PERSONNEL O.____
RECORDS & FILES BR.______________
PHOTOSTAT________________________
COM-MARIANAS_____________________

#################################

FOR:
Signature_______ ACTION___________
Information_____ Note & Return____
Initials________ Dispatch_________
Comment & File_____________
Concurrence______________________

IMPERIAL JAPANESE GOVERNMENT

CENTRAL LIAISON OFFICE

PMR 147 22 July 1946

TO : Japanese Liaison: G-2, GHQ, SCAP.

SUBJECT : Record of YAMASHITA Shiro.

1. Reference: Check Sheet LNO 2281 dated 9 July 1946, subject: "Record."

PMR Letter No. 138 dated 20 July 1946, subject: "Record of MATSUSHITA Shiro."

2. Captain MATSUSHITA Shiro may presumably be YAMASHITA Shiro and YAMASHITA Shiro's recordsis as follows:

Date of the Birth: 25 Feb. 1910.

Military and Biographical History:

1 Aug. 1941: Commissioned to Veterinary Capt., and attached to the Quarantine Stables of the Kwantung Army.

T. Kagoshima

T. KAGOSHIMA,
Military Section,
Political Division,
Central Liaison Office.

#330

MIR 330

IMPERIAL JAPANESE GOVERNMENT

CENTRAL LIAISON OFFICE

PMR 147 22 July 1946

TO : Japanese Liaison: G-2, GHQ, SCAP.

SUBJECT : Record of YAMASHITA Shiro.

1. Reference: Check Sheet LNC 2281 dated 9 July 1946, subject: "Record."

PMR Letter No. 138 dated 20 July 1946, subject: "Record of MATSUSHITA Shiro."

2. Captain MATSUSHITA Shiro may presumably be YAMASHITA Shiro and YAMASHITA Shiro's record is as follows:

Date of the Birth: 25 Feb. 1910.

Military and Biographical History:

1 Aug. 1941: Commissioned to Veterinary Capt., and attached to the Quarantine Stables of the Kwantung Army.

T. KAGOSHIMA,
Military Section,
Political Division,
Central Liaison Office.

IMPERIAL JAPANESE GOVERNMENT

CENTRAL LIAISON OFFICE

PMR 164 30 July 1946

TO : Japanese Liaison: G-2, GHQ, SCAP.

SUBJECT : Records of YAMASHITA Shiro.

1. Reference: a. Check Sheet LNO 2281 dated 9 July 1946, subject: "Records."

b. PMR Letter No. 138 dated 20 July 1946, subject: "Records of MATSUSHITA Shiro."

c. PMR Letter No. 147 dated 22 July 1946, subject: "Records of YAMASHITA Shiro."

2. The supplementary records of YAMASHITA Shiro are herewith submitted as per enclosure.

T. Kagoshima

T. KAGOSHIMA,
Military Section,
Political Division,
Central Liaison Office.

Enclosure: YAMASHITA Shiro's Military and Biographical History.

YAMASHITA SHIRO'S MILITARY AND BIOGRAPHICAL HISTORY

Domicile: 2, Haranaka, Kotakura, Nishigo-Mura , Nishishirakawa-Gun, Fukushima Prefecture.

Date of Birth: 20 Feb. 1910.

1. Biographical Career:

Mar. 1932:	Graduated from the Morioka Higher Agricultural and Forestry School.
Mar. 1932:	Employed by the Koshin Co. at Hikawashita, Koishikawaku, Tokyo City.
Jan. 1938:	Discharged from the above Co. for military service.
12 Nov. 1945:	Served at the Animal-breeding Sect. of Shirakawa pasture (which belonged to the Central Bushiness encouraging Office, Cultivation Bureau. Agricultural and Forestry Ministry)

2. Military Career:

1 Feb. 1933:	Entered the 2nd Transport Btn. as a candidate for a reserve Officer.
30 Nov. 1936:	Discharged as time expired.
13 Mar. 1936:	The 3rd class Veterinary.
15 Feb. 1937:	Commissioned to Veterinary 2nd Lieut.
13 Jul. 1937:	Enrolled to 26th Field Art. Regt.
30 Sept. 1938:	Commissioned to Veterinary 1st Lieut.
16 Jul. 1941:	Attached to Quarantine Stable, Kwangtung Army.
1 Aug. 1941:	Commissioned to Veterinary Captain.
2 Sept. 1945:	Discharged.

IMPERIAL JAPANESE GOVERNMENT

CENTRAL LIAISON OFFICE

PMR 195 13 August 1946

TO : GENERAL HEADQUARTERS OF THE SUPREME COMMANDER FOR THE ALLIED POWERS.

SUBJECT : Educational History of YAMASHITA Shiro.

1. Reference: a. Check Sheet LNO 2281 dated 9 July 1946, subject: "Records."

b. PMR Letter No. 138 dated 20 July 1946, subject: "Records of MATSUSHITA Shiro."

c. PMR Letter No. 147 dated 22 July 1946, subject: "Record of YAMASHITA Shiro."

d. PMR Letter No. 164 dated 30 July 1946, subject: "Records of YAMASHITA Shiro."

2. The educational history of YAMASHITA Shiro, a portion of his biographical history, is supplementally submitted herewith as per enclosure.

T. Kagoshima

T. KAGOSHIMA,
Military Section,
Political Division,
Central Liaison Office.

Enclosure: Educational History of YAMASHITA Shiro.

MIR 330

EDUCATIONAL HISTORY OF
YAMASHITA SHIRO

1 Apr. 1916:	Entered into the primary school in Nishigo-Mura, Nishishirakawa-Gun, Fukushima Prefecture,
1 Apr. 1921:	Changed to the Shirakawa second primary school in the same district.
1 Apr. 1922:	Entered into the higher course of the Shirakawa first primary school.
Apr. 1922:	Changed to the Kasuga primary school in Mukden City, Manchukuo.
25 Mar. 1924:	Graduated from the higher course of the above school.
1 Apr. 1924:	Entered into the Mukden middle school.
1 Apr. 1926:	Changed to the third year grade of the Fukushima Prefectural Fukushima middle school.
18 Mar. 1929:	Graduated from the above school.
10 Apr. 1929:	Entered into the Morioka higher agricultural and forestry school (the veterinary course), in Iwate Prefecture.
Mar. 1932:	Graduated from the above school.

MIR # 330

9.8 8 Aug. 1946: Inv. Div. No. 230, Report of Investigation Division, Legal Section, GHQ, SCAP, by: Capt. Joseph F. SARTIANO, 0-1321253, Inf.; 14609, BMS YI SI, DIGEST OF LETTER TO: Allied General Headquarters, FROM: NISHIMURA (西村)

资料出处：National Archives of the United States, R331, B1434.

内容点评：本资料为 1946 年 8 月 8 日盟军总司令部法务局调查科 Joseph F. Sartiano 上尉提交的编号 330 调查报告，附长野县西村投寄东京盟军总司令部涉外局的告发信函及内容摘要翻译：告发日军 100 部队人体实验。法务局调查科编号 330 调查报告为有关日本细菌战的调查报告。

Date: 6 August, 1946

Report of Investigation Division, Legal Section, GHQ, SCAP.

Inv. Div. No. 330	CRD No.	Report by: Capt. Joseph F. SARTIANO 0-1321253, Inf.

Title: Nishimura -FLU-, Nagano Ken.

Synopsis of facts: Nishimura accuses former Army veterinarians of infecting Prisoners of War with glanders, a contagious and destructive disease in MOKOTAN, CHINA, HSINKING PROV. Major YAMAGUCHI, MONJI, Gen. WAKAMATSU, YUJIRO, Capt. MATSUSHITA, SHIRO, Lt. Col. HOSAKA, YASUTARO and KINO, TAKESHI.

- P -

Details at Tokyo:

This investigation is predicated upon a translated letter known as ATIS document number 14609, from Nishimura - Nagano Ken. No first name, no date or full address. A check of CRD files JA 19-218 and JA 19-242 showed only a copy of Nishimura's letter.

He claims that Prisoners bodies were dissected in an open field near MOKOTAN, CHINA, HSINKING PROV., and also were infected with diseases for experimental purposes.

The accused are all graduates of the Tokyo Military Veterinarian school and worked in Hsinking Prov. as unit veterinarians, treating horses and mules for the Kwantung Army.

A signed statement by YAMAGUCHI, MONJI, Miyagi Ken, Shibata-Gun-Murata machi, one of the accused, brings out the fact that although there was experimental work being done in Hsinking, at no time were POWs brought in for experiments. There were POWs in the area, but their experiments were done on animals, mainly on horses and mules, and at no time were there any Prisoners brought in for any treatment.

Another accused officer, Lt. Col. HOSAKA, Yasataro, Setagaya-Tomogawa, Okusawa-Machi, 3 chome, 45 Tokyo, was also interviewed and the result of his interrogation also brought out the fact that only horses and mules were ever treated.

UNDEVELOPED LEADS:

The Tokyo office will find out the full name and address of Nishimura and bring him in for interrogation, - the other mentioned officers will also be interrogated and statements taken from them. The Fukuoka office has been notified to interrogate KINO, Takeshi who lives in Miyazaka Ken, Koto Gun, TAKANABE Machi.

- PENDING -

Distribution:
1 Pros.
1 CRD (Encl)
3 Inv.

Do not write in this space.

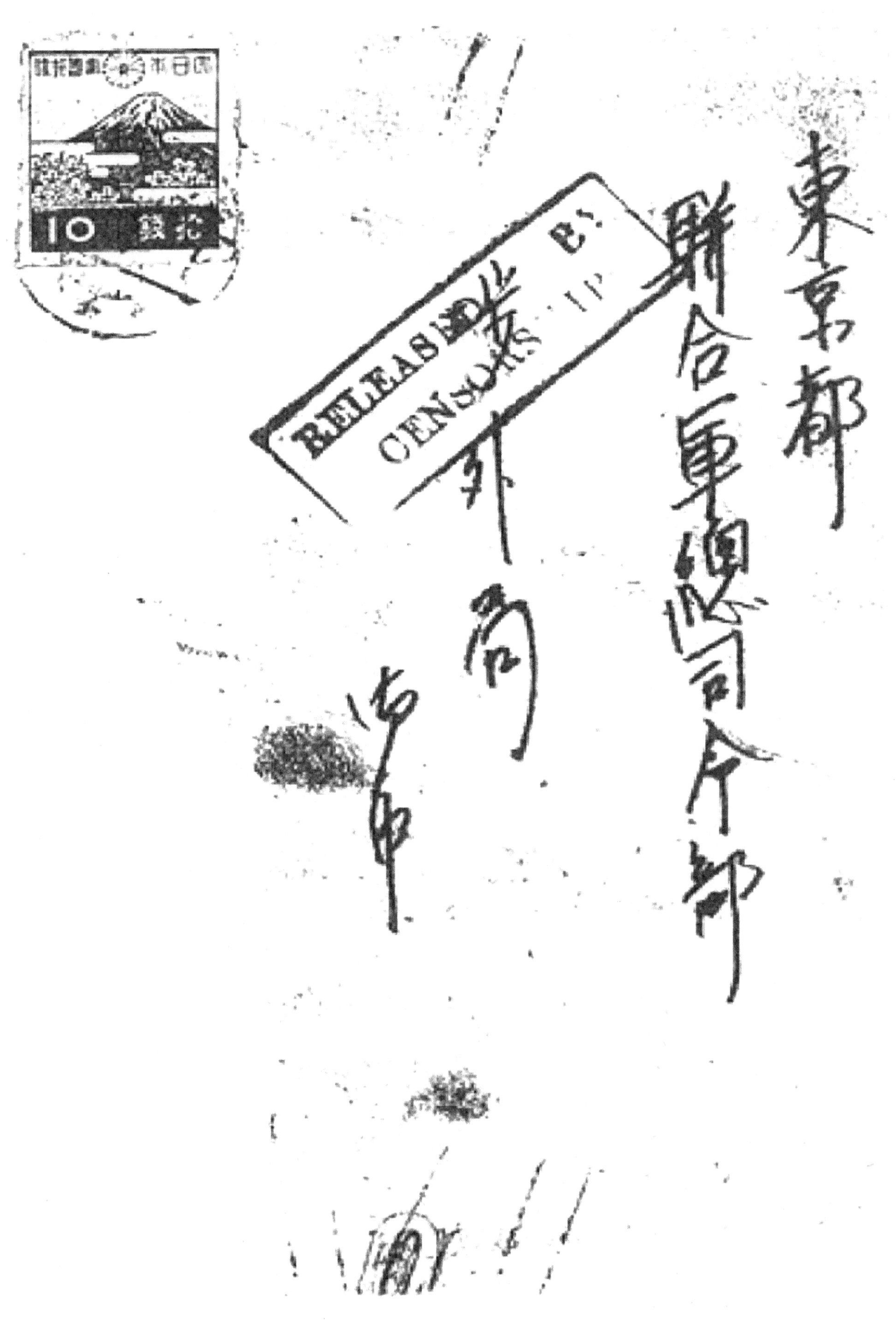

大日本帝國郵便
10 錢
RELEASED BY
CENSORSHIP
東京都
聯合軍總司令部

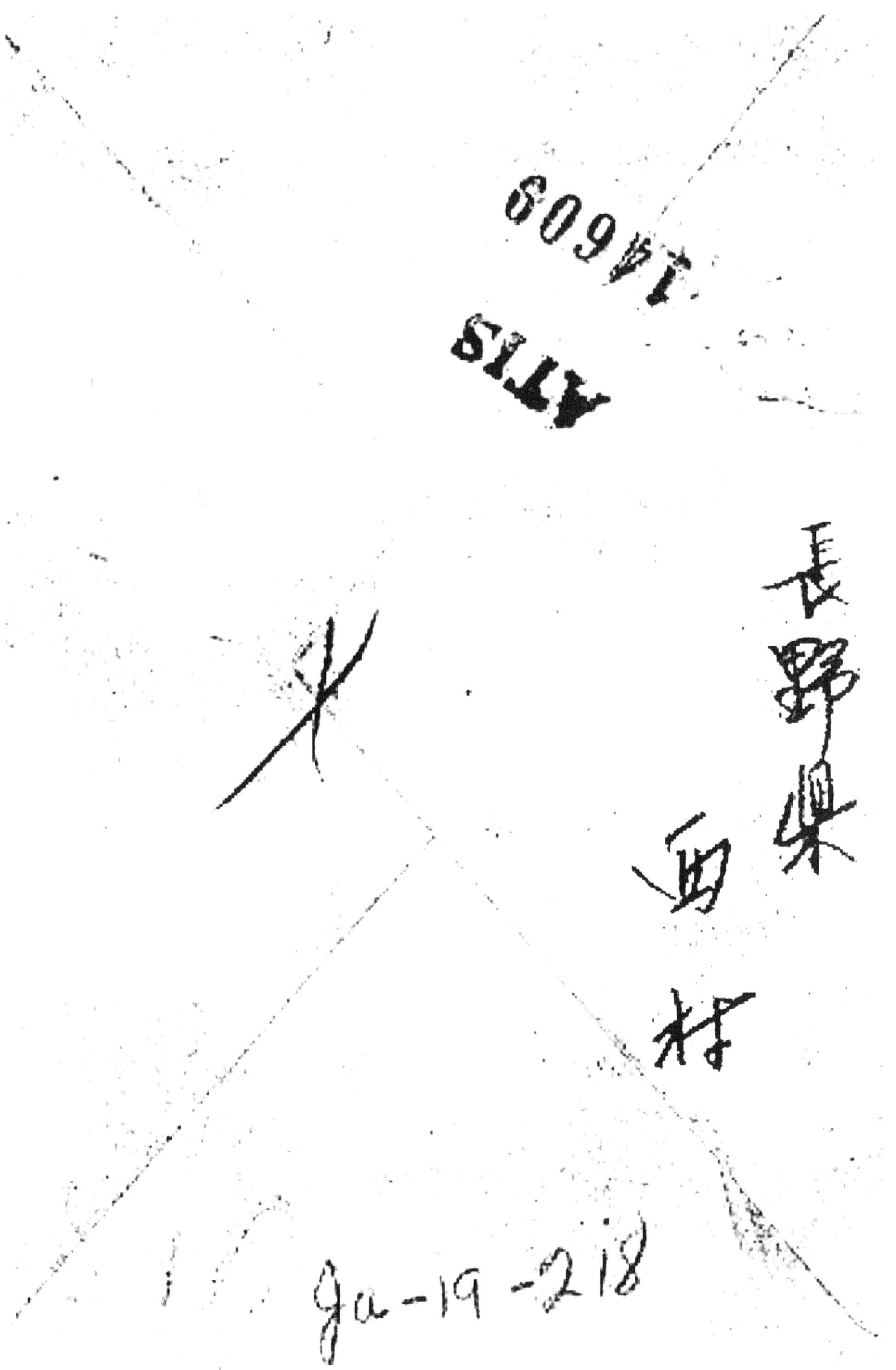
ATIS
14609
長野集
西村
Ja-19-218

同じ

戦争犯罪人ヲ通告ス

氏名　陸軍中佐　山口本治

原住所　宮城県柴田郡村田町

右ノ者ハ我方ノ各国捕虜ヲ細菌感染

試験ニ供シ野外ニ於テ解剖セリ

試験ニ供セル細菌ハ鼻疽菌ナリ

本実験ノ指導者並ニ主ナル協力者次ノ如シ

陸軍少将　若松有次郎　当県萩市ニ居住ス

〃　中佐　保坂

〃　大尉　松下四郎　栃木県ノ

右犯罪者ノ早急ナル逮捕ヲ乞フ

14609 BMS/YI SI

GENERAL HEADQUARTERS
SUPREME COMMANDER FOR THE ALLIED POWERS
MILITARY INTELLIGENCE SECTION, GENERAL STAFF
ALLIED TRANSLATOR AND INTERPRETER SECTION

NOTE: Translation directed by the Commander-in-Chief.

DIGEST OF LETTER

TO: Allied General Headquarters.

FROM: NISHIMURA (西 村). NAGANO-Ken.
(No date.)

The writer states that the following named persons infected prisoners of war with glanders (TN. A contagious and destructive disease of horses, mules, etc which may be transmitted to dogs, goats, sheeps and man) as an experiment, and dissected their bodies in an open field. Their names are as follow: Former Major YAMAGUCHI, Honji (山口 本治) of MIYAGI-Ken, SHIBATA-Gun, MURATA-Machi. Former Major General WAKAMATSU, Yujiro (若松有次郎). Former Lieutenant Colnel YASAKA (保坂). Former Captain MATSUSHITA, Shiro (松下 四郎). HOSAKA

YAMAGUCHI-KEN HAGI-SHI- TONYO YAMASHITA

Murata - 15 mi so. of Sendai

LT-COL YASUTARO HOSAKA

INV. 330

(SENDAI AREA)

[illegible]-19-210

9.9 23 Aug. 1946: Report Letter and Translation on War Criminals, TO: CI&E, GHQ, SCAP, FROM: Takeshi Nishimura（西 村 武）TO: Sadao MASUMORI（增 森 定 夫）, Public Safety Section, Prefectural Office, Sendai City（仙 台 市）, FROM: Takeshi Nishimura（西 村 武）; Report Letter and Translation, To Chief, Military Government, From a Repatriated Soldier

资料出处：National Archives of the United States, R331, B1434.

内容点评：本资料包括 1946 年 8 月 23 日长野县东筑摩郡里山边村西村武投寄东京盟军总司令部民间情报部告发日军细菌战战争犯罪人的信函及译文；吉冈町西村武投寄仙台市县广防犯课的增森定夫，告发细菌战犯罪人的明信片一张；一名复员军人投寄占领军司令官告发细菌战战争犯罪的信函及其译文。

LEGAL SECTION

ROUTING SLIP

DATE: ____
FROM: ____ TIME: ____

TO:

CHIEF SEC. ____ DOC.ANAL. ____
EX. O. ____ SUPPLY ____
ADM.O. ____ BRITISH ____
PROS.DIV. ____ AUSTRALIAN ____
INVES.DIV. ____ CANADIAN ____
APPREHENSION ____ NEW ZEALAND ____
LAW DIV. ____ DUTCH ____
LIAISON ____ CHINESE ____
P.R.O. ____ PERSONNEL O. ____
RECORDS & FILES BR. ✓ ____
PHOTOSTAT ____
COM-MARIANAS ____

FOR:
Signature ____ ACTION ____
Information ____ Note & Return ____
Initials ____ Dispatch ____
Comment & Concurrence ____ File ✓ ____

DECLASSIFIED
Authority NND 775011
BY Lewis NARS, Date 5/8/78

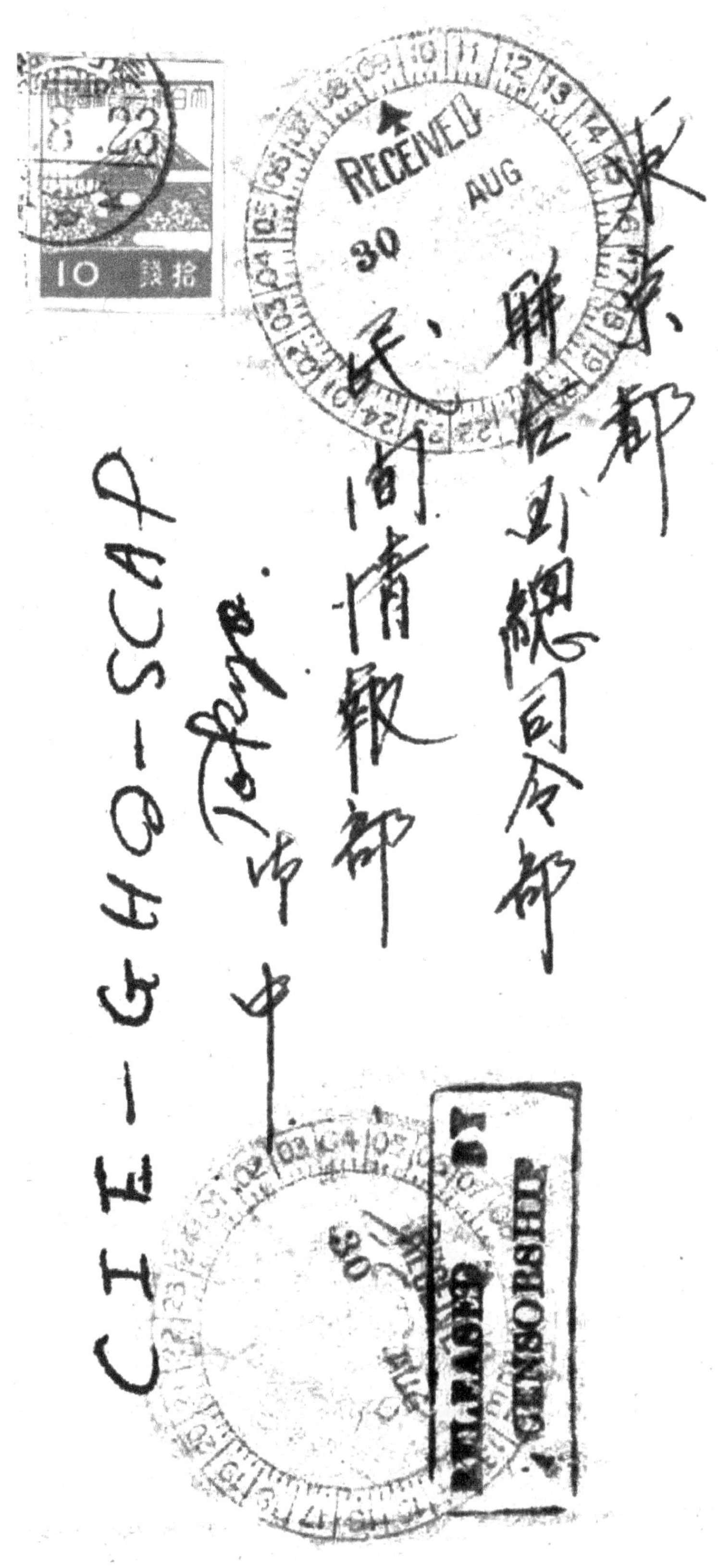
10 銭拾
RECEIVED
30 AUG
東京都
聯合國總司令部
民間情報部
CIE-GHQ-SCAP
RELEASED BY
CENSORSHIP

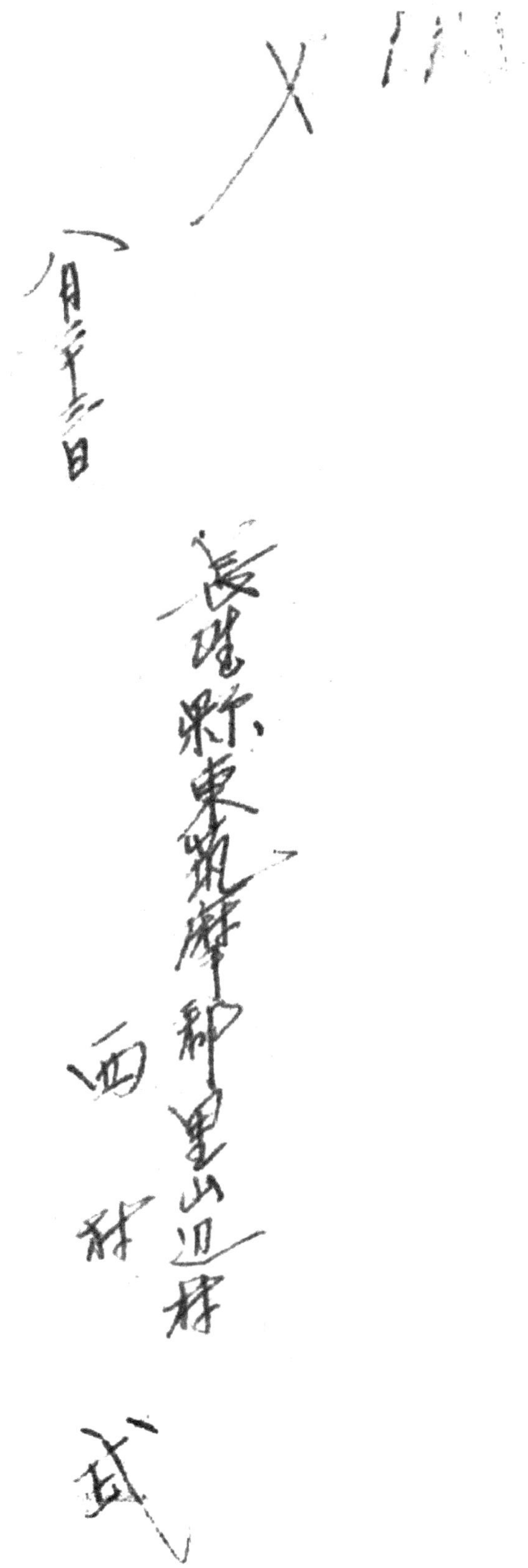

戦争犯罪人ト通告ス

陸軍獣医少佐　山口本治　宮城県柴田郡村田町

陸軍獣医少将　若松有次郎　山口県大津郡萩市

陸軍獣医中佐　保坂　不詳

右の者満洲国新京第一〇〇部隊郊外解剖場に於て捕虜多数を

獣疫の実験に供し解剖せり

実験に関係する者尚ほ多数あるも右の者調査にて判明せり

本実験に関しては多数の証人あり

昭和二十一年八月二十三日

通告者

山村　戊

聯合国民間情報部長殿

Satoyamabe-mura, Higashi Tsukuma-gun,

Nagano Prefecture

Aug. 23 1946

CI&E, GHQ, SCAP

Report on War Climinals.

Motoji Yamaguchi, a former veterinary surgeon major

Address: Murata-cho, Shibata-gun, Miyagi Prefecture

Yujiro Wakamatsu, a former veterinary surgeon major-general

Address: Hagi-shi, Otsu-gun, Yamaguchi Prefecture

Hozaka, a former veterinary surgeon lieutenant-colonel

Address Unknown

The above veterinary surgeons dissected many war prisoners of the Allied Forces at the outdoor dissecting ground of No. 100 Army Corps at Hsinking (Changchum), Manchuria, as their inspections of the cattle plague. If you would investigate these criminals, you will find many other persons who have participated to the dissections. There are a number of the witness of the inspections.

Yours truly

Takeshi Nishimura

Satoyamabe-mura, Higashi Tsukuma-gun,

Nagano Prefecture.

Aug. 23 1946

CI&E, GHQ, SCAP

Report on War Climinals.

Motoji Yamaguchi, a former veterinary surgeon major

Address: Murata-cho, Shibata-gun, Miyagi Prefecture

Yujiro Wakamatsu, a former veterinary surgeon major-general

Address: Hagi-shi, Otsu-gun, Yamaguchi Prefecture

Hozaka, a former veterinary surgeon lieutenant-colonel

Address Unknown

The above veterinary surgeons dissected many war prisoners of the Allied Forces at the outdoor dissecting ground of No. 100 Army Corps at Hsinking (Changchum), Manchuria, as their inspections of the cattle plague. If you would investigate these criminals, you will find many other persons who have participated to the dissections. There are a number of the witness of the inspections.

Yours truly

Takeshi Nishimura

郵便はがき

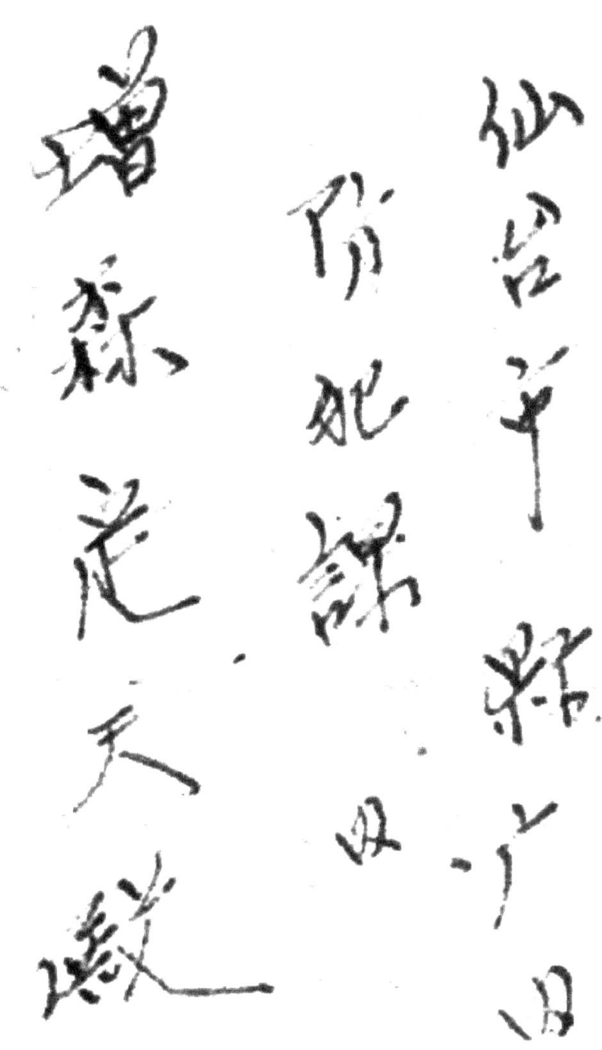

山口本治　宮城縣柴田郡村田町

防疫給水部　部隊名（石井部隊）

部隊長　石井四郎軍医中将

右往時迄に部隊長名御通知申上ます

TO: Sadao MASUMORI
Public Saftey Section,
Prefectural Office,
Sendai City.

FROM: Takeishi NISHIMURA
Yoshioka-cho

I hereby report the address and the name of the UNIT COMMANDER of the following person:

Motoji YAMAGUCHI, Murata-cho, Shibata-gun, Miyagi-ken.

(ISHII UNIT) Sanitary WATER SECTION.

COMMANDER: ISHII (fnu), M.D. Lt.General.

I certify this to be a true translation:

Toshiro Inouye

Toshiro INOUE,WDC.
Investigation Div.
Legal Section,
GHQ, SCAP.

1

新憲法も公布され占領軍の援助により
日本にとって唯一の花民主主義であり
民主化しつつあるのでありますことに喜ばし
しいことであります、しかし問題の財閥
軍閥のごときは、いかがでありましょう軍閥
の如きは日本にまだ多くの戦争主義者
がかくれて居ります國民の第一に感ずるの
は元ハルビンにて残虐行為主なる犯罪
捕虜虐殺、傳染病菌散布等
多々國際法違反したるところの石井部
隊 隊長石井中将以下書務課長、副官
等以下將校は終戦直前満洲より

Forget me not

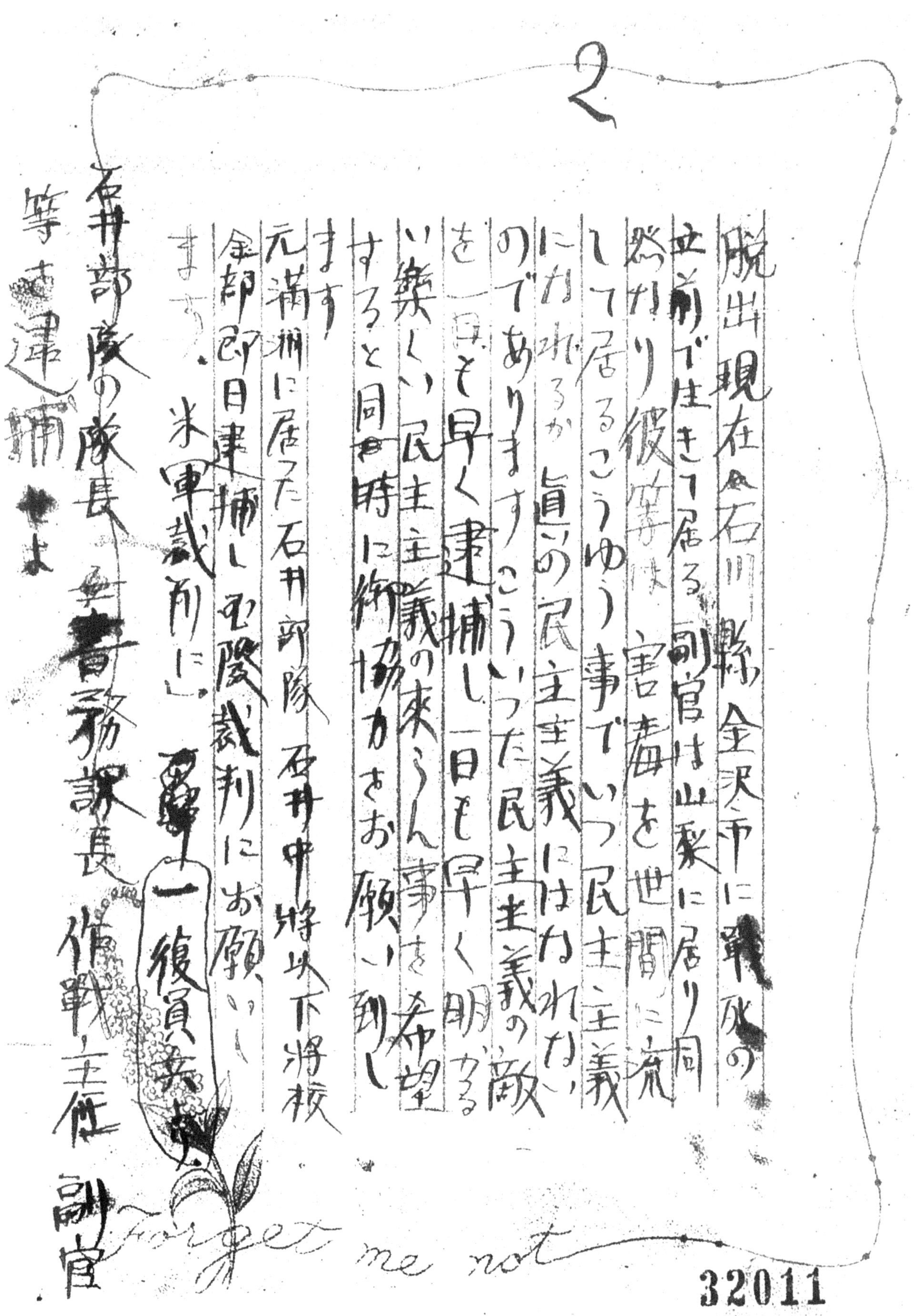

2

脱出現在石川県金沢市に戦死の
並前で生きて居る 副官は山梨に居り同
然かり彼等は害毒を世間に流
して居るこうゆう事でいつ民主主義
になれるか 真の民主主義にはなれない
のでありますこういった民主主義の敵
を一日も早く逮捕し一日も早く明かる
い楽しい民主主義の来らん事を希望
すると同時に御協力をお願い致し
ます
元満州に居った石井部隊 石井中将以下将校
全部即日逮捕し軍隊裁判にお願いし
ます 米軍裁判に
石井部隊の隊長 軍医務課長 作戦主任 副官
等を逮捕せよ

一復員兵

forget me not

32011

TRANSLATION

From a repatriated soldier.

To Chief, Military Government,

It is a matter of a great happiness that Japan is going to be democratised by the help of the Occupation forces after the new constitution has proclamated. But what have become of the "Zaibatsu" (financial giants) and "Gunbatsu" (Military clan). As for "Gunbatsu" there are still many war-advocaters hiding in Japan. What has become of the men who, violating international law, committed atrocities at "Harupin" such as slaughter of war-prisoners, dissemination of infections bacillus and etc. Those men are the officers of the Ishii detachment including lieutenant general Ishii, chief of general affairs section, and adjutant. They escaped from Manchuria just before the end of the war and they (or the general, it is not clear by the Japanese sentence) are living in Kanazawa city, Ishikawa prefecture disguising themselves as they were supposed dead at front. The adjutant is in Yamanashi prefecture under the same disguse. They are spreading evil influence on the nation. If we leave them as they are the true democratization cannot be achieved. I hope you will arrest those enemies of democracy and we will expect the time when true pleasant democracy will be realized. We also beg your cooperation on this matter. Please arrest all the officers including lieutenant general Ishii of the Ishii detachment that stayed in Manchuria and have them tried at the international tribunal. I will repeat again. Arrest the chief, the chief of general affairs section, the chief of strategic section, the adjutant of the Ishii detachment.

From a repatriated soldier.

9.10　4 Sep. 1946: Inv. Div. No. 330, Report of Investigation Division, Legal Section, GHQ, SCAP, HAROLD A. SMALL, Civilian Investigator

资料出处： National Archives of the United States, R331, B1434.

内容点评： 本资料为 1946 年 9 月 4 日盟军总司令部法务局调查科 Harold A. Small 提交的编号 330 调查报告。

Date: **4 September 1946**

Report of Investigation Division, Legal Section, GHQ, SCAP.

Inv. Div. No. 330	CRD No.	Report by: HAROLD A. SMALL, Civilian Investigator.

Title: Honji YAMAGUCHI, Yujiro WAKAMATSU, YASUZAKA, (FNU), Yasutaro HOSAKA, Shiro MATSUSHITA alias Shiro YAMASHITA.

VICTIM: Unknown.

Synopsis of facts: Request for military and biographical histories of subjects complied with by Japanese Government as regards Yujiro WAKAMATSU, Shiro YAMASHITA and Yasutaro HOSAKA.

\- P -

Reference: Report of 2d Lt. John R. EGLSAER dated 27 June 1946, Subject: Takeshi KINO.

DETAILS:

On 6 July 1946 Major L. H. BARNARD, Investigation Division, requested the complete military and biographical histories of the following former Japanese Army officers:

Honji YAMAGUCHI, former Major (IJA)
Shiro MATSUSHITA, former Captain (IJA)
(FNU) YASUZAKA, former Lt. Col. (IJA)
Yujiro WAKAMATSU, former Major General (IJA)
(FNU) HOSAKA, former Major (IJA)

On 22 July 1946 the Central Liaison Office submitted a partial report on one, Shiro YAMASHITA, presuming this person to be Shiro MATSUSHITA, noted above. This CLO report is attached to the CRD copy of this report, and reads as follows:

Date of Birth : 25 February 1910.
1 August 1941 : Commissioned to Veterinary Captain, and attached to the Quarantine Stables of the Kwantung Army.

Agent's Note:

The home address of Shiro YAMASHITA, was not included in the reports submitted by CLO. A request has been made for this information through CRD.

Distribution:

1 Prosecution Division
1 CRD (Encl) ✓
1 Fukuoka Office
1 Yamaguchi Office
3 Investigation Division

Do not write in this space.

- 2 -

A supplementary report on Shiro YAMASHITA containing his educational history was submitted by CLO on 13 August 1945. This report is attached to the CRD copy.

On 22 July 1946, the CLO submitted a report on the military and biographical history and present whereabout of Yujiro WAKAMATSU. This report, which is reproduced below, is attached to the CRD copy:

Date of Birth : 1 February 1897.

Military and Biographical History

1922	:	Graduated the Agricultural Department of the Tokyo Imperial University.
(Date Unknown)	:	Served at the Epidemic Research Institute.
(" ")	:	Stationed in Germany.
(" ")	:	Appointed to a staff of the Military Service Bureau of the War Ministry.
(" ")	:	Appointed to a teacher of the Army Veterinary School.
(" ")	:	Appointed to the Chief of the Veterinary Branch of the 13th Army.
1 July 1942	:	Appointed to the Chief of Quarantine Stables of the Kwantung Army.

Present Location: 173 Tsuchihara, Hagi-Shi, Yamaguchi Prefecture.

On 22 July 1946, the CLO submitted the home address and military and biographical history of Yasutaro HOSAKA. This report is attached to the CRD copy. HOSAKA's home address and biographical history from 1 August 1941 to 1 March 1945 are reproduced below:

Domicile : 41 Yoka-Machi, Kofu-Shi, Yamanashi Prefecture.
Date of Birth : 29 September 1908.

Military and Biographical History

1 August 1941	:	Commissioned to Veterinary Major.
31 March 1942	:	Appointed to the staff of the Reasearch Division of the Army Veterinary School.
20 August 1942	:	Appointed to the staff of the Veterinary Branch of the Kwantung Defence Army.
22 June 1944	:	Appointed to the staff of the Quarantine Stables of the Kwantung Army.
1 March 1945	:	Commissioned to Veterinary Lt. Col.

UNDEVELOPED LEADS:

The Hiroshima Office at Hagi-Shi, Yamaguchi Ken will interrogate Yujiro WAKAMATSU concerning his activities as Chief of the Quarantine Stables of the Kwantung Army. Will obtain from WAKAMATSU the names and present whereabouts of all officers connected with the Quarantine Stables, Kwantung Army.

MIR #520

The Tokyo Office at Kofu Shi, Yamanashi Ken will interrogate Yasutaro HOSAKA concerning his activities as a member of the staff of the Veterinary Branch of the Kwantung Army.

Will report on the present whereabouts and biographical and military history of Henji YAMAGUCHI as soon as this information becomes available.

Will report on the present whereabouts of Shiro YAMASHITA as soon as a report is submitted by CLO.

-PENDING-

MIR #330

9.11　14 Oct. 1946: Inv. Div. No. 330, Report of Investigation Division, Legal Section, GHQ, SCAP, by L. H. Barnard, Maj., Inf. 0-191597

资料出处：National Archives of the United States, R331, B1434.

内容点评：本资料为 1946 年 10 月 14 日盟军总司令部法务局调查科 L. H. Barnard 少校提交的编号 330 调查报告。

Date: 14 October 1946

Report of Investigation Division, Legal Section, GHQ, SCAP.

Inv. Div. No. 330	CRD No.	Report by: L. H. Barnard, Maj., Inf. 0-191597

Title: CHANGED:
Honji YAMAGUCHI; Yujiro WAKAMATSU; YASUZAKA (FNU); Yasutaro HOSAKA, alias Yasutaro HOZAKA; Shiro MATSUSHITA; and Shiro YAMASHITA.

Synopsis of facts:

Military and biographical historiesof YAMAGUCHI and YAMASHITA set out. NISHIMURA allegesPrisoners of War were dissected at dissecting ground No. 100 Hainking, Manchuria.

- P -

Reference: Report of Harold A. Small, dated 4 September 1946.

DETAILS:

At Tokyo:

The title of this report is being changed to reflect the alias HOZAKA for Yasutaro HOSAKA, as reflected in the communication of NISHIMURA referred to later in this report.

On 24 and 30 July, respectively, T. KAGOSHIMA, Military Section, Political Division, Central Liaison Office, of the Japanese Government, forwarded the military and biographical histories of Honji YAMAGUCHI and Shiro YAMASHITA, as reflected in the official filesof the Japanese Government. They read as follows:

Honji YAMAGUCHI:

Domicile: 2375 Murakami-Cho, Iwafuna-Gun, Niigata Prefecture.

Date of Birth: 18 Jan 1915.

Military and Biographical History:
Mar. 1938: Graduated the Veterinary Faculty of the Agricultural Department of the Tokyo Imperial University.

201

Distribution:
1 Prosecution
1 CRD (encl)
1 Chinese Division
1 Fukuoka
1 Osaka (Mr. Donnell)
1 Duffy
3 Inv. Div. (File 330)

Do not write in this space.
B

1 Apr. 1938: Appointed to Veterinary Cadet and attached to the 16th Cavalry Regiment.
30 June. 1938: Commissioned to Veterinary 1st Lt.
12 Dec 1938: Attached to the Reserve Unit of the 10th Cavalry Regt.
24 Sept 1940: Designated to the staff of the Veterinary Branch of the 10th Division.
1 Mar. 1941: Commissioned to Veterinary Capt.
1 Apr. 1942: Attached to the Military Veterinary Material Depot.
1 Dec. 1943: Commissioned to Veterinary Maj.
29 Jan 1944: Attached to the Quarantine Stables of the Kwantung Army.
24 Aug. 1945: Attached to the Reserve Unit of the 26th Field Artillery Regiment.

Shiro YAMASHITA:

Domicile: 2, Haranaka, Kotakira, Nishigo-Mura, Nishishirakawa-Gun, Fukushima Prefecture.

Date of Birth: 20 Feb. 1910.

1. Biographical Career:

Mar. 1932: Graduated from the Morioka Higher Agricultural and Forestry School.
Mar. 1932: Employed by the Koshin Co. at Kihawashita, Koishikawaku, Tokyo City.
Jan. 1938: Discharged from the above Co. for military service.
12 Nov. 1945: Served at the Animal-breeding Sect. of Shirakawa pasture (which belonged to the Central Bushiness encouraging Office, Cultivation Bureau, Agricultural and Forestry Ministry).

2. Military Career:

1 Feb. 1933: Entered the 2nd Transport Btn. as a candidate for a reserve Officer.
30 Nov. 1936: Discharged astime expired.
13 Mar. 1936: The 3rd class Veterinary.
15 Feb. 1937: Commissioned to Veterinary 2nd Lieut.
13 Jul. 1937: Enrolled to 26th Field Art. Regt.
30 Sept 1938: Commissioned to Veterinary 1st Lieut.
16 Jul. 1941: Attached to Quarantine Stable, Kwantung Army.
1 Aug. 1941: Commissioned to Veterinary Captain.
2 Sept. 1945: Discharged.

The originals of the above referred-to communications are being transmitted to the Criminal Registry Division with copies of this report.

On 23 August, 1946, Takeshi NISHIMURA, giving his address as Nagano-Ken, Hagashi Tsukuma-gun, Satoyaemabe-mura, forwarded a communication to the CIE Section of SCAP reading as follows:

Report on War Criminals.

Motogji Yamaguchi, a former veterinary surgeon major

Address: Murata-cho, Shibata-gun, Miyagi Prefecture

Yujiro Wakamatsu, a former veterinary sufgeon major-general

Address: Hagi-shi, Otsu-gun, Yamaguchi Prefecture

Hozaka, a former veterinary surgeon lieutenant-colonel

Address: Unknown

The above veterinayy surgeons dissected many war prisoners of the Allied Forces at the outdoor dissecting ground of No. 100 Army Corps at Hsinking (Changchun), Manchuria, as their inspections of the cattle plague. If you would investigate these criminals, you will find many other persons who have participated to the dissections. There are a number of the witness of the inspections.

This was substantially the same information as is reflected in the report of Capt. Joseph F. SARTIANO in this matter, dated 8 August 1946.

UNDEVELOPED LEADS:

The Osaka Office -- At Hagashi Yamaguchi-Ken -- Will interrogate Yujiro WAKAMATSU concerning his activities as Chief of the Quarantine of the Kwantung Armu and obtain from WAKAMATSU the names and present locations of all officers connected with the Kwantung stables.

The Tokyo Office -- At Tokyo -- Will report the results of the demand placed on the Japanese Government for the military and biographical histories of WAKAMATSU, YASUZAKA, HOSAKA, and MATSUSHITA.

The Tokyo Office -- At Satoyaemabe-mura, Nagano-ken -- Will locate and interview Takeshi NISHIMURA, presently reported residing at Satoyaemabe-mura, Higashi Tsukuma-gun, Nagano Prefecture, for full information he may have concerning the nature of the atrocities committed, the identities of the individuals committing same, and the individuals who witnessed same.

P E N D I N G

9.12 5 Nov. 1946: Inv. Div. No. 330, Report of Investigation Division, Legal Section, GHQ, SCAP, by L. H. Barnard, Maj. Inf. 0-191597; 4 Nov. 1946: 京都市吉田町上木寛より手紙: マッカーサー司令部御中

资料出处： National Archives of the United States, R331, B1434.

内容点评： 本资料为 1946 年 11 月 5 日盟军总司令部法务局调查科 L. H. Barnard 少校提交的编号 330 细菌战有关调查报告，附 1946 年 11 月 4 日京都市吉田町上木宽（Hiroshi Ueki）投寄麦克阿瑟司令部告发石井四郎的信函。

Date: 5 November 1946

Report of Investigation Division, Legal Section, GHQ, SCAP.

Inv. Div. No. 330 | CRD No. | Report by: L. H. Barnard, Maj. Inf. 0-191597

Changed:

Title: Motoji YAMAGUCHI alias Henji YAMAGUCHI; Yujiro WAKAMATSU; YASUZAKA (FNU); Yasutaro HOSAKA alias Yasutara HOZAKA; Shiro MATSUSHIDA alias Shiro YAMASHITA; Lt. General Shiro ISHII.

Synopsis of facts:

UEKI alleges ISHII established large scale human experimental station at Harbin during the war where brutal experiments on Allied Prisoners were made. Japanese Government directed to furnish military and biographical history of subject.

\- P -

Reference: Report of Harold A. Small, dated 4 September 1946.

DETAILS:

At Tokyo:

The title of this report is changed to reflect the addition of Lt. General Shiro ISHII as a subject of this of this investigation.

On 4 October 1946, Hiroshi UEKI, residing at Kyoto-shi, Yoshida-cho, directed a letter to General MacArthur which had been translated as ATIS Document No. 23836 and the original and translation of same are being retained in the Investigation Division file in this matter.

UEKI alleged that during the present war, Lt. General Shiro ISHII, an army medical doctor, established a large scale human experimental station in the suburbs of HARBIN. He allegedly acted as commander of the fictitious KAMO unit and executed brutal experiments on many Allied Prisoners of War. According to UEKI, at the time the war terminated, it was no secret that he destroyed the experiment station and the evidences of his activities. UEKI further alleged that ISHII considered the placing of his name on a war crime suspect list as inevitable and has been using bribes to escape the consequences of his acts.

According to the information contained in UEKI's communication, he is a physician who was conscripted by the Japanese Army.

Distribution:

1 Prosecution
1 CRD
1 Fukuoka
1 Osaka
1 Sapporo
1 Chinese Division
3 Inv. Div. (File #330)

Do not write in this space.

A directive has been issued to the Japanese Government through Assistant Chief of Staff, G-2, Japanese Liaison, to furnish the full military and biographical history of ISHII and the results of this demand will be set forth in the next investigative report in this matter.

In view of the fact that allegations of a similar nature had been received from numerous sources, a review of this file has been conducted and the following recapitulation is made:

On 26 June 1946, Takeshi KINO was interviewed by the Fukuoka office of the Legal Section at which time he executed a statement referred to in the report of Lt. John R. Eglsaer, dated 27 June 1946. KINO admitted that he had served in the Japanese Army and had been stationed in Manchuria, and was discharged from the military service in 1943, becoming a civilian employee of the Kwantung Army Stables. He stated that he heard a rumor to the effect that humans were being infected with glanders and then being dissected for experimental purposes but could not recall whether he had heard that these experiments were being conducted on Prisoners of War or Chinese Coolies. He further stated that the "ISHII" unit at Harbin was making experiments on this disease and may have been guilty of the acts. KINO stated that the experiments conducted by that station were of a secret nature; that he was not personally cognizant of the extent to which they were carried.

An individual, giving his name only as NISHIMURA of Nagano-ken, sent an undated letter to Allied Headquarters alleging that Prisoners of War had been infected with glanders by former Major Honji YAMAGUCHI, Major General Yujiro WAKAMATSU, Lt. Colonel YASUZAKA and Captain MATSUSHITA.

To date, unsuccessful efforts have been made to locate and interview ISHIMURA.

The report of Captain Joseph F. Sartiano, dated 8 August 1946, discloses that Motoji YAMAGUCHI, who is allegedly reported as Honji YAMAGUCHI was inducted into the army as a Probational Officer of the 16th Cavalry in the capacity of a Veterinarian on 20 April 1938 and subsequently joined the 10th Cavalry which moved to Jamusu, Manchuria. YAMAGUCHI was promoted to the grade of Captain in 1940 and in 1942 to the Tokyo Military Veterinary School where he majored in pathology at which time he went to Hsinking, China with the Kwantung Army Horse Disease Prevention Unit as a veterinarian. He remained there until 12 August 1945 when his unit retreated to Seoule, Korea. He denied that any experiments were conducted on humans but stated that experiments were conducted on guinea pigs, rabbits and horses.

YAMAGUCHI acknowledged knowing NISHIMURA, who, he stated, was also a veterinarian and who resides in Nagana-ken and formerly concocted serums at the No. 3 station. YAMAGUCHI stated that he at one time reprimanded NISHIMURA for having stolen some food and a few bottles of glucose.

In an effort to locate NISHIMURA, a directive has been sent to the Japanese Government to furnish his military and biographical history. Upon the receipt of this information, a lead will be set out to locate and interview him for specific information concerning the allegations contained in his letter.

- 2 -

UNDEVELOPED LEADS:

The Osaka Office -- At Kyoto -- Will locate and interview Hiroshi UEKI, presently reported residing in Kyoto-shi, Yoshita-cho, and obtain a complete and exhaustive statement from him concerning his knowledge of the matter of the experiments which were allegedly conducted upon Prisoners of War at the HARBIN experimental station.

At Hagi-shi, Yamaguchi-ken,-will locate and interview Shiro YAMASHITA, presently reported residing at 173 Tsuchirara, Hagi-shi, Yamaguchi-ken, concerning his knowledge of the experiments conducted on Prisoners of War.

For the information of the Osaka Office, the service record of WAKAMATSU as set forth in reference report, discloses that he graduated from the Agricultural Department of the Tokyo Imperial University in 1922, subsequently served at the Epidemic Research Institute, had a tour of duty in Germany, served with the Military Service Bureau of the War Ministry, was a former instructor in the Army Veterinary School, was former Chief of the Veterinary Branch of the 13th Army and on 1 July 1942 became Chief of the Quarantine Stables of the Kwantung Army.

The Tokyo Office -- at Tokyo -- Will report the result of the demand placed on the Japanese Government for the military and biographical history of ISHIMURA and set forth appropriate leads for the location and interview of this individual.

Will report the result of the demand placed on the Japanese Government for the military and biographical history of YAMAGUCHI, YAMASHITA, and ISHII.

At Kofu -- Will locate and interview Tatsutaro HOSAKA, presently reported residing at 41 Yoka-machi, Kofu-shi, Yamanashi-ken, concerning his knowledge of the illegal experiments reportedly conducted by the staff of the Quarantine Stables of the Kwantung Army. For the information of the agent conducting this interview, the service record of HOSAKA as reflected in reference report discloses that he was commissioned a Major in the Veterinary Corps on 1 August 1941 and on 31 March 1942 was appointed to the staff of the Research Division of the Army Veterinary School. On 20 August 1942, he was appointed to the staff of the Veterinary Branch of the Kwantung Defense Army and on 22 June 1944 he was appointed to the staff of the Quarantine Stables of the Kwantung Army. He became a Lt. Colonel in the Veterinary Corps on 1 March 1945.

At Tokyo -- Will confer with the Chinese Division for the purpose of ascertaining whether they have any information concerning the alleged atrocities committed on Prisoners of War or Chinese Coolies, as indicated in the body of this report.

P E N D I N G

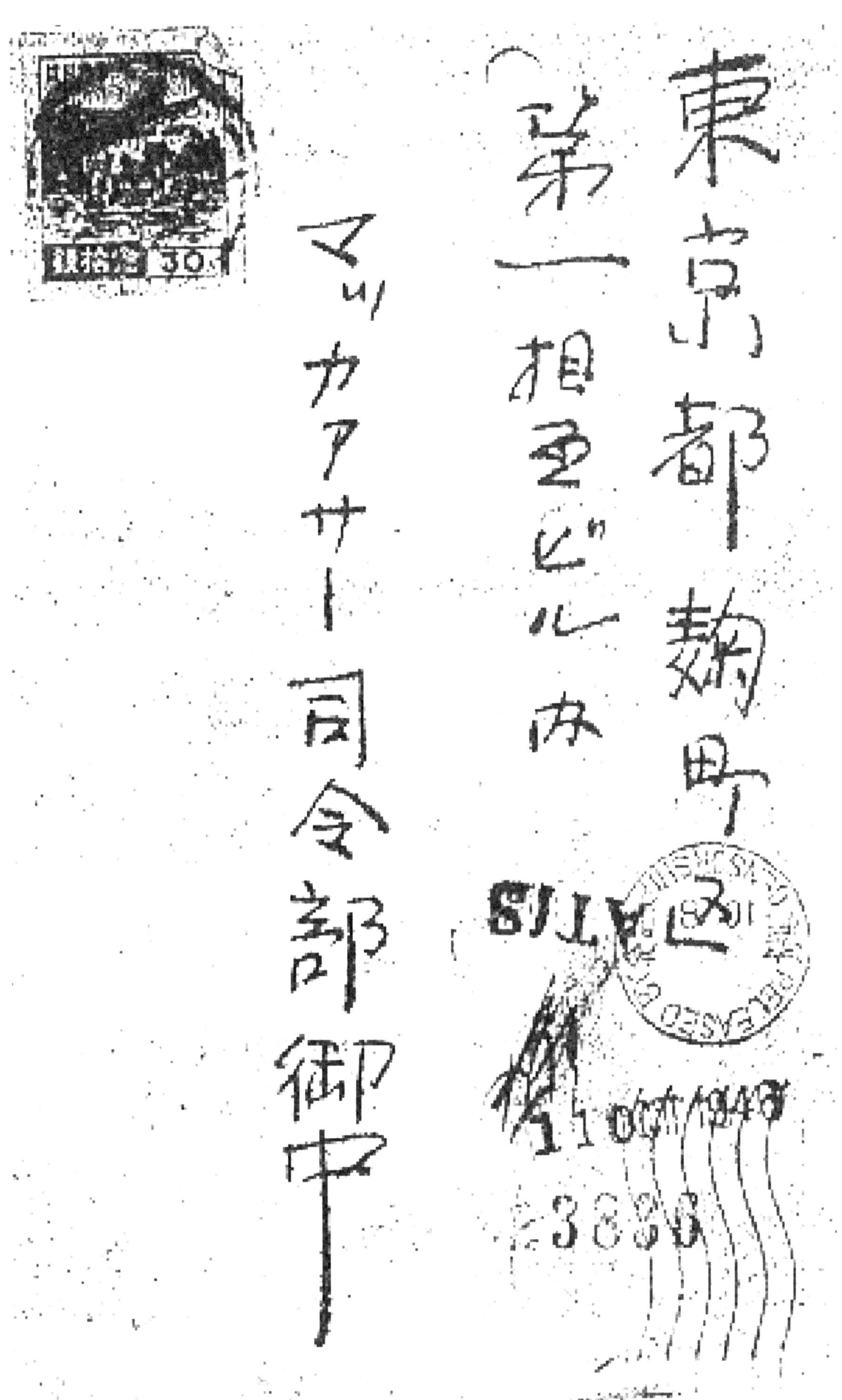

東京都麹町区
（第一相互ビル内
マッカアサー司令部御中

京都市吉田町
上木宜人

前陸軍々医中将石井四郎ガ今回ノ戦時中
ハルビン郊外ニ大規模ノ人間生体実験所ヲ設
カモ
加茂部隊ノ変名ノ下ニ　加茂部隊或ハトシニ
多数ノ聯合軍捕虜ニ対シ残酷ナル生体実験ヲ施
終戦時此等施設ヲバ破壊シテ其証拠ヲ消サントセシ
ハ公然ノ秘密トシテ我国民ノ能ク知リテ居ル[illegible]
サレバ彼ガ数月前貴司令部ヨリ戦犯容疑者トシテ
指名サレタルヲ新聞ニテ知リタル国民ハ当然ノ結果デアルト
其経過ヲ注意シ居リタルニ近来彼ハ多額ノワイロ金ヲ
使ヒ其罪ヲノガレントシテ大運動ヲシテ居ルトノコトデアル
私ハ平和愛好者ノ一人トシテ又聯合軍最高司令部ヲ
最モ崇敬スル日本人ノ一人トシテ司令部ノ権威ノタメニモ
右石井ノ審問ノ経過ヲ公表サレンコトヲ願フモノデアル

十月四日

元軍医トシテ召集サレタル
一人ヨリ

マッカアサー司令部御中

9.13 8 Nov. 1946: Inv. Div. No. 330, Report of Investigation Division, Legal Section, GHQ, SCAP, by L.H. Barnard, Maj. Inf. 0-191597; 3 Sep. 1946: Report Letter and Translation, TO: CI&E, GHQ, FROM: Koriyama-shi, Fukushima Prefecture: Contribution Concerning Surgeon Lt. Gen. Shiro Ishii

资料出处： National Archives of the United States, R331, B1434.

内容点评： 本资料为 1946 年 11 月 8 日盟军总司令部法务局调查科 L. H. Barnard 少校提交的编号 330 调查报告，附 1946 年 9 月 3 日自福岛县郡山市投寄盟军总司令部民间情报部门告发石井四郎的匿名信及译文。

Date: 8 November 1946

Report of Investigation Division, Legal Section, GHQ, SCAP.

Inv. Div. No. 330	CRD No.	Report by: L. H. Barnard, Maj. Inf. 0-191597

Title: Motoji YAMAGUCHI with aliases, et al

Synopsis of facts:

Anonymous letter alleges Lt. General Shiro ISHII engaged in activities while in China which would characterize him as a war criminal and involve one member of the Imperial family.

- P -

Reference: Report of Major L. H. Barnard, dated 5 November 1946.

DETAILS:

At Tokyo:

An anonymous letter, dated 3 September 1946, giving an address of Koriyama-shi, Fukushima-ken, was sent to the CI&E Section of SCAP, where a translation was obtained and the original and translation forwarded to the Legal Section for appropriate action.

The original and copies of the translation of same are being transmitted to the Criminal Registry Division with their copy of this report.

The letter reads as follows:

"CI&E, GHQ

Contribution concerning Surgeon Lt.Gen. Shiro Ishii.

I was forced to work in the army for a long time only for victory recently was demobilized without belongings.

People treat me cold-heartedly and I have no job at present, when inflation is rampant. Moreover, I have many family members to feed. This is the whole reward for me, who worked whole-heartedly at the risk of my life.

Distribution:
1 Prosecution ✓
1 CRD (Encl)
1 Fukuoka
1 Osaka
1 Sapporo
1 Chinese Division
3 Inv. Div. (File #330)

Do not write in this space.

B

One year after the termination of war, my living has become more and more difficult. Gradually I have began to lose hope of living through it.

Japan is now endeavouring to become a peaceful country. To realize this aim, militarists must be eradicated completely. But the cabinets since the end of the war have strove to conceal them as best as they could. Now I want to tell you the case of Lt. Gen. Ishii as an example.

A repatriate from Manchuria reported in the newspaper that he was shot to death, but this is not a fact, this article was made by the order of the government and nothing else. He was a well-known militarist and enemy of humanity. He established the Epidemic Prevention and Water Supply Section of Kwantong army. What did he do through this section and what did he plan? I was once attached to his corps, so I know quite well about his work. Militarists are afraid of his summon, as the secrets will be revealed by it. His summoning will provide evidence and data against 'A' class war criminal suspects and even one Imperial family member will be affected. So the cabinets, especially the Foreign Ministry, ex-Army Ministry. Demobilization Board and Liaison Office have endeavored to make this case lost in oblivion. I believe that it is utterly necessary to judge him and those who planned and worked with him fairly for the establishment of truly peaceful country.

I know quite well about him and his corps and the atrocities committed by them.

If you want my help, I will work as best as I can for the investigation of this case.

I have strict confidence to correspond to your expectation, if you permit me certain number of days and expenditures for investigation.

As to details, I want to meet you to consult with you. If you want to make me do this work, please put the following advertisement in the Nippon Keizai Press within 3 days after the arrival of this letter to you.

'Attendance Order'

'Shiro Ishii is required to appear in person on ---day Sept, 1946.

CI&E, GHQ, SCAP."

The request contained in the letter that the writer be contacted through the Keizai Press, could not have been complied with even had it been desirable, inasmuch as the original letter had not been translated within the specified time.

This information is being included in this report as another indication of the mounting complaints concerning the alleged activities of General ISHII and his associates at the Kwantung Experimental Stables in China, principals among which are alleged to have been infecting Prisoners of War with glanders for experimental purposes.

UNDEVELOPED LEADS:

The Osaka Office -- At Kyoto -- Will locate and interview Hiroshi UEKI, presently reported residing in Kyoto-shi, Yoshita-cho, and obtain a complete and exhaustive statement from him concerning his knowledge of the matter of the experiments which were allegedly conducted upon Prisoners of War at the HARBIN experimental station.

At Hagi-shi, Yamaguchi-ken, -- will locate and interview Shiro YAMASHITA, presently reported residing at 173 Tsuchirara, Hagi-shi. Yamaguchi-ken, concerning his knowledge of the experiments conducted on Prisoners of War.

For the information of the Osaka Office, the service record of WAKAMATSU as set forth in reference report, discloses that he graduated from the Agricultural Department of the Tokyo Imperial University in 1922, subsequently served at the Epidemic Research Institute, had a tour of duty in Germany, served with the Military Service Bureau of the War Ministry, was a former instructor in the Army Veterinary School, was former Chief of the Veterinary Branch of the 13th Army and on 1 July 1942 became Chief of the Quarantine Stables of the Kwantung Army.

The Tokyo Office -- At Tokyo -- Will report the result of the demand placed on the Japanese Government for the military and biographical history of ISHIMURA and set forth appropirate leads for the location and interview of this individual.

Will report the result of the demand placed on the Japanese Government for the military and biographical history of YAMAGUCHI, YAMASHITA, and ISHII.

At Kofu -- Will locate and interview Yatsutaro HOSAKA, presently reported residing at 41 Yoka-machi, Kofu-shi, Yamanashi-ken, concerning his knowledge of the illegal experiments reportedly conducted by the staff of the Quarantine Stables of the Kwantung Army. For the information of the agent conducting this interview, the service record of HOSAKA as reflected in reference report discloses that he was commissioned a Major in the Veterinary Corps on 1 August 1941 and on 31 March 1942 was appointed to the staff of the Research Division of the Army Veterinary School. On 20 August 1942, he was appointed to the staff of the Veterinary Branch of the Kwantung Defense Army and on 22 June 1944 he was appointed to the staff of the Quarantine Stables of the Kwantung Army. He became a Lt. Colonel in the Veterinary Corps on 1 March 1945.

At Tokyo -- Will confer with the Chinese Division for the purpose of ascertaining whether they have any information concerning the alleged atrocities committed on Prisoners of War or Chinese Coolies, as indicated in the body of this report.

P E N D I N G

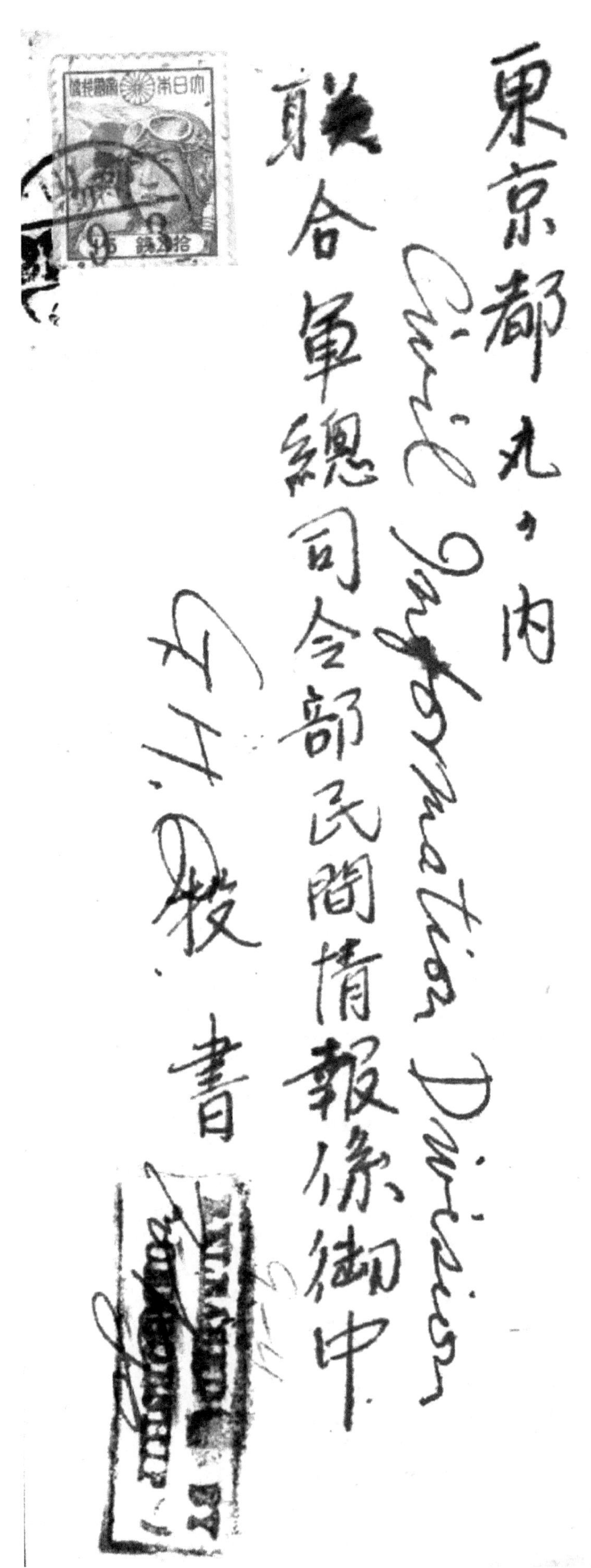

東京都丸ノ内
聯合軍總司令部民間情報係御中
Civil Information Division
F.H.殿　書

石井四郎軍醫中將に關する投書

勝ち抜く爲だと長い間軍隊生活を強要せられ
着のみ着のまゝで復員してみれば昨日に變る社会
の冷酷の扱ひ家業は失はれ 然も昨今のインフレ
と就職難 資金を借りたくとも借す人とてなく
十余名の家族を抱への生活苦……これが生命を
さゝげて國家に奉仕して來た私たちに與へられた
報酬の全部でした
終戰一ヶ年凡ゆる努力を傾注して來ましたが
私たち一家の經濟は愈々窮迫するばかり…此の
儘の狀態で推移せんか生活の破綻は
もう直き訪れるでせう

私は次第に生きる希望を失ひかけて參りました
私は時折死の幻影にとりつかれます。
何か刺戟があったら或はそれに突進するでせう

かうした生活に陷入れたのは無謀な戰爭を敢てした
軍国主義者に外なりません
日本は今民主的平和國家として生れ變らうとしてゐます。
ほんとうに平和國家となる爲には軍國主義信奉者は
完全に掃拭せられなければなりません 然し
終戰後の各内閣は極力之が隱蔽と保護に
力を傾けてゐるのです。
その一例は既に召喚命令の出た石井軍醫中將の

如きそれで有ます 過日の新聞には満洲よりの一歸還者の談として彼は満洲で銃殺されたと書いてゐました それは如何に虚偽に終始してゐるものであるか私はよく知つてゐるのです
それは政府の指令に依る宣傳以外の何物でも有ません
彼は有名な軍国主義者でした 典型的国家主義崇拜者でした そして又人道の敵でも有ました
それが故に彼は関東軍防疫給水部なるものを創設したのでした 彼は此處で何をやつたか そして何を計画してゐたか
私は彼の部隊に過去に於て勤務した事があつたのでよく知つてゐるのです
石井四郎中將の召換に依つてその内容は白日下に暴露されることは國家主義者共の如何に虞れることか それが故に事実を隠蔽秘隠して居るのです
彼の召喚はA級戰犯者に眞に不利な事実を提供致しませう 更に皇族の一員にさへも累系を及ぼすものなのです
それが故に終戦後内閣就中外務及陸軍大臣終戦連絡事務局並に復員廳は殊更に事實を闇にほうむらうとしてゐるのです
悪德に充ちた彼等を擁護し反面何等の罪の

ない私たちが犠牲にならねばならない こんな不合理な事は有ません
彼の悪虐無道の行爲を摘決し廣く輿論に訴へ 彼と共に計画し或は関聯した者たちの罪悪は公正な神の裁きを受けしむることこそ眞の平和國家建設の上から其の前提とならねばありません。
私は石井のこと、彼の長たりし部隊の内容と世期の惨虐行爲の数々、構成分子等一切の秘密を知つてゐます。
更に終戦後如何になつたか……これも調査次第で判明致しませう

若し御希望なれば 私は本件調査の爲尽し得る限りの御援助御協力をしたいと思つて居ります。
私に若干の日子と調査費用を御恵與下さるならば必ず御期待に副ひ得る確信を有します
詳細に亘っては御面談致し度存じます
若し幸ひに調査の大役お命じ下さるならば本書到着3日以内に日本産経新聞紙上に裏面の如き出頭廣告御掲示方御願ひ申上げます。

以上

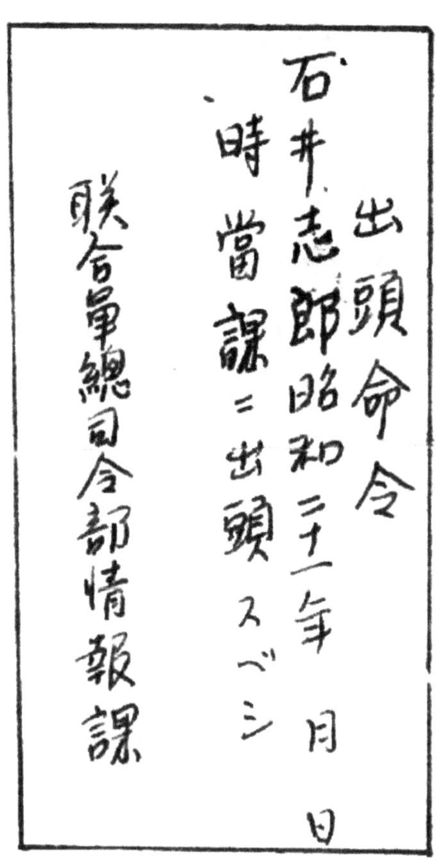
出頭命令

石井志郎昭和二十一年　月　日

時當課ニ出頭スベシ

联合軍總司令部情報課

联合軍總司令部情報部長殿

親展

Koriyama-shi, Fukushima Prefecture

Sept. 3 1946

CI&E, GHQ

Contribution concerning Surgeon Lt.Gen. Shiro Ishii.

I was forced to work in the army for a long time only for victory reventlyl was demobilized without belongings.

People treat me cold-heartedly and I have no job at present, when inflation is rampant. Moreover, I have many family members to feed. This is the whole reward for me, who worked whole-heartedly at the risk of my life.

One year after the termination of war, my living has become more and more difficult. Gradually I have began to lose hope of living through it.

Japan is now endeavouring to become a peaceful country. To realize this aim, militarists must be eradicated completely, But the cabinets since the end of the war have strove to conceal them as best as they could. Now I want to tell you the case of Lt. Gen. Ishii as an example.

A repatriate from Manchuria reported in the newspaper that he was shot to death, but this is not a fact, this article was made by the order of the government and nothing else. He was a well-known militarist and enemy of humanity. He established the Epidemic Prevention and Water Supply Section of Kwantong army. What did he do through this section and what did he plan? I was once attached to his corps, so I know quite well about his work. Militarists are afraid of his summon, as the secrets will be revealved by it. His summoning will provide evidence and data against 'A' class war criminal suspects and even one Imperial family member will be affected.

So the cabinets, especially the Foreign Ministry, ex-Army Ministry. Demobilization Board and Liaison Office have endeavoured to make this case lost in oblivion.

I believe that it is utterly necessary to judge him and those who planned and worked with him fairly for the establishment of truly peaceful country.

I know quite well about him and his corps and the atrocities committed by them.

If you want my help, I will work as best as I can for the investigation of this case.

I have strict confidence to correspond to your expectation, if you permit me certain number of days and expenditures for investigation.

As to details, I want to meet you to consult with you. If you want to make me do this work, please put the following advertisement in the Nippon Keizai Press within 3 days after the arrival of this letter to you.

'Attendance order'

'Shiro Ishii is required to appear in person on---day, Sept,1946.

CI&E, GHQ, SCAP.

9.14 12 Nov. 1946: Inv. Div. No. 330, Report of Investigation Division, Legal Section, GHQ, SCAP, by H. KANEMITSU

资料出处： National Archives of the United States, R331, B1434.

内容点评： 本资料为1946年11月12日盟军总司令部法务局H. KANEMITSU提交的编号330细菌战有关调查报告。

GENERAL HEADQUARTERS
SUPREME COMMANDER FOR THE ALLIED POWERS
AND
UNITED STATES ARMY FORCES, PACIFIC

ROUTING SLIP

FROM: G-2 JAP LIAISON DATE: 15 Nov 1946

TO:

Commander-in-Chief	Ordnance
Aide de Camp	Prov Marshal
Chief of Staff	Pub Relations
Deputy C of S AFPAC	Quartermaster
Deputy C of S SCAP	Signal
Secy, General Staff	Sp Services
G-1	Transp
G-2	
G-3	Civ Comm
G-4	Civ Int
Adjutant General ✓ (1)	Civ I&E
Antiaircraft	Civ Transp
Cent Purch	Civ Prop Cust
Chaplain	Diplomatic
Chemical	E&S
Civ Personnel	Gen Acct'g
Engineer	Gen Proc
Fiscal	Government
Hq Comdt	Int'l Pros
I&E	Legal ✓ (2)
Inspector General	Nat Resources
Judge Advocate	Public H&W
Medical	Stat & Rpts

FOR:

Approval	Note and Return
Comment or Concurrence	Dist'n Desired ✓ (1)
Information	Signature
Initials	Dispatch
Issuance of Orders	Attachment of Reference
Necessary Action ✓ (2)	File

JWJ

AFPAC AGO Form No. (14) (12 Sep 46)

Date: **12 November 1946**

Report of Investigation Division, Legal Section, GHQ, SCAP.

Inv. Div. No. **330** CRD No. Report by: **N. Kanemitsu**

Title: **Motoji YAMAGUCHI, et al.**

Synopsis of facts:

HOSAKA's relatives advise he is presently residing in Tokyo.

\- P -

Reference: Report of Major L. H. Barnard, dated 8 November 1946.

DETAILS:

At Kofu:

Reporting agent proceeded to Kofu-shi on 7 November 1946 and reported to Capt. KOPKE of Yamanashi Military Government Team.

A search was initiated at HOSAKA's (alias HOZAKA), registered address given by the Japanese Government as 41 Yoka-machi, Kofu-shi, Yamanashi-ken, with negative results. Subject left this home approximately 15 years ago. The home had since then been sold and then destroyed by air raids.

A check was made of HOSAKA's registry of name and a relative, SUEKI, was located and interviewed. SUEKI admitted receiving a letter from HOSAKA and gave his address as 3-45 Tamagawa Okuzawa-cho, Setagaya-ku, Tokyo. Telephone number given as Denenchofu 3234. HOSAKA is at present residing in the home of his brother, Bunzo.

UNDEVELOPED LEADS:

The Osaka Office — At Hagi-shi, Yamaguchi-ken — Will interrogate Yujiro WAKAMATSU concerning his activities as Chief of the Quarantine Stables of the Kwantung Army and obtain from WAKAMATSU the names and present locations of all the officers connected with the Kwantung stables.

At Kyoto — Will locate and interview Hiroshi UEKI, presently reported residing in Kyoto-shi, Yoshita-cho, and obtain a complete and ex-

Distribution:
1 Prosecution
1 CRD
1 Fukuoka
1 Osaka
1 Sapporo
1 Chinese Division
3 Inv. Div. (File 330)

Do not write in this space.

B

haustive statement from him concerning his knowledge of the matter of the experiments which were allegedly conducted upon Prisoners of War at the Harbin experimental station.

At Hagi-shi, Yamaguchi-ken — Will locate and interview Shiro YAMASHITA, presently reported residing at 173 Tsuchirara, Hagi-shi, Yamaguchi-ken, concerning his knowledge of the experiments conducted on the Prisonersof War.

For the information of the Osaka Office, the service record of WAKAMATSU, as set forth in reference report, discloses that he graduated from the Agricultural Department of the Tokyo Imperial University in 1922, subsequently served in the Epidemic Research Institute, had a tour of duty in Germany, served with the Military Service Bureau of the War Ministry, was former instructor in the Army Veterinary School, was former Chief of the Veterinary Branch of the 13th Army and on 1 July 1942 became Chief of the Quarantine Stables of the Kwantung Army.

The Tokyo Office — At Tokyo — Will report the results of the demand placed on the Japanese Government for the military and biographical history of NISHIMURA and set forth appropriate leads for the location and interview of this individual.

Will report the result of the demand placed on the Japanese Government for the military and biographical history of YAMAGUCHI, YAMASHITA, and ISHII.

Will confer with the Chinese Division for the purpose of ascertaining whether they have any information concerning the alleged atrocities committed on Prisoners of War or Chinese coolies, as indicated in report of Major L. H. Barnard, dated 8 November 1946.

The Tokyo Office — At Satoyaemabe-mura, Nagano-ken — Will locate and interview Takeshi NISHIMURA, presently reported residing at Sateyaemabe-mura, Higashi Tsukuura-gun, Nagano-ken, for full information he may have concerning the nature of the atrocities committed, the identities of the individuals committing same, and the individuals who witnessed same.

P E N D I N G

9.15 15 Nov. 1946: PMR 439, Records of ISHII Shiro, T. NOBORI, Military Section, Political Division, Central Liaison Office

资料出处： National Archives of the United States, R331, B1434.

内容点评： 本资料为1946年11月15日日本战后联络中央事务局政治部军事课向盟军总司令部提交的石井四郎履历。

IMPERIAL JAPANESE GOVERNMENT

CENTRAL LIAISON OFFICE

PMR 439 15 November 1946

TO : GENERAL HEADQUARTERS OF THE SUPREME COMMANDER FOR THE ALLIED POWERS.

SUBJECT : Records of ISHII Shiro.

1. Reference: Check Sheet LS-Z 3704 dated 5 November 1946, subject: "Request for Records."

2. The military and biographical history as well as the official domicile and present whereabouts of ISHII Shiro is submitted herewith as per enclosure.

T. Nobori
T. NOBORI,
Military Section,
Political Division,
Central Liaison Office.

Enclosure: A report as indicated above.

MILITARY AND BIOGRAPHICAL HISTORY OF ISHI SHIRO

Domicile: 1382 Osato, Chiyoda-Mura, Sambu-Gun, Chiba Pref.

Present Address: 77 Wakamatsu-Cho, Ushigome-Ku, Tokyo Pref.

Date of Birth: 25 June 1892.

Military History:

Promotion:

Apr. 1921:	First Lieutenant, A.M.C.
20 Aug. 1924:	Captain, A.M.C.
1 Aug. 1930:	Major, A.M.C.
1 Aug. 1935:	Lt. Colonel, A.M.C.
1 Mar. 1938:	Colonel, A.M.C.
1 Mar. 1941:	Maj. Gen., A.M.C.
1 Mar. 1945:	Lt. Gen., A.M.C.
1 Dec. 1945:	Transferred to reserve corps.

Appointment:

Apr. 1921:	Attached to 3rd Imperial Guard Inf. Regt.
1 Aug. 1922:	Attached to Tokyo First Army Hospital.
1 Apr. 1924:	Graduated Graduate School of Kyoto Imperial University. Attached to Kyoto Army Hospital.
From Apr. 1928 To Apr. 1930:	Sent abroad to study.
1 Aug. 1930:	Instructor of Army Medical School.
1 Aug. 1936:	Chief of Epidemics Prevention Bureau of Kwantung Army and instructor of Army Medical School.
1 Aug. 1940:	Chief of Epidemics Prevention and Water Supply Bureau of Kwantung Army and instructor of Army Medical School.
1 Aug. 1942:	Medical Chief of 1st Army.

1 Aug. 1943: Instructor of Army Medical School.

1 Mar. 1945: Chief of Epidemics Prevention and Water Supply Bureau of Kwantung Army.

Biographical History:

1 Apr. 1916: Entered Medical Dept. of Kyoto Imperial University.

Dec. 1920: Graduated above university.

1 Apr. 1924: Entered Graduate School of Kyoto Imperial University and specialized bacteriology, serum, and prevention of epidemics.

NOTE: The above information is furnished by the statement of the subject person.

9.16 20 Nov. 1946: Inv. Div. No. 91, Report of Investigation Division, Legal Section, GHQ, SCAP, by L.H. Barnard, Maj. Inf. 0-191597, Title: Lt. General Shiro ISHII

资料出处：National Archives of the United States, R331, B1434.

内容点评：本资料为1946年11月20日盟军总司令部法务局L. H. Barnard少校提交的编号330调查报告，题目：中将石井四郎。

Date: 20 November 1946

Report of Investigation Division, Legal Section, GHQ, SCAP.

Inv. Div. No 91 | CRD No. | Report by: L. H. Barnard, Maj. Inf. 0-191597

Title: Lt. General Shiro ISHII

Synopsis of facts:

IMAJI alleges ISHII conducted secret laboratory near Harbin where humans were inoculated with glanders. Communist Party alleges research work for same was conducted at Tokyo and Kyoto Imperial University Medical Laboratories. Technical Intelligence G-2, War Department, is of opinion Communists reports are unfounded. Case #91 is being consolidated with File #330.

- C -

DETAILS:

At Tokyo:

This investigation was initially predicated upon a letter from the Youths Liberal League, Chiba-ken, Sambu-gun, Chiyoda-mura, alleging that Shiro ISHII was engaged in large scale research work of disease as a combat weapon. This communication was translated by ATIS as their document #14249 and the original and translations of same are being retained in the Investigation Division file in this matter.

On 15 December 1945, an individual giving his name as Setsu IMAJI, Shinmachi, Setagaya-ku, Tokyo, forwarded a letter to CIS which was translated by ATIS as their document #2035 and a copy of same was delivered to the Legal Section. This communication read as follows:

"SUBJECT: The following notes are for your reference concerning the activities at the Secret Laboratories of the former Army Medical School.

1. This laboratory headed by Medics Lieutenant General ISHII, Shiro was outwardly conducting researches on bacteria and water purification while secretly they had employed technicians covering a very wide field for military purposes. This

Distribution

1 Prosecution
1 CRD
1 Niigata Office ✓
1 Fukuoka Office
3 Inv. Div. (File #330)
1 Inv. Div. (File #91)

Do not write in this space.

secret laboratories was first established near the HAIIN ( ) River Railway Station of the Manchurian HAIRAKU ( ) line. ISHII, Shiro then a Major General, had assumed the alias of TOGO, Hajime and all other officers also went under aliases. Later they moved to the plains on the outskirts of HARBIN and continued their activites.

2. Their most atrocious act was to use humans instead of animals for their research on bacteria. Although the majorities of the victims were convicted criminals there were also innocent farmers, Russian interpreter, officers of the Communist Army, women and children. At HAIIN River alone there were over a thousand victims of experiments conducted on horse glanders bacteria, Hidatsu Sakin ( ), Tansokin ( ), pestilence bacteria and other strong poisons, also as a result of experiments on contagious diseases, starvation reaction, reactions to electricity and certain medicine many were victimized. Moreover, General HISHIO, Yoshizo, who has been been called a war criminal, once investigated this laboratory when he was the Chief of Staff of the KWANTUNG Army (1935).

3. There was no change in the position of ISHII, Shiro, as virtual dictator of this plant, and along with the Laboratory Staff members he even controlled the following economic actions.

4. Machinery such as the water filter machine and microscopes were purchased under the name of The Japan Special Factory Inc. (KURITSU, Mitsuichi, Wakamatsu Cho, Ushigome-ku, TOKYO-to acted as representative). Altho this factory was managed alone by KURITSU, Mitsuichi at the start, it was later incorporated and ISHII, Shiro and his cohorts reaped hugh profits by receiving dividends under the names of dummy stockholders (their wives and relatives).

The entire fortune of ISHII, Shiro and his Laboratory Staff members was accumulated from the illegal profits gained from the by-products of their atrocious deeds. Moreover, because of the fact that ISHII's wife was the daughter of ARAKI, Torasaburo, President of the Peers School, ISHII was very intimate with the Former War Minister ARAKI, Tadao and received unlimited help from him.

5. Persons responsible for the Atrocious Acts:

1. Medics Lieutenant General ISHII, Shiro, President of the Army Medical School from 1932 to 1945.
2. Medics Colonel NISHIMURA, Eiji.
3. Medics Lieutenant Colonel SAKAKURA, Jun
4. Medics Lieutenant Colonel ONODERA, Yoshio
5. Civilian not on the regular staff. A certain Professor at the Nagasaki Medical College.
6. Civilian not on the regular staff ISHIYAMA, Kinzo
7. Medics Colonel, HOHO, Enryo
8. Civilian, KURITSU, Matsuichi
9. Civilian not on the regular staff, SUZUKI, - ---
10. " " " " " , SAKURAI, Kanichi
11. " " " " " , IIDA, ------
12. " " " " " , YAKIZAWA, Yukinara

-

13. Technician, SHINBO, SHINICHI
14. " , TAKAHASHI, Yoshiichi

The above statements are a rough outline of the actions of ISHII Shiro and his group. According to investigation, new facts and developments can be expected."

On 14 December 1945, the OCCIO transmitted a copy of the following memorandum:

"MEMORANDUM FOR THE OFFICER IN CHARGE:

Subject: Memorandum from Japanese Communist Party.

The following memorandum was received by the Research & Analysis Section from the Japanese Communist Party. It is copied below without change in language. The report is in two sections, the second part relating to General (Rtd.) ISHIHARA Kanji. A quick check of the names mentioned in the first part of the report, relating to Japanese bacteriological warfare, revealed no record in CIS.

'ACTIVITY OF ISHII B.K.A. CORPS

'Ishii B.K.A. (Bacterial War Army) was established in Harbin under commandership of Lieutenant-General Shiro Ishii. A large bacterial laboratory built in Harbin, succeeded in cultivating pest in 1944, December. Pest was applied to Manchurians, in Moukden was applied to several American citizens captured during war. For experiment sake, rats implanted with pest were dispersed in and around Moukden, as a result of which it was proved successfull. When Ishii after these experiments was about to start actual manufacturing in large scale war termination was declared. Japanese army bombarded the laboratory wherein most precious documents, equipments were destroyed together with hundreds of laboratory members engaged in study. The research works were conducted in cooperation with Tokyo and Kioto Imperial Universities medical laboratories.

'Most leading personel engaged in this research were Rinnosuke Shoji and Hisato Yoshimura in the Laboratory and Kiyu Ogata of Chiba Medical University assisted from outside. In 1944 spring Ryoichi Naito succeeded to Ishii. Most of medical institutes, universities were mobilised for the purpose, which are:

'Densenbyo Kenkyusho: Saburo Kojima
Shogo Hosoya
Hidetake Yahagi
Kioto Imperial University: Kozo Kunimoto
Shiro Kasahara
Medical Bureau of War Ministry: Lieut.-General Hiroshi Kanbayashi
Lieut.-Colonel Hiraga
Asaoka
Kaji
Maj.-Colonel Otaguro
Akuzuki

- 3 -

'Rinnosuke Shoji is Professor of Kioto University concurrently Prof. 6f Shamasu University (Manchuria) under whose guidance Dr. Kyugo Sasakawa, Professor Ko Inouye, Iyemori worked as assistants.

'There is a Medical Doctor in Kioto City by name of Minowada Masuzo who also participated in the research.

'Kioto Imperial University: Teiji Hoshino
Shun Mashita (dead)
Shogo Funaoka
Senri Araki

Osaka University: Ryojun Kinoshita
Eiji Taniguchi

Chief of General Affairs Department of Ishii Corps was Lieut.-General Tanabe.

'Kanji Ishihara

'One of leading supporters of his movement is Miyazaki, former Managing Director of S.M.R. Research Buro. Ishihara is connected with Katsuzo Nishi who hold peculiar influence among Imperial family for instance Prince Higashikuni, Prince Chichibu. Nishi was once Director of Electric Buro of Tokyo Municipal Government, later retired and started famous 'Nishi's Health Engineering Method' and won a great popularity. His method was prohibited by Government in accusation that his method has no medical basis.'"

On 3 December 1945, the Metropolitan Unit No. 80 of the CIC submitted a summary of information concerning Dr. Shiro ISHII residing at Chioda-mura, Yamatake-gun, Chiba-ken:

"The following information was obtained from Confidential Informant 80-11 of this office, during the course of an investigation:

On 10 November 1945, SUBJECT, allegedly a large landowner in Chiba Prefecture and a former Lt. General of the Army Surgeon's Corps of the Japanese Army, was proclaimed dead and his funeral observed in Chioda-mura, Yamatake-gun, Chiba. This death is alleged false by Informant 80-11, and it is claimed that ISII has gone underground with the aid of the Village Headman of Chioda-mura, and intends to carry on anti-democratic activities.

It is claimed that SUBJECT was the Commanding Officer of the Ishii Detachment of the Surgeon's Corps during the war; that he had his assistants inject bubonic plague bacilli into the bodies of some Chinese in Harbin, China and some Americans in Mukden, China as an experiment; that the SUBJECT carried out a similar experiment in Canton, China, and that as a result of his carelessness there the bubonic plague ravaged the city."

On 15 March 1946, Captain William R. Gill submitted a memorandum to the effect that Lt. Colonel Thompson, who had been called by Technical Intelligence of G-2 to investigate the matter of Lt. General ISHII, had been contacted and expressed the opinion that the present belief of the Technical Intelligence Section was that most of the Communists reports submitted in this matter were not true and that Lt. General ISHII is innocent of the charges against him. Captain Gill indicated that Lt. General ISHII's address at that time was 77, Wakamatsu-cho, Ushigome-ku, Tokyo.

In view of the fact that considerable investigation has been conducted in this matter in File #330 in which General ISHII's name was recently added as a subject in that case, all investigation in File #91 is being discontinued, the case closed and further investigation of ISHII is being conducted under File #330.

C L O S E D

- 5 -

9.17 27 Nov. 1946: Inv. Div. No. 330, Report of Investigation Division, Legal Section, GHQ, SCAP, by Taro SHIMOMURA

资料出处： National Archives of the United States, R331, B1434.

内容点评： 本资料为1946年11月27日盟军总司令部法务局Taro SHIMOMURA提交的编号330调查报告。

Date: 27 November 1946

Report of Investigation Division, Legal Section, GHQ, SCAP.

Inv. Div. No. 330 | CRD No. | Report by: Taro Shimomura

Title: Motoji YAMAGUCHI, et al.

Synopsis of facts:

Interview of Motoji YAMAGUCHI. He stated that he never conducted experiments on human beings. Personnel of the Kwantung Army Quarantine Stables set forth as stated by YAMAGUCHI.

- P -

Reference: Report of Major L. H. Barnard, dated 14 October 1946.

DETAILS:

At Niigata - the Niigata Office:

On 4 November 1946, the Niigata office interrogated Motoji YAMAGUCHI at the 87th Military Government Headquarters in Niigata City with the following results:

Name: Motoji YAMAGUCHI
Age: 32
Address: Miyagi-ken, Shibata-gun, Murata-machi, Otsuki-shita, #61.

Attended the Tokyo Imperial University and graduated from the Veterinary Department in 1938.

In April 1938, he was called into the Japanese Army as a veterinarian with the rank of Probationary Officer.

From August 1940 to March 1942, he was attached to the 10th Cavalry Regiment, 10th Division in Jamusu, Manchuria.

From March 1944 to 12 August 1945, he was attached to the Kwantung Army Quarantine Stables at Hsingking, Manchuria.

Distribution:
1 Prosecution
1 CRD ✓
1 Fukuoka
1 Osaka
1 Capt. Powell
1 Chinese Division
1 Niigata Office
3 Inv. Div. (File #330)

Do not write in this space.
B

The unit designation, No. 100 Army Corps, is the same as the Kwantung Army Quarantine Stables. This unit designation was made after the war started as a military precaution.

Subject states that the cattle plague was prevelent in Manchuria the year around but was worse on or about April 1944, shortly after his arrival at the Quarantine Stables. They directed the outlying stations to take proper measures by isolating the diseased cattle and vaccinating the cattle in the vicinity. To the best of his knowledge, this disease (cattle plague) is not contracted by human beings even when the meat of the diseased cattle is eaten by them. Subject denies ever conducting experiments on human beings and also states that he never saw any Prisoners of War at the Quarantine Stables while he was there.

The members of the staff at this Kwantung Army Quarantine Stables at Hsingking were:

Rank	Name
Major General	Yujiro WAKAMATSU
Lt. Colonel	Yasutaro HOSAKA
Major	Motoji YAMAGUCHI
Captain	Tokio MACHIDA
Captain	Yukenobu OKI
Captain	Shiro YAMASHITA
Captain	Hironobu MATSUYAMA
Captain	Kaiichi NAKAJIMA
Captain	Korin KANEDA
1st Lieutenant	Usaburo SATO
1st Lieutenant	Shoji MARUYAMA
1st Lieutenant	Shin SAKATA
1st Lieutenant	Shiro MATSUYAMA
1st Lieutenant	Bunson SASAKI
1st Lieutenant	Keitaro ANDO
2nd Lieutenant	Noboru SATO
2nd Lieutenant	Junji KUROSAKI
2nd Lieutenant	Toshiro MATSUI
2nd Lieutenant	Jiro GOTO
Civilian equivalent to Lt. Colonel	(FNU) SHISHIDO
do	Yutaka ONO
do	(FNU) IDA
do	Shin AKIYAMA
do	(FNU) FUJITA
Civilian equivalent to Major	(FNU) KATO
do	Yutaka MURAKAMI
Civilian equivalent to Captain	(FNU) MITSUDA
Civilian equivalent to 2nd Lieutenant	(FNU) SHOJI
do	(FNU) MATSUI

The above information is to be checked against the report by the Osaka Office on the interrogation of Major General WAKAMATSU.

The Nagano Prefectural Police Department reported that Takeshi NISHIMURA does not reside at Sateyaemabe-mura, Higashi-Tsukuma-gun, Nagano-ken, but that he can be located through the Veterinary Laboratory of the Tohoku Imperial University in Sendai, Miyagi-ken.

UNDEVELOPED LEADS:

The Osaka Office -- At Hagi-shi, Yamaguchi-ken -- Will interrogate Yujiro WAKAMATSU concerning his activities as Chief of the Quarantine Stables of the Kwantung Army and obtain from WAKAMATSU the names and present locations of all the officers connected with the Kwantung Stables.

At Kyoto -- Will locate and interview Hiroshi UEKI, presently reported residing in Kyoto-shi, Yoshita-cho, and obtain a complete statement from him concerning his knowledge of the matter of the experiments which were allegedly conducted upon Prisoners of War at the Harbin experimental station.

At Hagi-shi, Yamaguchi-ken -- Will locate and interview Shiro YAMASHITA presently reported residing at 173 Tsuchirara, Hagi-shi, Yamaguchi-ken, concerning his knowledge of the experiments conducted on the Prisoners of War.

For the information of the Osaka Office, the service record of WAKAMATSU as set forth in report of Harold A. Small dated 4 September 1946, discloses that he graduated from the Agricultural Department of the Tokyo Imperial University in 1922, subsequently served in the Epidemic Research Institute, had a tour of duty in Germany, served with the Military Service Bureau of the War Ministry, was former instructor in the Army Veterinary School, was former Chief of the Veterinary Branch of the 13th Army and on 1 July 1942, became Chief of the Quarantine Stables of the Kwantung Army.

The Tokyo Office -- At Tokyo -- Will report the result of the demand placed on the Japanese Government for the military and biographical history of NISHIMURA and set forth appropriate leads for the location and interview of this individual.

Will report the result of the demand placed on the Japanese Government for the military and biographical history of YAMAGUCHI, YAMASHITA, and ISHII.

Will confer with the Chinese Division for the purpose of ascertaining whether they have any information concerning the alleged atrocities committed on Prisoners of War or Chinese coolies, as indicated in the report of Major L. H. Barnard, dated 8 November 1946.

The Sendai Office -- At Tohoku Imperial University -- Will locate and interview Takeshi NISHIMURA, presently reported working at the Veterinary Laboratory of the Tohoku Imperial University at Sendai, for full information he may have concerning the nature of the atrocities committed, the identities of the individuals comitting same, and the individuals who witnessed same.

PENDING

9.18 29 Nov. 1946: PMR 481, TO: GENERAL HEADQUARTERS OF THE SUPREME COMMANDER FOR THE ALLIED POWERS, Records of NISHIMURA Takeshi, FROM: T. NOBORI, Military Section, Political Division, Central Liaison Office

资料出处：National Archives of the United States, R331, B1434.

内容点评：本资料为 1946 年 11 月 29 日日本战后联络中央事务局政治部军事课提交盟军总司令部的西村武（NISHIMURA Takeshi）履历。

IMPERIAL JAPANESE GOVERNMENT

CENTRAL LIAISON OFFICE

PMR 481 29 November 1946

TO : GENERAL HEADQUARTERS OF THE SUPREME COMMANDER FOR THE ALLIED POWERS.

SUBJECT : Recoeds of NISHIMURA Takeshi.

1. Reference; Check Sheet LS-Z 3707 dated 5 November 1946, subject: "Request for Records".

2. The military and biographical history etc. of NISHIMURA Takeshi are submitted herewith as per enclosure.

T. Nobori

T. NOBORI,
Military Section,
Political Division,
Central Liaison Office.

Enclosure: A report as indicated above.

MILITARY AND BIOGRAPHICAL HISTORY OF NISHIMURA TAKESHI

Domicile: 2642, Wada-Mura, Higashi-chikuma-Gun, Nagano Pref.

Present Address: Epidemic prevention laboratory of Tohoku Imperial University, Yoshioka-Cho, Kurokawa-Gun, Miyagi Pref.

Date of Birth: 29 November 1914.

25 Mar 1935: Graduated Nippon Veterinary School, Tokyo.

2 Oct. 1935: Licensed veterinary surgeon.

16 Mar.1938: "Rikugun Gite" (Army Engineer) Attached to Central China Expeditionary Army Hq.

4 Apr.1938: Served at Temporary Horse Epidemic Prevention Yard of Central China Expeditionary Army.

10 May 1939: Served at Horse Epidemic Prevention Yard, Central China.

18 Sept.1940: Entered Shanghai Army Hospital.

22 Nov.1940: Returned to Japan.

9 Dec.1940: Entered Kanazawa Army Hospital.

[illegible] Mar.1941: Released from hospital.

31 Mar.1941: Attached to Veterinary Material Main Depot.

12 July 1941: Attached to home unit hq. of 3rd Div. as member of 15th Horse Epidemic Prevention Yard.

16 July 1941: Left Ujina port.

25 July 1941: Arrived at Tungninghsien, Manchuria.

1 May 1942: Attached to Horse Epidemic Prevention Yard of Kwangtung Army.

Note: 1.No information is available since May 1942 due to the lack of record.
2.The above information is furnished by Nagano Local Assistance Bureau.

9.19 2 Dec. 1946: Interrogation of Dr. Kiyoshi OTA, Interrogator: Major Owen V. Keller, Cml. C.

资料出处：National Archives of the United States, R331, B1434.

内容点评：本资料为 1946 年 12 月 2 日美军太平洋部队远东化学战部队少校 Owen V. Keller 对大田澄（Kiyoshi OTA）的讯问记录。

SECRET

O-310

GENERAL HEADQUARTERS
UNITED STATES ARMY FORCES, PACIFIC
OFFICE OF THE CHIEF CHEMICAL OFFICER

APO 500
2 December 1946

Interrogation of Dr. Kiyoshi Ota 333041

Dr. Kiyoshi Ota was interrogated in the Chemical Section, GHQ, Room 409, Mitsubishi Shoji Building, on 13 November 1946. In a recent interrogation of Lt. Gen. Kitano, the name of Dr. Ota was presented as having been associated with the Pinfang Institute of the Kwantung Army.

Persons Present: Dr. Kiyoshi Ota
Major Owen V. Keller, Cml C., Interrogator
Mr. T. Yagisawa, Interpreter
Mr. T. Emoto, Demobilization Ministry of Japan

Q. This interrogation is called not for any reason of persecution of war criminals, but for intelligence purposes along the line of bacterial warfare. We only want to make our records complete along with other records already in our file. I am trying to make a complete biographical record of you.

. Will you give us your full name and nationality?
A. My name is Kiyoshi Ota. I was a Medical Colonel. I am Japanese.

Q. What is the date of your birth?
A. I was born June 2nd, 1897.

Q. Your place of birth?
A. No. 1806 Chinto, Hagi City, Yamaguchi Prefecture.

Q. What is your present address?
A. I am now living in the same town as above, only the block number is different, which is 2502.

Q. Tell me about your education after you got into college, with dates.
A. I will start out with my education at the Okayama Medical College. I entered this medical college in 1916, and graduated from it in 1920 after finishing the 4 years' full course.

Q. Any other school after that?
A. I continued the study of medicine in the Army Medical College. I entered in 1922 and spent 1 year in the study of bacteriology. In 1923 I left the college.

Then in 1930 I entered the Medical Department of the Seoul Imperial University and graduated from it in 1932, spending two years in the study of pathology.

Q. Going back to your first college education at Okayama, what was the subject you took there?
A. I received education in fundamentals of general medicine and clinical practices.

SECRET

SECRET

Q. Did you hold any position in these years after you graduated from your first medical education until you entered the Army Medical College?

A. After graduation from the Okayama Medical College, I joined the Army.

Q. To what unit were you assigned first?

A. In 1920 I was assigned to the Third Imperial Guard Infantry Regiment. For the first 4 months in the army I was given general military training as a soldier, then I was assigned to the 44th Infantry Regiment stationed at Kochi, Shikoku. I was Medical Duty Officer and in charge of general medical affairs of the regiment.

Q. What was your rank then?

A. In October 1920 I was commissioned Medical 2nd Lieutenant. In 1922 I was transferred to the Hiroshima Army Hospital and did the routine clinical work, giving medical treatment to the soldiers hospitalised there. I stayed in the hospital there until I entered the Army Medical College in 1922. While I was studying in the Army Medical College I was promoted to Medical First Lieutenant. It was in December 1923. In August 1924 I was transferred to the Japanese Army Hospital at Tientsin in China.

Q. What was the nature of your task there?

A. My duty was partly to look after the administration of the hospital and partly clinical work, giving medical treatment to the sick and wounded soldiers.

In 1927 I was promoted to Medical Captain and was assigned to the 13th Infantry Regiment at Kumamoto. My duty was to take care of the general medical affairs of the regiment.

In October 1929 I was transferred to the Seoul Army Hospital, Korea. This time my duty was to treat the patients who contracted infectious diseases. During my tenure at this hospital I entered the Medical Department of the Seoul Imperial University. I did my work at the hospital in the morning and studied at the university in the afternoon. Pathology was the subject I took, but I specialised in the study of Immunology.

In January 1933 I was transferred to the First Army Hospital in Tokyo, my main duty being to administer to hospitalised soldiers at the Atami Sanitorium.

In 1934 I was transferred to the Army Medical College where my chief duty was administrative work of the college, but part of my time I spent in the section which manufactures vaccines. In August of the same year I was promoted to Medical Major.

In August 1936 I was transferred to the Pinfang Army Institute of the Kwantung Army (the section of Prevention of Diseases and Water Supply). I was in charge of the section of general affairs, that is, the general administration of the institute.

During my tenure at this institute, I was appointed Commanding Officer of a Field Unit of Prevention of Diseases and Water Supply temp-

SECRET

orarily organized by the Kwantung Army and sent out to Tientsin. I headed this field unit from June 1937 to December 1937. The task of this unit was to prevent the occurrence of infectious diseases and to supply purified water to the field army. In January 1938 I returned to the Pinfang Institute and resumed my former duty of administration.

In 1941 I was promoted to Medical Full Colonel.

From the expedition to Central China I returned to my former task at the Pinfang Institute, in 1943. I remained at this institute until the end of the last war.

Q. While at work at the Pinfang Institute did you run across any epidemic or infectious diseases which particularly attracted your attention?
A. In Northern China at one time there broke out at Tangu a large number of cholera cases.

Q. I am interested to know any infectious disease cases which you thought unusual or extraordinary. I mean those cases that occurred in an unusually great number or in the areas where they were least expected.
A. I cannot think of any such cases that answer your question. Speaking of infectious diseases that came under my attention, the most frequent ones were (1) Typhoid, (2) Black Plague, (3) Irruptive Typhus, they are common infectious diseases in all Manchuria and China. The infectious diseases that occurred in unusual number in China were cholera, malaria, dysentary, typhus and typhoid fever.

Q. Were there not any particularly abnormal epidemic or infectious disease cases— cases which made you suspect them of being man-made diseases, deliberately caused by some enemy sabotage against the Japanese army?
A. I do not have any first-hand information of such cases. As my task was chiefly on the administrative side, what information I came across was only a hearsay and I cannot vouch for its accuracy. On certain occasions I heard that our army captured Russian secret agents carrying on them some ampules containing such bacteria as anthrax, black plague, typhus, etc.

Q. Can you give me some more details about that incident?
A. At Hailar quite unexpectedly a large number of horses and cattle contracted anthrax and died. Investigation was started by the Japanese authorities, but could not ascertain where the germs were brought from. Shortly after this incident, a Russian secret agent was caught by the Japanese army and was found to have on him some supplies, that is, ampules containing the germs of anthrax which led us to suppose that the cattle anthrax was deliberately caused by Russian bacterial sabotage.

Q. When was it that this occurred?
A. It was around [illegible] or [illegible]. My memory is vague about this. Any way though conclusive evidence was lacking, the circumstances attending this incident made us suspect that this was caused by the Russian hand.

Q. You might tell us any similar epidemics or infectious cases along this line you have in mind.

SECRET

33304 1-4

SECRET

A. This was another second hand information. In the fall of 1937 a large number of cholera cases broke out in the Japanese Army at Hozan near Shanghai. Then the Japanese were fighting with Chinese and drove them out from the Hozan town. After the capture of the town cholera cases occurred among the Japanese soldiers who drank water from a certain well in the town. By investigation the well was found to contain cholera contaminated vessels, from which we surmised that the Chinese army, when evacuating the town, had thrown into the well the well the contaminated vessels with an idea to disseminate the germs a among the Japanese.

Q. How large was the occurrence?
A. I do not know, but I was told quite a number of Japanese soldiers contracted cholera in this incident.

Q. Do you know of any other similar cases?
A. All other epidemic or infectious cases were of minor nature and not extraordinary. These two instances I have just mentioned are the only outstanding ones I have in mind.

Q. Are you informed of the bacterial warfare activities of the Japanese Army?
A. My understanding is that the Japanese Army had made researches and experiments in bacterial warfare only for the purpose of establishing effective measures to counteract the enemy's offensive bacterial attacks. But since all these works were conducted strictly secretly, no outsiders were allowed to have any information about them. Being on an administrative staff, I was not authorized to know anything definitely about them. I was often told by my friends that the subject matter in such experiment, being living bacteria, the work was extremely difficult.

The main objective of their bacterial experiment being the discovery and establishment of effective means of defense against enemy's bacterial warfare, some defensive devices were worked out. For example, intestinal infectious disease, that is diseases that spread by oral contamination, could easily be spread by contaminating the drinking water. To counteract this, we developed and manufactured completely disinfected water filters and provided the field armies with them.

They also made researches in the improvement of the quality of vaccines and manufactured improved vaccines and distributed them among the army.

Q. Don't you know anything as to what the Japanese Army did in the way of preparation for offensive use of bacteria?
A. Being an administrative officer, I took care of all business pertaining to requisitions, procurement, storing of all supplies and materials needed by the Pingfang Institute. To the best of my knowledge I can assure you that the Pingfang Institute had never procured or accumulated supplies and materials which were needed for offensive use of bacterial warfare, at least during my tenure. I never received any

4

SECRET

instructions for the procurement of such supplies and materials. I know of no store rooms where they might have been accumulated.

Q. Possibly you may know something about the bacterial bombs, the ones they made and experimented upon at the Institute.

A. Yes, I heard of such bombs made for experimental purpose. They were known among the staffs concerned by the name of "I" Bombs, "Ro" Bombs, "Ha" Bombs and "Uji" Bombs, and I know they conducted some experiments with them. But they were manufactured and tested in order to ascertain to what extent disease germs could be effectively spread by means of bombs, eventually to determine what would be the best counter-measure against them. Again I would say that the final objective of the experiments with those bacterial bombs was establishment of defensive means in bacterial warfare.

Another circumstance that confirms my statement were the small amounts of such bacterial bombs stored in the Institute--just enough to conduct experiments with them. If the Japanese Army had an intention of making offensive use of bacteria, they should have manufactured and stored a sufficient quantity of the necessary bacterial arms and ammunitions somewhere, but as I said before I do not know of any such stores.

Q. Are you familiar with any of the results of the experiments of bacterial warfare made at the Institute?

A. No. All such experiments being carried out secretly and no outsiders were authorised to have any information on them, I do not know.

As to the bacterial bombs themselves, I had on one or two occasions only a passing glimpse of them. Never had a chance to have a good look at them.

However, Major Hinofuji, one who I understand is coming to this section for an interrogation one of these days, may have some data on the results of bacterial bomb experiments. He used to be one of the officers responsible for the testing of such bacterial bombs.

Beside the administrative works, I was at one time at the head of the Fourth Section of the Institite-- a section responsible for the manufacture of various types of vaccines. I held that position for about 18 months from February 1943 to September 1944.

Q. You might tell me if you have ever written papers on your scientific achievements or researches. Any articles published? That I may have them on our record together with other information in our files.

A. Yes, among the subjects of my study, the one on which I made a concentrated study was the problem of the bacterial colony and the changing conditions of such a colony. I wrote a paper summarizing the results of my study and on the merits of it I was conferred Doctor's Degree of Medicine in 1943. This problem of bacterial colony has an important bearing on the problem of the improvement of various antigens and vaccines and their manufacture.

As a corollary to the above study I also studied and wrote on the problem of the antagonism of bacteria, in other words, the influence

SECRET

SECRET

of one kind of bacteria upon another in the manufacture of vaccines.

Q. Did you write and publish any other papers?
A. No, I am not a good writer, all other papers I wrote were just routine reports I had to submit to my superior officers.

Q. Are you connected with any scientific or other public organizations?
A. No, I have no affiliation with any public organizations. As I spent most of my time in the army, I practically lost contact with the purely scientific and other circles. Before I went to Manchuria I was on the membership of the Japan Micro-biological Association, but during my army life I fell out of contact with the Association. But in the army I was on the Research Committee for the Improvement of Disease Preventive Solutions.

Q. This is a subject a little deviated from our main line. But in order to make our record complete, I want to know your idea on political matters. Have you any political affiliation?
A. I have no affiliation with any political parties.

Q. Still you might have some idea of your own on politics?
A. I know nothing about politics. I am not interested in them. But regarding the present political conditions in Japan I mayhave a thing or two to say.

Q. That is what I am interested to know?
A. From my point of view as a medical practitioner I see a lot of things to be changed in the present medical system of Japan. A thoroughgoing reform in the system must be effected.

The present medical problems cannot be solved without the collaboration of the general political efforts to solve the problem of food, housing and clothing.

The medical profession in the past was concerned primarily with the cure of diseases, but in the future medicine whould be devoted more to the prevention of diseases. In the medical education more stress should be placed upon the teaching of preventive medicine.

And the goal of the preventive medicine can only be realized with the simultaneous betterment of the general living conditions of the people, improvement of their food, housing, and clothing.

Another thing I should like to see reformed is the pitiable inefficiency with which the government people are carrying on their business. Now that I am a civilian, I am more impressed as never before by the inefficiency of those government clerks and officials. They should be taught how to serve people instead of bossing them.

Many people seem to be misguided by a wrong interpretation of the democratic way of living. What I understand by democracy is a sort of mutual assistance and cooperation, but in the mind of many people democracy is a sort of extreme individualism, a selfish pursuit of selfish interests.

6

SECRET

Under a democratic system the greatest happiness of the greatest number of people should be the final goal, but the people look at it differently; they seem to think that with democracy they have the freedom to do anything they please. They seek their personal profit at the sacrifice of the community.

Q. What is your opinion as to the type of government which would be best for Japan? Communist, Democratic, Socialist, or the old system of Emperor-Rule? Let's start with Communism. What do you think of it?

A. The Communistic government I do not approve of. I detest Communism. In my opinion I am inclined more to the support of the Emperor-Rule system as the most desirable form of government for Japan. However, I see that the old Emperor-Rule system had two sides--good and bad. In the first place this system had been a sort of stabilizing influence in the politics of Japan. No matter whatever political parties came in power, they were always subject to the Emperor. This has saved Japan from political catastrophe. In the second place, however, because of its conservative nature this system proved to be a drag upon the political progress of Japan. It checked the adoption of new political systems or policies no matter how beneficial they might have been to this country.

Another thing that I had always suspected and came home to me during the wartime is that in Japan scientific workers and engineers had not been given favorable treatment. They were not given full opportunitie to pursue their scientific researches and studies. A new order of things should have such a setup that these scientific workers would feel more at home in their work and study without any undue restraints.

Many important branches of industry are going on strike demanding higher wages, better standards of working conditions, and more latitude of control in their industry, but they seem to ignore the general welfare of the community. They should not sacrifice the Benefit of the community for the sake of their own business.

Q. One more question. What do you think of the United States? What is your opinion regarding the Occupation?

A. I have nothing special to say except that so far as my observation goes, the United States is managing their occupation in a very friendly, generous spirit, and with an unusual amount of success.

If I am allowed to make a comment, I should like to see the SCAP take a more active attitude in the matter of the internal politics of Japan, stepping in where the Japanese government seemed too powerless to deal with their business, so that, where necessary, more drastic reforms could be effected without delay. Without the active assistance and guidance of the United States, the present government would be too incompetent to effect any revolutionary reconstructions.

Q. When were you repatriated?

A. I had been suffering from kidney trouble and returned to Japan soon after the end of the war and had been laid up at home until I was formally demobilized from the army in February, 1946.

33304

7

SECRET

Q. What foreign languages do you speak?
A. I studied English for 5 years in the high school. I can read and write it but cannot speak it so well. In the college I studied German, which is a sort of official foreign language in medicine, and can read, write, and speak it, but not so fluently.

O. V. KELLER
Major, Cml C.

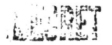

9.20 3 Dec. 1946: Inv. Div. No. 330, Report of Investigation Division, Legal Section, GHQ, SCAP, by John C. Donnell

资料出处： National Archives of the United States, R331, B1434.

内容点评： 本资料为 1946 年 12 月 3 日由盟军总司令部法务局调查科 John C. Donnell 提交的编号 330 调查报告，包括若松有次郎少将讯问记录。

Date: 3 December 1946

Report of Investigation Division, Legal Section, GHQ, SCAP.

Inv. Div. No. 330	CRD No.	Report by: John C. Donnell

Title: Honji YAMAGUCHI; Yujiro WAKAMATSU; YASUZAKA (FNU); Yasutaro HOSAKA, alias Yasutaro HOZAKA; Shiro MATSUSHITA; Shiro YAMASHITA; MACHIDA (FNU); OKI (FNU); and NAKAJIMA (FNU).

Synopsis of facts:

Former Major General Yujiro WAKAMATSU, interrogated at Kure, denied that any humans had been injected with glanders or dissected in Kwantung Army Quarantine Stables research on animal diseases during the war. Two Japanese research assistants died after accidentally contracting the disease, but their bodies were not dissected, and further details of their cases were not known by WAKAMATSU. Brief information furnished on Takeshi NISHIMURA, who supplied the initial lead in this case. Names of three more Quarantine Stables officers, furnished by WAKAMATSU. Japanese Government ordered to furnish biographical histories on these three former officers.

- P -

Reference: Report by Harold A. Small, dated 4 September 1946.
Reports by Major L. H. Barnard, dated 14 October 1946 and 29 October 1946.

DETAILS:

At Tokyo:

Interrogation of Yujiro WAKAMATSU was predicated on an undeveloped lead set out in the above-cited report by H. A. Small, requiring details concerning WAKAMATSU's activities as Chief of the Quarantine Stables of the Kwantung Army and names and present whereabouts of all officers connected with the Quarantine Stables. (WAKAMATSU and his staff were alleged to have dissected POWs in their research on cattle plague [glanders] at an outdoor dissecting ground at Hsinking, Manchuria, according to a letter sent to one Takeshi KINO by Takeshi NISHIMURA, and again in a communication forwarded to the CIE Section of SCAP on 23 August 1946 by NISHIMURA, who gave his address as Nagano-ken, Higashi Tsukuma-gun, Stacyasmabe-mura.)

Distribution:	Do not write in this space.
1 CRD 1 Prosecution 1 Niigata 1 Osaka ✓ 1 Hiroshima 1 Chinese Division 3 Inv. Div. (File 330)	

At Kure, Hiroshima-ken:

WAKAMATSU was interrogated at the Kure Police Station on 28 October 1946. A sworn statement was not taken. WAKAMATSU denied that the Quarantine Stables had ever engaged in experimental injections of any humans. WAKAMATSU stated substantially as follows:

WAKAMATSU, 50 years old, resides at Yamaguchi-ken, Hagi-shi, Tsuchihara, #172. He is a veterinarian, unemployed. He stated that all during the war the Mukden Quarantine Stables, located at Hsinkiang Province, had conducted research on the prevention and treatment of glanders and anthrax, diseases which had been very destructive to the Quantung Army's horse stock. Various immunizations, notably pyridine and pus from infected animals, had been tried on dogs, marmots, and rabbits. Further experimentation on mules and horses was being started when the war ended. It was found that untreated animals suffering from chronic glanders lived for two or three years, and those suffering from the acute condition lived only one or two months. Pyridine was found to be of some value in treating horses, but pus from infected animals apparently had no effect, positive or negative, on the animals' condition.

WAKAMATSU claimed that no humans, POWs, Chinese, nor Japanese, had ever been given any kind of injection in this research program, nor had any humans been dissected in the study of the disease. He stated that it was common knowledge at the Quarantine Stables that an unknown number of Manchurians herding horses had died of glanders contracted from infected animals, but he claimed he knew no details of any of these deaths. He stated that two Japanese research workers in the Quarantine Stables died after accidentally contracting the disease in their work. One of these Japanese worked in the laboratory at Mukden, Laoning Province, and the other worked at Hsinking, Kirin Province. WAKAMATSU claimed that these men's bodies were not dissected or examined post mortem; but he said he had no knowledge of their names nor the length of their illnesses, nor other details of their cases.

WAKAMATSU stated he had no knowledge of glanders or other animal disease research which may have been carried on at Harbin by the ISHII Unit, commanded by Major General Chuzo ISHII. The ISHII Unit was a Medical Corps organization in contradistinction to the Veterinarian Unit commanded by WAKAMATSU. He claimed that there had been no lateral dissemination of research reports between these units. All research findings were transmitted to higher headquarters, WAKAMATSU said, and he claimed he had not received information on animal disease work done by the ISHII Unit.

WAKAMATSU named the following officers as having been attached to the Quarantine Stables:

Lt. Col. Yasutaro HOSAKA, believed to be living in Tokyo
Capt. MACHIDA (FNU) " " " " " Nagano-ken
Capt. OKI (FNU) " " " " " Hokkaido
Capt. NAKAJIMA (FNU) " " " " " Aichi-ken
Capt. Shiro YAMASHITA " " " " " Tochigi-ken

When questioned concerning Takeshi NISHIMURA (who furnished the original lead in this case), WAKAMATSU responded that NISHIMURA had been a civilian technician (gite) attached to the Unit under his command. He stated that NISHIMURA was first attached to the Kwantung Army in 1937 and 1938; that he was assigned to duty in the Shanghai Quarantine Stables for about a year sometime during 1939 and 1940; that he returned to Japan for about a year, and was subsequently reassigned to the Kwantung Army from sometime in 1942 until the end of the war. The military unit to which he was last attached, according to WAKAMATSU, was the 17th Area Army under Kwantung Army Headquarters.

WAKAMATSU stated he last saw NISHIMURA at a meeting at Senzaki, Yamaguchi-ken, in March 1946, of Japanese who were demonstrating for resumption of repatriation of Japanese soldiers from the Russian-held areas of Korea and Manchuria. He believed that NISHIMURA's home was in Nagano-ken. He described NISHIMURA as being about 30 years old, about 5'6" tall, slender build, wore glasses, and was married.

AGENT's NOTES: WAKAMATSU appeared to be withholding information. He would probably yield more information if confronted with specific details of the allegations outlined in NISHIMURA's letter to CIE.

At Tokyo:

A request for full military and biographical data on Captain NAKAJIMA (FNU), Captain OKI (FNU), and Captain MACHIDA (FNU) from the Japanese Government through Japanese Liaison, AC of S, G-2, was submitted to CRD on this date. (Biographical histories on the other Quarantine Stable officers named by WAKAMATSU -- Major YAMAGUCHI, Lt. Col. HOSAKA, and Captain Shiro YAMASHITA-- have already been furnished by the Japanese Government andincorporated in this file.)

UNDEVELOPED LEADS:

The Niigata Office -- At Satoyaemabe-mura, Nagano-ken -- Will locate and interrogate Takeshi NISHIMURA, reportedly residing at Satoyaemabe-mura, Higashi Tsukuma-gun, Nagano Prefecture, for full information on the atrocities he alleged had been committed by staff members of the Kwantung Army Quarantine Stables, and the identities of perpetrators, victims, and witnesses.

TheTokyo Office -- At Tokyo -- Will report on the results of the demand placed on the Japanese Government for the military and biographical histories of MACHIDA, OKI, and NAKAJIMA, and also on the previous demand for biographical histories of Takeshi NISHIMURA, Lt. Col. YASUZAKA (FNU), and Captain Shiro MATSUSHITA.

Will confer with the Chinese Division for the purpose of ascertaining whether they have any information concerning the alleged atrocities committed on POW or Chinese coolies, as indicated in report of Major Barnard, dated 8 November 1946.

The Osaka Office -- At Kyoto -- Will locate and interview Hiroshi UEKI, presently reported residing in Kyoto-shi, Yoshita-cho, and obtain a complete and exhaustive statement from him concerning his knowledge of the matter of the experiments which were allegedly conducted upon POWs at the Harbin experimental station.

The Hiroshima Office -- At Hagi-shi, Yamaguchi-ken -- Will interrogate and interview Shiro YAMASHITA, presently reported residing at 173 Tsuchirara, Hagi-shi, Yamaguchi-ken, concerning his knowledge of the experiments conducted on the POWs.

P E N D I N G

9.21 24 Jan. 1947: Translation of Transcription of the Interrogation of NISHIMURA Takeshi, E. H. POWELL, Capt., Inf., Investigating Officer, Legal Section, GHQ, SCAP; Inv. Div. No. 330, Report of Investigation Division, Legal Section, GHQ, SCAP, by Capt. E. H. Powel, 0234393, Inf.

资料出处： National Archives of the United States, R331, B1434.

内容点评： 本资料为 1947 年 1 月 24 日盟军总司令部法务局调查科 E. H. Powell 上尉提交的编号 330 调查报告，附日本仙台市西村武（NISHIMURA Takeshi）讯问记录。

Date: 24 January 1947

Report of Investigation Division, Legal Section, GHQ, SCAP.

Inv. Div. No.	CRD No.	Report by:
330		Capt. E. H. POWELL, 0234393, Inf.

Title:
Motoji YAMAGUCHI, et al.

Synopsis of facts:

Interview of Takeji NISHIMURA set out. NISHIMURA stated he did not participate in any illegal experiments on human beings. Stated he heard Group No. 2 Kwantung Army Quarantine Stables conducted experiments on human beings. Stated Major General Yujiro WAKAMATSU was directly responsible for the alleged experiments on human beings. Gave the name of Takshi KINO as the actual witness to these atrocities. Accused YAMAGUCHI and HOSAKA as having participated.

-P-

Reference: Report of Taro Shimomura, dated 27 November 1946.

DETAILS:

At Sendai:

A verbal interview was held with Takeshi NISHIMURA, 24 January 1947, in the Sendai Office, Hq. IX Corps, and his sworn statement set out:

"Takeshi NISHIMURA, having been duly sworn, testified in the Legal Section, GHQ, SCAP, Sendai Office, located in the Headquarters Building, Headquarters IX Corps, Sendai, Japan, on January 24, 1947, as follows:

Q. State your name, age, place of birth, and present address?
A. NISHIMURA, Takeshi, age 34, born in Japan, and I live at:
Miyagi-ken, Kurokawa-gun, Yoshioka-machi,
Tohoku, Teidai, Igakubu, Boeki, Kenkyubu.

Q. Were you ever in the Japanese Army?
A. No. I was a civilian attached to the Army.

Q. In what capacity did you serve?
A. I was a veterinarian.

Distribution:

1 Prosecution
1 CRD (Encl)
1 Fukuoka
1 Osaka
1 Sendai
1 Chinese Division
1 Niigata
3 Inv. Div (File 330)
1 British Division

Do not write in this space.

15

Q. What college did you graduate from?
A. Tokyo Veterinarian School in 1935. I have a diploma as a veterinarian.

Q. Did you serve with the Kwantung Army Quarantine Stables in Manchuria?
A. Yes I did.

Q. State the dates?
A. From August 1935 to August 1945. I went from Manchuria to Korea and then sent to Japan.

Q. During the time you were in Manchuria did you see any prisoners of war?
A. Yes, I saw some prisoners of war during 1945. Some were Chinese but I do not know what the others were.

Q. Where did you see the prisoners of war?
A. It was in Choshun, Manchuria.

Q. Did you ever see any sick prisoners of war?
A. I don't know if they were sick or not, but they appeared to be weak and fatigued out.

Q. What caused them to appear in that condition?
A. I believe it was caused by poor food and living conditions.

Q. Was the cattle plague prevalent in Manchuria then?
A. Yes, and it was very common the cattle plague.

Q. In what year did the cattle plague appear to be most severe?
A. I can't say what year, but it was bad all of the time.

Q. Did you work at the quarantine stables?
A. I was working at the experimental laboratory.

Q. Did you work at the HARBIN Experimental Station?
A. No, I did not.

Q. Who had charge of the HARBIN Experimental Station?
A. I don't know.

Q. Did you see any experiments being conducted upon prisoners of war?
A. I heard from my friends that they did carry on experiments with human beings at the HARBIN Station. Also, I heard from my friends that they conducted experiments on human beings at my station.

Q. Which station were you employed?
A. The men were assigned by groups. Group Nol, Group No.2, and Group No.3. Experiments on human beings was conducted by Group No. 2, and I was assigned to Group No. 3.

Q. Who had charge of Group No. 2?
A. Motoji YAMAGUCHI was the first in charge, but later on he was relieved by Lieut-Colonel Yasutaro HOSAKA.

Q. What rank did YAMAGUCHI have?
A. He was a Major.

Q. Do you know where YAMAGUCHI resides at the present?
A. He lives in Miyagi-ken some place, but I don't know his exact address.

-2-

Q. Where does Yasutaro HOSAKA reside?
A. I don't remember but it might be in Okayama-ken.

Q. Do you know of any witnesses who say YAMAGUCHI and HOSAKA conduct the experiments?
A. Yes, KINO, Takeshi. This man said he actually saw the experiments going on one day on human beings. Another man by the name of OUCHI, Mamoru, said he saw some pictures of the experiments.

Q. Where does KINO, Takeshi, reside?
A. Miyazaki-ken, Kotsu-gun, Takanabe-machi, Aza, Hagihara. He is the only one that I know of that actually saw the experiments.

Q. Where does OUCHI reside?
A. Nagano-ken, Kamiminochi-gun, Tsuwa-mura.

Q. Do you knew what kind of experiments they made?
A. I heard that they injected a fluid containing germs taken from horses that had the plague in the human beings, and in some cases they mixed these germs in the human being's food. This in turn caused a disease known as "glanders" (Bisobyo). I am not too sure of this process. This disease was very contagious, and there was no known cure for it.

Q. How long were these experiments conducted?
A. I think about six months.

Q. Do you know how many human beings these experiments were conducted on?
A. I heard that they used about twenty human beings. This was very secret. I could not even enter this station myself.

Q. Do you know under whose orders YAMAGUCHI and HOSAKA conducted these experiments?
A. Major General WAKAMATSU, Yujiro.

Q. Do you know where GeneralWAKAMATSU resides?
A. Yamaguchi-ken, Hagi-shi, Uyehara-machi, % Fujita.

Q. Did you see any pictures of the victims?
A. No, but my friend OUCHI told me that he saw pictures.

Q. Were these victims of this virus all Chinese?
A. Some were Chinese and others were occidentals.

Q. Were there any deaths resulting from the virus injections?
A. I heard that most all of them died after they had received the injections or ate the food thatcontained the germs. After death they would perform an autopsy to learn the cause of death, nature and extent of the disease. They may have killed the patients first, or they may have waited until the virus killed them then performed the autopsy. This was all so secret I don't know all of the details, but my friend KINO could tell you all about it.

Q. Do you know of any other atrocities?
A. It is possible that they may have carried on similar experiments, but I am not definite about it. I heard that they did conduct similar experiments at the HARBIN Station.

Q. What types of experiments was conducted in your laboratory?

A. We were trying to improve the cure of glanders, and to determine what caused the disease.

Q. Did KINO tell you that he actually saw YAMAGUCHI and HOSAKA conducting the experiments?
A. He said he saw the autopsy being performed on the bodies, but he did not mention to me the names of the people who were performing the autopsy.

Q. What did OUCHI say the pictures looked like?
A. He said the pictures were taken of the dead bodies after the autopsy.

Q. Would you be willing to appear in court and state the hearsay evidence you have presented in this interrogation?
A. Yes, I would be willing to appear in court and state what I know about about these illegal experiments.

Q. What rank did KINO and OUCHI hold?
A. They were civilians attached to the Army.

Q. Are you sure you have told me all of the names of people who participated in these illegal experiments?
A. There is only one name, and that is of the commanding officer of the HARBIN Experimental Station, and I will go to my home and write you a letter and tell you who he was, as I have forgotten his name.

Q. Did you ever read any news in the local papers concerning the HARBIN Experimental Station?
A. I read an article in the "Tokyo Mainichi" or the "Asahi Shimbun" about the HARBIN Experimental Station. This article appeared in the newspapers some time between January 1-20, 1946. I was residing in Nagano Pref. at that time.

Q. Are you definitely sure that you did not participate in any illegal experiments yourself?
A. I did not participate in any illegal experiments.

Q. Do you have anything further to say in this interrogation?
A. The following named officers and civilians were members of Group No. 2:

Captain Tokio MACHIDA(Address unknown by me)
Captain Yukenobu OKI (May reside in Hokkaido)
Captain Kaiichi NAKAJIMA (May reside in Tokyo)
Captain Korin KANEDA (address unknown)
1st Lt. Bungo SASAKI (Address unknown by me)
1st Lt. Keitaro ANDO (May reside in Tokyo)
Civilian SHISHIDO (fnu) Address unknown by me
Civilian Kiyoshi IDA (May reside in Tokyo)
Civilian Fumiya KATO (Address unknown by me)
Civilian Yutaka MURAKAMI (Address unknown by me)
Civilian Masayuki MITSUDA (May reside in Fukuoka)
Civilian MATSUI (fnu) (Address unknown by me)

Group No. 2 was sub-divided, and it is possible that all of the above named personnel did not participate in the illegal experiments. I think that this is all of the information I can give you concerning the operations of the Experimental station in Manchuria."

UNDEVELOPED LEADS:

The Hiroshima Office -- At Yamaguchi-ken, Hagi-shi, Uyehara-machi (% Fujita) - Will locate and obtain a sworn statement from Major General Yujiro WAKAMATSU, regarding his knowledge of any violations of the Rules of Land Warfare, with special reference to the illegal experiments on human beings at the Kwantung Quarantine Stables in Manchuria, and other atrocities.

At OKAYAMA-ken -- Will locate and obtain a sworn statement from Lieut-Colonel Yasutaro HOSAKA, regarding his knowledge of any violations of the Rules of Land Warfare, with special reference to the illegal experiments on human beings alleged to have been conducted at the Kwantung Army Quarantine Stables in Manchuria, and/or other atrocities.

The Niigata Office -- At NAGANO-ken -- Will locate and obtain a sworn statement from Major Motoji YAMAGUCHI regarding his knowledge of any violations of the Rules of Land Warfare, with special reference to his participations in the illegal experiments on the human beings at the Kwantung Army Stables in Manchuria and/or other atrocities.

The Fukuoka Office - At Nagano-ken, Kamiminochi-gun, Tsuwa-mura - Will locate and carefully interview Mamoru OUCHI, and obtain a sworn statement from him regarding his knowledge of the illegal experiments on human beings at the Kwantung Army Stables in Manchuria, and/or other atrocities.

At Miyazaki-ken, Kotou-gun, Takanabe-machi, Aza, Hagihara -- Will locate and carefully interview and obtain a sworn statement from Takeshi KINO regarding his knowledge of the illegal experiments conducted on the human beings at the Kwantung Army Quarantine Stables in Manchuria, and/or other atrocities.

Will check the indices of the Criminal Registery Division of the foregoing personnel, and if negative results are obtained, will place a demand on the Japanese Government for the military and biographical history of same.

Will check the indices of the Criminal Registery Division of the following named personnel, and if negative results are obtained, will place a demand on the Japanese Government for the military and biographical history of same. At the appropriate time will set out leads as to insure these Japanese are interviewed and investigated, as it is alleged they formed the greater part of Group No. 2, which is alleged to have performed most of the illegal experiments on the human beings at the Kwantung Army Quarantine Stables in Manchuria:

Captain Tokio MACHIDA	Captain Yukenobu OKI
Captain Kaiichi NAKAJIMA	Civ. Kiyoshi IDA
Captain Korin KANEDA	Civ. Fumiya KATO
1st Lt. Bunzo SASAKI	Civ. Yutaka MURAKAMI
1st Lt. Keitaro ANDO	Civ. Masayuke MITSUDA
Civl SHISHIDO (fnu)	Civ. MATSUI (fnu)

Will check with the Editor of the "Tokyo Mainichi" newspaper concerning an article that is alleged to have appeared in that newspaper between January 1-20, 1946, about the operation of the HARBIN Experimental Station in Manchuria.

The Sendai Office -- At Sendai -- Will report the name of the commanding officer of the HARBIN Experimental Station when available.

P E N D I N G

~~CONFIDENTIAL~~

ALLIED OCCUPATION FORCES)
CITY OF Sendai)

I, NISHIMURA Takeshi, being duly sworn on oath, state that I had read to me and understood the translation of the foregoing transcription of my interrogation and all answers contained therein, consisting of four pages are true to the best of my knowledge and belief.

西村 武 (西村)
NISHIMURA Takeshi
(Signature of Witness)

Subscribed and sworn to before me this 24 day of January 1947

E H Powell
E. H. POWELL, Capt., Inf.
Investigating officer, Legal Section, GHQ, SCAP.

ALLIED OCCUPATION FORCES)
CITY OF Sendai)

I, Thomas T. Yoshimura, being duly sworn on oath, state that I truly translated the questions and answers given from English to Japanese and from Japanese to English respectively, and that after being transcribed, I truly translated the foregoing deposition containing four pages, to the witness; that the witness thereupon in my presence affixed his signature thereto.

Thomas T. Yoshimura
THOMAS T. YOSHIMURA Pvt TIS
(Name) (Rank) (Arm)

Subscribed and sworn to before me this 24 day of January 1947

E H Powell
E. H. POWELL, Capt., Inf.
Investigating officer, Legal Section, GHQ, SCAP.

ALLIED OCCUPATION FORCES)
CITY OF Sendai)

I, ERNEST HENRY POWELL certify that on the 24 day of January 1947, personally appeared before me Takeshi NISHIMURA and according to Thomas T. Yoshimura gave the foregoing answers to the several questions set forth therein; that after his testimony had been transcribed the said Takeshi NISHIMURA had read to him by the said interpreter the same and affixed his signature thereto in my presence.

E H Powell
E. H. POWELL, Capt., Inf.
Investigating officer, Legal Sect GHQ SCAP

Takeshi NISHIMURA, having been duly sworn, testified in the Legal Section, GHQ, SCAP, Sendai Office, located in the Headquarters Building, Headquarters IX Corps, Sendai, Japan, on January 23, 1947, as follows:

Q. State your name, age, place of birth, and present address?
A. NISHIMURA, Takeshi, age 34, born in Japan, and I live at:
Miyagi-ken, Kurokawa-gun, Yoshioka-machi,
Tohoku, Teidai, Igakubu, Boeki, Kenkyubu.

Q. Were you ever in the Japanese Army?
A. No. I was a civilian attached to the Army.

Q. In what capacity did you serve?
A. I was a Veterinarian.

Q. What college did you graduate from?
A. Toyko Veterinarian School in 1935. I have a deploma as a Veterinarian.

Q. Did you serve with the Kwantung Army Quarantine Stables in Manchuria?
A. Yes I did.

Q. State the dates?
A. From August 1935 to August 1946. I went from Manchuria to Korea and then sent to Japan.

Q. During the time you were in Manchuria did you see any prisoners of war?
A. Yes, I saw some prisoners of war during 1945. Some were Chinese but I do not know what the others were.

Q. Where did you see the prisoners of war?
A. It was in Choshun, Manchuria.

Q. Did you ever see any sick prisoners of war?
A. I dont know if they were sick or not, but they appeared to be weak and fatigued out.

Q. What caused them to appear in that condition?
A. I believe it was caused by poor food and living conditions.

Q. Was the cattle plague prevelent in Manchuria then?
A. Yes, and it was very common the cattle plague.

Q. In what year did the cattle plague appear most serere?
A. I cant say what year, but it was bad all of the time.

Q. Did you work at the quarantine stables?
A. I was working at the experimental labratory.

Q. Did you work at the HARBIN Experimental Station?
A. No, I did not.

-1- 

Q. Who had charge of the HARBIN experimental Station?
A. I dont know.

Q. Did you see any experiments being conducted upon prisoners of war?
A. I heard from my friends that they did carry on experiments with human beings at the HARBIN Station. Also, I heard from my friends that they conducted experiments on human beings at my station.

Q. Which station were you employed?
A. The men were assigned by groups. Group No. 1, Group No. 2, and Group No. 3. Experiments on human beings was conducted by Group No. 2, and I was assigned to Group No. 3.

Q. Who had charge of Group No. 2?
A. Motoji YAMAGUCHI was the first in charge, but later on he was relieved by Lieut-Colonel Yasutaro HOSAKA.

Q. What rank did YAMAGUCHI have?
A. He was a Major.

Q. Do you know where YAMAGUCHI resides at the present?
A. He lives in Miyagi-ken some place, but I dont know his exact address.

Q. Where does Yasutaro HOSAKA reside?
A. I dont remember but it might be in Okayama-ken.

Q. Do you know of any witnesses who saw YAMAGUCHI and HOSAKA conduct the experiments?
A. Yes, KINO, Takeshi. This man said he actually saw the experiments going on one day on human beings. Another man by the name of OUCHI, Mamoru, said he saw some pictures of the experiments.

Q. Where does KINO, Takeshi, reside?
A. Miyazaki-ken, Kotou-gun, Takanabe-machi, Aza, Hagihara. He is the only one that I know of that actually saw the experiments.

Q. Where does OUCHI reside?
A. Nagano-ken, Kamiminochi-gun, Tsuwa-mura.

Q. Do you know what kind of experiments they made?
A. I heard that they injected a fluid containing germs taken from horses that had the plague in the human beings, and in some cases they mixed these germs in the human being's food. This in turn caused a disease known as "glanders" (Bisobyo). I am not too sure of this process. This disease was very contagious, and there was no known cure for it.

-2-

Q. How long were these experiments conducted?
A. I think about six months.

Q. Do you know how many human beings these experiments were conducted on?
A. I heard they used about twenty human beings. This was very secret. I could not even enter this station myself.

Q. Do you know under whos orders YAMAGUCHI and HOSAKA conducted these experiments?
A. Major General WAKAMATSU, Yujiro.

Q. Do you know where General WAKAMATSU resides?
A. Yamaguchi-ken, Hagi-shi, Uyehara-machi, c/o Fujita.

Q. Did you see any pictures of the victims?
A. No, but my friend OUCHI told me that he saw the pictures.

Q. Were these victims of this virus all Chinese?
A. Some were Chinese and others were occidentals.

Q. Were there any deaths resulting from the virus injections?
A. I heard that most all of them died after they had received the injections or ate the food that contained the germs. After death they would perform an autopsy to learn the cause of death, nature and extent of the disease. They may have killed the patients first, or they may have waited until the virus killed them then performed the autopsy. This was all so secret I dont know all of the details, but my friend KINO could tell you all about it.

Q. Do you know af any other atrocities?
A. It is possible that they mave have carried on similiar experiments , but I am not definite about it. I heard that they did conduct similiar experiments at the HARBIN Station.

Q. What types of experiments was conducted in your labaratory?
A. We were trying to improve the cure of glanders, and to determine what caused the disease.

Q. Did KINO tell you that he actually saw YAMAGUCHI and HOSAKA conducting the experiments?
A. He said he saw the autopsy being performed on the bodies, but he did not mention to me the names of the people who were performing the autopsy.

Q. What did OUCHI say the pictures looked like?
A. He said the pictures was taken of the dead bodies after the autopsy.

-3-

Q. Would you be willing to appear in court and state the hear say evidence you have presented in this interrogation?

A. Yes I would be willing to appear in court and state what I know about these illegal experiments.

Q. What rank did KINO and OUCHI hold?
A. They were civilians attached to the Army.

Q. Are you sure you have told me all of the names of people who participated in these illegal experiments?

A. There is only one name, and that is of the commanding officer of the HARBIN Experimental Station, and I will go to my home and write you a letter and tell you who he was, as I have forgotten his name.

Q. Did you ever read any news in the local papers concerning the HARBIN Experimental Station?
A. I read an article in the "Toyko Mainichi" or the "Asahi Shimbun" about the HARBIN Experimental Station. This article appeared in the newspaper some time between January 1-20, 1946. I was residing in Nagano Prefecture at that time.

Q. Are you definitely sure that you did not participate in any illegal experiments yourself?
A. I did not participate in any illegal experiments.

Q. Do you have anything further to say in this interrogation?
A. The following named officers and civilians were members of Group No. 2:

Captain Tokio MACHIDA (Address unknown by me)
Captain Yukenobu OKI (May reside in Hokkaido)
Captain Kaiichi NAKAJIMA (May reside in Tokyo)
Captain Korin KANEDA (Address unknown)
1st Lieut Bunzo SASAKI (Address unknown by me)
1st Lieut Keitaro ANDO (May reside in Tokyo)
Civilian SHISHIDO (FNU) (Address unknown by me)
Civilian Kiyoshi IDA (May reside in Tokyo)
Civilian Fumiya KATO (Address unknown by me)
Civilian Yutaka MURAKAMI (Address unknown by me)
Civilian Masayuki MITSUDA (May reside in Fukuoka)
Civilian MATSUI (FNU) (Address unknown by me)

Group No. 2 was sub-divided, and it is possible that all of the above named personnel did not participate in in the illegal experiments. I think that this is all the information I can give you concerning the operations of the experimental station in Manchuria.

西村 武 (seal: 西村)
NISHIMURA, Takeshi

9.22 27 Jan. 1947: Inv. Div. No. 330, Report of Investigation Division, Legal Section, GHQ, SCAP: by Neal R. Smith, 1st Lt., Inf.

资料出处：National Archives of the United States, R331, B1434.

内容点评：本资料为 1947 年 1 月 27 日盟军总司令部法务局调查科 Neal R. Smith 中尉提交的编号 330 调查报告：中岛与町田履历。

Date: 27 January 1947

Report of Investigation Division, Legal Section, GHQ, SCAP.

Inv. Div. No. 330	CRD No.	Report by: Neal R. Smith, 1st Lt., Inf.

Title: Motoji YAMAGUCHI et al

Synopsis of facts:

Military and biographical histories of NAKAJIMA and MACHIDA set out.

- P -

Reference: Report by Major L. H. Barnard dated 9 December 1946.

DETAILS:

At Tokyo:

On 28 December 1946 and 20 January 1947, respectively, T. Norori and Y. Amano, respectively, submitted the following military and biographical histories of Tokio MACHIDA and Seiichi NAKAJIMA, the originals of which are being transmitted to the Criminal Registry Division with their copy of this report:

Military and Biographical History of
Tokio MACHIDA

Domicile: 90, Gorobei-shinden-Mura, Kita-saku-Gun, Nagano Pref.
Present Address: Same as above.
Date of Birth: 4 December 1919.
Military History:
20 Jan. 1942: Entered replacement unit of Imperial Transport Regt.
20 Mar. 1942: Vet. 2nd Lt.
4 Apr. 1942: Entered Military Veterinary School.
7 Nov. 1942: Graduated from the above school. Attached to 18th Inf. Regt.
2 Aug. 1943: Vet. 1st Lt.
1 Dec. 1943: Attached to veterinary dept. of 29th Div.
19 Feb. 1944: Attached to Remount Epidemic Prevention Dept. of Kwangtung Army.
10 June 1945: Vet. Capt.
30 Aug. 1945: Attached to Art. Replacement Unit of Seoul Divisional District.
15 Oct. 1945: Landed at Sasebo and demobilized.
Biographical History:
26 Dec. 1941: Graduated from Tokyo Higher Agricultural School.
16 Oct. 1945: Engaged in farming at home.
30 Apr. 1946: Served at Nagano Prefectural Agriculture Association.

Distribution:
1 Prosecution Div.
1 CRD (2 Encl)
1 Osaka
1 Hiroshima
1 Niigata
1 Chinese Division
1 Sappore
3 Inv. Div. (File 330)

Do not write in this space.

Note: The above information is furnished by Nagano Local Assistance Bureau.

Military and Biographical History of
Seiichi NAKAJIMA

Domicile: 510 Kami-Asahina, Asahina-Mura, Ogasa-Gun, Shizuoka Prefecture.
Present Address: Same as above.
Date of Birth: 25 October 1907
Military History:
Promotion:
15 Sept. 1942: 2nd Lt., Veterinary.
15 Sept. 1944: Lt., Veterinary.
Appointment:
14 July 1941: Mobilized to the Chūbu 8th Unit.
18 July 1941: Army Veterinary Probational Officer.
3 Aug. 1941: Attached to the 1292 Unit in Manchuria.
3 Apr. 1943: Attached to the 1st Area Army.
19 Aug. 1945: Commanding Officer of Transport of the families of personnel of the 1st Area Army.
21 Aug. 1946: Demobilized.
Biographical History:
26 Mar. 1922: Finished the Higher Course of the Sugayama Primary School.
24 Mar. 1926: Graduated from the Nakaizumi Agricultural School in Shizuoka Pref.
1 May 1927: Assistant teacher in the Niino Higher Primary School.
25 Mar. 1928: Resigned
8 Apr. 1928: Entered the Training Course of the Agricultural Supplementary School.
16 Mar. 1929: Finished the above.
31 Mar. 1929: Appointed teacher of the Ogasa Primary School.
18 Sept.1933: Appointed teacher of the Ikeshinden Agricultural School.
30 Mar. 1939: Passed the examination for License of Veterinarian.
1 Apr. 1940: Appointed teacher of Public Business School.

UNDEVELOPED LEADS:

Osaka Office -- At Kyoto -- Will locate and interview Hiroshi UEKI, presently reported residing at Kyoto-shi, Yoshita-cho, and obtain a complete and exhaustive statement from him concerning his knowledge of the matter of the experiments which were allegedly conducted upon POWs at the Harbin Experimental Station.

Hiroshima Office -- At Hagi-Shi, Yamaguchi-Ken -- Will locate and interview Shiro YAMASHITA, presently reported residing at 173 Tsuchirara, Hagi-Shi, Yamaguchi-Ken, concerning his knowledge of the experiments conducted on the POWs.

Niigata Office -- At Satoyaenabe-Mura, Nagano-Ken -- Will locate and interview Takeshi NISHIMURA, presently reported residing at Satoyaenabe-Mura, Higashi Tsukuura-Gun, Nagano-Ken, for full information concerning the nature of the atrocities committed, the identities of the individuals committing same, and the individuals who witnessed same.

At Gorobei-Shinden-Mura, Nagano-Ken -- Will locate and interview Tokio MACHIDA, presently reported residing at 90, Gorobei-Shinden, Kita-Saku-Gun, Nagano-Ken, and obtain from him a complete and exhaustive statement concerning his knowledge of the atrocities committed against POWs at the Harbin Experimental Station.

Tokyo Office -- At Tokyo -- Will interrogate Seiichi NAKAJIMA, presently reported residing at 510, Kami-Asahina, Asahina-Mura, Ogasa-Gun, Shizuoka-Pref., concerning his knowledge of atrocities committed at Harbin Experimental Station, names of individuals committing same, and names of individuals witnessing same.

P E N D I N G

- 2 -

9.23 28 Jan. 1947: Inv. Div. No. 330, Report of Investigation Division, Legal Section, GHQ, SCAP, by Neal R. Smith, 1st Lt., Inf.

资料出处: National Archives of the United States, R331, B1434.

内容点评: 本资料为 1947 年 1 月 28 日盟军总司令部法务局调查科 Neal R. Smith 中尉提交的编号 330 调查报告：内藤良一首次供述石井四郎在哈尔滨实验站用战俘做细菌战实验。

Date: 28 January 1947

Report of Investigation Division, Legal Section, GHQ, SCAP.

Inv. Div. No. 330	CRD No.	Report by: Neal R. Smith 1st Lt., Inf.

Title: Motoji YAMAGUCHI

Synopsis of facts: Ryoichi NAITO alleges that Shiro ISHII used POWs for his research work in bacterial warfare conducted at the Harbin experimental station. NAITO, formerly a faculty member at the Tokyo Army Medical College, gives roster of former microbiologists working with ISHII.

-P-

Reference: Report by Major L. H. Barnard dated 9 December 1946

DETAILS:

At Tokyo:

On 24 January 1947, Ryoichi NAITO, formerly a Lt. Col. in the Japanese Surgeons Corps was interrogated by the reporting agent in connection with the alleged atrocities committed by the ISHII B.K.A. (Bacterial War Army) at the Harbin experimental station.

A check of CRD indices revealed no information regarding Ryoichi NAITO.

Investigation Division files revealed that neither an Investigation nor an interrogation had been requested or conducted on the subject individual.

Ryoichi NAITO was called for interrogation because of the fact that: NAITO was a member of the faculty at theTokyo Army Medical College from 1939 until 1942 and from 1943 until the end of the war; that Shiro ISHII was OIC at said College; that Tokyo Army Medical College did research work for the ISHII B.K.A.(Bacterial War Army). During an interrogation that took place on 24 January 1947, NAITO gave the following voluntary statement, the original of which is being transmitted to Criminal Registry Division with their copy of this report:

Distribution:
1 CRD (encl)
1 Prosecution
1 Osaka
1 Hiroshima
1 Niigata
1 Fukuoka
1 Sapporo
1 Chinese Div.
3 Inv. Div (File 330)

Do not write in this space.

" I, Ryoichi NAITO, being sworn to speak the truth conscientiously, concealing nothing whatsoever, testified as follows in Room 835, Meiji Bldg., Tokyo, Japan, on 24 January 1947:

Q. State your full name, age, address, nationality, marital status, religion and occupation.
A. Ryoichi NAITO, 42 years of age, Osaka-Prefecture, Mishima-gun, Ibaraki-machi, Tonomachi, Japanese, married, christian, Doctor.

Q. Were you ever a member of the Japanese Surgeons Corps?
A. Yes.

Q. Give a summary of your Military Career?
A. I graduated from the Kyoto Imperial University in 1931 and was appointed a Lieutenant in the medical Corps in the same year. From 1931 until 1932, I took a post graduate course at the Tokyo Army Medical College. During the period 1932 until 1933 I was assigned as Battalion Surgeon in the 11th Inf. Regt. From 1933 until 1934 I was attached to the 27th Inf. Reg. as Bn. surgeon. From January 1934 until April the same year I was with the 25th Inf. Regt. In April 1934 I took a two year course at Kyoto Imperial University ending in March 1936. From 1936 until March 1937 I was a member of the Tokyo Army Medical College. In March 1937 I was sent to Russia as a language Officer and remained until February, 1938, when I was transferred to Berlin. On 2 December 1938 I entered the United States to study microbiology. I returned to Japan in March 1939. From 1939 until 1942 I was assistant Professor at the Tokyo Army Medical College and in 1942 became a member of Water Purification at Singapore. From 1942 until 1943 I was with the Supply Section of the South Army in Singapore. I was on the faculty at Tokyo Army Medical College from 1943 until 1945 when I retired.

Q. Were you ever connected with Lt. General Shiro ISHII?
A. Yes, I was at the Tokyo Army Medical College which was under the supervision of ISHII.

Q. What was ISHII's mission?
A. ISHII's chief mission was Bacterial Warfare and was divided into two sections, Offensive and Defensive.
Under Offensive came:
a. Mass production of bacteria.
b. Distribution of virus into enemy territory.
1. Airplane, etc.
c. Virulence
Under Defensive:
a. Vaccination
b. Water Purification
c. Disinfection
d. Organization.

Reports are that ISHII was using the water purification phase of defensive research to cover up on the Offensive research. ISHII was chief of the Harbin Troops and also chief of the Army Medical College. He would be at Harbin for three-fourths of the year and at Tokyo Medical College for the other 1/4. Whenever he returned to Tokyo he tried to hide his realpurpose by saying that his experiments were being conducted in secrecy. The only way we could learn about ISHII's work was when his men from the Harbin unit would return to Tokyo. Rumors that circulated all through

Rumors that circulated all through Japan were such that led us to believe that he was using humans for his experiments. ISHII was very famous among the professors in Japan and they also heard these rumors. The experiments were being conducted in Bacterial Warfare and could and probably did include most every kind of disease. Other animals used were goats, dogs, cats, pigs, cow, horses, etc. I think these rumors were true about using humans for experiments for the following reasons: that some of the vaccines prefected could only be called successful after observing the results obtained after innoculating humans with the disease and the vaccine; that men returning from the Harbin would tell me of humans being used for the experiments and that ISHII had established his laboratory in Harbin where he could obtain POWs for his experiments. The same tests could have been conducted in Tokyo without the use of POWs with more accurate results because of the more modern equipment, etc. but ISHII choose Harbin where he could work in secrecy. Harbin was the only place that he could obtain POWs without inteference.

Major Hajime TOGO was the alias used by ISHII during the course of his experiments in Harbin. His older brother, who acted in the capacity of private secretary to ISHII, and was with him fromthe start of his career until the end of the war, used the alias of HOSOYA. Rumors were to the effect that all of ISHII's officers used aliases while working at the secret laboratory.

I first heard of the alias used by ISHII in April 1936 from members of the "TOGO" troops returning from Harbin. They talked of the TOGO troops and because I had never heard of the "TOGO" troops I inquired about them and was informed that it was the ISHII unit in Harbin. ISHII had been conducting the secret laboratory since he first arrived in Harbin in 1934.

The idea of Bacterial Warfare was soley that of ISHII. He came back from Europe in 1930 and immediately initiated steps for financing Bacterial War-fare, both Offensive and Defensive. Most microbiologists in Japan were connected in some way or another with ISHII's work. He mobilized most of the Universities in Japan to help in research for his unit. In addition to the Tokyo Army Medical College, there were the Kyoto Imperial University, Tokyo Imperial University, Infectious Disease Research Laboratory, Tokyo, etc.

The following is a list of men who served on ISHII's staff at Harbin:

General Shiro ISHII	Commanding Officer
Maj.Gen.Hitoshi KIKUCHI	Chief, 1st Section
Col. Kiyoshi OTA	Chief, 3rd "
Col. Hatushige IKARI	Chief, 2nd "
Col. (fnu) NAGAYAMA	Chief, Clinical "
Col. Tomasada MASUDA	Chief, Administration
Maj. (fnu) HIRASAWA	Test Pilot(Aeronavigation)
Col. Takashi MURAKA MI	Chief, Education
Col. Saburo SONODA	" "
Col. Kokan IMAZU	" Administration
Col. Masataka KITAGAWA	", 2nd Section (deceased)
Col. (fnu) EGUCHI	" 4th "
Maj. Yashiyasu MASUDA	Pharmacy
Maj. (fnu) TANABE	Chief, General Affairs
Maj. (fnu) TAKAHASHI	" " "

Eng. 2nd Class Hotori WATANABE	Research conductant (Bacteria)
Eng. 6th Class Hideo FUKATI	Common Member
Eng. 6th Class Tachio ISHIKAWA	Common Member
Eng. 2nd Class Koji ANDO	Chief, Darien Dispatch (Darien EISEI KENKYSHO)
Eng. 2nd Class Zen KAWAKAMI	", 1st Section

The next list are those men connected with Tokyo Army College during the period 1942 until 1945:

General Shiro ISHII	Chief
Col. Hitoshi KIKUCHI	Bacteriology
Col. Tomasuda MASUDA	General Affairs
Col. Takatomo INOUE	Bacteriology
Col. Enryo HOJO	Water Purification
Col. (fnu) SATO	Member
Lt. Col. Ryoichi NAITO	Water Purification
Lt. Col. Katsushige IDEI	Serumand Vaccine
Maj. Jun-Ichi KANEKO	Serum
Maj. Yoshifumi TSUYAMA	Disinfection
Eng. 5th Class Haru HASHIMOTO	Bacteriology

It can be noted that men are listed as section chiefs. ISHII had eight sections in his Harbin unit. They are as follows:

1. Study (science)	5. Administration
2. Study (bacteria) Offensive	6. Education
3. Manufacture of serum. Defensive	7. Clinical
4. Study (water supply)	8. Supply.

I will now give you a list of men who will be able to inform more exactly the work of ISHII.

1934 - 1935

Col. TAKATOMO INOUE	Now chief of NARA Govt.(KOKUITSU) Hospital.
Col. Kiyoshi OTA	Residence not known.

1936 - 1942

Lt. Col. Kiyoshi HAYAKAWA	Now a member of KOSHUEISEIIN (Public health)
Maj. Yukimasa YAGISAWA	Member of Japan Penicillin Society
Col (fnu) IKARI	Residence not known.

General Masaji KITANO, successor to ISHII when ISHII was removed to be Chief Surgeon of 1st Army must be able to tell you everything on organization, equipment, etc., of the Harbin unit.

Mr. Mitsuichi MIYAMOTO	Chief owner of the Nihon TOKUSHU-KYOGO Co. Ltd. Minami -Shiagawa, 3 Chome, Tokyo.

The above man was sole agent who was allowed to go to the Harbin Unit. He supplied or sold every necessary equipment to the unit and should be able to give you full information regarding the unit.

Q. Do you have anything else to add that might be of value to the statement?
A. Nothing, but if ISHII was guilty of using human beings for his experiments I think that he should be punished.

S. Ryoichi NAITO"

-4-

NAITO's statement reflects that ISHII used the Water Purification phase of Defensive research to cover up his research and experimentation conducted in the Offensive phase of Bacterial warfare.

To substantiate his allegation that ISHII used HUMANS for his experimental research, NAITO states, "I think these rumors were true about using HUMANS for experiments for the following reasons; that some of the vaccines perfected could only be called successful after observing the results obtained after innoculating HUMANS with the disease and the vaccine; that men re turning from the Harbin unit would tell me of HUMANS being used for experiments and that ISHII had established his laboratory in Harbin where he could obtain POW's for his experiments. --ISHII choose Harbin where he could work in secrecy".

This allegation by NAITO adds one more complaint to the numerous allegations of ISHII using POW's for his experimental work in Bacterial Warfare conducted at the Harbin experimental station as found in Inv. Div. Case #330. It can be noted that the allegation by NAITO is the first not from an anonymous source.

The Chinese Division, Legal Section, was contacted by the reporting agent as per Undeveloped Lead set out in Report by Major L. H. Barnard, dated 9 December 1946. This agent was informed that the Chinese Division had nothing in their files on the atrocities committed at the Harbin experimental station but that an investigation has been conducted by the Chinese Government and a copy of the investigation would be forwarded to this office as soon as possible.

UNDEVELOPED LEADS:

The Tokyo Office -- At Tokyo -- Will locate and interview Masaji KITANO, presently reported residing at Setagayu-ku, Daita-machi, Itchome, #5, Tokyo, and obtain from him a completeand exhaustive statement concerning his knowledge of the atrocities committed at the Harbin experimental station.

At Tokyo -- Will interrogate Tomasada MASUDA, residing at Chiba-Pref., Kimuzu-gun, Akimoto-mura, Nishihisaku, #289, concerning the location of the secret laboratory in Harbin, type of experiments and research conducted, methods used in the experiments and personnel involved in the researchwork.

At Tokyo -- Will report on the demand placed on the Japanese Government for the military and biographical histories of former General Masaji KITANO and former General Hitoshi KIKUCHI.

The Osaka Office -- At Kyoto -- Will locate and interview Hiroshi UEKI, reported residing at Kyoto-shi, Yoshita-cho, and obtain from him a complete statement concerning his knowledge of the matter of the experiments which were allegedly conducted upon POWs at the Harbin experimental station.

The Nagoya Office -- At Uozu-mura, Toyama-ken, -- Will interview Jun-ichi KANEKO, Toyama-Pref., Uozu-mura, Takata-machi, #18, and obtain from him a complete and exhaustive statement concerning the atrocities committed at the Harbin experimental station, Names of individuals who committed same and names of individuals witnessing same.

The Hiroshima Office -- At Hagi-shi Yamaguchi-ken -- Will locate and interview Shiro YAMASHITA, presently reported residing at 173 Tsuchirara, Hagi-shi, Yamaguchi-ken, concerning his knowledge of the atrocities committed at the Harbin experimental station.

At Hagi-shi, Yamaguchi-ken -- Will locate and interview Kiyoshi OTA, formerly chief of Serum Section of the Harbin experimental station, presently reported residing at Yamaguchi-ken, Hagi-shi, Chinto, #2502, Concerning the manner in which the serum was produced, type of serum, research methods, testing methods of serum, in an attempt to uncover atrocities committed at the Harbin experimental station.

At Fukuki-mura, Hiroshima-ken -- Will locate and interview Dr. Nobukazu HINOFUJI, presently reported residing at Hiroshima-ken, Asa-gun, Fukuki-mura, Umagi, #640, concerning his knowledge of the atrocities committed at the Harbin Experimental station during his tour of duty at said station.

The Niigata Office -- At Satoyaenabe-mura, Nagano-ken -- Will locate and interview Takeshi NISHIMURA, presently reported residing at Nagano-ken, Satoyaenabe-mura, Higashi-Tsukuura-gun, and obtain from him an exhaustive statement covering full information concerning the nature of the atrocities committed, names of individuals committing same, and names of individuals who witnessed same.

P E N D I N G

9.24 6 Feb. 1947: Inv. Div. No. 330, Report of Investigation Division, Legal Section, GHQ, SCAP, by Mr. Roy T. Yoshida

资料出处： National Archives of the United States, R331, B1434.

内容点评： 本资料为 1947 年 2 月 6 日盟军总司令部法务局调查科 Roy T. Yoshida 提交的编号 330 调查报告。

Date: 6 February 1947

Report of Investigation Division, Legal Section, GHQ, SCAP. , Osaka Branch.

Inv. Div. No. 330	CRD No.	Report by: Mr. Roy T. Yoshida

Title: Motoji YAMAGUCHI et al

Synopsis of facts: Hiroshi UEKI, could not be located at address given in reference report.

- P -

REFERENCE:

Report of 1st Lt Neal R. Smith, dated 27 January 1947.

DETAILS:

At Osaka:

On 18 November 1946, the Osaka Branch Office received a report #330 by Mr. H. Kanemitsu, dated 12 November 1946. The Osaka Office was requested to locate Hiroshi UEKI and obtain a complete and exhaustive statement from him concerning his knowledge of the matter of the experiments which were allegedly conducted upon Prisoners of War at the Harbin Experimental Station in Manchuria.

The address given for Hiroshi UEKI in the reference report was Kyoto-shi, Yoshida-cho. However, it was found on investigation that there are several Yoshida-cho in Kyoto-shi and it was impossible to locate Hiroshi UEKI, but in order to make an exhaustive search for UEKI, this agent ordered the Central Demobilization Liaison Office to contact the Kyoto Prefecture Office and have the Police check all the Neighborhood Associations in every Yoshida-cho, in an effort to locate Hiroshi UEKI or to find a more complete address.

On 24 January 1947, the Central Demobilization Liaison Office submitted following report regarding the course of investigation concerning Hiroshi UEKI.

24 January 1947
Chufuku "sho" No. 10.

To Mr. Roy Yoshida
Investigator, Legal Section,
GHQ, SCAP, Osaka Branch Office.

RE COURSE OF INVESTIGATION ON UEKI, Hiroshi

Distribution:

1 - Prosecution
1 - CRD
1 - Hiroshima
1 - Niigata
1 - Chinese Division
1 - Sapporo
3 - Inv. Div. (File #330)
1 - Withdrawn for Osaka files.
1 - Fukuoka
1 - Sendai
1 - Nagoya

Do not write in this space.

3

a) Course of investigation: On 20 November 1946, this office sent telegram to the man in caption at Yoshida-machi, Kyoto City, but received a report from the post office of that locality that the existence of this man in his locality is unknown.

b) On November 22nd 1946, established connection with detective Kazono, Detective Section of Kyoto Prefecture and received his response saying that with only Yoshida-cho investigation is impossible.

c) Again on November 26th 1946, we requested the same man to make investigation in Yoshida-cho, Kyoto City. On November 29th received his reply to the effect that the man in question is not living there.

d) On December 2nd, we repeated the same request to Kazono, and this time also, he replied that such a man is not living there.

e) On December 6th established connection with Kyoto Local Assistance Bureau, and requested Mr. Koroyasu, Investigation Dept. to investigate on the man in caption and received his response saying that the man corresponding to is not living.

f) From December 13th to 16th, our official Morioka went to Kyoto and made investigation by himself but could not find him. To make things sure, he obtained certificate of respective block Association Chiefs to certifying the no-existence of the corresponding man.

g) We then inquired of an Official in Sakyo Ward Office in Kyoto, and had him check the list of Electors, but still was unable to find him.

/s/ Shoroku SHOJI
Chief of Public Relations Sub-Sec
Chubu Demobilization Liaison Off

- -

The Police and Prefecture authorities of Kyoto have been instructed to communicate with this office if any further information on Hiroshi UEKI is uncovered.

Upon a thorough check with the various Japanese agencies in Kyoto, the reporting agent feels that when UEKI directed a letter to General MacArthur, the author used a fictitious name and a false address to avoid detection.

Osaka Branch Office has completed an exhaustive search for Hiroshi UEKI in the Kyoto and Osaka areas with negative results.

UNDEVELOPED LEADS:

Tokyo Office:
At Tokyo - Will recheck UEKI's letter to General MacArthur, dated 4 October 1946, reference report of Maj L.H. Barnard, dated 5 November 1946, to see if there is a more detailed address.

Will check the indices of the Criminal Registery Division of the foregoing personnel, and if negative results are obtained, will place a demand on the Japanese Government for the military and biographical history of same.

Will check the indices of the Criminal Registery Division of the following named personnel, and if negative results are obtained, will place a demand on the Japanese Government for the military and biographical history of same. At the appropriate time will set out leads as to insure these Japanese are interviewed and investigated, as it is alleged they formed the greater part of Group No. 2, which is alleged to have performed most of the illegal experiments on the human beings at the Kwantung Army Quarantine Stables in Manchuria;

Captain Tokio MACHIDA	Captain Yukenobu OKI
Captain Kaiichi NAKAJIMA	Civ. Kiyoshi IDA
Captain Korin KANEDA	Civ. Fumiya KATO
1st Lt. Bunzo SASAKI	Civ. Yutaka MURAKAMI
1st Lt. Keitaro ANDO	Civ. Masayuke MITSUDA
Civ. SHISHIDO (FNU)	Civ. MATSUI (FNU)

Will check with the Editor of the "Tokyo Mainichi" newspaper concerning an article that is alleged to have appeared in that newspaper between January 1-20, 1946, about the operation of the HARBIN Experimental Station in Manchuria.

Nagoya Office:

At Shizuoka-ken - Will interrogate Seiichi NAKAJIMA presently reported residing at 510, Kami Asahina, Asahina-mura, Ogasa-gun, Shizuoka-ken, concerning his knowledge of atrocities committed at Harbin Experimental Station, names of individuals committed same, and names of individuals witnessing same.

Niigata Office:

At Gorobei-Shinden-mura, Nagano-ken - Will locate and interview Toko MACHIDA, presently reported residing at 90, Gorobei-Shinden-mura, Kita-Saku-gun, Nagano-ken, and obtain from him a complete and exhaustive statement concerning his knowledge of the atrocities committed against POWs at the Harbin Experimental Station.

At Nagano-ken - Will locate and obtain a sworn statement from Major Motoji YAMAGUCHI regarding his knowledge of any violations of the Rules of Land Warfare, with special reference to his participations in the illegal experiments on the human beings at the Kwantung Army Stables in Manchuria and/or other atrocities.

At Nagano-ken, Kamiminochi-gun, Tsuwa-mura - Will locate and carefully interview Mamoru OUCHI, and obtain a sworn statement from him regarding his knowledge of the illegal experiments on human beings at the Kwantung Army Stables in Manchuria, and/or other atrocities.

Hiroshima Office:

At Hagi-shi, Yamaguchi-ken- Will locate and interrogate Shiro YAMASHITA, presently reported residing at 173 Tsuchirara, Hagi-shi, Yamaguchi-ken, concerning his knowledge of the Experiments conducted on the POWs at the Harbin Experimental Station.

At Yamaguchi-ken, Hagi-shi, Uyahara-machi (% Fujita) - Will locate and obtain a sworn statement from Major General Yujiro WAKAMATSU, regarding his knowledge of any violations of the Rules of Land Warfare, with special reference to the illegal experiments on human beings at the Kwantung Quarantine Stables in Manchuria, and other atrocities.

Fukuoka Office:

At Miyazaki-ken, Kotou-gun, Takanabe-machi, Aza, Hagihara - Will locate and carefully interview and obtain a sworn statement from Takeshi KINO regarding his knowledge of the illegal experiments conducted on the human beings at the Kwantung Army Quarantine Stables in Manchuria, and/or other atrocities.

Sendai Office:

At Sendai - Will report the name of the Commanding Officer of the Harbin Experimental Station when available.

P E N D I N G

9.25 25 Feb. 1947: Inv. Div. No. 330, Report of Investigation Division, Legal Section, GHQ, SCAP, by Ernest H. Powell Capt., Inf., 0-234393

资料出处： National Archives of the United States, R331, B1434.

内容点评： 本资料为1947年2月25日盟军总司令部法务局调查科Ernest H. Powell上尉提交的编号330调查报告。

Date: 25 February 1947

Report of Investigation Division, Legal Section, GHQ, SCAP.

Inv. Div. No. 330	CRD No.	Report by: Ernest B. Powell Capt., Inf. 0-234393

Title: Motoji YAMAGUCHI et al

Synopsis of facts:

The name of the former Commanding Officer at HARBIN EXPERIMENTAL STATION unknown.

- P -

Reference: Report by Mr. Roy T. YOSHIDA 6 February 1947.

DETAILS:

At Sendai:

Takeshi NISHIMURA, Miyagi-ken, Kurokawa-gun, Yoshioka-machi, Tohoku, Teidai, Igakubu, Boeki, Kenkyubu, stated under oath that Motoji YAMAGUCHI, then a Major, had charge of Group No. 2. He further stated that Group No. 2 made the experiments on human beings. He stated that he did not know who the commanding officer of the Experimental station was.

According to the files in this office, there is no further information in this case. This office can be of no further assistance in determining the namesof the Commanding Officer, HARBIN EXPERIMENTAL STATION.

UNDEVELOPED LEADS:

The Tokyo Office -- At Tokyo -- Will recheck UEKI's letter to General MacArthur, dated 4 October 1946, reference report of Major L. H. Barnard, dated 5 November 1946, to see if there is a more detailed address.

Will check the indices of the Criminal Registry Division of the foregoing personnel, and if negative results are obtained, will place a demand on the Japanese Government for themilitary and biographical history of same.

Will check the indices of the Criminal Registry Division of the following-named personnel, and ifnegative results are obtained, will place a demand on the Japanese Government for themilitary and biographical history of same.

Distribution:
1 Prosecution
1 CRD
1 Hiroshima
1 Niigata
1 Chinese Division
1 Sapporo
3 Inv. Div. (File 330)
1 Fukuoka
1 Sendai
1 Nagoya

Do not write in this space.

At the appropriate time will set out leads as to insure these Japanese are interviewed and investigated, as it is alleged they formed the greater part of Group No. 2, which is alleged to have performed most of the illegal experiments on the human beings at the Kwantung Army quarantine stables in Manchuria;

Captain Tokio MACHIDA	Captain Uukenobu OKI
Captain Kaiichi NAKAJIMA	Civ. Kiyoshi IDA
Captain Korin KANEDA	Civ. Fumiya KATO
1st Lt. Bunzo SASAKI	Civ. Yutaka MURAKAMI
1st Lt. Keitaĝe ANDO	Civ. Masayuke MITSUDA
Civ. SHISHIDO (FNU)	Civ. MATSUI (FNU)

Will check with the Editor of the "Tokyo Mainichi" newspaper concerning an article that isalleged to have appeared in that newspaper between January 1-20, 1946, about theoperation ofthe HARBIN E xperimental Station in Manchuria.

Nagoya Office;

At Shizuoka-ken -- Will interrogate Seiichi NAKAJIMA presently reported residing at 510, Kami Asahina, Asahina-mura, Ogasa-gun, Shizuoka-ken, concerning his knowledge of atrocities commited at Harbin Experimental Station, names of individuals committed sam e, and names of individuals witnessing same.

Niigata Office;

At Gorobei-Shinden-mura, Nagano-ken -- Will locate and interview Toka MACHIDA, presently reported residing at 90, Gorobei-Shinden-mura, Kita-Saku-gun, Nagano-ken, and obtain from him a complete and exhaustive statement concerning his knowledge of the atrocities committed against POWs at the Harbin Experimental Station.

At Nagano-ken -- Will locate and obtain a sworn statement from Major Motoji YAMAGUCHI regarding his knowledge of any violations of the Rules of Land Warfare, with special reference to hi s participations in the illgal experiments on the human beings at the Kwantung Army Stables in Manchuria and/or other atrocities.

At Nagano-ken, Kamimonochi-gun, Tsuwa-mura -- Will locate and carefully interview Mamoru OUCHI, and obtain a sworn statement from him regarding his knowledge of the illegal experiments on human beings at the Kwantung Army Stables in Manchuria and/or other atrocities.

Hiroshima Office;

At Hagi-shi, Yamaguchi-ken -- Will locate andinterrogate Shiro YAMASHITA, presently reported residing at 173 Tsuchirara, Hagi-shi, Yamaguchi-ken, concerning hisknowledge of the Experiments conducted on the POWs at the Harbin Experimental Station.

At Yamaguchi-ken, Hagi-shi, Uyahara-machi (% Fujita) -- Will locate and obtain a sworn statement from Major General Yujiro WAKAMATSU, regarding his knowledge of any violations of the Rules of Land Warfare, with special reference to theillegal experiments on human beings at the Kwantung Quarantine Stables in Mancuria, and other atrocities.

Fukuoka Office;

At Miyazaki-ken, Kotou-gun, Takanabe-machi, Aza, Hagihara -- Will locate and carefully interview and obtain a sworn statement from Takeshi KINO regarding his knowledge of the illegal experiments conducted on the human beings at the Kwantung Army Quarantine Stables in Manchuria and /or other atrocities.

P E N D I N G

9.26 6 Mar. 1947: Inv. Div. No. 330, Report of Investigation Division, Legal Section, GHQ, SCAP, Joseph F. Sartiano Capt., Inf.

资料出处：National Archives of the United States, R331, B1434.

内容点评：本资料为 1947 年 3 月 6 日盟军总司令部法务局调查科 Joseph F. Sartiano 上尉提交的编号 330 调查报告：1947 年 3 月 5 日福冈纪野猛（Takeshi Kino）讯问记录。

Date: 6 March 1947

Report of Investigation Division, Legal Section, GHQ, SCAP.

Inv. Div. No. 330	CRD No.	Report by: Joseph F. Sartiano Capt., Inf.

Title: Motoji YAMAGUCHI

Synopsis of facts: Takeshi KINO, denies participation in the experiments but admits hearing that General WAKAMATSU, was responsible for the death of thirteen (13) men as the result of secret experiments carried on at Group # 2 under WAKAMATSU, further states that YAMAGUCHI, also helped in the experiments.

-P-

REFERENCE: Report of Lt., Neal R. Smith, dated 28 January 1947.

DETAILS:

At Fukuoka:

On 6 March 1947, Takeshi KINO, was summoned for interrogation concerning his knowledge and possible participation in the experiments carried out at the Kwantung Army, Quarantine Stables in Manchuria.

Takeshi KINO's complete signed statement is attached as (Ex. A).

UNDEVELOPED LEADS:

The Tokyo Office--At Tokyo--Will locate and interview Masaji KITANO, presently reported residing at Setagayu-ku, Daita-machi, 1 chome, 5 Banchi, Tokyo, and obtain from him a complete and exhaustive statement concerning his knowledge of the atrocities committed at the Harbin experimental station.

Will interrogate Tomasada MASUDA, residing at Chiba-ken, Kimuzu-gun, Akimoto-mura, Nishihiaaku, #289, concerning the location of the secret laboratory in Harbin, type of experiments and research conducted, methods used in the experiments and personnel involved in the researchwork.

Distribution:

1 Prosecution
1 CRD
1 Osaka
1 Niigata
1 Fukuoka
1 Yamaguchi
1 Sapporo
1 Chinese Div.
Inv. Div. (File 330)
1- British Div
1 Sendai

Do not write in this space.

Will report on the demand placed on the Japanese Goverment for the military and biographical histories of former General Masaji KITANO, and former General Hitoshi KIKUCHI.

The Osaka Office--At Kyoto--Will locate and interview Hiroshi UEKI, reported residing at Kyoto-shi, Yoshita-cho, and obtain from him a complete statement concerning his knowledge of the matter of the experiments which were allegedly conducted upon POW's at the Harbin experimental station.

The Nagoya Office--At Uozu-mura, Toyama-ken--Will interview Junichi KANEKO, Toyama-ken, Uozu-mura, Takata-machi, #18, and obtain from him a complete and exhaustive statement concerning the atrocities committed at the Harbin experimental station, Names of individuals who committed same and names of individuals witnessing same.

The Yamaguchi Office--At Hagi-shi, Yamaguchi-ken, Will locate and interview Shiro YAMASHITA, presently reported residing at 173 Tsuchirara, Hagi-shi, Yamaguchi-ken, concerning his knowledge of the atrocities committed at the Harbin experimental station.

Will locate and interview Kiyoshi OTA, formely Chief of Serum Section of the Harbin experimental station, presently reported residing at Yamaguchi-ken, Hagi-shi, Chinto, #2502, concerning the manner in which the serum was produced, type of serum, research methods, testing methods of serum, in an attempt to uncover atrocitie committed at the Harbin experimental station.

Will locate and interview Dr. Nobimaru HINOFUJI, presently reported residing at Hiroshima-ken, Asa-gun, Fukuki-mura, Umagi, #640, concerning his knowldege of the atrocities committed at the Harbin Experimental station during his tour of duty at said station.

The Niigata Office--At Satoyaenabe-mura, Nagono-ken--Will locate and interview Takeshi NISHIMURA, presently reported residing at Nagano-ken, Satoyaenabe-mura, Higashi-Tsukaura-gun, and obtain from him and exhaustive statement covering full information concerning the nature of the atrocities committed, names of individuals committing same, and names of individuals who witnessed same.

----------P-E-N-D-I-N-G----------

54 A - Statement of Takeshi KINO

ALLIED OCCUPATION FORCES)
CITY OF FUKUOKA)

I, Takeshi KINO, being duly sworn on oath, state that I had read to me and understood the translation of the foregoing transcription of my interrogation and all answers contained therein, consisting of 3 pages are true to the best of my knowledge and belief.

Takeshi Kino
(Signature of Witness)

Subscribed and sworn to before me this 5 day of March 1947

Joseph F. Sartiano
Joseph F. Sartiano, Capt. Inf.
Investigating Officer
Legal Section, GHQ., SCAP.

ALLIED OCCUPATION FORCES)
CITY OF FUKUOKA)

I, George M. Yasutake, being duly sworn on oath, state that I truly translated the questions and answers given from English to Japanese, and from Japanese to English respectively, and that after being transcribed, I truly translated the foregoing deposition containing 3 pages, to the witness; that the witness thereupon in my presence affixed his signature thereto.

George M Yasutake
George M. Yasutake T/(Arm)
(Name) (Rank)

Subscribed and sworn to before me this 5 day of March 1947.

Joseph F. Sartiano
Joseph F. Sartiano, Capt. Inf.
Investigating Officer
Legal Section, GHQ., SCAP.

ALLIED OCCUPATION FORCES)
CITY OF FUKUOKA)

I, Joseph F. Sartiano, Capt. Inf., certify that on the 5 day of March, 1947, personally appeared before us Takeshi KINO, and according to George M. Yasutake gave the foregoing answers to the several questions set forth therein; that after his testimony had been transcribed the said Takeshi KINO, had read to him by the said interpreter the same and affixed his signature thereto in my presence.

Joseph F. Sartiano
Joseph F. Sartiano, Capt. Inf.
Investigating Officer
Legal Section, GHQ., SCAP.

FUKUOKA CITY, FUKUOKA KEN, KYUSHU, JAPAN
5 MARCH 7
194

Q State your name, age address and profession.
T.K. A. KINO, Takeshi, 29 years of age, Miyazaki-ken, Koyu-gun, Takanabe-machi, INARI-machi, Veternarian.
Q Give a brief history of your military career.
T.K. A. 10 Feb. 1940: Conscripted into Army; Kumamoto 6th Cav.
28 Feb. 1940: sent to Haeraru, Manchuria.
Nov. 1940 : sent to Russia to study Russian Lang.
6 April 1943: Discharged.
Q What did you do prior to your army career?
A. I was with the KWANTUNG Army Stables at Shinkio Manchuria. in the capacity of Veternarian.
Q What type of work was conducted at the KWANTUNG Army Stables?
A Study of Epidemics on animals.
Q Were KWANTUNG and HARBIN connected in any way ?
A No, KWNATUNG worked on Horses and HARBIN experimented on Humans.
Q Did you ever hear of General Shiro ISHII ?
A Yes.
Q Was he in charge of KWANTUNG ?
A No.
Q Who was CO at KWANTUNG ?
a Maj. Gen. Yujiro WAKAMATSU.
Q What sort of experiments were conducted at KWANTUNG?
a Main work was mainly on animals. I heard that before V J day there was a laboratory that experimented on Humans but as I was never allowed in that section because of my low rank I dont know how true this was.

紀 野 猛

In June 1938 I went to Kanto Gun in Shinkio Manchuria, as a veternarian, and was attatched to KWANTUNG Army Stables. I was doing disecting work on horses and studying the cause of their death. I was a specialist in that line.

Q While you were attatched to the stables, did you ever see experiments performed on Humans ?

a No, I never actually saw experiments performed on Humans, however, one day I was at my place of work and saw a stretcher carried past which carried the body of what was unmistakably a human. I know this because it was too small for a horse and too large for any other type animal, therefore it had to be a human. I have heard many rumors though from other men that experiments had been conducted and will give you a list of the men that I know had acsess to the place where the experiments were conducted. They were : Maj. Gen. Yujiro WAKAMATSU

Lt. Col. HOSAKA

Major Motoharu YAMAGUCHI

Civilian Spec. Keiko MATSUI

Captain Kaichi NAKAGIMA

Civilian Spec. Tetsu YOSHIKAWA

I heard these rumors from a civilian attatched to the army named MITOMO (fnu). I am sure that MITOMO used to work with the above-mentioned men and was ordered to mention this to no-one.

Q Why did MITOMO talk to you and tell you about the experiments when he had orders no to do so?

a. Through curiosity I wanted to know what was going on and I asked MITOMO who was of lower rank than I and he to tell me because he was a subordinate, I asked" did you kill someone during an experi-

紀野猛

ment"and he answered that they had. ~~Wexwerexbothxusedxfromx timextoxtimexyxbyxthexhighxrankingxofficersxandxwhenxIxwasxnotx availablexMITOMOxwasxusedx~~

Q What else did MITOMO tell you of the death ?

A Knowing that he (MITOMO) was under orders notto speak of the incident, and also knowing that MITOMO would get into serious trouble if he said, or told,anything else, I didn't ask him the details.

Q What other incidents do you remeber of the same nature?

A I did not attempt to learn anything that was going on after that because of the orders that the man had concerning the experiments.

Q What can you tell me about the men that you named as having knowledge of the experiments?

A Tetsu YOSHIKAWA would be able to tell you more concerning these experiments because he was directly connected with them.

Q What sort of work did YOSHIKAWA do?

A I dont know.

Q Then how do yu happen to know that YOSHIKAWA was connected with the labotatory that experimented on humans ?

A I ~~knowxfor~~ positively know that YOSHIKAWA was working in that section because I used to talk to him.

Q Did you ever talk about your work ?

A No, we always talked about other things.

Q What about the other men that you mentioned ?

A I cant tell you about the others because they were of higher rank and I never talked to them.

紀野猛

Q Was MATSUI of higher rank ?

A Yes.

Q Do you know of any unusual incidents that happened while you were stationed at the KWANTUNG Stables ?

A. One day, Captain NAKAJIMA, YOSHIKAWA and two or thee others had a screen between my work place and where they were working and were conducting some sort of an experiment. Near where they were working they had a grave dug that was too small for a horse and too large for any other animal and it was my opinion that it was for a human being. There was also a photographer present where they were conducting the experiment.

Q The humans that you speak of, were they POW's, civilians, and what nationality?

A I never saw the experiments but I think that they were Russians.

Q Why do you think they were Russians?

A Because Japan and Russia were at war, therefore I think that they were Russian POWs.

Q When did these incident occur ?

A I think in 1945.

Q I did not know that Russia and Japan were at war in 1945,.

A. Due to the fact that there were so many Russians in Manchuria perhaps the persons that were in custody of the Kempei Tai were used, but Russia and Japan were not at war in 1945.

Q Did you ever hear of POWs being injected with " Glanders" ?

紀野猛

and then disected for experiments?

A. Yes I heard rumors to that effect but I dont know whether they are true. I have also seen the ~~guards~~ persons who performed the exper. carry food to the guard house.

Q. What were the rumors that you heard ?

A. I dont know how true these rumors were but I heard that they put somethimg into the prisoners food and they also injected the prisoners with some sort of fluid.

Q. Did any of the men die as a result of the exeriments?

A. I heard that about ~~fifteen~~ twelve of the pows died as a result of the experiments.

Q. How do you know all this when you previously told me that you had no acsess to what was going on because of yur low rank?

A. Due to the fact that rumors spread and once I heard of something I liked to listen and find out the results.

Q. Who were the men responsible for these experiments, other than the ones you have already named ?

紀野猛

I, Takeshi KINO, after being duly sworn to speak the truth conscientiously adding nothing or concealing nothing whatsoever, testified at the Legal Section Office, Fukuoka, Kyushu, Japan, this 5th day of March 1947, as follows:

Q. Please state your full name, age, and address?
A. Takeshi KINO, age 29, address Miyazaki-ken, Koyu-gun, Takanabe-machi, Inari-machi.

Q. What is your present occupation?
A. A veterinarian.

Q. Give us a brief history of your military career?
A. February 10, 1940 Called into the army, at Kumamoto, 6th Cav. Regt.
February 28, 1940 Haeraru, Manchuria, 836th Unit (Regt.).
November , 1940 Harbin to study Russian Language.
June 6, 1941 Back to the 836th Unit. (The 836th Unit were scouts for mechanezed units).
April 6, 1943 Discharged.
I was working as a civilian employee at the Kwantung Army Quarantine Stables from June 6, 1938, to February 10, 1940, when I went into the army. I received my discharge in Manchuria in April 6, 1943, and went back to the Kwantung Army Quarantine Stables located at Mokaton, which is close to Shin Kyo, until August 10, 1945.

Q. Did you ever hear of POW's being infected with "GLANDERS DISEASE" and then dissected for experiments?
A. I heard rumors that experiments of that sort were being preformed, but I don't know if they were POW's or Coolies (Chinese labors) that were being used.

Q. Exactly what were the rumors that you heard?
A. I heard others saying that about thirteen (13) persons had been injected with the disease, but I didn't hear about their being dissected. It may have been about January 1945, that I heard about this.

Q. How many of these men died as the result of the experiment?
A. They all died from the experiment.

Q. Who was responsible for these experiments?
A. General WAKAMATSU, Yujiro.

Q. Did you help in these experiments?
A. No.

Q. Who else besides WAKAMATSU, helped in the experiments?
A. I heard that YAMAGUCHI, helped WAKAMATSU.

Q. Who did you hear this rumor from?
A. There was a lot of talk going on in camp about these experiments.

Q. Just what did these experiments consist of?
A. I don't know, everything was done secretly, therefore only the higher officials knew about them.

Q. Weren't you curious about these experiments?
A. Yes, but we were not allowed to inquire.

9A

T.K

Q. Who was the Commanding Officer of the stables?
A. Major General Yujiro WAKAMATSU. His home address is Yamguchi-ken, Otsu-gun, Hagishi, Tsuchihara 172. Care of Naoto FUJITA.

Q. Who was in charge of the experiment section?
A. Major HOSAKA.

Q. Who else do you remember that was in the Experiment Section?
A. Major YAMAGUCHI, Captains, OHKI, NAKAJIMA, YAMASHITA, TOBA, 1st Lieutenants, NAKAJIMA, TAKIZAWA, SASAKI, and 2nd Lieutenants, GOTO, TOYOKI, NISHIYAMA. There were about 300 persons in the experiment section and about 30 officers, I was not in that section so this is all I can think of.

Q. Do you know the address of Major YAMAGUCHI?
A. No, I do not.

Q. Do you know Lt. Col., YASUZAKA?
A. I8ve been at this stable close to ten (10) years but I've never heard of YASUZAKA.

Q. Do you know Capt., Shiro MATSUSHITA?
A. I haven't heard of him either.

Q. Did you ever work under General ISHII?
A. No, I was under General WAKAMATSU.

Q. Did you ever participate in any experiments during your stay in the Kwantung Army?
A. Yes, only on horses.

Q. Describe these experiments?
A. It required the dissection of the horses to study glander deseases.

Q. Did you ever see or take part in any experiments of that sort on human beings?
A. Never.

Q. Do you know Takeshi NISHIMURA?
A. Yes, he is a good friend of mine.

Q. NISHIMURA says that you were a witness in some of these experiments, is that true?
A. I am sure that he is mistaken or probably mistook my name for another.

Q. Then you think that NISHIMURA is lying in accusing you?
A. I don't think that NISHIMURA is the type that would lie, but it is possible that he misunderstood the rumors at the camp.

Q. Then why is NISHIMURA mentioning your name as having witnessed the experiment?
A. I remember that one day, I told NISHIMURA, that I thought I saw the body of a human being in a sack passing by my stables, he may have misunderstood that remark therefore, thinks that i probably took part in the experiment.

Q. Did you ever hear your name mentioned a having witnessed the experiments at the camp?
A. Never.

44

T.K.

-3-

Q. Did you ever witness any experiments conducted on human beings by General WAKAMATSU?
A. No, I was a civilian with a low rank, therefore was not permitted to work or see the work of the higher officers.

Q. Did you ever see any POW's, dead or alive during your stay at the camp?
A. None whatsoever.

Q. How about Chinese and Russian laborers?
A. Yes, there were many Chinese laborers, but I never saw any Russians.

Q. Do you think Major HOSAKA knows about persons being injected with GLANDERS and then dissected?
A. Yes, he should know, because he worked for WAKAMATSU. There was a section of the Experimental Station where they carried out secret experiments and the only ones allowed was the C. O. and persons directly connected with experiment. So they may have made such an experiment.

Q. Who else would know about these experiments?
A. One day a civilian by the name MITOMO, told me that he took part in dissecting human beings but warned me not to say anything about it as it was very secrative.

Q. Who was MITOMO's immediate superior?
A. Major YAMAGUCHI.

Q. Did MITOMO tell you anything more in detail about the dissecting of human beings.
A. Nothing more.

Q. Have you anything further to add to your statement?
A. Nothing.

Takeshi Kino
Takeshi KINO

9A

9.27 11 Mar. 1947: Inv. Div. No. 330, Report of Investigation Division, Legal Section, GHQ, SCAP, Neal R. Smith, 1st Lt., Inf.

资料出处：National Archives of the United States, R331, B1434.

内容点评：本资料为 1947 年 3 月 11 日盟军总司令部法务局调查科 Neal R. Smith 中尉提交的编号 330 调查报告，包括此日纪野猛再讯问记录。

Date: 11 March 1947

Report of Investigation Division, Legal Section, GHQ, SCAP.

Inv. Div. No. 330	CRD No.	Report by: Neal R. Smith, 1st Lt., Inf.

Title: Motoji YAMAGUCHI, et al.

Synopsis of facts:
GCD Intercept reflects that members of the Research Institute of Animals were ordered to remain in China by the 8TH ROUTE ARMY (China Communist Army) for purpose of reestablishing the Institute. Statement obtained from KINO names persons in charge of conducting experiments on humans at KWANTUNG Army Stables. Mail cover placed on KINO and NISHIMURA. Military and biographical history of OKI set out. Communication names Unit Commander of HARBIN Experimental Station.

- P -

Reference: Report of Capt. Joseph Sartiano dated 6 March 1947.

DETAILS:

At Tokyo:

On 10 February 1947, Tatsuzo INOUE giving his address as 63-1 Umemoto-cho, Hyogo-ku, Kobe-shi, (Japan), directed a letter to Ichiro MOTOMURA, 15 Shimizu-cho, Sasebo-shi, which was intercepted by a CCD, who forwarded a copy identified as JP/OSA/43312 to Legal Section for necessary action. The following communication was passed and is being transmitted to Criminal Registry Division with their copy of this report:

"MOCHIDA, TAJIMA, YAMASHITA, and FUJITA, the members of our JUKEN (Ex: Research Institute of Animals) were ordered to remain for the purpose of reestablishing the organization. FUJITA came back to Japan, but the others are still in their office, I suppose. As they desired to remain, I did not advise them to return home, UJIIE, KUWAHARA, the members of our branch office at Harbin, SAKAI, a member of the Mongolian Quarantine Office, and TOMIOKA, a member of the Tsitsihar Quarantine Office, went to Tsitsihar with their families, by order of the 8th Route Army (Chinese Communist Army) on the day before the Japanese in Harbin left there."

"After the surrender, the members of our laboratory earned their own living as shoemaker, a sweet red-bean bun salesman and a broker; some of them ran a tea room, a circulating library, and a manufactury of homespun cloths or sausage and so on I had to take care of sixty boys, members of the Volunteer

Distribution:	Do not write in this space.
1 CRD (Encl) 1 Prosecution Div. 1 Sendai 1 Niigata 1 Sapporo 1 Yamaguchi 1 Osaka 1 Fukuoka 1 Nagoya 1 Chinese Div. 3 Inv. Div. (File 330)	

Training Corps, whom I rescued from the Soviet Army, and at last found jobs for them in a brewery and another industrial company. My subordinates in the Institute sold their belongings and clothes to support themselves and fought against the Soviet troops, 8th Route Army, urged by their earnest desire to return home in safety.

On the morning of January 5, 1946, I was taken prisoner by Soviet Troops and was provided with only a piece of Russian bread and a glass of water a day during January. Mr. Takeda, the chief of the section of general affairs, was with me in the prison. I was arrested and closely examined, on suspicion of being the chief secretary of KYOWAKAI (the Harmony Association, a Japanese semi-official organization in Manchuria) and Mr. TAKEDA never returned, and is now missing. I thought I might be sent to Siberia, but fortunately I was acquitted. But to make matters worse, after returning home, my legs ached so that I could not stand up and I was ill in bed with heart-disease through February and March, due to undernourishment. I started from Mukden on August 20th with MOMOSE and his family, and arrived in Kobe on October 1st, with nothing but a rucksack."

. . . .

YAMASHITA, named by INOUE, is the only one that can be found in the indices of the Investigation Division.

On 11 March 1947, the Reporting Agent interrogated Takeshi KINO as per Undeveloped Lead set out in report of investigation by Capt. N. H. Powell dated 24 January 1947. KINO was named during an interrogation of Takeshi NISHIMURA as having witnessed experiments performed on prisoners of war at the KWANTUNG Army Stables. The original of the following statement obtained from KINO, is being transmitted to Criminal Registry Division with their copy of this report:

Q. State your name, age, address and profession.
A. KINO, Takeshi, 29 years of age, Miyazaki-ken, Koyu-gun, Takanabe-machi, Veternarian.

Q. Give a brief history of your military career.
A. 10 Feb. 1940: Conscripted into Army; Kumamoto 6th Cav.
28 Feb. 1940: Sent to Haeraru, Manchuria.
Nov. 1940: Sent to Russia to study Russian Language.
6 Apr. 1943: Discharged.

Q. What did you do prior to your army career?
A. I was with the KWANTUNG Army Stables at Shinkio Manchuria, in the capacity of Veternarian.

Q. What type of work was conducted at the KWANTUNG Army Stables?
A. Study of Epidemics on animals.

Q. Were KWANTUNG and HARBIN connected in any way?
A. No, KWANTUNG worked on horses and HARBIN experimented on humans.

Q. Did you ever hear of General Shiro ISHII?
A. Yes.

Q. Was he in charge of KWANTUNG?
A. No.

Q. Who was CO at KWANTUNG?
A. Major General Yujiro WAKAMATSU.

- 2 -

Q. What sort of experiments were conducted at KWANTUNG?
A. Main work was mainly on animals. I heard that before V J Day there was a laboratory that experimented on humans but as I was never allowed in that section because of my low rank, I don't know how true this was. In June 1938, I went to Kanto Gun in Shinkio Manchuria, as a Veternarian, and was attached to KWANTUNG Army Stables. I was doing dissecting work on horses and studying the cause of their death. I was a specialist in that line.

Q. While you were attached to the stables, did you ever see experiments performed on humans?
A. No, I never actually saw experiments performed on humans, however, one day I was at my place of work and saw a stretcher carried past which carried the body of what was unmistakably a human. I know this because it was too small for a horse and too large for any other type of animal, therefore it had to be a human. I have heard many rumors through other men that experiments had been conducted and will give you a list of the men that I know had excess to the place where the experiments were conducted. They were:

Lt. Col. HOSAKA
Major Motoharu YAMAGUCHI
Civilian Spec. Keiko MATSUI
Captain Kaichi NAKAJIMA
Civilian Spec. Tetsu YOSHIKAWA

I heard these rumors from a civilian attached to the army named MITOMO (fnu). I am sure that MITOMO used to work with the above mentioned men and was ordered to mention this to no one.

Q. Why did MITOMO talk to you and tell you about the experiments? When he had orders not to do so?
A. Through curiosity I wanted to know what was going on and I asked MITOMO who was of lower rank than I and he told me because he was a subordinate. I asked, "Did you kill someone during an experiment?" and he answered that they had.

Q. What else did MITOMO tell you of the death?
A. Knowing that he (MITOMO) was under orders not to speak of the incident, and also knowing that MITOMO would get into serious trouble if he said, or told, anything else, I didn't ask him the details.

Q. What other incidents do you remember of the same nature?
A. I did not attempt to learn anything that was going on after that because of the orders that the men had concerning the experiments.

Q. What can you tell me about the men that you named as having knowledge of the experiments?
A. Tetsu YOSHIKAWA would be able to tell you more concerning these experiments because he was directly connected with them.

Q. What sort of work did YOSHIKAWA do?
A. I don't know.

Q. Then how do you happen to know that YOSHIKAWA was connected with the laboratory that experimented on humans?
A. I positively know that YOSHIKAWA was working in that section because I used to talk to him.

Q. Did you ever talk about your work?
A. No, we always talked about other things.

Q. What about the other men that you mentioned?

A. I can't tell you about the others because they were of higher rank and I never talked to them.

Q. Was MATSUI of higher rank?
A. Yes.

Q. Do you know of any unusual incidents that happened while you were stationed at the KWANTUNG Stables?
A. One day, Captain NAKAJIMA, YOSHIKAWA, and two or three others had a screen between my work place and where they were working and were conducting some sort of an experiment. Near where they were working they had a grave dug that was too small for a horse and too large for any other animal and it was my opinion that it was for a humanbeing. There was also a photographer where they were conducting the experiment.

Q. The humans that you speak of, were they POWs, civilians, and what nationality?
A. I never saw the experiments but I think they were Russians.

Q. Why do you think they were Russians?
A. Because Japan and Russia were at war, therefore, I think that they were Russian POWs.

Q. When did these incidents occur?
A. I think in 1945.

Q. I did not know that Russia and Japan were at war in 1945.
A. Due to the fact that there were so many Russians in Manchuria perhaps the persons that were in custody of the Kempei Tai were used, but Russia and Japan were not at war in 1945.

Q. Did you ever hear of POWs being injected with "Glanders"? And then dissected for experiments?
A. Yes, I heard rumors to that effect but I don't know whether they are true. I have also seen the persons who performed the experiments carrying food to the guard house.

Q. What were the rumors that you heard?
A. I don't know how true these rumors were, but I heard that they put something into the prisoners food and they also injected the prisoners with some sort of fluid.

Q. Did any of the men die as a result of the experiments?
A. I heard that about twelve (12) of the POWs died as a result of the experiments.

Q. How do you know all this when you previously told me that you had no access to what was going on because of your low rank?
A. Due to the fact that rumors spread and once I heard of something I liked to listen and find out the results.

Q. Who were the men responsible for these experiments, other than the one's you have already named?
A. Yujiro WAKAMATSU was in direct command of the unit, therefore, I think that he would be the responsible person.

Q. Do you know where WAKAMATSU lives at the present time?
A. Yamaguchi-ken, Otsu-gun, Hagi-shi, Tsuchihara, 172.

Q. Do you correspond with him?
A. No, I do not.

Q. Then how do you happen to know his address?
A. When we left Manchuria, WAKAMATSU left before everyone else and we were

interested in knowing how we could get in touch with him when we needed advice.

Q. What sort of advice would you want from WAKAMATSU?
A. WAKAMATSU was the Unit Commander and we might want to know how to get out family back to the mainland.

Q. Have you seen WAKAMATSU since you came back to Japan?
A. Yes, two or three times.

Q. What did you talk about when you met?
A. About bringing back my family from Manchuria.

Q. How long have you been back in Japan?
A. Since November 1945.

Q. Since you have been back, have you seen, talked or corresponded to any member of the unit other than NISHIMURA and WAKAMATSU?
A. Yes, I also met, and corresponded with Tokio OTSUKA and my section chief, Yutaka ONO.

Q. Where do these men live?
A. OTSUKA lives at Kumomoto-ken, Otsu-gun; ONO resides at Yokohama, Tsurumi-ku, Namamugi-cho, c/o Isamu KADOMA.

Q. What was OTSUKA's position?
A. We both were in the same unit. OTSUKA was a Vet. in my stable.

Q. What was the general correspondence when you wrote.
A. About our families.

Q. Do you know Tatsuzo INOUE, MOCHIDA, TAJIMA, YAMASHITA, FUJITA, UJIIE, TOMIOKA, KUWAHARA or TAKEDA?
A. I know a Shiro YAMASHITA, FUJITA and UJIIE. They all worked at the Institute.

Q. Do you know anything about the work of these men?
A. YAMASHITA was in charge of General Affairs, the FUJITA that I knew was in charge of Intendance; UJIIE was working under YOSHIKAWA.

Q. What was the administrative set-up of the KWANTUNG Army Stables?
A. There were three (3) sections. 1st Section was in charge of all animals in the KWANTUNG Stables; 2nd Section was research; 3rd Section manufacture of Serum, and a Headquarters Section. Yujiro WAKAMATSU was Commanding Officer, YAMAGUCHI was Chief of 1st Section; HOSAKA was Chief of 2nd Section; YAMAGUCHI was also Chief of 3rd Section and YAMASHITA was in charge of Headquarters.

Q. Who else worked in the Research Section?
A. There were six (6) sub-sections under the Research Section. I can't remember the first five but the sixth was headed by YAMAGUCHI and doing the secret work.

Q. Then in your opinion, it was the sixth sub-section in Research that was doing the research on human beings?
A. According to rumors, yes.

Q. Do you know anyone else working in the sixth sub-section other than YAMAGUCHI?
A. Only the one's that I have previously named, Civilian Specialist Keiko MATSUI, Civilian Specialist Tetsu YOSHIKAWA and Major Motoharu YAMAGUCHI.

Q. Do you know where MITOMO is living at the present time?
A. I don't know but I think he lives somewhere in the Tokyo area.

Q. Do you have anything else to add to your statement that you think would be of value?
A. No.

/s/ Takeshi KINO

. . . .

On 18 February 1947, T. Katsube, Chief of Liaison Section, Central Liaison Office of the Japanese Government, forwarded the following military and biographical history of Masami OKI, identified as CLO #1021(PM), the original of which is being transmitted to Criminal Registry Division with their copy of this report:

Domicile: 3,266 Ooaza Nomi, Toyoe-mura, Toyota-gun, Hiroshima Prefecture.
Date of Birth: 11 February 1917.
Military Personal History:
Promotion:
13 Mar. 1942: Veterinary Second Lieutenant.
Appointment:
10 Jan. 1938: Entered the Replenishment Unit of the 41st Infantry Regiment.
2 May 1938: Military Reserve Officer Candidate.
3 Aug. 1939: Transferred to the 232nd Infantry Regiment.
9 Oct. 1939: Dispatched to Central China.
27 Apr. 1941: Attached to the Sick Horse Depot of the 39th Division.

From this time forward, there is no record concerning his military career.

Biographical History:
12 May 1935: Finished the whole course of the Hiroshima Prefectural Saijyo Agricultural School.

(Note) This follows the military career register. He is not yet demobilized.

. . . . . .

On 10 March 1947, a mail cover was placed on Takeshi KINO and Takeshi NISHIMURA for a period of sixty days starting from 10 March 1947. It can be noted from the above report that KINO and NISHIMURA were co-workers at the KWANTUNG Army Stables and according to KINO they correspond quite regularly.

At Sendai:

On 13 February 1947, Captain E. H. Powell, Agent in charge of the Sendai office, submitted to the Tokyo office a communication received from Sadao MASUMORI, Public Safety Section, Prefectural Office, Sendai City, written by Takeishi NISHIMURA, Yoshioka-cho, which contains the name of the Unit Commander of the HARBIN Experimental Station. The original of the following translation is being transmitted to Criminal Registry Division with their copy of this report:

I hereby report the address and the name of the UNIT COMMANDER of the following person:

Motoji YAMAGUCHI, Murata-cho, Shibata-gun, Miyagi-ken.
(ISHII UNIT) Sanitary Water Section.
COMMANDER: ISHII (fnu), M.D. Lt. General.

Report of Investigation by Major L. H. Barnard dated 20 November 1946 contains the above information.

UNDEVELOPED LEADS:

Tokyo Office -- At Tokyo -- Will locate and interview Masaji KITANO, presently reported residing at Setagayu-ku, Daita-machi, 1 Chome, 5, and obtain from him a complete and exhaustive statement concerning his knowledge of the atrocities committed at the HARBIN Experimental Station. At Chiba-ken, Kimusu-gun -- Will locate and interro-

- 6 -

gate Tomasada MASUDA, residing at Chiba-Ken, Kimusu-Gun, Akimoto-Mura, Nishihiaaku, 289, concerning the location of the HARBIN Secret Laboratory, type of experiments and research conducted, methods used in the experiments and personnel involved in the research work.

Will report on the demand placed on the Japanese Government for the military and biographical history of former generals KITANO and KIKUCHI.

Will interview Tatsuzo INOUE upon his arrival in Tokyo, concerning CCD Intercept in which he stated that certain members of the Research Institute for Animals were ordered to remain in China, and obtain a complete and exhaustive statement concerning the nature of the Institute and it's connection with the KWANTUNG Army Stables. (Agent's Note: CCD Intercept referred to is identified as JP/OSA/43312 and contained in above report.)

Osaka Office — At Kobe-Shi, Hyogo-Ku — Will locate Tatsuzo INOUE, presently reported residing at 63-1 Umemoto-Cho, Hyogo-Ku, Kobe-Shi, and upon locating INOUE will take appropriate action to assure his arrival at the Tokyo Office of Legal Section for interrogation.

At Kyoto — With aid of Kyoto police, will continue the search for Hiroshi UEKI reported residing at Kyoto-Shi, Yoshida-Cho, and upon locating UEKI will take appropriate action to assure his arrival in Tokyo at the office of Legal Section for interrogation in connection with the HARBIN Experimental Station.

Nagoya Office -- At Uozu-Mura, Toyama-Ken -- Will locate and interview Junichi KANEKO, Toyama-Ken, Uozu-Mura, Takata-Machi, 18, and obtain from him a complete and exhaustive statement concerning the atrocities committed at the HARBIN Experimental Station, names of individuals who committed same and names of individuals who witnessed same.

At Shizuoka-Ken -- Will locate and interview Seeichi NAKAJIMA, presently reported residing at Shizuoka-Ken, Ogasa-Gun, Asahina-Mura, Asahina Kami, 510, and obtain from him a complete and exhaustive statement concerning his knowledge of the atrocities committed at the HARBIN Experimental Station.

Niigata Office — At Gorobei-shinden-machi, Nagano-ken, — Will locate and interview Tokio MACHIDA, presently reported residing at Nagano-ken, Kita-Saku-gun, Gorobei-Shinden-mura, 90, and obtain from him a complete and exhaustive statement concerning his knowledge of the atrocities committed at the HARBIN Experimental Station; said interrogation to include the names of individuals conducting the experiments, individuals witnessing the experiments and the type of experiments conducted.

At Nagano-Ken — Will locate Motoji YAMAGUCHI, former Major General in charge of the KWANTUNG Army Stables and upon location of subject, take appropriate action to assure his arrival at the Tokyo Office for interrogation.

At Nagano-Ken, Kamiminochi-Gun, Tsuwa-Mura — Will locate and interview Mamoru OUCHI and obtain a sworn statement concerning his knowledge of the alleged experiments conducted on humans at the KWANTUNG Army Stables.

Yamaguchi Office -- At Hagi-Shi — Will locate and interview Shiro YAMASHITA, presently reported residing at 173 Tsuchirara, Hagi-shi, Yamaguchi-Ken, and obtain from him a complete and exhaustive statement concerning his knowledge of the atrocities committed at the KWANTUNG Army Stables and/or any other atrocities committed at said stables.

At Yamaguchi-Ken, Hagi-Shi — Will locate former Major General Yujiro WAKAMATSU, presently reported residing at Yamaguchi-Ken, Hagi-Shi, Uyahara-Machi, c/o FUJITA, and after locating subject, will take appropriate action to assure his arrival to the Tokyo Office for interrogation in regards to atrocities committed at the KWANTUNG Army Stables.

At Tokyo — Will locate and interview MITOMO (fnu) who was alleged to have participated in the experiments involving humans at the KWANTUNG Army Stables.

Q. Where do these men live ?

A. OTSUKA lives at Kumomoto-ken, Otsu-gun. ONO resides at Yokohama , Tsurumi-ku, Namamugi-cho, c/o Isamu KADOMA.

Q. What was OTSUKA's position ?

A. We both were in the same unit. OTSUKA was a Vet. in my stable.

Q. What was the general correspondence when you wrote.

A. About our families.

Q. Do you know Tatsuzo INOUE, MOCHIDA, TAJIMA, YAMASHITA, FUJITA, UJIIE, TOMIOKA,KUWAHARA or TAKEDA ?

A. I know a Shiro YAMASHITA, FUJITA and UJIIE, they all worked at the institute.

Q. Do you know anything about the work of these men?

A. YAMASHITA was in chage of General Affairs, the FUJITA that I knew was in charge of Intendance; UJIIE was working under YOSHIKAWA.

Q. What was the administrative set up of the KWANTUNG Army Stables ?

A. There were three(3) Section, 1st Section was in charge of all animals in the KWANTUNG Stables; 2nd Section was research; 3rd Section manufacture of Serum, and a Headquarters Section. Yujiro WAKAMATSU was Commanding Officer, YAMAGUCHI was Chief of 1st Section; HOSAKA was Chief of 2nd Section; YAMAGUCHI was also Chief of 3rd Section and YAMASHITA was in charge of Headquarters.

Q. Who else worked in Research Section ?

A. There were six(6) sub-sections under the Research Section. I cant remember the first five but the sixth was headed by YAMAGUCHI and doing the secret work.

Q. Then in your opinion, it was the sixth sub-section in Research that was doing the research on Human Beings ?

A. According to rumors, yes.

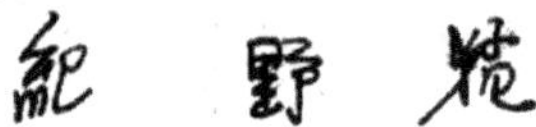

Q. Do you know anyone else working in the sixth sub-section other than YAMAGUCHI ?

A. Only the ones that I have previously named, Civilian Specialist Keiko MATSUI, Civilian Specialist Tetsu YOSHIKAWA and Major Motoharu YAMAGUCHI.

Q. Do you know where MITOMO is living at the present time ?

A. I don't know but I think he lives somewhere in the Tokyo area.

Q. Do you have anything else to add to your statement that you think would be of value ?

A. No.

Takeshi Kino

Takeshi KINO

ALLIED OCCUPATION FORCES)

CITY OF TOKYO)

I, Takeshi KINO, being duly sworn on oath, state that I had read to me and understood the translation of the foregoing transcription of my interrogation, consisting of eight (8) pages, and they are true to the best of my knowledge and belief.

Takeshi Kino

Takeshi KINO

Subscribed and sworn to before me this 11 day of March 1947.

Neal R. Smith

Neal R. Smith, 1st Lt., Inf.
Investigating Officer,
Legal Section, GHQ, SCAP.

9.28 17 Mar. 1947: Inv. Div. No. 330, Report of Investigation Division, Legal Section, GHQ, SCAP, by Neal R. Smith, 1st Lt., Inf.

资料出处：National Archives of the United States, R331, B1434.

内容点评：本资料为 1947 年 3 月 17 日盟军总司令部法务局调查科 Neal R. Smith 中尉提交的编号 330 调查报告，包括增田知贞（Tomosada Masuda）讯问记录。

Date: 17 March 1947

Report of Investigation Division, Legal Section, GHQ, SCAP.

Inv. Div. No. 330	CRD No.	Report by: Neal R. Smith, 1st Lt., Inf.

Title: Motoji YAMAGUCHI, et al.

Synopsis of facts:
Location and authenticity of HARBIN Secret Laboratory established.
Responsible persons named.

\- P -

Reference: Report by Lt. N. R. Smith dated 11 March 1947.

DETAILS:

At Tokyo:

On 13 March 1947, Tomosada MASUDA, former Colonel assigned to the HARBIN Experimental Laboratory, was interrogated by the Reporting Agent in connection with the location, type of research and persons connected with the alleged secret laboratory located at the HARBIN Experimental Laboratory.

The following voluntary statement was obtained from MASUDA, the original of which is being retained in Investigation Division file pertaining to this matter:

Q. State your full name, age, address and profession.
A. Tomosada MASUDA, 47 years of age, Chiba-Ken, Kimitsu-Gun, Akimoto-Mura, Nishi Hikasa, 289, Doctor.

Q. Give a summary of your military career.
A. 30 June 1926: Lt. Medical Doctor, 22nd Regiment.
1 Apr. 1929: Post Grad. student at Kyoto Imperial University, Microbe Bacteriology Institute.
1 Apr. 1931: Medical Captain in 9th Regiment.
1 Aug. 1931: Prof. at Army Medical College at Tokyo.
Apr. 1933: Was sent as military attache to Berlin, Germany. Student at the Institute of experimental of Cell Culture.
June 1934: Transferred to Paris Army Medical College of Val de Grace as student Officer Attache.
June 1935: Came back to 4th Inf. Imperial Guard Unit, Tokyo.
Aug. 1936: Made Major and worked on War Ministry Medical Bureau at Tokyo.
Aug. 1937: Left for Manchuria. KWANTUNG Army Prevention Unit under

Distribution:
1 CRD
1 Prosecution Div.
1 Sendai
1 Niigata ✓
1 Sapporo
1 Yamaguchi
1 Osaka
1 Fukuoka
1 Nagoya
1 Chinese Div.
3 Inv. Div. (File 330)

Do not write in this space.

Col. ISHII, Shiro.

Aug. 1938: Transferred to Middle China as Chief of 7th Field Water Supply Unit.

15 Apr. 1939: Water Supply Unit in Middle China under Col. ISHII, made Lt. Col. April 1939.

July 1941: Made Prof. at Army Medical College at Tokyo and came back to Japan in August.

Aug. 1942: Promoted to Colonel.

Mar. 1943: Division Medical Doctor of 31st Division and transferred to Burma.
Became Chief Officer of the Japanese Burma Expeditionary Army and studied the prevention on Malaria for 2 years.

Mar. 1945: Member of the Medical Bureau of General Headquarters of South Expeditionary Army located in Saigon, French China.

May 1945: Received orders to report to KWANTUNG Army Water Supply and Preventional Bureau under ISHII. Reached Manchuria in middle of July 1945 and was Chief of Water Supply up to end of the War.

Q. What were your duties while stationed in Manchuria under ISHII?
A. My first duties were general affairs and at the same time I was experimenting on Typhiod Fever. That was while I was with the unit from 1937 until 1938.

Q. What were your duties when you returned in 1945?
A. I reached Manchuria in July 1945 and the following month the war ended.

Q. Didn't you do anything from July until August?
A. I was in Heijo North Korea for 10 days on a trip, before I had a chance to get organized with the unit the war ended.

Q. What sort of an organization did ISHII have in HARBIN?
A. Contagious Disease Prevention, Water Supply and Purification, Manufacture and Study of Water Purification Equipment, Filter Systems for Water Purification. Also vaccine and serum manufacturing.

Q. Where was the Unit located?
A. Twenty (20) miles from HARBIN at a place called PINGFUN.

Q. Have you ever heard of Hajime TOGO?
A. I have heard of the TOGO Unit.

Q. What was the TOGO Unit?
A. I don't know.

Q. Was it true that ISHII operated a secret laboratory where he conducted experiments on Bacterial Warfare?
A. Yes.

Q. Where was the laboratory located?
A. PINFUN, Manchuria.

Q. What sort of research was conducted?
A. Defense of Bacterial Warfare.

Q. Wasn't he also experimenting in Offensive Bacterial Warfare?
A. In order to have a defense in Bacterial Warfare, he first had to have an offense.

Q. Do you know of anything that went on at the secret laboratory?
A. In 1934-35-36, they were experimenting on bacterial bombs at the secret laboratory, but that is all that I know of.

Q. Who were the men connected with the secret laboratory?
A. ISHII had full charge, working with him were Kiyoshi OTA and Hatushige IKARI.

Q. Do you have anything else to add to your statement?
A. No.

UNDEVELOPED LEADS:

Tokyo Office -- At Tokyo -- Will report on the demand placed on the Japanese Government for the military and biographical history of former generals, KITANO and KIKUCHI.

At Kyoto -- With aid of Kyoto Police, will continue the search for Hiroshi UEKI reported residing at Kyoto-Shi, Yoshida-Cho, and upon locating UEKI will take appropriate action to assure his arrival in Tokyo at the office of Legal Section for interrogation in connection with the HARBIN Experimental Station.

Nagoya Office -- At Uozu-Mura, Toyama-Ken -- Will locate and interview Junichi KANEKO, Toyama-Ken, Uozu-Mura, Takata-Machi, 12, and obtain from him a complete and exhaustive statement concerning the atrocities committed at the HARBIN Experimental Station, names of individuals who committed same and names of individuals who witnessed same.

At Shizuoka-Ken -- Will locate and interview Seeichi NAKAJIMA, presently reported residing at Shizuoka-Ken, Ogasa-Gun, Asahina-Mura, Asahina Kami, 510, and obtain from him a complete and exhaustive statement concerning his knowledge of the atrocities committed at the HARBIN Experimental Station.

Niigata Office -- At Gorobei-shinden-machi, Nagano-ken, -- Will locate and interview Tokio MACHIDA, presently reported residing at Nagano-ken, Kita-Saku-gun, Gorobei-Shinden-Mura, 90, and obtain from him a complete and exhaustive statement concerning his knowledge of the atrocities committed at the HARBIN Experimental Station; said interrogation to include the names of individuals conducting the experiments, individuals witnessing the experiments and the type of experiments conducted.

At Nagano-Ken -- Will locate Motoji YAMAGUCHI, former Major General in charge of the KWANTUNG Army Stables and upon location of subject, take appropriate action to assure his arrival at the Tokyo office for interrogation.

At Nagano-Ken, Kamiminochi-Gun, Tsuwa-Mura -- Will locate and interview Mamoru OUCHI and obtain a sworn statement concerning his knowledge of the alleged experiments conducted on humans at the KWANTUNG Army Stables.

Yamaguchi Office -- At Hagi-Shi -- Will locate and interview Shiro YAMASHITA, presently reported residing at 173 Tsuchirara, Hagi-Shi, Yamaguchi-Ken, and obtain from him a complete and exhaustive statement concerning his knowledge of the atrocities committed at the KWANTUNG Army Stables and/or any other atrocities committed at said stables.

At Yamaguchi-Ken, Hagi-Shi -- Will locate former Major General Yujiro WAKAMATSU, presently reported residing at Yamaguchi-Ken, Hagi-Shi, Uyahara-Machi, c/o FUJITA, and after locating subject, will take appropriate action to assure his arrival to the Tokyo Office for interrogation in regards to atrocities committed at the KWANTUNG Army Stables.

At Tokyo -- Will locate and interview MITOMO (fnu) who was alleged to have participated in the experiments involving humans at the KWANTUNG Army Stables.

P E N D I N G

9.29 17 Mar.: 1947: Inv. Div. No. 330, Report of Investigation Division, Legal Section, GHQ, SCAP, by John A. Duffy, Civilian Investigator

资料出处： National Archives of the United States, R331, B1434.

内容点评： 本资料为 1947 年 3 月 17 日盟军总司令部法务局行政调查官 John A. Duffy 提交的编号 330 调查报告，包括长野县新潟办公室对大内守（Mamoru Ouchi）和町田时男（Tokio Machida）讯问记录。报告指出，目前的调查结果显示为相关于一大规模计划的战略性细菌战的发动。

Date: 17 March 1947

Report of Investigation Division, Legal Section, GHQ, SCAP

Inv. Div. No. 330	CRD No.	Report by: John A. Duffy Civilian Investigator

Title: Motoji YAMAGUCHI, et al.

Synopsis of Facts: Interview of Mamoru OUCHI and Tokio MACHIDA set out. Summarization of investigations to date--experiments conducted on Prisoners of War at Kwantung Army Quarantine Stables part of plan of strategic bacterial warfare.

- P -

References: Report of 1st Lt Neal R. Smith, dated 27 Jan 47.
Capt. Ernest Powell 25 Feb 47.
Roy T. Yoshida 6 Feb 47.
1st Lt Neal R. Smith 28 Jan 47.
Capt E. H. Powell 24 Jan 47.
Maj. L. H. Barnard 9 Dec 46.
John C. Donnell 3 Dec 46.
Maj. L. H. Barnard 29 Nov 46.
Taro Shimomura 27 Nov 46.
Maj. L. H. Barnard 14 Oct 46.

DETAILS:

The Niigata Office - At Nagano-ken - interviewed Mamoru OUCHI on 14 March 1947 and Tokio MACHIDA on 15 March 1947. Statements were taken from both individuals, and are as follows:

I, Mamoru OUCHI, being duly sworn to speak the truth, conscientiously, adding nothing and concealing nothing whatsoever, testified at the Nagano Military Government HDQ, Nagano City, on the 14 March 1947, as follows:

Q. - Please state your full name, age, religion and address.
A. - Mamoru OUCHI, 34 years of age, Buddhist, address: Nagano-ken; Kami Mizuuchi-gun; Tsuwa-mura; 486.

1 Pros Div
1 G.S (Incls)
1 Fukuoka
1 Osaka
1 Sendai
1 Niigata
1 Yamaguchi
1 Sapporo
1 Chinese Div
1 Nagoya
1 British Div
3 Inv Div File 330
1 Col Carpenter

Q. - Were you in the Japanese Army in Manchuria?
A. - I was a civilian attached to the Army.

Q. - With what unit and for how long did you serve?
A. - I was with the 100th Unit, later the 25,207th Unit which is the same as the Kwantung Army Quarantine Stables, from May 1940 to 16 August 1945.

Q. - Did you know Takeshi NISHIMURA?
A. - Yes.

Q. - Did you know Motoji YAMAGUCHI?
A. - Yes.

Q. - How and where were you associated with these two men?
A. - I knew YAMAGUCHI by sight only, I never talked to him, he was a Major and was in charge of the 2nd Division of the 2nd Section and was later put in charge of the Section. Then he was transferred to the 3rd Section and later to the 1st Section. I saw NISHIMURA quite frequently after my arrival and talked to him for the first time in March 1943 at a meeting of men from Nagano Prefecture. We returned to Japan together on the 16 August 1945. He was a civilian attached to the 3rd Section.

Q. - During the time you were in Manchuria, did you ever see any Prisoners of War?
A. - I never saw any of them, but I heard they were there.

Q. - How close to the Kwantung Stables were these prisoners?
A. - According to what I heard there were about ten prisoners in the guard house on the post.

Q. - During the time you were in Manchuria the cattle plague was very severe, was it not?
A. - I do not know anything about cattle plague, I was a blacksmith until April 1945 and then went into the office where they kept the medical supplies. The diseases I heard about were TANSO (Anthrax) and BISO (Glanders) which affect horses and can also be contracted by man.

Q. - Were these two diseases you mentioned prevalent among the horses at your station?
A. - At our station BISO was more prevalent then TANSO. Other stations would send us cases of both diseases.

Q. - With regard to these diseases did you ever see any experiments being conducted on Prisoners of War?
A. - I never saw any experiments being conducted, but I heard that this had been done from Nobuo TERANISHI, I believe his home is in AKITA-KEN.

Q. - What did you hear from TERANISHI regarding these experiments?
A. - TERANISHI was a photographer and took pictures of PW's who had been killed or died and he showed me a picture of one. He said that BISO had been injected into the PW and he had died. He showed me this picture in July or August of 1944 but did not say when it had been taken. This photo was taken after an autopsy had been performed, the face was blacked out and the body had been incised from about the end of the ribs down to and including the crotch, and this incision was open exposing all parts of the body and stomach.

Q. - What unit conducted these experiments?
A. - The 2nd Division of the 2nd Section.

Q. - Who was in charge of the unit?
A. - Major Motoji YAMAGUCHI.

Q. - How are you sure this was the body of a Prisoner of War?
A. - From seeing the picture I would say it was the body of a Russian or some other Caucasian.

Q. - Did TERANISHI tell you he witnessed the experiment?
A. - No, and I believe he was called to take the picture after the experiment had been conducted. Tokio MACHIDA who was in charge of the 3rd Division would know more about this. Tokio OTSUKA (add: Kyushu, Kumamoto-ken) who worked in the 3rd Division since I went there, should know some of the experiments conducted in the 2nd division.

Q. - Do you have anything further to add to your statement at this time?
A. - No.

I, Tokio MACHIDA, being duly sworn to speak the truth conscientiously, adding nothing and concealing nothing whatsoever, testified at the Nagano Military Government HDQ, Nagano City on the 15 March 1947 as follows:

Q. - State your full name, age, religion and address.
A. - Tokio MACHIDA, 29 years of age, Buddhist, address: Nagano-ken, Nagano-shi, Motoyoshi-cho, 481 c/o FUKUSHOIN Permanent domicile: Nagano-ken, Kita Saku-gun, Gorobei, Shinden-mura, 81.

Q. - Did you serve with the Japanese Army at the Kwantung Quarantine Stables in Manchuria?
A. - Yes.

Q. - What was your rank and position?
A. - I was a veterinarian 1st Lt. when I arrived and was later promoted to Captain. I joined this unit 2 April 1944 and remained until August 1945.

Q. - What was the unit designation of this organization and its disposition.
A. - This was the 100th unit of the Kwantung Army and it was divided into four sections, one Administrative and three experimental sections.

Q. - To what section were you assigned and what were the specific duties of that section?
A. - I was assigned to the 3rd division of the 2nd section. The duties of this section were:
The treatment and cure of TANSO (Anthrax), BISO (Glanders), DENSEN SEISHIN KETSU (A contagious disease that reduces the blood count in animals) (Experiments to determine how it is contracted), KANKATSUSEIGANIN (A disease affecting the eyes of horses, and causes blindness).

Q. - What type of experiments were being conducted to determine the origin of these diseases and their cures if any?
A. - BISO - was injected into healthy horses. ZURO-PHAPIRIZIN, ZURUPAGUANIJIN, and SEPHALANCHIN were tried as cures, but all the animals died. Autopsies were performed post mortem to determine exact effect of disease and serums on animals organism, such as liver, stomach, etc.
TANSO - was not handled by me. It was handled by the 1st division.
DENSEN SEISHIN KETSU - AMIGUDARIN was injected, negative results.
KANKATSUSEIGANIN - A solution containing vitamin "C" was injected into the water of the eye, negative results.

Q. - Who was in charge of this section?
A. - Lt. Col. Tomio NAKAYAMA (killed in plane crash Sept. 44). He was replaced by Lt. Col. Yasutaro HOSAKA.

Q. - Were you ever attached to or did you ever do any work for the HARBIN Experimental Station?
A. - I was never attached to the HARBIN Station, but one time when they were conducting an experiment I went along with the 6th division of the 2nd section who had some connection with the HARBIN Station.

Q. - What was the nature of this experiment?
A. - We sprayed cow plague germ and YOTO by airplane over a small herd of cattle and sheep. This was to determine if the animals would contract the disease.

Q. - What were the results of this experiment?
A. - Two out of fifteen of the cattle caught the disease. The sheep were attacked by wolves, so it was impossible to continue the experiment or get any results from them.

Q. - When did this experiment take place?
A. - September 1944.

Q. - Was this the only time you did any work for the HARBIN Station?
A. - Yes, this was the only time I had anything to do with this station.

Q. - Who else from the Kwantung stables went on this experiment:
A. - Major General Yujiro WAKAMATSU; Lt. Col. Yasutaro HOSAKA; Major Motoji YAMAGUCHI; Capt Toshiyuki OGI; (FNU) MITSUDA, Civilian; (FNU) MATSUI Civilian; (FNU) IDA Civilian; and 1st Lt. Bunson SASAKI.

Q. - Who was there from HARBIN?
A. - The Commanding Officer (Not ISHII) and two others, whose names I do not know.

Q. - Who came from Tokyo?
A. - Lt. Col. NAKAYAMA and one other (NU).

Q. - On this experimental work in the treatment and cure of BISO who else in your section and division conducted experiments with you?
A. - Lt. Col. Yasutaro HOSAKA — Civ. Hideo SHISHIDO
Major Motoji YAMAGUCHI — Civ. Yutaka ONO
Captain Toshiyuki OGI — Civ. Fumiya KATO
1st Lt. Korin KANEDA — 2nd Lt. (FNU) TOYOKI
1st Lt. Nobuo UEDA — 2nd Lt. Jiro GOTO
1st Lt. Bunson SASAKI — Civ. Masayuke MITSUDA

Q. - These twelve men and yourself were primarily interested in the treatment and cure of BISO, is that true?
A. - Yes.

Q. - How successful would you say your experiments were?
A. - We didn't have any success.

Q. - During what year or what part of a year was this disease the most severe?
A. - There was no noticeable increase or decrease before or during the time I was there.

Q. - At the Kwantung stables was there a Prisoner of War Camp or was the regular guard house used for these prisoners?
A. - I heard that there were Prisoners of War in the guard house.

Q. - Did you ever see any of these Prisoners of War?
A. - No.

Q. - With regard to this cattle plague, what sort of experiments were conducted on human beings at Kwantung stables?

A. - There were no experiments conducted on human beings with regard to the cattle plague.

Q. - Are you absolutely sure of this?
A. - Yes, I am sure of this.

Q. - Couldn't these experiments have taken place without your knowledge?
A. - I can't say that I knew everything that went on there, but I don't think these experiments happened.

Q. - Were any experiments conducted on human beings with BISO?
A. - Not as far as I know.

Q. - A few months after you arrived at Kwantung weren't the bodies of some dead Prisoners of War taken into the experimental lab and autopsies performed on them?
A. - I never heard or saw of any autopsy being performed on Prisoners of War.

Q. - Do you know Takeshi NISHIMURA?
A. - Yes.

Q. - Did NISHIMURA work in the same section with you?
A. - No.

Q. - What reaction would BISO have if injected into a man?
A. - I don't know how this would react.

Q. - How many prisoners of war did you hear were on the post at Kwantung?
A. - I dont know how many, there were two cells.

Q. - At the end of the war, what Nationality soldiers took over the Kwantung stables?
A. - I dont know.

Q. - Why dont you know?
A. - I left on the 15 August.

Q. - Where did you go to?
A. - To KEIJO, the capital city of Korea.

Q. - To whom were the Prisoners of War turned over to after the war?
A. - I dont know.

Q. - Weren't the Prisoners in the guard house released at the end of the war?
A. - I dont know.

Q. - Do you still deny any knowledge or part in the conduction of experiments of BISO on Prisoners of War?
A. - I know nothing about anything like this happening.

Q. - In conducting an autopsy on an animal such as a horse in what manner is the incision made?
A. - First the left foreleg is cut off, then the left hind leg is cut off. The incision is started at the ribs and continued through the center of the abdomen down through and including the crotch, then a cross incision is made through the abdomen so as to expose the intestines for examination. Next the legs are cut to examine the joints. Then the head is incised and the brain examined.

Q. - When healthy horses were injected with BISO about how long did they live?
A. - The disease took effect in about twelve hours. Only a few of the horses died, so the rest had to be killed to find out what effect it had on their organs.

Q. - How long do men live who contract BISO?
A. - According to what I have read about a week.

Q. - Didn't you ever see anyone who had this disease?
A. - No.

Q. - Didn't any of the men on your base die of this disease?
A. - No.

Q. - To what HDQ did all the research reports of your findings go?
A. - To the Kwantung Army HDQ.

Q. - Didn't you and YAMAGUCHI agree to conduct the experiments on human beings and keep it secret?
A. - No. The only experiment that we were told to keep secret about was when we made the trip to HARBIN and sprayed the herds.

Q. - Who told you to keep this a secret?
A. - General WAKAMATSU.

Q. - What reason did he give for wanting to keep this secret?
A. - Because of the bacterial strategy.

Q. - Is there anything else you wish to add to your statement?
A. - No.

The investigation of this case to date, and excerpts from testimonies of witnesses and alleged perpetrators of the causes of deaths of Prisoners of War at the Kwantung Army Quarantine Stables, reflect this to have been part of a large scale plan for the instigation of strategic bacterial warfare.

The original informant, Takeshi NISHIMURA, alleged that former high ranking officers of the Kwantung Quarantine Stables injected "BISO" glanders into Prisoners of War in a secret experiment conducted at the Kwantung Stables. Major Motoji YAMAGUCHI was the alleged perpetrator and originator of the experiment.

When interrogated on 4 November 1946, by the Niigata Office, Motoji YAMAGUCHI emphatically denied that any such experiment had been conducted; and further stated that diseases that they were experimenting with at the Kwantung Stables, such as Cattle Plague, Anthrax and Glanders, could not be contracted by human beings. He also denied the presence of any Prisoners of War at the Kwantung Stables post.

This testimony of YAMAGUCHI is entirely false, due to the fact that these above-mentioned diseases are highly contagious and very easily contracted by humans. Other veterinarians and witnesses state that the fear of the men contracting these diseases was one of the major problems of the station. Witnesses also claim to have been well aware of Prisoners of War on the post. There was no special camp set aside for them, and they were confined in the post guard house.

The Yamaguchi Office interviewed former Major General Yujiro WAKAMATSU on 28 October 1946. He was Commanding Officer of the Kwantung Stables. He stated that it was common knowledge at the Kwantung Stables that an unknown number of Manchurians herding horses had died of Glanders contracted from infected animals, and that two Japanese research workers died after accidentally contracting the disease in their work. WAKAMATSU denied that any Prisoners of War had been injected with Glanders or that any dissections had been made on post mortem examinations.

Captain Powell interviewed Takeshi NISHIMURA at SENDAI on 24 January 1947, with the following results:
He stated that he had seen Prisoners of War at the Quarantine Stables, some of whom were Chinese and others whose nationalities he could not identify. He further stated that these prisoners appeared weak and fatigued out, and attributed their condition to poor food and living conditions. NISHIMURA said that Takeshi KINO actually saw the experiments being conducted on the Prisoners of War, and that KINO told him about this. He also stated that Mamoru OUCHI saw some pictures relative to these experiments. KINO told him that (BISO) Glanders extracted from horses had been injected into the Prisoners and, in some cases, had been mixed in their food. He was not too sure of the exact details, but is positive of the experiments having taken place on about twenty Prisoners of War. This experiment was very secretive, and all other workers were forbidden to enter this part of the station at the time. He stated that, after the Prisoners had died of the disease, autopsies were performed on the bodies to learn the cause of death and the nature and extent of harm done to the vital organs of the body by the disease.

Lt Neal R. Smith interviewed Ryoichi NAITO on 24 January 1947. He stated that Lt General Shiro ISHII was in charge of preparatory experiments for the purpose of conducting strategic bacterial warfare, and that these experiments were divided into offensive and defensive actions. In the offensive action, they were to discover a formula for the mass production of bacteria and its ultimate distribution into enemy territory by airplanes. In the defensive program, they were to set up the proper systems of vaccination, water purification, disinfection, and organization. He contends that ISHII mobilized most of the universities in Japan to help him. Some of these schools are: Tokyo Army Medical College, Kyoto Imperial University, Tokyo Imperial University, Infectious Disease Research Laboratories, Tokyo, and many others. NAITO claims that ISHII must have used human beings for some of his experiments because, he says, "Some of the vaccines perfected could only be called successful after observing the results obtained after innoculating humans with the disease and the vaccine; men returning from the Harbine Experimental Station would tell me of humans being used for the experiments, and that ISHII had established his laboratory in HARBIN where he could obtain Prisoners of War for his experiments". Mitsuichi MIYAMOTO, chief owner of the Nihon Tokushu Kyogo Company, Ltd, Minami Shinagawa, 3-chome, Tokyo, was the sole agent who supplied all the necessary equipment to the Harbin Experimental Station.

The Niigata Office interviewed Mamoru OUCHI at Nagano City on 14 March 1947. He stated that he had heard of the injection of (BISO) Glanders into Prisoners of War, and that autopsies had been performed on the bodies after they had died. OUCHI states that Nobuo TERANISHI photographed the bodies of these Prisoners of War after the autopsies had been performed and that, on or about July or August 1944, showed him a picture of one of the autopsies. He described this photograph as follows: The face had been blacked out and the body had been incised from the ribs down to and including the crotch, through the center of the abdomen. The abdomen had been crosswise incised, exposing all parts of the stomach, etc. OUCHI said that this was the picture of a white man, probably a Russian or some other nationality.

Tokio MACHIDA was interviewed at NAGANO CITY on 15 March 1947. He denies knowledge or part in any experiments conducted on human beings, or any autopsies having been performed. He stated that he was primarily interested in the treatment and cure of (BISO) Glanders, and devoted all his time to this work. He admits taking part in a secret experiment conducted at the Harbin Station, the purpose of which was to study the effect of spraying animals from an airplane with Cattle Plague and a disease known as YOTO. The reason for this being a secret experiment was because of the bacterial strategy.

The original statements of OUCHI and MACHIDA are being transmitted to the Criminal Registry Division with their copy of this report.

UNDEVELOPED LEADS:

The Osaka Office -- At Kyoto -- Will locate and interview Hiroshi UEKI, presently reported residing at Kyoto-shi, Yoshita-cho, and obtain a complete and exhaustive statement from him concerning his knowledge of the matter of the experiments which were allegedly conducted upon Prisoners of War at the Harbin Experimental Station.

The Yamaguchi Office -- At Hagi-Shi, Yamaguchi-Ken -- Will locate and interview Shiro YAMASHITA, presently reported residing at 173 Tsuchiwara, Hagi-Shi, Yamaguchi-Ken, concerning his knowledge of the experiments conducted on the Prisoners of War.

The Nagoya Office -- at Ogasa-Gun -- Will interrogate Seiichi NAKAJIMA, presently reported residing at 510, Kami-Asahina, Asahina-Mura, Ogasa-Gun, Shizuoka Prefecture, concerning his knowledge of atrocities committed at Harbin Experimental Station, the names of individuals committing same, and names of individuals witnessing same.

Will confer with Prosecution Division to determine what further investigation will be necessary and what steps will be taken in this case.

P E N D I N G

9.30　4 Apr. 1947: Inv. Div. No. 330, Report of Investigation Division, Legal Section, GHQ, SCAP, by Neal R. Smith, 1st Lt., Inf.

资料出处：National Archives of the United States, R331, B1434.

内容点评：本资料为 1947 年 4 月 4 日盟军总司令部法务局调查科 Neal R. Smith 中尉提交的编号 330 调查报告，为该部门细菌战有关调查阶段性报告，提出法务局的调查是为追究用盟军人员进行违法人体实验的战争犯罪者，并送交审判。关东军军马防疫厂与关东军防疫给水部进行的战俘人体实验显示实施战略性细菌战的大规模计划。

CONFIDENTIAL

Date: 4 April 1947

Report of Investigation Division, Legal Section, GHQ, SCAP.

Inv. Div. No. 330	CRD No.	Report by: Neal R. Smith, 1st Lt., Inf.

Title: Motoji YAMAGUCHI alias Honji YAMAGUCHI, Yujiro WAKAMATSU, YASAZUKA (fnu), Yasutaro HOSAKA alias Yasutara HOZAKA, Shiro MATSUSHIDA alias Shiro YAMASHITA, Shiro ISHII alias Hajime TOGO.

Synopsis of facts:

Report of Investigation Division Case #330 to date. Experiments conducted on POWs at KWANTUNG Army Stables and Army Water Purification and Supply Unit reflect plan of Bacterial Warfare.

\- P -

Reference: Reports of Maj. L. H. Barnard dated 14 October 1946, 5 November 1946, 8 November 1946, 20 November 1946, 29 November 1946, 9 December 1946; Report of Taro Shimomura dated 27 November 1946; Report of John C. Donnell dated 3 December 1946; Report of Capt. E. H. Powell dated 24 January 1947; Report of Lt. N. R. Smith dated 27 January 1947, 28 January 1947, 11 March 1947, 17 March 1947; Report of Maj. J. F. Sartiano dated 6 March 1947; Report of John A. Duffy dated 17 March 1947; and Report of Robert M. Ousley dated 19 March 1947.

DETAILS:

At Tokyo:

In view of the fact that G-2, GHQ, SCAP, has requested a report on the progress in investigation in the case of Shiro ISHII, former Lieutenant General, I.J.A., a review of the investigation to date has been made and the following chronological report is submitted.

This investigation was originally predicated upon the receipt of an undated letter from a person giving his name as NISHIMURA which reflects that members of the I.J.A. infected POWs with glanders and then dissected their bodies as an experiment. Named as responsible for the experiments were: former Major Honji YAMAGUCHI, former Major General Yujiro WAKAMATSU, former Lt. General Yasuzaka (fnu) and Capt. Shiro MATSUSHIDA. The original and translation of this letter can be found in the indices of the Criminal Registry Division in File JA 19-218.

On 3 December 1945, Metropolitan Unit #80 of the CIC submitted a summary of information concerning Shiro ISHII residing in Chioda-Mura, Yamatake-Gun, Chiba-Ken. The information was obtained from confidential informant 80-11 of that office who stated that ISHII, allegedly a large land owner in Chiba Prefecture and formerly a Lieutenant

Distribution:
1 CRD
1 Prosecution Div.
1 Niigata
1 Osaka
1 Fukuoka
1 Nagoya
1 Sendai
1 Sapporo
1 Yamaguchi
1 G-2 (Col. McQuail)
1 Col. Carpenter
3 Inv. Div. (File 330)

Do not write in this space.

CONFIDENTIAL

CONFIDENTIAL

General of the Army Surgeons Corps of the Japanese Army, was proclaimed dead and his funeral observed in Chioda-Mura, Yamatake-Gun, Chiba-Ken, on 10 November 1945. The informant alleged that the death was false and claimed that ISHII had gone underground with the aid of the village head man of Chioda-Mura, with intentions of carrying on anti-democratic activities. The informant also claimed that ISHII was the Commanding Officer of the ISHII Detachment of the Surgeons Corps during the war and that through a result of his carelessness, after injecting Bubonic Plague Bacilli into the bodies of some Chinese in Canton, China, a Bubonic Plague ravaged that city.

On 14 December 1945, OCCIO transmitted a copy of a memorandum from the Japanese Communist Party with reference to Japanese Bacteriological Warfare. This communication reveals the activities of the ISHII B.K.A. It reflects that the B.K.A. was established in Harbin under the commandership of Lt. General Shiro ISHII. In 1944, the B.K.A. succeeded in cultivating pests which was applied to Manchurian and several American citizens captured during the war. ISHII was alleged to have started actual manufacture of pestilence bacteria on a large scale when war termination was declared. It is further stated that the Japanese Army bombarded the laboratory, destroying documents, equipment and hundreds of laboratory members engaged in study. The research work was conducted in cooperation with Tokyo and Kyoto Imperial Universities medical laboratories.

The memorandum also alleges that the leading personnel engaged in the research were Rinnosuke SHOJI and Hisato YOSHIMURA from the laboratory and Kiyu OGATA of the Chiba Medical University. Medical Universities and Institutes mobilized for the purpose, were: Densenbyo Kenkyusho, Tokyo; Kyoto Imperial University; Medical Bureau of War Ministry; and Chiba Medical University.

On 15 December 1945, an individual giving his name as Setsu IMAJI, Shinmachi, Setagaya-Ku, Tokyo, forwarded a letter to CIS which was translated by ATIS as their Document #2035 and a copy of same was delivered to Legal Section. The communication reflects that ISHII outwardly conducting research on Water Purification, was secretly conducting research on Bacterial Warfare. A secret laboratory was established near the Haiin River Railway Station of the Manchurian-Hairal Line. Shiro ISHII, then a Major General, assumed the alias of Hajime TOGO. The communication reflects that the atrocious acts was to use humans instead of animals for their research on bacteria. It is alleged that although the majority of the victims were convicted criminals, there were also innocent farmers, officers of the Communist Army, women and children and over a thousand victims of the experiments conducted on horse glanders bacteria, pestilence bacteria and other strong poisons. The communication also sets out the fact that ISHII's wife was the daughter of Torasaburo ARAKI, president of the Peers School and was very intimate with former War Minister Tadao ARAKI, thus receiving unlimited help from him. It can also be noted that the communication states that machinery such as water filter machines and microscopes were purchased under the name of the Japan Special Factory, Incorporated, with Mitsuichi KURITSU acting as representative. The factory was managed by KURITSU at the start of operations but was later incorporated and ISHII and his cohorts reaped huge profits by receiving dividends under the names of dummy stockholders.

On 10 February 1946, an individual giving his name as Takeshi KINO, Miyazaki-Ken, Koto-Gun, Tanabe-Machi, directed a letter to Legal Section which reflected that certain residents of Hagi-Shi, Yamaguchi-Ken, were responsible for using Allied POWs as human guinea pigs at an experimental station at Mokotan, Hsinking, China. He named Yujiro WAKAMATSU, Shiro YAMASHITA, Yasutaro HOSAKA and Motoji YAMAGUCHI, former veterinarians of the I.J.A. The original and translation of this letter is contained in the indices of the Criminal Registry Division, Legal Section, and can be found in File JA 19-242.

On 26 June 1946, Takeshi KINO was interrogated at the 6th Marine Division Headquarters in Fukuoka by Lt. John Eglsear and a signed statement was obtained from KINO as set out in the report of said agent dated 27 June 1946. KINO admitted that he had

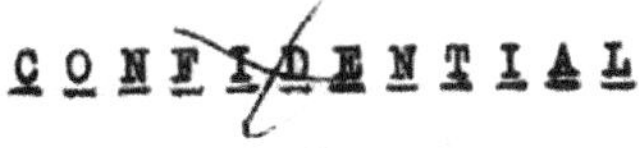

CONFIDENTIAL

served in the Japanese Army and had been stationed in Manchuria and was discharged from military service in 1943 becoming a civilian employee of the KWANTUNG Army Stables. He stated that he had heard rumors to the effect that humans were being infected with glanders and then being dissected for experimental purposes but could not recall whether he had heard that these experiments were being conducted on prisoners of war or Chinese coolies. He further stated that the ISHII Unit at Harbin was making experiments on this disease and may have been responsible for the acts. KINO stated that the experiments conducted by that station were of a secret nature; that he was not personally cognizant of the extent to which they were carried.

The report of Capt. Joseph Sartiano dated 8 August 1946, disclosed that Motoji YAMAGUCHI who is allegedly reported as Honji YAMAGUCHI, was inducted into the army as a Probationary Officer of the 16th Cavalry, in the capacity of Veterinarian on 20 April 1938 and subsequently joined the 10th Cavalry which moved to Jamusu, Manchuria. YAMAGUCHI was promoted to Captain in 1940 and in 1942 to the Tokyo Military Veterinary School where he majored in Pathology at which time he went to Hsinking, China, with the KWANTUNG Army Horse Disease Prevention Unit as a Veterinarian. He remained there until 12 August 1945 when his unit retreated to Seoul, Korea. He denied that any experiments had been conducted on humans but stated that experiments were conducted on guinea pigs, rabbits, horses and various types of other animals. YAMAGUCHI acknowledged knowing NISHIMURA, who, he stated, was also a Veterinarian and formerly concocted serums at the No. 3 Station. YAMAGUCHI stated that at one time he had reprimanded NISHIMURA for having stolen some food and a few bottles of glucose.

On 23 August 1946, Takeshi NISHIMURA, giving his address as Nagano-Ken, Hagashi Tsukuma-Gun, Satoyanaebe-Mura, forwarded a communication to CI&E Section of SCAP and is set out in report of Maj. L. H. Barnard dated 14 October 1946 as follows:

Report on War Criminals.

Motogji YAMAGUCHI, a former veterinary surgeon major

Address: Murata-Cho, Shibata-Gun, Miyagi Prefecture

Yujiro WAKAMATSU, a former veterinary surgeon major-general

Address: Nagi-Shi, Otsu-Gun, Yamaguchi Prefecture

HOZAKA, a former veterinary surgeon lieutenant-colonel

Address: Unknown

The above veterinary surgeons dissected many war prisoners of the Allied Forces at the outdoor dissecting ground of No. 100 Army Corps at Hsinking (Changchun), Manchuria, as their inspections of the cattle plague. If you would investigate these criminals, you will find many other persons who have participated to the dissections. There are a number of the witness of the inspections.

On 4 October 1946, Hiroshi UEKI, giving his address as Kyoto-Shi, Yoshida-Cho, directed a letter to General MacArthur which had been translated as ATIS Document # 23836, the original and translation of which are being retained in the Investigation Division file pertaining to this matter.

UEKI alleged that during the present war, Lt. General Shiro ISHII, an army medical doctor, established a large scale human experimental station in the suburbs of Harbin. He allegedly acted as commander of the fictitious KANO Unit and executed brutal experiments on many Allied POWs. According to UEKI, it was no secret that he destroyed the experimental station and evidence of his activities. UEKI further alleges that ISHII considered the placing of his name on a war crime suspect list as inevitable and has been using bribes to escape the consequences of his acts.

CONFIDENTIAL

CONFIDENTIAL

CI&E Section of SCAP received an anonymous letter dated 3 September 1946 giving only an address of Koriyama-Shi, Fukushima-Ken, which was translated by said CI&E Section, the original and translation was forwarded to Legal Section for necessary action. The communication was set out in report of Major L. H. Barnard dated 8 November 1946 as follows:

CI&E, GHQ

Contribution concerning Surgeon Lt. Gen. Shiro Ishii.

I was forced to work in the army for a long time only for victory recently was demobilized without belongings.

People trust me cold-heartedly and I have no job at present, when inflation is rampant. Moreover, I have many family members to feed. This is the whole reward for me, who worked whole-heartedly at the risk of my life.

One year after the termination of war, my living has become more and more difficult. Gradually I have began to lose hope of living through it.

Japan is now endeavouring to become a peaceful country. To realize this aim, militarists must be eradicated completely. But the cabinets since the end of the war have strove to conceal them as best as they coult. Now I want to tell you the case of Lt. Gen. Ishii as an example.

A repatriate from Manchuria reported in the newspaper that he was shot to death, but this is not a fact, this article was made by the order of the government and nothing else. He was a well-known militarist and enemy of humanity. He established the Epidemic Prevention and Water Supply Section of Kwantong Army. What did he do through this section and what did he plan? I was once attached to his corps, so I know quite well about his work. Militarists are afraid of his summon, as the secrets will be revealed by it. His summoning will provide evidence and data against 'A' class war criminal suspects and even one Imperial family member will be affected. So the cabinets, especially the Foreign Ministry, ex-Army Ministry, Demobilization Board and Liaison Office have endeavored to make this case lost in oblivion. I believe that it is utterly necessary to judge him and those who planned and worked with him fairly for the establishment of truly peaceful country.

I know quite well about him and his corps and the atrocities committed by them.

If you want my help, I will work as best as I can for the investigation of this case.

I have strict confidence to correspond to your expectation, if you permit me certain number of days and expenditures for investigation.

As to details, I want to meet you to consult with you. If you want to make me do this work, please put the following advertisement inthe Nippon Keizai Press within 3 days after the arrival of this letter to you.

'Attendance Order'

"Shiro Ishii is required to appear in person on ——day Sept. 1946

CI&E, GHQ, SCAP."

The request contained in the letter that the writer be contacted through the Keizai Press, could not have been complied with even had it been desirable, inasmuch as the original letter had not been translated within the specified time.

CONFIDENTIAL

CONFIDENTIAL

This information was included in this report as another indication of the mounting complaints concerning the alleged activities of General ISHII and his associates at the KWANTUNG Experimental Stables in China, principals among which are alleged to have been infecting Prisoners of War with glanders for experimental purposes.

Report of John C. Donnell dated 3 December 1946 sets out the interrogation of former Maj. General Hujiro WAKAMATSU; said WAKAMATSU stating that no humans, POWs, Chinese nor Japanese had ever been given any kind of injections in the research program, nor had any humans been dissected in the study of the disease. He stated that it was common knowledge at the Quarantine Stables that an unknown number of Manchurians had died of glanders contracted from herding diseased animals. He stated that two members of the research laboratory (Japanese) had died after accidentally contracting the disease in their work. One of the Japanese worked in the laboratory at Mukden and the other at Hsinking. WAKAMATSU claimed that these men's bodies were not dissected or examined post mortem; but he said that he had no knowledge of their names nor the length of illness, nor other details of their case. WAKAMATSU also stated that he had no knowledge of the research work being conducted by the ISHII Unit and claimed that there had been no lateral dissemination of research reports between these units. He further stated that all research reports were transmitted to higher headquarters.

On 24 January 1947, Capt. E. H. Powell, Agent in Charge of the Sendai Office of Legal Section, interviewed Takeshi NISHIMURA, former Veterinarian attached to the KWANTUNG Army Stables. NISHIMURA stated in his interview that he had never participated in illegal experiments but that Group #2 at the station conducted research and experimentation on humans. He further stated that Motoji YAMAGUCHI was in charge of Group #2 but was later relieved by former Lt. Colonel Yasutaro HOSAKA. He further stated that Takeshi KINO had actually witnessed these atrocities and that a man named Mamoru OUCHI had seen pictures of said experiments. NISHIMURA also stated that he had heard that most of the men died after receiving the injections at Group #2 and after death the bodies were dissected to determine the cause of death. The following names were set out by NISHIMURA as having been connected with Group #2:

Tokio MACHIDA, Capt.	SHISHIDO (fnu), Civilian
Yukenobu OKI, Capt.	Kiyoshi IDA, Civilian
Kaiichi NAKAJIMA, Capt.	Fumiya KATO, Civilian
Kerin KAMEDA, Capt.	Yutake MURAKAMI, Civilian
Bunzo SASAKI, 1st Lt.	Maseyuki MITSUDA, Civilian
Keitaro ANDO	MATSUI (fnu), Civilian

On 24 January 1947, the reporting agent interrogated Ryochi NAITO, formerly a Lt. Colonel and Officer in Charge of the Army Medical College, Tokyo, in connection with the experiments conducted by the college in conjunction with the research work of ISHII in Harbin. NAITO states that ISHII was using the water purification phase of defensive research as a cover-up in order to conduct his experiments in Bacterial Warfare. ISHII went to Harbin sometime in 1932 and started research in Bacterial Warfare. He further stated that the idea for Bacterial Warfare was solely that of ISHII and that he started initial steps for financing the project after he returned from a trip to Europe in 1930. NAITO also said that it was common knowledge among the microbiologists in Japan, all of whom were connected with ISHII, that humans were used for experimentation at the Harbin installation, and that ISHII used the alias of Hajime TOGO during the course of the experiments, as did all of his officers connected with the laboratory during their tour of duty. A list of personnel attached to the laboratory was obtained from NAITO and is set out here for those persons interested:

General Shiro ISHII	Commanding Officer
Maj. Gen. Hitoshi KIKUCHI	Chief, 1st Section
Col. Kiyoshi OTA	Chief, 3rd Section
Col. Hatshuge IKARI	Chief, 2nd Section
Col. (fnu) NAGAYAMA	Chief, Clinical
Col. Tomasada MASUDA	Chief, Administration
Maj. (fnu) HIRASAWA	Test Pilot
Col. Takashi MURAKAMI	Chief, Education
Col. Saburo SONADA	Chief, Education
Col. Kokan IMAZU	Chief, Administration
Col. Masataka KITAGAWA	Chief, 2nd Section
Col. (fnu) EGUCHI	Chief, 4th Section
Maj. Yashiyasu MASUDA	Pharmacy

CONFIDENTIAL

Maj. (fnu) TANABE	Chief, General Affairs
Maj. (fnu)TAKAHASHI	Chief, General Affairs
Eng. 2nd Class Hotori WATANABE	Research Conductant (Bacteria)
Eng. 6th Class Hideo FUKATI	Common Member
Eng. 6th Class Tachio ISHIKAWA	Common Member
Eng. 2nd Class Koji ANDO	Chief, DARIEN Dispatch (Darien EISEI KENKYSHO)

The following list of persons are alleged to have been connected with the Army Medical College, Tokyo:

General Shiro ISHII	Chief
Col. Hitoshi KIKUCHI	Bacteriology
Col. Tomasada MASUDA	General Affairs
Col. Takatomo INOUE	Bacteriology
Col. Enryo HOJO	Water Purification
Col. (fnu) SATO	Member
Lt. Col. Ryochi NAITO	Water Purification
Lt. Col. Katsushige IDEI	Serum and Vaccine
Maj. Jun-Ichi KANEKO	Serum
Maj. Yoshifumi TSUYAMA	Disinfection
Eng. 5th Class Haru HASHIMOTO	Bacteriology

The eight sections were named as follows: (1) Study (Science); (2) Study of Bacteria (offensive); (3) Manufacture of Serum (defensive); (4) Study of Water Supply; (5) Administration; (6) Education; (7) Clinical Section; and (8) Supply.

In report of Lt. N. R. Smith dated 27 January 1947, the military and biographical histories of Tokio MACHIDA and Siichi NAKAJIMA are set out. These two men are mentioned in report of Capt. E. H. Powell dated 24 January 1947, in which the interrogation of Takeshi NISHIMURA is set out in which NISHIMURA stated that the two men were members of the group that conducted experiments on humans, Group #2 at KWANTUNG Army Stables. The military histories of the two men give evidence that they were members of the KWANTUNG Stables; MACHIDA during the period 19 February 1944 until 30 August 1945; NAKAJIMA from 3 August 1941 until 19 August 1945.

Report of Roy T. Yoshida, Agent at Osaka Office, dated 6 February 1947, reveals that UEKI, writer who directed a letter to General MacArthur, as set out in report by Maj. L. H. Barnard dated 20 November 1946, cannot be located at the address given by the writer, Kyoto-Shi, Yoshida-Cho. The search for UEKI is being continued with the aid of the Japanese Police at Kyoto.

On 6 March 1947, Capt. Joseph Sartiano, Agent in Charge of the Fukuoka Office of Legal Section, interrogated Takeshi KINO, in connection with the alleged experiments conducted at the KWANTUNG Army Stables; said KINO named by Takeshi NISHIMURA, in an interview at Sendai by Capt. E. H. Powell as set out in report of investigation dated 24 January 1947, that KINO was a witness to the experiments. KINO, however, denied that he had ever witnessed or participated in the experiments but stated that he had heard that General WAKAMATSU was responsible for thirteen (13) deaths as a result of the experiments carried on under the supervision of Group #2. KINO further states that WAKAMATSU was a participant of the experiments.

On 11 March 1947, the reporting agent submitted a report containing a CCD Intercept written by a person giving his name as Tatsuso INOUE, Kobe-Shi, Hyogo-Ku, Umemoto-Cho, 63-1, which reflects that certain members of the Juken (Research Institute for Animals) were ordered to remain in China by the 8th Route Army (Chinese Communist Army) for the purpose of re-establishing the institute. Persons named by INOUE as having been ordered to remain in China were: MOCHIDA, TAJIMA, YAMASHITA, FUJITA, UIIJE, KUWHARA, SAKAI, and TOMIOKA. INOUE states that on 5 January 1946, he was taken prisoner by the Soviet Troops, and after a courts martial for being a suspected member of KYOWAKAI (a Japanese semi-official organization in Manchuria) was acquitted and returned to Japan. Also set out in the repot is the interrogation of Takeshi KINO which contains very little more information than received by Capt. Sartiano in his interview

CONFIDENTIAL

CONFIDENTIAL

with KINO as related in the foregoing paragraph. He did state, however, that he corresponded with NISHIMURA, and a mail cover was placed on both men with CCD. The military history of Masami OKI, formerly alleged to be Captain Yukenobu OKI, is set out and it was ascertained that OKI was a member of the KWANTUNG Army Stables from 27 April 1941 until the cessation of hostilities.

On 13 March 1947, Tomasada MASUDA, formerly Chief of General Affairs at the KWANTUNG Water Purification and Supply Unit, was interrogated, said interrogation set out in report of Lt. N. R. Smith dated 17 March 1947, and the location and authenticity of the secret laboratory operated by ISHII for his experiments in Bacterial Warfare was ascertained. MASUDA stated that his laboratory was located at PINGFUN, about twenty (20) miles from Harbin. He also stated that he knew that experiments were being conducted by Kiyoshi OTA, Hatusuge IKARI and ISHII and that the experiments were on Bacterial Bombs.

Robert M. Ousley, Agent in Charge of the Nagoya Office of Legal Section, interrogated Seiichi NAKAJIMA on 19 March 1947 and it was learned that said NAKAJIMA had never been at the KWANTUNG Water Purification Unit under ISHII but that he had been at the KWANTUNG Army Stables under the command of YAMAGUCHI. NAKAJIMA was named by NISHIMURA, in an interrogation conducted by Capt. E. H. Powell on 24 January 1947, as having been a member of Group #2, KWANTUNG Army Stables.

In an interview conducted by John A. Duffy, Agent in Charge of the Niigata Office, Mamoru OUCHI; named by KINO as having witnessed the illegal experiments, as set out in report of Lt. N. R. Smith dated 11 March 1947; stated that he was a blacksmith at the Army Stables and that two types of diseases were being experimented on at said stables. They were BISO (glanders) and TANSO (anthrax). He stated that he had never witnessed experiments being conducted on POWs but that he had heard of the experiments through Nobuo TERANISHI, a photographer who had taken pictures of the experiments. He further stated that he had seen a picture of one of the POWs after death and that the POW had been dissected after he died from being injected with BISO. OUCHI also named the same men responsible for the experiments as did KINO, those of Group #2 at the KWANTUNG Army Stables.

This agent is making every attempt to ascertain the connection between the hospitals in Japan who experimented on POWs, with the ISHII unit in HARBIN, and the KWANTUNG Army Stables in SHINKIO. To date, this agent has received communication from various sources which reflect that nine (9) hospitals in and around Tokyo were conducting experiments on POWs. It has also been brought to the attention of this agent that one organization in Northern Japan, operated by a doctor named ARIYAMA of Niigata Medical College was conducting experiments in artificial blood -- Western Army Headquarters at Fukuoka were conducting experiments on prisoner patients that followed no definite pattern. SHINAGAWA Army Hospital, SAGAMIGAHARA Army Hospital, and Tokyo 2nd Military Hospital in Tokyo, are all alleged to have conducted experiments on POW patients. It has been definitely extablished that the Infectious Disease Research Laboratory (DENSENBYO KENKYUSHO) and the Army Medical College, both located in Tokyo, were working in conjunction with the ISHII Unit, inasmuch as they were mobilized by ISHII for the purpose. The aforementioned institutions are being investigated as the following Investigation Division cases:

SAGAMIGAHARA Army Hospital	Inv. Div. #290
SHINAGAWA Army Hospital	Inv. Div. #1873
TOKYO 2nd Military Hospital	Inv. Div. #385
Infectious Disease Research Lab.	Inv. Div. #1117
Army Medical College	Inv. Div. #330 (connected with ISHII)
HUNCHUN Hospital	Inv. Div. #1387
Western Army Headquarters	Inv. Div. #420
Noburo ARIYAMA (Niigata Medical College)	Inv. Div. #997
KYUSHU Imperial University	Inv. Div. #604

It is evident that each of these hospitals and/or experimental laboratories was doing some sort of research work on prisoner patients, with orders for such experiments

CONFIDENTIAL

CONFIDENTIAL

and research work coming from some higher headquarters, but to date the source of these orders has not been ascertained.

This report covers the investigation to date and it can be noted from the foregoing review of the case, that Legal Section is interested only in those persons guilty of performing illegal experiments and atrocities against allied personnel, working towards the inevitable goal of classifying said persons as war criminals, and trying them as such. It is also evident, from testimonies of witnesses and alleged perpetrator CCD Intercepts and letters directed to the Supreme Commander, that the disease in which the research was conducted, PESTILENCE, GLANDERS and ANTHRAX, were conducted at both stations mentioned, KWANTUNG Water Purification and Supply Unit and KWANTUNG Army Quarantine Stables, and the trend of the research reflects that this was a part of a large scale plan for the initiation of strategic Bacterial Warfare. Inasmuch as this investigation concerns those persons who were experimenting in Bacterial Warfare, G-2, GHQ, SCAP, has directed that this file be re-classified as 'CONFIDENTIAL'.

UNDEVELOPED LEADS:

Tokyo Office -- At Tokyo -- Will report on the demand placed on the Japanese Government for the military and biographical history of former generals, Masaji KITANO and Hiroshi KIKUCHI.

At Tokyo -- Will locate and interview MITOMO (fnu) who was alleged to have participated in the experiments involving humans at the KWANTUNG Army Stables.

Osaka Office -- At Kyoto -- With the aid of the Kyoto Police, will continue the search for Hiroshi UEKI, alleged to be residing at Kyoto-Shi, Yoshida-Cho, and upon locating said UEKI, will take appropriate steps to assure his arrival at the Tokyo Office for interrogation in connection with the Harbin Experimental Station.

Nagoya Office -- At Uozu-Mura, Toyama-Ken -- Will locate and interview Junichi KANEKO, Toyama-Ken, Uozu-Mura, Takata-Machi, and obtain from him a complete and exhaustive statement concerning the atrocities committed at the Harbin Experimental Station, names of individuals committing same and names of individuals who witnessed same.

Niigata Office -- At Nagano-Ken -- Will locate Motoji YAMAGUCHI, former Major General in charge of the KWANTUNG Army Stables, and upon location of subject, will take appropriate action to assure his arrival at the Tokyo Office for interrogation in connection with said army stables.

Yamaguchi Office -- At Hagi-Shi -- Will locate and interview Shiro YAMASHITA, presently reported residing at 173, Tsuchirara, Hagi-Shi, Yamaguchi-Ken, and obtain from him a complete and exhaustive statement concerning his knowledge of the atrocities committed at the KWANTUNG Army Stables, to include names of persons responsible, names of witnesses and location of said atrocities.

At Hagi-Shi -- Will locate former Major General Yujiro WAKAMATSU, presently reported residing at Yamaguchi-Ken, Hagi-Shi, Uyehara-Machi, c/o FUJITA, and after locating subject, will take necessary action to assure his arrival at the Tokyo Office for interrogation in connection with the KWANTUNG Army Stables.

PENDING

CONFIDENTIAL

9.31 18 Apr. 1947: Inv. Div. No. 330, Report of Investigation Division, Legal Section, GHQ, SCAP, by: Neal R. Smith, 1st Lt., Inf.

资料出处： National Archives of the United States, R331, B1434.

内容点评： 本资料为 1947 年 4 月 18 日盟军总司令部法务局调查科 Neal R. Smith 中尉提交的编号 330 调查报告：今后细菌战调查将在 ATIS 中央讯问中心监管下，于东京办事处进行。由美军总参谋部直接命令（SWNCC 351/1），G–2 监管。必须保持高度机密以维护美国国家利益，避免困境。

SECRET

Date: 18 April 1947

Report of Investigation Division, Legal Section, GHQ, SCAP.

Inv. Div. No. 330	CRD No.	Report by: Neal R. Smith, 1st Lt., Inf.

Title: Motoji YAMAGUCHI

Synopsis of facts:
Future interrogations to be conducted at Tokyo Office under control of ATIS Central Interrogation Center. Case classified as secret.

\- P -

Reference: Report of Lt. N. R. Smith dated 4 April 1947.

DETAILS:

At Tokyo:

On 18 April 1947, Legal Section received the following Check Sheet from G-2 dated 17 April 1947, Subject: Legal Section, Investigation Division, Report 330.

1. Reference is made to Report of Investigative Division No. 330, LS, GHQ, SCAP, 4 Apr 47, subject: "MOTOJI YAMAGUCHI". This report contains information of Secret classification.

2. Your attention is invited to:

a. War Department Radio WX 95147, 24 July 1946, subject: "...U S Policy for International Co-ordination in Exploitation of Intelligence Targets...", with particular reference to par. 3 E and 5. (Copy of radio dispatched to LS by CN dated 12 March 1947).

b. SWNCC 351/1, 5 March 1947. (Copy delivered to Major King, 17 April 1947).

3. This investigation is one under direct Joint Chiefs of Staff order (SWNCC 351/1), and is under control of G-2. Every step, interrogation, or contact must be co-ordinated with this section. The utmost secrecy is essential in order to protect the interests of the United States and to guard against embarrassment.

4. It is requested that:

Distribution:	Do not write in this space.
1 CRD 1 Prosecution Div. 1 Niigata 1 Osaka 1 Fukuoka 1 Nagoya 1 Sendai 1 Sappore 1 Yamaguchi 1 G-2 (Attention: Col. McQuail) 1 Col. Carpenter 3 Inv. Div. (File 330)	

SECRET

SECRET

a. No action be taken on prosecution or any form of publicity of this case without G-2 concurrence. This is by direct orders of the C-in-C and CS.

b. Above report and allied papers be classified SECRET, and that all United States personnel concerned with case be so notified.

c. Additional information obtained be distributed to G-2.

d. Particular efforts be made to obtain documents or photographs.

e. Further interrogations to be conducted under control of ATIS Central Interrogation Center.

* * * * *

With reference to Paragraph 4-e of the above Check Sheet, all future interrogations will be conducted at the Tokyo Office under control of ATIS Central Interrogation Center and previous Undeveloped Leads set out for the field offices are cancelled.

UNDEVELOPED LEADS:

Tokyo Office -- At Tokyo -- Will report on the demand placed on the Japanese Government for the military and biographical histories of former Generals Masaji KITANO and Hiroshi KIKUCHI.

At Tokyo -- Will locate and interview Mitomo (fnu) who is alleged to have participated in the experiments involving humans at the KWANTUNG Army Stables.

Osaka Office -- At Kyoto -- With the aid of the Kyoto police, will continue the search for Hiroshi UEKI alleged to be residing at Kyoto Shi, Yoshida Cho, and upon locating said UEKI, will take appropriate steps to assure his arrival at the Tokyo Office for interrogation in connection with the Harbin Experimental Station.

Nagoya Office -- At Uozu Mura, Toyama Ken -- Will locate Junichi KANEKO, Toyama Ken, Uozu Mura, Takata Machi and take appropriate steps to assure his arrival at the Tokyo Office for purpose of interrogation.

Yamaguchi Office -- At Hagi Shi -- Will locate Shiro YAMASHITA presently reported residing at 173 Tsuchirara, Hagi-Shi, Yamaguchi Ken, and take appropriate steps to assure his arrival in Tokyo for interrogation.

At Hagi Shi -- Will locate former Maj. General Yujiro WAKAMATSU presently reported residing at Yamaguchi Ken, Hagi Shi, Yuehara Machi, c/o FUJITA, and after locating Subject, will take necessary action to assure his arrival in Tokyo for interrogation in connection with KWANTUNG Army Stables.

PENDING

SECRET

9.32 3 Jun. 1947: INCOMING MESSAGE NR: WAR 99277, FROM: WAR (WDSCA WO), TO: CINCFE (FOR CARPENTER LEGAL SECT FOR ACTION)

资料出处: National Archives of the United States, R331, B1434.

内容点评: 本资料为 1947 年 6 月 3 日美国陆军部发送盟军总司令部法务局长官 Carpenter 电文：石井愿意详告细菌战项目，如果给予书面文件保证其本人、上司、下属免于追究战争犯罪责任；要求提交有关可能构成任何对于石井等人战争犯罪证据和指控的详细情报。

FAR EAST COMMAND
GENERAL HEADQUARTERS, ~~U. S. ARMY FORCES, PACIFIC~~
ADJUTANT GENERAL'S OFFICE
RADIO AND CABLE CENTER

INCOMING MESSAGE

~~Top Secret~~
PRIORITY 3 June 47

DECLASSIFIED PER JCS LTR OF 20 AUG. 75

FROM : WAR (WDSCA WO)

TO : CINCFE (FOR CARPENTER LEGAL SECT FOR ACTION)

NR : WAR 99277

Fol is extract of rad from CINCFE dtd 6 May 47, nr C-52423 "Experiments of humans were known to and described by 3 Japanese and confirmed tacitly by Ishii; Field trials against Chinese Army took place on at least 3 occasions; scope of program indicated by report of reliable informant Matsuda that 400 kilograms of dried anthrax organisms destroyed at Pingfan in Aug 45; and research on use of BW against plant life was carried out. Reluctant statements by Ishii indicate he had superiors (possibly Gen Staff) who knew and auth the program. Ishii states that if guaranteed immunity from 'War Crimes' in documentary form for himself, superiors and subordinates, he can describe program in detail. Ishii claims to have extensive theoretical high-level knowledge including strategic and tactical use of BW on defense and offense, backed by some research on best BW agents to employ by geographical areas of Far East, and use of BW in cold climates." It is imperative that you furn this office by cable soonest detailed info on all possible War Crimes evidence or charges against Ishii or any member of groups referred to in above extract for consideration in conference here concerning this matter. Specifically what evidence of War Crimes is now in possession of US auth against Ishii or any member of groups for whom he has requested guarantee of immunity. Which of our allies have

10905 ~~Top Secret~~ PRIORITY

"Paraphrase not required. Handle as ~~TOP SECRET~~ correspondence per par 51 i and 60 a (4) AR 380-5."

-1-

Handling and transmission of literal plain text of this message as correspondence of the same classification has been authorized by the War Department in accordance with the provisions of paragraphs 16-C, 18-E, 53-A, 53-D (1) (2) (3), and 60-A (1) (2) (3) (4), AR 380-5, 6 March 1946.

COPY NO. 14

"WC" 150 INDEXED BY MacARTHUR ARCHIVES

WAR 80671 refs
C-53169 replies

9.33 6 Jun. 1947: C-53169, FROM: CINCEF (CARPENTER, LEGAL SECTION, SCAP), TO: WAR (WDSCA WO)

资料出处：National Archives of the United States, R331, B1434.

内容点评：本资料为 1947 年 6 月 6 日法务局长官 Alva C. Carpenter 回复陆军部电文：石井等均未包括在等候远东国际军事法庭审判的主要日本战争犯罪者中。国际检察局美国检察官 Frank S. Tavernner，Jr. 告知：苏联在押的石井下属少将川岛清、少佐柄泽十三夫、中将秦彦三郎的供述，以及中国原卫生总署总长金宝善的证词已在国际检察局备案，涉及细菌实验、攻击等。

SECRET

CONFIDENTIAL

6 JUNE 1947

U70431

CINCFE (CARPENTER, LEGAL SECTION, SCAP)

WAR (WDSCA WC) . . . . PRIORITY

PAREN C-53169 PAREN REURAD WAR NINE NINE TWO SEVEN SEVEN CMA THREE JUNE ONE NINE FOUR SEVEN CLN PARA ONE THE REPORTS AND FILES OF THE LEGAL SECTION ON ISHII AND HIS COWORKERS ARE BASED ON ANONYMOUS LETTERS CMA HEARSAY AFFIDAVITS AND RUMORS PD THE LEGAL SECTION INTERROGATIONS CMA TO DATE CMA OF THE NUMEROUS PERSONS CONCERNED WITH THE BAKER WILLIAM PROJECT IN CHINA CMA DO NOT REVEAL SUFFICIENT EVIDENCE TO SUPPORT WAR CRIME CHARGES PD THE ALLEGED VICTIMS ARE OF UNKNOWN IDENTITY PD UNCONFIRMED ALLEGATIONS ARE TO THE EFFECT THAT CRIMINALS CMA FARMERS CMA WOMEN AND CHILDREN WERE USED FOR BAKER WILLIAM EXPERIMENTAL PURPOSES PD THE JAPANESE COMMUNIST PARTY ALLEGES THAT QUOTE ISHII BAKER KING ABLE QUOTE PAREN BACTERIAL WAR ARMY PAREN CONDUCTED EXPERIMENTS ON CAPTURED AMERICANS IN MUKDEN AND THAT SIMULTANEOUSLY CMA RESEARCH ON SIMILAR LINES WAS CONDUCTED IN TOKYO AND KYOTO PD PARA TWO NONE OF ISHIIS SUBORDINATES ARE CHARGED OR HELD AS WAR CRIME SUSPECTS CMA NOR IS THERE SUFFICIENT EVIDENCE ON FILE AGAINST THEM PD ISHIIS POSSIBLE SUPERIORS CMA WHO ARE NOW ON TRIAL BEFORE ITEM MIKE TARE FOX EASY CMA INCLUDE UNCLE MIKE EASY ZEBRA UNCLE CMA COMMANDER CMA KWANTUNG ARMY CMA ONE NINE THREE NINE DASH FOUR FOUR CMA MIKE ITEM NAN ABLE MIKE

CONFIDENTIAL PRIORITY COPY NO 7.

CONFIDENTIAL

6 JUNE 1947 LS

PAGE 2

CINCFE

WAR (WDSCA WC) . . . . PRIORITY

ITEM CMA COMMANDER CMA KWANTUNG ARMY ONE NINE THREE FOUR DASH THREE SIX CMA KOISO CMA CHIEF OF STAFF CMA KWANTUNG ARMY ONE NINE THREE TWO DASH THREE FOUR CMA TOJO CMA CHIEF OF STAFF CMA KWANTUNG ARMY ONE NINE THREE SEVEN DASH THREE EIGHT PD PARA THREE NONE OF OUR ALLIES TO DATE HAVE FILED WAR CRIMES CHARGES AGAINST ISHII OR ANY OF HIS ASSOCIATES PD PARA FOUR NEITHER ISHII NOR HIS ASSOCIATES ARE INCLUDED AMONG MAJOR JAPANESE WAR CRIMINALS AWAITING TRIAL PD PARA FIVE THIS MATTER COORDINATED WITH TAVENNER OF ITEM PETER SUGAR CMA WHO REPORTS AS FOLLOWS CLN ABLE PD MAJOR GENERAL KAWASHIMA CMA KIYOSHI CMA AND MAJOR KARAZAWA CMA TOMIO SUBORDINATES OF ISHII CMA ARE HELD BY THE SOVIETS CMA PRESUMABLY AS WAR CRIMINAL SUSPECTS PD NO SUBORDINATES ARE CHARGED OR HELD BY UNCLE SUGAR AS WAR CRIME SUSPECTS PD AFFIDAVITS OF ABOVE DASH MENTIONED SUBORDINATES AND OF LIEUTENANT GENERAL HATA CMA HIKOSABURO CMA CHIEF OF STAFF CMA KWANTUNG ARMY CMA AND DOCTOR PETER ZEBRA KING CMA ARE ON FILE IN ITEM PETER SUGAR PD BAKER PD KAWASHIMA AFFIDAVIT ALLEGES DETACHMENT HAD SECRET DUTY OF RESEARCH OF VIRUS FOR THE PURPOSE OF USING THEM IN WAR AND EXPERIMENTS WERE CONDUCTED PD ISHII CALLED ATTENTION OF HIS STAFF TO INSTRUCTIONS FROM GENERAL STAFF IN TOKYO TO IMPROVE VIRUS WAR

IDENTIAL

PRIORITY

CONFIDENTIAL

6 JUNE 1947

PAGE 3

CINCFE

WAR (WDSCA WC) . . . . .PRIORITY

RESEARCHES PD CHARLIE PD KARAZAWA AFFIDAVIT STATES THAT ISHII DETACHMENT EXPERIMENTED AS TO MOST EFFECTIVE VIRUS CMA GERM CULTIVATION CMA THE WAY OF INFECTION CMA DISPERSING GERMS AS MEANS OF ATTACK CMA LARGE DASH SCALE PRODUCTION OF VIRUS CMA PRESERVATION OF VIRUS CMA AND DISCOVERY OF PREVENTIVE MATERIALS PD DOG PD HATA AFFIDAVIT STATES THAT ISHII WAS VERY ANXIOUSLY CONTROLLING DETACHMENT UNDER THE INSTRUCTION OF GENERAL STAFF IN ORDER TO FIND OUT NEW VIRUS AND PREVENTIVE MATERIALS CMA BUT IT DOES NOT STATE THAT THE GENERAL STAFF INTENDED TO RESORT TO BACTERIA WARFARE PD EASY PD THE AFFIDAVIT OF DOCTOR PETER ZEBRA KING REFLECTS THAT JAPANESE PLANES SCATTERED WHEAT GRAINS AT NINGPO OCTOBER TWO NINE CMA ONE NINE FOUR NAUGHT CMA AT CHUHSIN OCTOBER FOUR CMA ONE NINE FOUR NAUGHT CMA AT KINGHWA ON NOVEMBER TWO EIGHT CMA ONE NINE FOUR NAUGHT CMA AND CHANGTEH ON NOVEMBER FOUR CMA ONE NINE FOUR NAUGHT CMA AND SHORTLY AFTER EACH OCCURREN BUBONIC PLAGUE APPEARED PD FOX PD SINCE CERTAIN OF ISHII SUPERIOR ARE NOW ON TRIAL FOR MAJOR WAR CRIMES BEFORE ITEM MIKE TARE FOX EASY CMA USE OF THIS MATERIAL WAS CONSIDERED BY ITEM PETER SUGAR AND DECISION WAS REACHED BY ITEM PETER SUGAR IN DECEMBER ONE NIN FOUR SIX ON THE BASIS OF INFORMATION THEN AVAILABLE THAT THESE

CONFIDENTIAL

[illegible] PRIORITY

CONFIDENTIAL

6 JUNE 1947

PAGE 4

CINCFE

WAR (WDSCA WC) . . . . PRIORITY

WITNESSES SHOULD NOT BE PRODUCED CMA AS EVIDENCE WAS NOT SUFFICIENT TO CONNECT ANY OF THESE ACCUSED WITH ISHIIS DETACHMENT SECRET ACTIVITIES CMA THE TRIBUNAL HAVING ANNOUNCED PRIOR THERETO THAT EVIDENCE RELATING TO ATROCITIES AND PRISONERS OF WAR WOULD NOT BE RECEIVED IN THE ABSENCE OF AN ASSURANCE BY THE PROSECUTION THAT THE ACCUSED OR SOME OF THEM COULD BE ASSOCIATED WITH THE ACTS CHARGED PD THE SOVIET PROSECUTOR PROBABLY WILL ENDEAVOR IN CROSS DASH EXAMINATION OF ONE OR MORE ACCUSED TO LAY FOUNDATION FOR THE USE IN REBUTTAL OF THE ABOVE DASH MENTIONED EVIDENCE AND OTHER EVIDENCE WHICH MAY HAVE RESULTED FROM THEIR INDEPENDENT INVESTIGATION.

OFFICIAL:

R. M. LEVY
COLONEL, AGD
ADJUTANT GENERAL

APPROVED BY:

ALVA C. CARPENTER
CHIEF
LEGAL SECTION

9.33 附　录 1　D9307 INTERROGATION REPORT, Chief of the Medical Dept., Kwantung Army, Lt. General KAJITSUKA, Ryuji（梶塚隆二）, Army Medical Department

资料出处：The University of Virginia Law Library, the Personal Papers of Frank S. Tavenner, Jr. and Official Records from the IMTFE, 1945-1948, Box 2, US.

内容点评：本资料为国际检察局文件编号 9307，关东军军医部部长梶塚隆二讯问记录。

DOC. 9307

INTERROGATION REPORT

Prisoner of War Chief of the Medical Dept., Kwantung Army
Lt. General KAJITSUKA, Ryuji,
Army Medical Department

The person being interrogated was warned beforehand that when making a statement as a prisoner of war, he will bear the responsibilities according to the U.S.S.R. Criminal Law No. 95.

Q. What is your medical speciality?

A. Bacteriology.

Q. What was your duty in the Kwantung Army and from when did you serve?

A. From December, 1939, I was assigned as Chief of the Medical Department of the Kwantung Army, Major General, Medical Department. I was promoted to Lieutenant General in 1942. From September, 1942, until March, 1945, I served concurrently as Chief of the Medical Supply Department of the Kwantung Army. I was relieved from this last position in March, 1945, being replaced by Colonel OGAWA. I served as Chief of the Medical Department of the Kwantung Army until September 5, 1945, when I became a prisoner of the Red Army.

Q. What was the scope of your duties as Chief of the Medical Department, Kwantung Army, and as Chief of the Medical Supply Department of the same Army?

A. As Chief of the Medical Department, Kwantung Army, my duties were as follows:

1. Military sanitation (Food, clothing, quarters).
2. Medical examinations in units and hospitals.
3. Health education.
4. Transportation of patients.
5. Supply of sanitation materials.
6. Sanitation within the Headquarters of the Kwantung Army.

My duties as Chief of the Medical Supply Department, Kwantung Army, were actually the same as those as Chief of Medical Department. My authority extended not only to the Kwantung Army Headquarters, and to the 1st and 2d Area Armies, but also to other independent units and special service units directly under the control of the Commanding Officer of the Kwantung Army.

Q. Were all the sanitation facilities, organs, laboratories and units of the Kwantung Army in Manchuria under your leadership.

A. During my tour of duty, especially during the time I was serving two positions concurrently, sanitation facilities and organs, medical examinations and research of disease prevention were under my leadership, but units and organs which were conducting research for the preparation of bacterial warfare were not.

Q. What was the unit not under your command, which was conducting preparations for bacterial warfare?

A. As far as I know, the Kwantung Army Water Purification and Supply Unit was the only unit concerned with the problem of bacterial warfare preparations. This unit was stationed at PINGFANG about 20 km. southeast of HARBIN. The unit was established in 1935-1936 and was under the command of Medical Colonel ISHII, Shiro. In August, 1942, he was replaced as the unit commander by Major General KITANO, Seiji (later Lieutenant General) of the Medical Department. But in February, 1945, before the war against Soviet Russia, Major General ISHII again became the unit commander.

Q. Was the reason this unit was not under your command because this unit was conducting research on the method and preparation of bacterial warfare? Were there other reasons?

A. Yes. The research and preparation of bacillus weapons were outside the scope of my duties. That is why I was not in command of this unit.

Q. What do you know about the work done by this unit?

A. I know that this unit did the following:

1. Research of unknown contagious disease germs in Manchuria.
2. Prevention of contagious disease in units.
3. Manufacture of preventive vaccines and serum for the purpose of preventing contagious diseases.
4. Direction and education of water supply and purification.
5. Research and manufacture of sanitary water filters.
6. Epidemic prevention education of officers and non-commissioned officers of the Sanitation Department within the Kwantung Army.

7. Research on examinations and treatments of contagious diseases.

Among these problems I had connection with treatment and prevention of diseases. This unit was conducting research in the field of bacterial warfare, but I had no connection in that field. I only know that this unit conducted research on the following:

1. Chances of survival of bacilli dropped from air.
2. Bacillus-bombs, their effects and the altitude of releasing them.
3. Contagion through water and its counter-measure.
4. Contagion through food and its counter-measure.
5. Individual constitutions in relation to bacilli-infections.

Q. What are the positive results obtained by the unit in its preparation and research of bacterial methods?

A. Although I don't know the details, I can say the following: When bacilli are dropped from a high altitude, they die. The effective altitude limit is 500 M. Furthermore, it is difficult to hit the target from a high altitude. When bacilli are used as weapons, they are dangerous also to friendly troops. When bacillus bombs explode, most of the bacilli die and lose their effectiveness. However, some types of bacilli such as those of anthrax alone keep their vitality. I must add that it is necessary to drop bombs from a low altitude for accurate hits. Quite a bit of research was made on the 3d and 4th items above, especially with regard to the counter-measures. It was decided that these methods are most effective when carried out by saboteurs. Detailed research was made on the problem of individual constitutions, but complete results could not be obtained. This was due to the fact that KAWAKAMI, a pathologist who was directing this research, died of illness in 1944 while in the midst of the research.

Q. What methods were used in carrying out research on the last item?

A. I do not know the details of the research but I heard from Unit Commander KITANO that many soldiers, both healthy and those who were contagious disease patients were used for the research.

Q. Were only Japanese soldiers use, or were other people used?

A. I did not hear that they used other people besides Japanese soldiers.

Q. As the leader of the unit, under whose substantial control was Major General ISHII?

A. He was directly under the control of the Commanding Officer of the Kwantung Army.

Q. In that case, did Major General ISHII receive all orders directly from the Commanding Officer or did he receive them from persons within the Headquarters?

A. Orders pertaining to bacterial warfare preparations were issued by Section I of the Kwantung Army, Headquarters Staff Section in the name of the Commanding Officer.

Q. Did, in addition to the Commander, Section I of the Kwantung Army Staff Section know about the results of the work done by the ISHII Unit?

A. Naturally, the results of the research should have been known not only to the Commanding Officer, but also to the Chief of Section I of the Staff Section and his subordinate staff in charge of this work. However, I do not think they knew about the details of the research.

Q. During your tour of duty with the Kwantung Army Headquarters, who was the Commanding Officer of the Kwantung Army, and who was the Chief of Section I?

A. General UMEZU was the Commander from October, 1939, until June, 1944, after which it was General YAMADA unit the surrender. Colonel ARISUE was the Chief of the First Section until the autumn of 1940, after which Colonel TAMURA was the Chief until August (?), 1942. After that it was Colonel (now a Major General) MATSUMURA.

Q. Among the men you have named, who visited the ISHII Unit?

A. I believe the above mentioned men have visited the ISHII Unit at least once, but I cannot say so with accuracy.

Q. Then, were the actions of the ISHII Unit known not only through documents but also through visits?

A. Yes.

Q. To what degree was the ISHII Unit and the Unit Commander under the control of the Chief of Staff, Kwantung Army?

A. Since the Chief of Staff, Kwantung Army is between the Commander and Chief of First Section, he should know generally the duties assigned to the unit.

Q. Who were the men among the former Chiefs of Staff, Kwantung Army, who visited the ISHII Unit?

A. I believe all the Chiefs of Staff have visited the unit at least once for the purpose of recognizing the unit. However, the present Chief of Staff HATA alone must not have visited the unit yet, as he had no time to spare after taking the post.

Q. Have you ever visited the ISHII Unit? If so, state the number of times and the dates.

A. I visited this unit three times. The first time was April-May, 1940; the second time was April-May, 1941; and the third time was September-October, 1943.

Q. What was your objects in visiting this unit?

A. The first time was for the first inspection tour of the unit as Chief of the Medical Department, Kwantung Army. The second visit was made because at that time many cases of tuberculosis broke out in units within the Kwantung Army and desiring preventive measures against this disease, and since this unit was assigned to give mass education to the medical officers of the Army on tuberculosis prevention, I went to see the actual situation. The third visit was made while I was making an inspection tour of units besides those in HARBIN, and I went to see the research being made on the SUNWU Fever (an infectuous hemorrhage fever) which was discovered at the time.

Q. Who went with you when you visited the ISHII Unit?

A. I was accompanied the first and second time by a member of the Army Medical Department, Lieutenant Colonel (Colonel, on the second trip) KONNO, Hisao. I was accompanied on the third trip by a section member Colonel MAKI, Yuzuru a Medical Officer.

Q. At the beginning of the interrogation, you stated that you did not control the ISHII Unit and that you did not have any connections with it. How do you explain the fact whereby you now say that you visited the unit since you had a certain degree of interest in the work being done by the unit?

A. There were many competent researchers in the ISHII Unit, and I was not able to direct them with my knowledge. However, if you consider my requesting the prevention of contagious disease such as requesting counter-measure be taken against outbreaks of tuberculosis, or requesting research be made on other contagious diseases and their causes, or my requesting research be made on preventive measures, or if you consider my requesting the manufacture of preventive vaccines as directions (T.N. commands), then I will not deny it.

Q. Was the existence of this unit concealed as a military medical research organ? And what designation did the unit use?

A. In documents, this unit used an anonymous designation, Manchuria 731st Unit. But the designation was Water Supply and Purification Unit, Kwantung Army.

Q. If this unit was in charge of Water Supply and Purification only, does it not come under your command?

A. Naturally, yes.

Q. Then, did this unit carry out research on methods and preparations for bacterial warfare under the designation as Water Supply and Purification Unit of the Kwantung Army?

A. This unit chiefly carried out work concerned with prevention of contagious diseases, and in part carried out research on chemical warfare preparations. However, the latter did not come under my jurisdiction.

Q. When visiting the ISHII Unit, were you interested in the objects of study in the laboratory as well as the study regarding the patients?

A. When I visited the ISHII Unit I was introduced to the Bacteriological Laboratory as well as the room where vaccine and serum were being manufactured. I also saw the isolated wards for infectious cases. I remember, however, of only one Japanese civilian employee being there at the time. There was also an isolation hospital in this unit. It was in HARBIN city1 There were about 30 sick Japanese soldiers there at the time.

Q. How many sick wards were there in the ISHII Unit's laboratory? Further, how many sick beds were there in the sick wards?

A. According to my memory there were about 10 sick beds. The hospital in the city had about 50 sick beds. I believe there were about 10 large and small sized sick wards here.

Q. We are interested in the results of artificial germiculture, especially in regard to mass production. How about this?

A. It is difficult to reply in detail as to what results the ISHII Unit obtained in regard to the artificial culture of bacteria. I know that a study was being made regarding mass production, but I cannot say anything about the results thereof. Furthermore, research work was conducted regarding insects such as fleas, flies and ticks.

Q. What measures were the ISHII Unit expected to adopt at the time of the KAN-TOKU-EN /T.N. Special Maneuvers of the Kwantung Army/?

A. At the time of the KAN-TOKU-EN the ISHII Unit was to have assumed a leading role in regard to the Army's water supply and purification as well as epidemic prevention.

Q. What actual duties were to be performed by the ISHII Unit?

A. The ISHII Unit had various duties, such as research regarding the causes of infectious diseases, manufacture of various vaccines, repairing of sanitary water filters, education regarding epidemic prevention, etc.

Q. What actually took place in the ISHII Unit at the KAN-TOKU-EN in 1941 when the Kwantung Army adopted emergency and important measures?

A. Two or three water supply and purification corps to be attached to the Army were organized by the personnel of the ISHII Unit. Similar corps to be attached to the Division were dispatched after being organized in Japan proper. The number of personnel of these corps was from 200 to 300.

Q. What other measures were taken by the ISHII Unit at the time of the KAN-TOKU-EN?

A. The unit's duties did not, as a whole, differ considerably from those of the days prior to the KAN-TOKU-EN.

Q. Where were you introduced to Major General KAWASHIMA for the first time?

A. I got to know him from his captain days.

Q. When did you get to know Major General KAWASHIMA as a member of the ISHII Unit?

-7-

A. In 1940 (41).

Q. In what duties was he engaged then?

A. I believe that he was then in charge of Administration, Investigation and Personnel, etc.

Ryuji KAJIWARA
Army 1st Lieut. (med.)

Examiner: Capt. NIKICHIN /phonetic/

Interpreter: Priachenko /phonetic/
Ogorodenif /phonetic/

Stenographer: Chimafeewa /phonetic/

(This translation is correct but it has not been approved for reproduction without further checking.)

9.33 附　录 2　D9308 STATEMENT OF Former Chief of Staff of the Kwantung Army, Lt. General HATA, Hikosaburo（秦彦三郎）, Oct. 10, 1946

资料出处： The University of Virginia Law Library, the Personal Papers of Frank S. Tavenner, Jr. and Official Records from the IMTFE, 1945-1948, Box 2, US.

内容点评： 本资料为 1946 年 10 月 10 日国际检察局文件编号 9308，关东军总参谋长秦彦三郎证词。

DOC. 9308

STATEMENT

of

Former Chief of Staff of the Kwantung Army, Lieutenant General HATA, Hikosaburo.

Q. In what year and in what position did you serve with the Japanese Army General Staff Headquarters?

A. I served as Sub-Chief of the Army General Staff from April, 1943, to April, 1945. From 1920 to 1922 I served in the Second Section (Intelligence) of the Army General Staff as first lieutenant, and in 1926 in the European Division of the same Second Section of the General Staff, and from spring, 1929, to 1930, and again in 1933 in the same European Division of the Second Section.

Q. What sort of duties did you carry out as Sub-Chief of the Japanese Army General Staff?

A. For two years I assisted throughout the Chief of the General Staff concerning the draft and practise of the operations of the Pacific War. I had no subordinate section of my own. Sometimes I received special duties from the Chief of the General Staff, concerning the preparation of operations for the Pacific Theatre against U.S.A., Britain and the Netherlands, and carried them out.

Q. Explain in detail what matters you carried out concerning the operations against the Allied Forces.

A. At that time I participated in evacuating Japanese forcex which were forced to retreat due to the pressure of British and American forces on the Commanders Islands. I also took part with the Japanese forces defending the line of Burma, Sumatra, Java, Borneo, Thailand and French Indo-China. Then we were forced to give up the Commanders Islands. As a result, there were at that time, differences of opinions between Army and Naval leaders, but later in September, 1943, according to the Army's opinion, it was decided to retreat to the second line, or the line of the Kuriles, Iwo, Saipan, Guam, New Guinea, Western Java, Sumatra, Borneo and Burma. Early in February, 1944, the American forces effected a landing on part of the Marshall Islands and, as its result, our Navy's main force retreated from Truk to the Northwestern

Pacific. In May, Americans landed at Hollandia in New Guinea and in June they occupied Saipan and later Guam. In September 1944, they landed at the Morotai Island and, in October, Leyte. They landed at Manila in 1945, Iwo Jima in February, Okinawa in April of the same year, and until that time I served in the General Staff Office. For two years our greatest hardship was the insufficiency of the air forces and the ocean transportation, especially so since our Navy was heavily damaged at the battle lost on and near Leyte Island. Later as the traffic between Japan and oil producing Sumatra was cut off, Japan was destined to expect the reversal after the battle of Leyte Island was lost.

Q. Who was holding control over the weapons of the Japanese Army? What bearing did you have in this matter?

A. The weapons were under the control by the War Ministry. We received the necessary arms from them and distributed to the armies. I was looking after the distribution of arms to the armies.

Q. You, therefore, know thoroughly about all sorts of arms. Don't you?

A. The matters regarding various weapons were governed by the Military Ordnance Headquarters. Of course, I know the sorts of them used by the Army.

Q. What were the secret weapons the Japanese Army used or prepared to use in the field?

A. The first of the secret weapons of the Japanese Army was plane of special type which carried a baby plane manned by the death-defying flyer, on its fuselage (a mother and baby plane). When the mother plane gets near to its target, it was to let the baby plane off and the baby was to hit the target as a human bomb. The Navy prepared certain special service submarine boats. The boats were driven by death-faring sailor and were to hit the submerged part of the target as a human torpedo. We also prepared gas shrapnels as a special material for war but we never used them. We prepared them for revenge in case of the Allied forces should initiate gas fighting.

Q. In expectation of losing the war what the General Staff Headquarters of Japan planned to offer to the enemy as a final blow?

A. The General Staff Headquarters was firmly determined to fight to the last man.

Q. Tell me about the top secret weapons especially as to the materials on bacterial strategy prepared by the General Staff Headquarters of Japan in case they were awared that the defeat was unavoidable.

A. We had nothing doing with the problem of applying bacterial materials on war as long as I was on duties with the General Headquarters. We were of the opinion that if we were to fight inland for defence the application of bacteria by ourselves was inconceivable from the view points of the dense population of our own and also of the injuries that the public would have to suffer in case of it was taken up by the enemies in revenge. It was, therefore, was considered that the bacterial strategy was only feasible in such occupied area where it was far remoted from the interior and under certain special situation, by sending a detachment of a strategic corps deep to the rear of the enemy and making it to scatter the germs of contagious disease.

Q. What preparatory works did the Japanese Army General Staff practise in order to apply bacterial materials to warfare?

A. I don't know anything in detail of when the Japanese Army began to study bacterial materials. The matters concerning the study and experiment in the application of bacterial materials to warfare were in the charge of the 1st Division of the Army General Staff, and recently, the matters were directed by Lieutenant General MIYAZAKI. They were also in the direct charge of the 2d section of the 1st Division, a section which was recently led by Major General AMANO. The subject in question was at the same time carried on under the guidance of the Military Affairs Bureau of the War Ministry. In other words, the matter was directly led by Lieutenant General YOSHIZUMI, Chief of the Military Affairs Bureau, and in practise dealt with by Colonel ARAO himself, Chief of the Military Affairs Section. The Medical Bureau of the War Ministry was also related with the study of bacterial materials.

Q. What organization was directly engaged in the study of the materials for bacterial warfare?

A. There is the Army Medical School in Tokyo. The school gives a special and professional education to those who have been sent there after graduation from medical schools. It is in reality a university and not a mere school. While the Military Affairs Bureau of the War Ministry dealt with the materials, establishments and intendance, the Medical Bureau and the school above-mentioned were in charge of the study and experiment of materials for bacterial warfare. The school had its own special laboratory. Afterward various armies established a special unit of disease prevention and water supply in their respective organizations, and the measures and preparations for bacterial warfare were studied. For instance, the Kwantung Army in Manchuria, the China Expeditionary Forces and the whole army in the south were in possession of such special units.

Q. Do you know the names of the above-mentioned three chiefs of the Epidemic Prevention and Water Supply Department?

A. I do not know the names of the Department Chiefs of the Expeditionary Forces to China and the Southern Whole Army. The chief of the Epidemic Prevention and Water Supply Department of the Kwantung Army in Manchuria was Medical Lieutenant General ISHII.

Q. To whom was the aforesaid Epidemic Prevention and Water Supply Department subordinated to?

A. The Department was directly subordinated to the army commander. Lieutenant General ISHII was, accordingly, subordinated to the Commander of the Kwantung Army. He had been subordinated finally to General YAMADA, but up to July 1944 to General UMEZU, the Commander of the Kwantung Army. Concerning the problem of the preparation for bacterial warfare, Lieutenant General ISHII kept direct connection with the authorities in TOKYO.

Q. Did you know the principle in the tactical application of the materials for bacterial warfare which had been manufactured by the First Section of the Japanese General Staff Headquarters?

A. What I knew personally about this problem was that there was the possibility of applying the materials for bacterial warfare only in the following cases: To use them behind the enemy in a strategic view, or mix them in water before retreat for the purpose of spreading them to communicate diseases or cause infectious diseases among men and domestic animals by communicating the diseases to animals or insects.

Q. Did you know the concrete plan of the Japanese Army for applying the materials for bacterial warfare?

-4-

A. I did not know the concrete plan for applying the materials for bacterial warfare. I knew personally that there was an unofficial opinion that such materials could not be used except in the special cases as above mentioned.

HATA, Hikosaburō

ACKNOWLEDGEMENT

HARBIN

Oct. 10, 1946

I, P.O.W. Lieutenant General HATA, Hikosaburo hand the Military Investigator Captain Peters the acknowledgement stating that I certify only the truth as witness for the case of the leading war criminals. I have been given previous notice that if I make any false statements, I will be penalized in accordance with the U.S.S.R. Criminal Law Article 95.

HATA, Hikosaburo

This acknowledgement is received by

Military Investigator
Captain Peters

Under the guidance of the Headquarters of the General Staff and the Medical Bureau Lieutenant General ISHII very earnestly led the Special Unit of the Kwantung Army to find new germs and preventive materials against the epidemic. For this purpose there was a special laboratory and appropriate staff members. I do not know the final result of the discovery.

This interrogation was recorded in my words and was translated into Japanese for me.

HATA, Hikosaburo

Military Investigator: Colonel KUDRYAVCHEV
Captain

Translator: PRYACHENKO

Stenographer: TMAFEEVA

(This translation is correct but it has not been approved for reproduction without further checking.)

9.33 附　录 3　4 April 1946：J. C. Fang, Acting Director, National Health Administration, Witness the Attached Statement of Dr. P. Z. King dated March 31, 1942

资料出处： The University of Virginia Law Library, the Personal Papers of Frank S. Tavenner, Jr. and Official Records from the IMTFE, 1945-1948, Box 2, US.

内容点评： 本资料为 1942 年 3 月 31 日中国卫生总署总长金宝善证词，及 1946 年 4 月 4 日中国卫生总署代理总长 J.C.Fang（方颐积）证明金宝善证词为正式公文。

WEI SHENG SHU
(National Health Administration)
The Republic of China

Telegraphic Address
Weishengshu or "5898"

Nanking

The foregoing copies of Statement of Dr. P. Z. King dated March 31, 1942 with Appendices 1, 2, 3, 4 and 5 attached and Statement of "Plague in Chekiang Province" are true and correct copies of the official reports and documents on file in the National Health Administration of the Republic of China.

Witness my signature and seal this 4th day of April 1946

/s/ J. C. Fang
Acting Director, National Health Administration

JAPANESE ATTEMPT AT BACTERIAL WARFARE IN CHINA

Up to the present time the practicability of bacterial warfare is little known to the public, because applicable experimental results, if available, are usually kept as a military secret. In the past, the artificial dissemination of diseased germs had been done for military purposes. The pollution of drinking water supplies by the introduction of diseased animals or other infected materials into the wells had been practised by retreating armies with the intention of causing epidemics of gastro-intestinal infections among the opposing troops in pursuit. Fortunately, such water-borne infections can be controlled with relative ease by boiling of all drinking water and disinfection by chemical means. Whether or not other infectious diseases could be intentionally spread by artificial means with deadly results in a wide area had not been demonstrated prior to the outbreak of the present Sino-Japanese War. However, in the last two years sufficient circumstantial evidence has been gathered to show that the Japanese have tried to use our people as guinea pigs for experimentation on the practicability of bacterial warfare. They have tried to produce epidemics of plague in the Free China by scattering plague-infected materials with aeroplanes. The facts thus far collected are as follows:

1. On October 29, 1940 bubonic plague for the first time occurred in Ningpo of Chekiang Province. The epidemic lasted a period of thirty-four days and claimed a total of ninety-nine victims. It was reported that on Oct. 27, 1940 Japanese planes raided Ningpo and scattered a considerable quantity of wheat grains over the port city. Although it was a curious fact to find "grains from heaven," yet no one at the time seemed to appreciate the enemy's intention and no thorough examination of the grains was made. All the plague victims were local residents. The diagnosis of plague was definitely confirmed by laboratory test. There was no excessive mortality among rats noticed before the epidemic outbreak; and despite of careful investigation no exogenous sources of infection could be discovered.

2. On Oct. 4, 1940 a Japanese plane visited Chü-hsien of Chekiang. After circling over the city for a short while, it scattered rice and wheat grains mixed with fleas over the western section of the city. There were many eye-witnesses, among whom was a man named Hsu, who collected some grains and dead fleas from the street outside of his own house and sent them to the local Air-raid Precautionary Corps for transmission to the Provincial Hygienic Laboratory for examination. The laboratory examination result was that "There were no pathogenic organisms found by bacteriological culture methods." However, on Nov. 12, thiry-eight days after the Japanese plane's visit, bubonic plague

appeared in the same area where the grains and fleas were found in abundance. The epidemic in Chü-hsien lasted twenty-four days resulting in twenty-one deaths. As far as available records show, plague never occurred in Chü-hsien before. After careful investigation of the situation it was believed that the strange visit of the enemy plane was the cause of the epidemic and the transmitting agent was the rat fleas, presumably infected with plague and definitely dropped by the enemy plane. As plague is primarily a disease of the rodents, the grains were probably used to attract the rats and expose them to the infected fleas mixed therein. It was regrettable that the fleas collected were not properly examined. Owing to deficient laboratory facilities, an animal inoculation test was not performed; otherwise it would have been possible to show whether or not the fleas were plague-infected, and a positive result would have been an irrefutable evidence against Japan.

3. On Nov. 28, 1940 when the plague epidemic in Ningpo and Chü-hsien was still in progress, three Japanese planes came to Kinghwa, an important commercial center situated between Ningpo and Chü-hsien, and there they dropped a large quantity of small granules, about the size of shrimp-eggs. These strange objects were collected and examined in a local hospital. The granules were more or less round, about 1 mm. in diameter, of whitish-yellow tinge, somewhat translucent with a certain amount of glistening reflection from the surface. When brought into contact with a drop of water on a glass slide, the granule began to swell to about twice its original size. In a small amount of water in a test-tube, with some agitation, it would break up into whitish flakes and later form a milky suspension. Microscopic examination of these granules revealed the presence of numerous gram-negative bacilli, with distinct bipolar staining in some of them and an abundance of involution forms, thus possessing the morphological characteristics of P. pestis, the causative organism of plague. When cultured in agar medium these gram-negative bacilli showed no growth; and because of inadequacy of laboratory facilities animal inoculation test could not be performed. Upon the receipt of such startling report from Kinghwa, the National Health Administration dispatched Dr. W. W. Yung, Director of the Department of Epidemic Prevention, Dr. H. M. Jettmar, epidemiologist, formerly of the League of Nations' Epidemic Commission, and other technical experts to investigate the situation. When arriving in Kinghwa early in January, 1941, they examined twenty-six of these granules and confirmed the previous observations, but inoculation test performed on guinea-pigs by Dr. Jettmar gave negative results. It is difficult to say whether or not the lapse of time and the method of preservation of the granules had something to do with the negative results from the animal inoculation test, which is a crucial test for P. pestis. At all events

no plague occurred in Kinghwa and it indicated that this particular Japanese experiment on bacterial warfare ended in failure.

4. On Nov. 4, 1941, at about 5 A.M. a long enemy plane appeared over Changteh of Hunan Province, flying very low, the morning being rather misty. Instead of bombs, wheat and rice grains, pieces of paper, cotton wadding and some unidentified particles were dropped. There were many eye-witnesses, including Mrs. E. J. Bannon, R. N., Superintendent of the local Presbyterian Hospital and other foreign residents in Changteh. After the "all clear" signal had been sounded at 5 P.M., some of these strange gifts from the enemy were collected and sent by the police to the local Presbyterian Hospital for examination, which revealed the presence of micro-organisms reported to resemble P. pestis. On Nov. 11, seven days later, the first clinical case of plague came to notice, then followed by five more cases within the same month, two cases in December, and the last case to date on January 13, 1942. The diagnosis of bubonic plague was definitely confirmed in one of the six cases in November by bacteriological culture method and animal inoculation test. According to the investigation of Dr. W. K. Chen, bacteriologist who had had special training in plague work in India and Dr. R. Pollitzer, epidemiologist of the National Health Administration and formerly of the League of Nations' Epidemic Commission, the Changteh plague epidemic was caused by enemy action because of the following strong circumstantial evidences:

(a) That Changteh has never been, as far as is known, afflicted by plague. During previous pandemics and severe epidemics elsewhere in China, this part of Hunan, nay this part of Central China in general, has never been known to come under the scourge of the disease.

(b) That the present outbreak may have been due to direct contiguous spread from neighboring plague-infected districts is also untenable on epidemiological grounds. Epidemiologically, plague spreads along transport routes for grain on which the rats feed. The nearest epidemic center to Changteh is Chu-hsien in Chekiang, about 2,000 kilometers away by land or river communication. Furthermore, Changteh, being a rice producing district, supplies rice to other districts and does not receive rice from other cities. Besides, all the cases occurring in Changteh were native inhabitants who had not been away from the city or its immediate environs at all.

(c) That all the cases came from the areas within the city where the strange objects dropped by enemy plane were found, and that among the wheat and rice grains and cotton rags there were most probably included infective vectors, probably fleas. The fleas were not noticed on the spot because they were not looked for and because the air-raid alarm lasted some twelve hours with the result that the fleas must have in the meantime escaped to other hiding places.

(d) That there was no apparent evidence of any excessive rat mortality before and for sometime after the "aerial incident." About two hundred rats were caught and examined during the months of November, and December, but no evidence of plague was found. However, toward the end of January and the first part of February this year, among seventy-eight rats examined there were eighteen with definite plague infection. As plague is primarily a disease of the rodents, the usual sequence of events is that an epizootic precedes an epidemic; but that did not take place in the present case. The infected fleas from the enemy plane must have first attacked men and a little later the rats.

(e) That all the first six human cases were infected within fifteen days after the "aerial incident" and that infected fleas are known to be able to survive under suitable conditions for weeks without feeding. The normal incubation period of bubonic plague is 3 to 7 days and may occasionally be prolonged to 8 or even 14 days. The time factor is certainly also a strong circumstantial evidence.

5. A serious epidemic of plague occurring in Suiyuan, Ningsha and Shensi Provinces has been recently reported. From the last week of January this year to date there have been some six hundred cases. According to a recent communique from the local military in the northwestern frontier, "a large number of sick rodents had been set free by the enemy in the epidemic area." However, considering the fact that plague is known to be enzootic among the native rodents in the Ordos region in Suiyuan, one must wait for confirmation of this report. Technical experts, including Dr. Y. N. Yang, Director of the Weishengshu Northwest Epidemic Prevention Bureau, have been sent there to investigate and help to control the epidemic.

The enumeration of facts thus far collected leads to the conclusion that the Japanese Army has attempted at bacterial warfare in China. In Chekiang and Hunan they had scattered from the air infective materials and succeeded in causing epidemic outbreaks of plague. Aside from temporary terrorization of the general population in the afflicted areas, this inhuman act of our enemy is most condemnable when one realizes that once the disease has taken root in the local rat population it will continue to infect men for many years to come. Fortunately, the mode of infection and the method of control of plague are known and it is possible to keep the disease in check by vigorous control measures. Our difficulty at present is the shortage of the anti-epidemic supplies required. The recent advance in chemotherapy has given us new drugs that are more or less effective for the treatment of plague cases, and they are sulfathiazole and allied sulphonomide compounds which China cannot as yet produce herself. For prevention, plague vaccine can be produced in considerable quantities by the Central Epidemic Prevention Bureau in Kunming and the Northwest Epidemic Prevention Bureau in Lanchow, provided the raw materials required for vaccine production such as peptone and agar-agar are available. Rat-proofing of all buildings and eradication of rats are fundamental control measures, but under war conditions they cannot be satisfactorily carried out. If rat poisons such as cyanogas and barium carbonate can be obtained from abroad in large quantities, deratilization campaigns may be launched in cities where rats are a menace.

P. Z. King, Director-General,

March 31, 1942 NATIONAL HEALTH ADMINISTRATION

Appendix 1

Presbyterian Hospital
Changteh, Hunan, Dec. 18, 1941

Dr. P. Z. King, Director-General
National Health Administration
Chungking

Dear Dr. King:

Following the initial outbreak of plague there appears to have been a lull in the situation, at least I have only heard of one case being reported within the past few days. Dr. Chang Wei of the Provincial Health Bureau who himself examined this case assures me that the patient who died within a period of two days was a plague victim.

The facts in connection with this outbreak appear to prove:

1) That unhulled grain and wheat found on the streets and roofs of houses in the city of Changteh following the visit of an enemy plane on the morning of November 4th was dropped from that plane. I might say in this connection that I watched the flight of the plane closely that morning. In appearance it was somewhat like an hydroplane and flew low over the city--lower than any plane has yet flown in the more than 20 bombings I have witnessed here.

2) That some of this grain was collected and brought to the hospital for examination.

3) That the laboratory report showed bacillus closely resembling that of plague.

4) That some ten days after the grain was dropped a young girl was brought to the hospital seriously ill, and that the symptoms indicated plague.

5) Smears taken from the bubos, and from spleen and liver after death, confirmed the diagnosis.

6) That on succeeding days other patients were examined and treated and that bacteriological examination showed plague bacilli present in each case.

7) Dr. W. K. Chen's report of his investigations and experiments appear to place the findings of plague bacilli beyond doubt.

8) Finally I might add that this is the first occasion during my long residence here (almost 30 years) that there has been an outbreak of plague in this area, or if it has occurred it has not been recognized as such.

9) If the facts be true, as I believe they are, there can be only one conclusion drawn and that is--that the enemy is now carrying on a ruthless and inhuman warfare against combatants and non-combatants alike. Truly a new way of spreading Japanese "culture."

Very sincerely yours,

(Signed) E. J. BANNAN, R. N.

Superintendent, Presbyterian Hospital, Changteh

Appendix 2

Weishengshu Anti-Epidemic Unit No. 14
Changteh, Hunan, December 30, 1941

Dr. P. Z. King, Director-General
National Health Administration
Chungking

Dear Sir:

I have the honour to report on the plague situation in Changteh as follows:

1) As unanimously stated by the inhabitants of Changteh, an enemy airplane, appearing in the morning of November 4th, 1941 and flying unusually low, scattered over certain parts of the city fairly large amounts of grain admixed to which were other materials as discussed below.

2) On November 12th a girl, 12 years of age, was admitted to the local Missionary Hospital in a most serious condition with high fever and delirium. She died the next day. Post mortem examination revealed the presence of swollen lumphatic glands on the left side of the neck but since eczema was present in this region, a local infection of the skin might have been the cause of the gland swelling. Be this as it may, it is certain that numerous gram-negative bacilli, showing the microscopic appearance of plague bacilli, were found in her blood during life and in smears made after death from the spleen.

3) This initial case was followed by six further plague cases confirmed by microscopical examination and in one instance also by culture and animal experiment, the last case being recorded on December 20th. Of these six patients five had inguinal buboes whilst the sixth presumably had septicaemic plague. All the above mentioned seven patients succumbed to the infection. They were all residents of Changteh.

4) In addition a number of suspicious cases was recorded but subsequent investigations make it probable that only one of these patients, dying on November 19th, might have actually suffered from (?) speticaemic plague.

5) Examination of small quantities of the grain dropped from the plane (the bulk of the grain had been collected and burnt as soon as possible) did not lead to definite results. I personally was shown on December 23rd two bouillon cultures made with this material. In smears from these cultures as

well as from the subcultures made under my supervision, gram-negative bacilli and cocci preponderated whilst the minority of gram-negative bacilli present did not show appearances characteristic for P. pestis. A guinea-pig infected on December 23rd with the combined material from these cultures and subcultures, remained well to date.

6) It might be emphasized, however, that these negative findings do by no means exclude a causal connection between the aerial attack on November 4th and the subsequent plague outbreak in Changteh. It should be noted in this connection that:

(a) Plague bacilli are not fit to subsist for appreciable length of time on inanimate objects or to grow and survive when cultivated together with such microorganisms as found in the present instance. The fact that we failed to find plague bacilli in the cultures in question does therefore not exclude that they were originally present on the grain.

(b) It must be moreover be kept in mind that the question whether or not the grain dropped from the plane was originally contaminated with plague bacilli, is not of such paramount importance as it would seem at first glance. The Indian Plague Commission and other investigators after them had little or even no success when trying to infect highly susceptible rodents including guinea-pigs under optimal laboratory conditions through prolonged contact with plague-contaminated inanimate objects or by feeding such animals with materials containing plentiful plague bacilli. That it would be possible to obtain better results when trying to utilise such methods in the case of human beings by throwing plague-contaminated materials from a plane, seems not likely.

On the other hand, it must be admitted that human infections would be likely to occur if the material dropped from the plane would serve as a vehicle for plague-infected fleas. Hence there is no doubt that the latter procedure would recommend itself to experts who think it fit to participate in bacterial warfare and I for one am led to assume that this method was used in the present instance. Support for this assumption is furnished by the statement made by several witnesses that the plane dropped besides grain also some other material or materials variously described as pieces of cotton or cloth, paper or pasteboard. Such materials, especially the first two, would offer good protection for fleas.

7) Further support for the assumption that the recent plague outbreak was due to enemy action is furnished by the following considerations:

(a) Observations as to the time and the place of the outbreak are well compatible with such assumption:

We have seen that the first victim was admitted to hospital on November 12th, i.e. 8 days after the aerial attack--a period of reasonable length, especially if infected fleas were involved which first had to seek for individuals to feed upon. It is known on the other hand that plague fleas may remain infective for weeks or even months.

The first six of the confirmed plague cases developed in persons living in two areas which had been copiously sprinkled with the materials dropped from the plane and only the seventh patient lived at some distance from one of these areas.

(b) If we temporarily dismiss for the sake of argument the assumption that the recent plague outbreak in Changteh was due to enemy action, we would be rather at loss to say how it could have originated. It must be noted in this connection that

(i) No previous outbreak of plague in Hunan is on record in modern times and the very intensive anti-epidemic work done in this province since the end of 1937 has shown no evidence whatsoever suggestive of plague.

(ii) The nearest foci from which plague infection could have been derived, are in Eastern Chekiang and Southern Kiangsi. It takes at least about 10 days to reach Changteh from either of these areas so that a person contracting plague infection in one of them and then starting on his journey to Changteh would be likely to fall ill before arrival. Such travellers have repeatedly to change from one transport vehicle to another and to stay overnight in the various stations en route; they have to use their own bedding during part of the journey at least. That they would carry along infected fleas on their persons or in their effects is therefore unlikely.

(iii) Changteh is situated on a river system entirely different from those in Chekiang or Southern Kiangsi so that direct traffic by boat which might lead to the transport of infected rats and/or fleas, is out of question.

(iv) The Changteh region produces rice and cotton so that it would be absurd to assume that such commodities, infested with plague rats and/or fleas would have been imported from elsewhere.

(c) As recently confirmed by our observations in Chekiang and Kiangsi, bubonic plague outbreaks in China are in most, if not in all, instances ushered in by a very considerable mortality of the local rats. No such rat falls have been observed in Changteh and we have not been able thus far to get any definite evidence that the local rats have become infected.

8) All the observations and considerations recorded above leave little if any room for doubt that the recent plague outbreak in Changteh was in causal connection with the aerial attack of November 4th.

9) It is reassuring that no further human case was reported during the last ten days but this does not exclude the possibility that further cases might occur.

10) It is impossible to decide at present whether or not the rats have become involved in the outbreak. As mentioned, so far no definite evidence of rat plague was found and it appears that the "Indian" rat fleas (X. cheopis) are infrequent at present. It must be kept in mind on the other hand that (a) Instances of rat plague, if existing, would be infrequent at the present junction and (b) Owing to untoward conditions (inclement weather and constant air alarms) we have been able so far to examine only limited numbers of rats. Prolonged observation will be necessary to decide this most important point.

Respectfully submitted by
(Signed) Dr. R. Pollitzer
(Signed) DR. R. POLLITZER

Epidemiologist,
NATIONAL HEALTH ADMINISTRATION

Appendix 3

Clinical and Autopsy Notes of the Proven Case of Bubonic Plague in Changteh

Name of Patient:	Kung Tsao-sheng
Date of Autopsy:	November 25, 1941
Place:	Isolation Hospital, Changteh
Operator:	Dr. W. K. Chen
First assistant:	Dr. Y. K. Hsueh
2nd Assistant:	Dr. B. Liu
Recorder:	Dr. C. C. Lee

Clinical History of the Patient:

The patient, a male of 28, lived in a small lane in front of the Kwan Miao Temple, and used to work in a village outside Changteh. He returned to the city on November 19th, 1941, on account of the death of his mother six or seven days before. The cause of her death was not definitely known (? tuberculosis - long standing illness with severe emaciation). He felt unwell in the evening of November 23rd, and experienced feverishness and headache with malaise at about 11 p.m. The next morning he complained of pain and tenderness in the right groin for which a Chinese plaster was applied. He vomitted once during the afternoon, and from then on his condition grew rapidly worse. Dr. C. C. Lee of the 4th Emergency Medical Service Training School and the 4th Sanitary Corps, was called in at 7 p.m. to see the patient, and found him to be dying. Important findings on examination were high fever, and enlarged and tender glands in the right inquinal region. Plague was strongly suspected. The patient was to have been sent to the Isolation Hospital, but he died at 8 p.m. before he could be removed. With the aid of the police, the body was brought to the Wei Sheng Yuan by 10 p.m. where disinfection of clothing and bedding was carried out in order to kill fleas. The plaster covering the groin was removed; cardiac puncture and aspiration of the right inguinal gland were performed for culture under sterile technique, and, since the light was inadequate, autopsy was postponed until the next morning. The body was laid in a coffin with the lid nailed down.

Autopsy Findings:

1. General Appearance: The cadaver was medium-sized and appeared very thin.

2. Skin: Face was slightly blue, and lips cyanotic. No petechial spots or flea-bite wounds were seen. Lesions resembling scabies in the right popliteal region.

3. Lymph Glands: The right inguinal glands were enlarged. Mesenteric lymph nodes also slightly enlarged.

4. Chest Findings: Lungs normal in gross appearance. There was fluid estimated at 20 cc. approximately in each pleural cavity. Pericardial effusion of about 20 cc. also present. Heart very flabby but not enlarged. Cardiac puncture through the right auricle performed under sterile technique and a few cc. of blood were obtained and inoculated on blood agar slant.

5. Abdominal Findings: Liver firm. Spleen enlarged to twice its normal size. Kidneys normal. Haemorrhagic spots seen on the surface of liver, spleen and intestine. No free fluid in the abdomen.

Bacteriological Findings:

Specimen of right inguinal glands, liver, spleen and blood were taken for direct smears, culture and animal tests.

1. Direct Smears: Carbol-thionin blue and Gram's method of staining were employed for all the smears. 50% ether in absolute alcohol was used for fixation. Under the microscope many oval-shaped Gram negative bacilli with their bipolar regions deeply stained were found.

2. Cultivation: Under sterile technique, specimens of cardiac blood, inguinal glands, liver and spleen of the patient were inoculated on blood agar slant of pH 7.6 and incubated in a wide-mouth thermos bottle. Temperature was regulated at 37° centigrade. Twenty-four hours later, many minute greyish-white opaque colonies were found on the surface of the media. All were pure cultures. Smear examination showed Gram negative bipolar staining organisms.

3. Animal Inoculation Test:

A. Guinea-pig No. 1. The animal was artificially infected by smearing splenic substance of the cadaver on its right flank which was newly shaven at 3 p.m. on November 25, 1941. (The splenic substance was found to have contained many gram negative bipolar staining bacilli). The animal began to develop symptoms at 8 p.m. on November 26th, and was found dead in the early morning of November 28th. Thus the incubation period was not more than 29 hours, and the whole course of the disease ran at most 32 hours.

Autopsy Findings:

1.	Skin:	Swelling and redness at the site of inoculation.
2.	Gland:	Bilateral enlargement of inguinal glands, more marked on the right side with congestion.
3.	Subcutaneous Tissues:	Edematous and congested. Haemorrhage at the site of inoculation.
4.	Chest Findings:	Not remarkable.
5.	Abdominal Findings:	Spleen enlarged and congested. Liver, kidneys and G.I. tract also congested.

Specimens of heart blood, liver, spleen and inguinal lymph glands were taken for smears and culture.

Microscopic examination of the stained smears (Carbol-thionin blue and Gram's stains) revealed Gram negative bipolar staining bacilli similar to those seen in the direct smears made of autopsy material from the patient.

Culture of these specimens on blood agar slants at pH 7.6 was made. Twenty-four hours later, pure cultures of similar organisms were found.

B. Guinea-pig No. 2. This animal was similarly treated as guinea-pig No. 1 at 9 a.m. on November 26th, but the inguinal gland of the cadaver was used instead. Symptoms were first noticed at 8 a.m. on November 28th, an incubation period of 47 hours. Death of the animal occurred 44 hours later (in the morning of November 30th).

Autopsy of the animal showed essentially the same gross pathological changes as those of guinea-pig No. 1. Direct smears of lymph glands, liver and spleen showed similar findings.

C. Guinea-pig No. 3. This time a pure culture of the organisms was used to smear on the newly shaven left flank of the guinea-pig. (The culture was obtained by growing the cadaver's heart blood on blood agar slant at pH 7.6 for 24 hours). The animal appeared to have become ill 45 hours later and was found dead in the early morning of November 30th. The course of the disease of the animal was, therefore, not more than 40 hours.

On autopsy, gross pathological changes were found to be similar to those of guinea-pigs Nos. 1 and 2 except that changes of lymph-glands and spleen were more pronounced.

Smear examination of heart blood, lymph-gland, liver and spleen yielded similar results.

Conclusion:

Clinical history, autopsy, findings and bacteriological findings prove the patient to be a case of bubonic plague, dying from septicaemic infection from Pasteurella Pestis.

(Signed) W. K. CHEN, M. D.

Head, Department of Laboratory Medicine,
Emergency Medical Service Training School,
Ministry of War;
Consultant, Chinese Red Cross Medical Relief Corps

Kweiyang,
December 12, 1941

Appendix 4

Clinical Notes of Cases in Changteh Suspected to be Plague

Case No. 1 (Tsai Tao-erh)

This patient, a girl of eleven living in Tsai Hung Sheng Charcoal Dealer Shop ( ), Kwan Miao Street, was said to have fallen ill on November 11, 1941 and was sent by the police to the Kwangteh Hospital at 7 a.m. the next day for treatment. On admission she was seen by Dr. H. H. Tan and was found delirious. Temperature 105.7° f. Eczema of the right ear. No glandular enlargement or tenderness. Few rales were heard in the chest. Abdominal findings were said to be normal. Blood smears (Wright and Gram's stains) showed organisms resembling P. pestis morphologically. Patient was then isolated and sulfanilamide treatment given. Her general condition turned from bad to worse in the morning of November 13th, when petechial spots of skin were noted. Blood smear examination was repeated and revealed the same result as before. At about 8 a.m. she died.

Essential features of autopsy were enlarged left infra-auricular lymph nodes. No sign of pneumonia; liver and spleen enlarged with hemorrhagic spots on their surfaces. Kidneys were also hemorrhagic. Splenic smear showed similar findings as the blood smear. Culture of the splenic substances was done in the Kwangteh Hospital but no definite report was obtained.

Case No. 2 (Tsai Yü-chen)

This was a woman of 27, living in Chang Ching Street ( ), East Gate district; she was said to have had an abrupt onset of fever on November 11th and died on the 13th. While her cortage was passage Tehshan, Dr. Kent of Red Cross Medical Relief Corps met it and made enquiry of the cause of her death. The above information led him to suspect plague. Post mortem liver puncture was done and smear examination showed organisms resembling P. pestis morphologically.

Case No. 3 (Nieh Shu-sheng)

This was a man of 58 living in No. 1, 3rd Ghia, 4th Pao, Chi Ming Cheng ( ), East Gate district. Developed high fever in the evening of November 12th, complained of pain and tenderness in the groin on November 13th. Aspiration of the enlarged groin gland was done by Dr. P. K. Chien of Red Cross Medical Relief Corps and smear examination (Wright stain) showed P. pestis like organisma. The patient died in the same evening.

Case No. 4 (Hsu Lao-san)

The patient was a man of 25, living in No. 5, 5th Chia, 5th Pao, Yun An Hsiang, Yang Chia Hsiang, East Gate district ( ). Became ill with fever and headache since November 12th. Seen by Dr. H. H. Tan and Dr. T. C. Fang, and found to have tender and enlarged groin lumph glands the next day. Aspiration of the gland was done in the Kwangteh Hospital and smear examination (Wright's stain) showed P. pestis like organisms.

Case No. 5 (Hu Chung-fa)

A man living in Chung Fa Hospital, Kwan Miao Street ( ). In the morning of November 19th, he went to the Wei Sheng Yuan complaining of being infected with plague and demanding treatment. He appeared, at that time, quite irritable and spoke somewhat incoherently. His pulse rate was rapid, but fever was not high. Groin glands were enlarged. Other findings were not recorded. He was immediately admitted to the Isolation Hospital. In the evening his temperature went up and he died.

Autopsy by Drs. H. H. Tang and M. N. Shih showed bluish discoloration of the skin, more marked over the chest and abdomen. No enlargement of lymph glands were noticed. Spleen was found to be slightly enlarged and other abdominal findings were not remarkable. Smear and culture of splenic material showed only Gram positive cocci and bacilli. It should be noted that Dr. Tan was working with inadequate culture media.

(Signed) W. K. CHEN, M. D.
Head, Department of Laboratory Medicine
Emergency Medical Service Training School,
Ministry of War;
Consultant, Chinese Red Cross Medical Relief Corps

Kweiyang
December 12, 1941

Appendix 5

Notes on Examination of Grain Dropped by Enemy Plane

Examination of a sample of grain dropped by the enemy plane over Changteh city on November 4, 5 a.m., 1941 and collected from the ground next morning and examined after an interval of fully 34 days.

Gross Examination: The sample consists of barley, rice and unidentified plant seeds.

Culture Examination: The sample was put into a sterile mortar and ground with 5 cc. sterile saline. This mixture was cultivated on blood agar slants and copper sulphate agar slants (all pH 7.6). After incubation at 37° C. for 24-48 hours, only contaminating organisms of staphylococci, B. coli and unidentified Grampositive bacilli with central spores were found; no P. pestis like organisms were found.

Animal Inoculation: Two cc. of the above mixture were injected subsutaneously into a guinea-pig on Dec. 8th, 1941 at 9 a.m. The testing animal died in the evening of Dec. 11th after showing no sign of illness.

Autopsy Findings: On the morning of Dec. 12th, autopsy of the dead animal was performed. Local inflamation, general congestion of subcutaneous tissue, inguinal lymph glands not enlarged, liver and spleen normal and not enlarged. Heart and lungs normal. Smears made from lymph gland, spleen and liver showed no P. pestis like organisms. Only Gram positive bacilli and some Gram negative bacilli were present.

Culture of heart blood of the dead animal showed unidentified Gram positive bacilli with central spores. P. pestis not found. Culture from the lymph nodes, spleen and liver showed pure culture of B. coli only. P. pestis also not found.

Conclusions: By culture and animal inoculation tests, P. pestis is not present in the sample.

(Signed) W. K. CHEN, M. D.
Head, Department of Laboratory Medicine,
Emergency Medical Service Training School
Ministry of War;
Consultant, Chinese Red Cross Medical Relief Corps

Kweiyang,
December 12, 1941

9.34　9 Jun. 1947: Intelligence Information on Bacteriological Warfare, CHECK SHEET, From: G-2, To: LS

资料出处：National Archives of the United States, R331, B1434.

内容点评：本资料为1947年6月9日盟军总司令部G-2送交法务局的G-2长官C. A. W.（Willoughby）与美化学部队司令电话纪要，题目：关于细菌战的情报。提及调查所获相关情报极其重要，不用于战争犯罪的审判。有关情报必须保密。

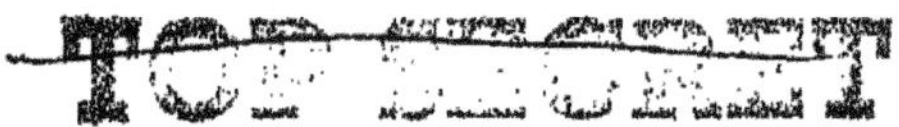

GENERAL HEADQUARTERS
FAR EAST COMMAND

CHECK SHEET

(Do not remove from attached sheets)

File No:

Subject: Intelligence Information on Bacteriological Warfare

Note No.

From: G-2 To: IS Date: 9 June 1947

1 Herewith extracts of telecon held by G-2 personnel with the Chief of Chemical Corps, WDSS, 2 June 1947, on the subject of B.W. These extracts indicate the extreme value of the intelligence information obtained and the danger of publicity on this subject:

"...Information most welcome and of course of prime importance. We await receipt of report with much interest..."

"...It is intention of mil int representative on SWNCC sub committee to recommend that information re B.W. given to us will not be divulged or used in war crimes trials..."

"...I consider it vital that we get the information and that secrecy (which would be impossible if war crimes trials were held) be maintained..."

"...The information so far indicates that investigation is producing most important data. It merits all necessary support, financial and otherwise..."

[signature]

AFPAC AGO Form No. 37

773434

9.35 22 Jun. 1947: INCOMING MESSAGE NR: WAR 80671, FROM: WAR (WDSCA WO), TO: CINCEF (CARPENTER LEGAL SECT); 23 Jun. 1947: INCOMING CLASSIFIED MESSAGE Nr: C53555, From: CINCFE Tokyo Japan, To: WDCSA

资料出处：National Archives of the United States, R331, B1434.

内容点评：本资料为 1947 年 6 月 22 日美国陆军部发送盟军总司令部法务局 Carpenter 电文，令迅速搞清国际检察局是否掌握证据，支持其主张石井等违反陆战法规。附 1947 年 6 月 23 日法务局回电 Nr: C53555。

CONFIDENTIAL

FAR EAST COMMAND
GENERAL HEADQUARTERS, U. S. ARMY FORCES, PACIFIC
ADJUTANT GENERAL'S OFFICE
RADIO AND CABLE CENTER

INCOMING MESSAGE

PRIORITY

22 Jun 47
21

FROM : WAR (WDSCA WC)

TO : CINCFE (CARPENTER LEGAL SECT)

NR : WAR 80671

Reurads May C 52423 June C 53169 ourad Jun WAR 99277.

Request soonest clarification and further details para 5 F urad C 53169 particularly IPS opinion as to whether evidence now in its possession warrants opinion that Japanese BW group headed by Ishii did violate rules of land warfare. We are satisfied evidence now in possession Legal Sect SCAP does not warrant such charge against and trial of Ishii and his group. Must have info re all possible proof re Ishii BW group participation in activities that could be considered War Crimes under rules of land warfare before reaching decision reurad C 52423 dtd 6 May 47.

NO SIG

R E V I S E D (22 JUN 47)

ACTION: LEGAL

INFORMATION: COMMANDER IN CHIEF, CHIEF OF STAFF, G-2

PRIORITY

TOO: 211536 Z
MCN: YA 74/21

"Paraphrase not required. Handle as TOP SECRET correspondence per par 51 i and 60 a (4) AR 380-5."

copy No 10 destroyed 26 Jun 47

Handling and transmission of literal plain text of this message as correspondence of the same classification has been authorized by the War Department in accordance with the provisions of paragraphs 16-C, 18-E, 53-A, 53-D (1) (2) (3), and 60-A (1) (2) (3) (4), AR 380-5, 6 March 1946.

COPY NO. 18

AG FILE 20

CONFIDENTIAL

17

WAR DEPARTMENT
CLASSIFIED MESSAGE CENTER
INCOMING CLASSIFIED MESSAGE

RECEIVED 23 JUN 1947

PARAPHRASE NOT REQUIRED. HANDLE AS TOP SECRET CORRESP... PARAS 511 and 60a (4), AR 380-5.

CONFIDENTIAL

From: CINCFE Tokyo Japan

To : WDCSA

Nr : C 53555 23 June 1947

Reurad WAR 80671, 22 June 1947, urgently recommend any action by WC be based SWNCC 351 line 1 with particular reference to paragraph 4. Any pressure will endanger present status of valuable BCW intelligence. Refer to Dr. Fell now returned to CWS.

End.

Directorate for Freedom of Information And Security Review
Office of the Assistant Secretary of Defense (Public Affairs)
Room 2C-757, Pentagon, Washington, D.C.

DOWNGRADED TO: 8 JUL 1977
CONFIDENTIAL on
DECLASSIFY on
Classified by

ACTION: Gen Noce

INFO: Gen Chamberlin, Gen Norstad, Gen Waitt

DECLASSIFIED BY ORDER OF THE SEC ARMY BY TAG PER 770475

CM IN 3575 (23 June 47) DTG 230813Z jy

CONFIDENTIAL

12

(17)

EXCLUDED FROM AUTOMATIC REGRADING DOD DIR 5200.10 DOES NOT APPLY

COPY NO.

THE MAKING OF AN EXACT COPY OF THIS MESSAGE IS FORBIDDEN

9.36 27 Jun. 1947: 250.401 War Crimes, 6-30/1856, No. C53663, From: CINCFE, To: WAR (WDSCA WC): JAPANESE WAR CRIMES TRIAL-(Scattered Wheat Grain over Ningbo)

资料出处： National Archives of the United States, R331, B1434.

内容点评： 本资料为 1947 年 6 月 27 日盟军总司令部法务局长官 Carpenter 发送美国陆军部的电文，题目：日本战争犯罪（在宁波上空撒播谷物）。提及 6 月 22 日与国际检察局 Tavenner 再次会谈，对方报告苏联在押日军战俘柄泽十三夫、川岛清的证词内容，称国际检察局认为根据以上情报，石井为首的日本细菌部队确实违反了陆战法规，而表明如此观点并非主张起诉与审理。

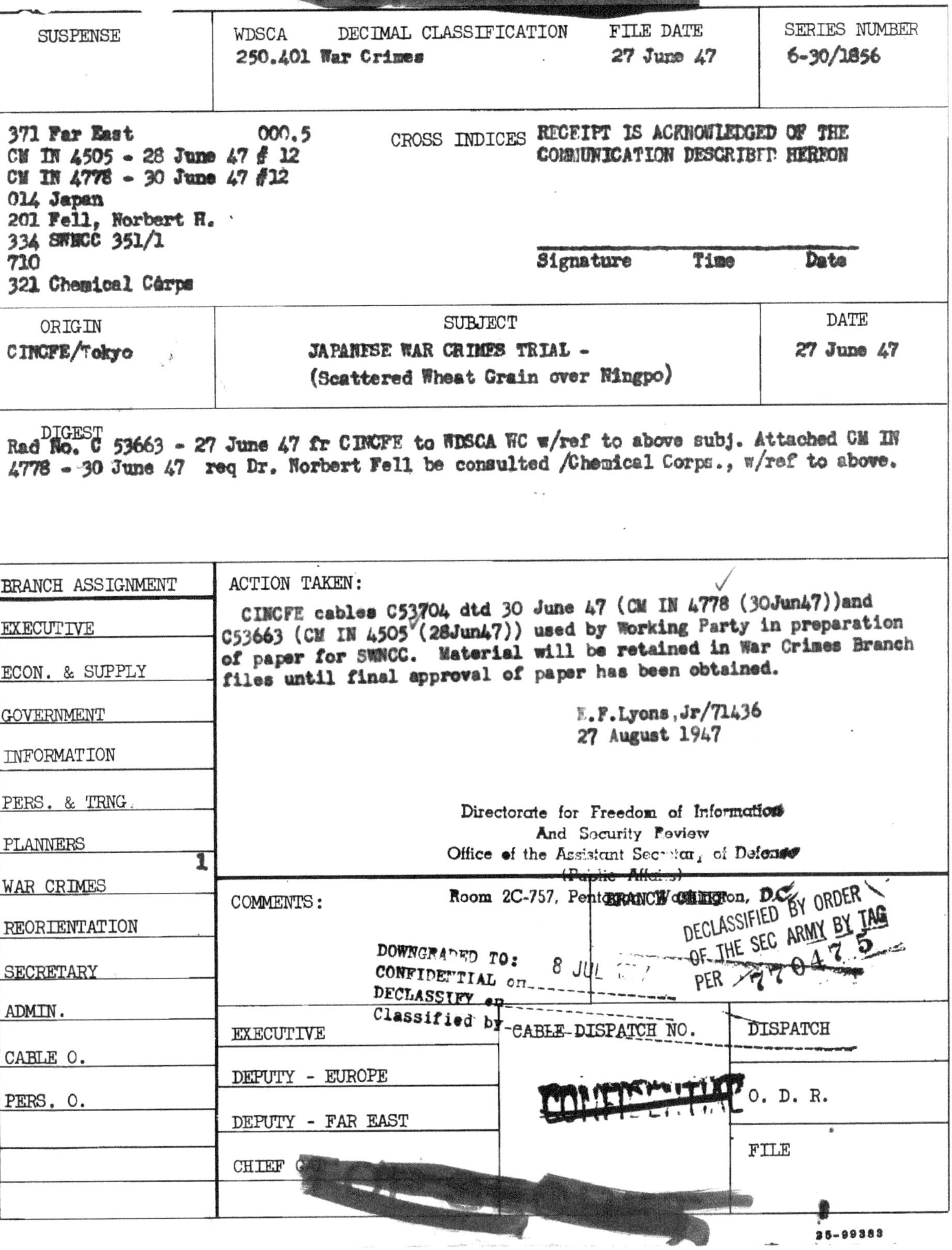

COMBINED ROUTING - INFORMATION - FILING FORM

SUSPENSE	WDSCA DECIMAL CLASSIFICATION 250.401 War Crimes	FILE DATE 27 June 47	SERIES NUMBER 6-30/1856

371 Far East 000.5
CM IN 4505 - 28 June 47 # 12
CM IN 4778 - 30 June 47 #12
014 Japan
201 Fell, Norbert H.
334 SWNCC 351/1
710
321 Chemical Corps

CROSS INDICES

RECEIPT IS ACKNOWLEDGED OF THE COMMUNICATION DESCRIBED HEREON

Signature Time Date

ORIGIN	SUBJECT	DATE
CINCFE/Tokyo	JAPANESE WAR CRIMES TRIAL - (Scattered Wheat Grain over Ningpo)	27 June 47

DIGEST

Rad No. C 53663 - 27 June 47 fr CINCFE to WDSCA WC w/ref to above subj. Attached CM IN 4778 - 30 June 47 req Dr. Norbert Fell be consulted /Chemical Corps., w/ref to above.

BRANCH ASSIGNMENT: EXECUTIVE / ECON. & SUPPLY / GOVERNMENT / INFORMATION / PERS. & TRNG. / PLANNERS / WAR CRIMES 1 / REORIENTATION / SECRETARY / ADMIN. / CABLE O. / PERS. O.

ACTION TAKEN:

CINCFE cables C53704 dtd 30 June 47 (CM IN 4778 (30Jun47))and C53663 (CM IN 4505 (28Jun47)) used by Working Party in preparation of paper for SWNCC. Material will be retained in War Crimes Branch files until final approval of paper has been obtained.

E.F.Lyons,Jr/71436
27 August 1947

Directorate for Freedom of Information And Security Review Office of the Assistant Secretary of Defense (Public Affairs) Room 2C-757, Pentagon, Washington, D.C.

COMMENTS: BRANCH CHIEF

DECLASSIFIED BY ORDER OF THE SEC ARMY BY TAG PER 770475

DOWNGRADED TO: CONFIDENTIAL on 8 JUL ... DECLASSIFY on Classified by

EXECUTIVE / DEPUTY - EUROPE / DEPUTY - FAR EAST / CHIEF

CABLE-DISPATCH NO.

CONFIDENTIAL

DISPATCH / O. D. R. / FILE

25-99383

THIS SLIP WILL NOT BE REMOVED
FROM BASIC COMMUNICATION
COMBINED ROUTING - INFORMATION - FILING FORM

SUSPENSE	WDSCA DECIMAL CLASSIFICATION	FILE DATE	SERIAL NUMBER
	250.401 War Crimes	27 June 47	6-30/1856

CONFIDENTIAL

371 Far East 000.5
CM IN 4505 - 28 June 47 # 12
CM IN 4778 - 30 June 47 #12
014 Japan
201 Fell, Norbert H.
334 SWNCC 351/1
710
321 Chemical Corps

CROSS INDICES

RECEIPT IS ACKNOWLEDGED OF THE COMMUNICATION DESCRIBED HEREON

Signature Time Date

ORIGIN	SUBJECT	DATE
CINCFE/Tokyo	JAPANESE WAR CRIMES TRIAL - (Scattered Wheat Grain over Ningpo)	27 June 47

DIGEST

Rad No. C 53663 - 27 June 47 fr CINCFE to WDSCA WC w/ref to above subj. Attached CM IN 4778 - 30 June 47 req Dr. Norbert Fell be consulted /Chemical Corps., w/ref to above.

BRANCH ASSIGNMENT: EXECUTIVE; ECON. & SUPPLY; GOVERNMENT; INFORMATION; PERS. & TRNG.; PLANNERS; WAR CRIMES; REORIENTATION; SECRETARY; ADMIN.; CABLE O.; PERS. O.

ACTION TAKEN:

CINCFE cables C53704 dtd 30 June 47 (CM IN 4778 (30Jun47))and C53663 (CM IN 4505 (28Jun47)) used by Working Party in preparation of paper for SWNCC. Material will be retained in War Crimes Branch files until final approval of paper has been obtained.

E.F.Lyons,Jr/1436
27 August 1947

Directorate for Freedom of Information And Security Review
Office of the Assistant Secretary of Defense (Public Affairs)
Room 2C-757, Pentagon, Washington, D.C.

COMMENTS:

DECLASSIFIED BY ORDER OF THE SEC ARMY BY TAG PER 770475

DOWNGRADED TO: CONFIDENTIAL on ... 1977
DECLASSIFY ON: ...
Classified by ...

EXECUTIVE	CABLE DISPATCH NO.	DISPATCH
DEPUTY - EUROPE		O. D. R.
DEPUTY - FAR EAST		FILE
CHIEF CAD		

CONFIDENTIAL

25-99383

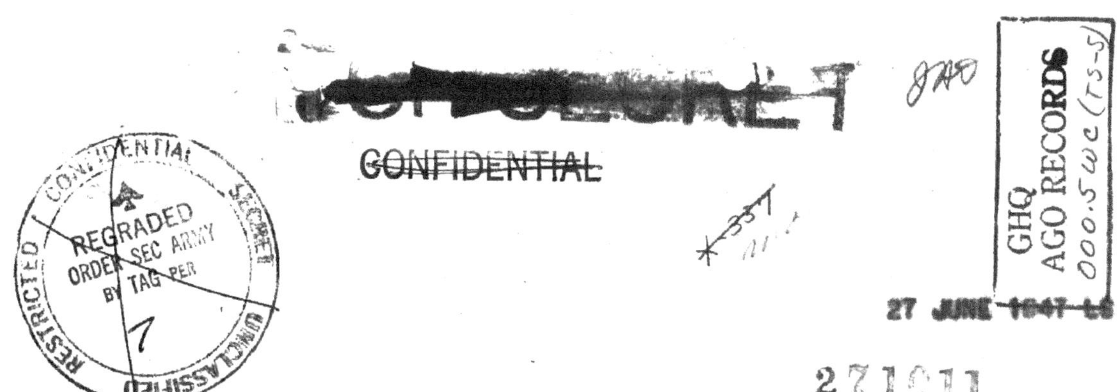

27 JUNE 1947 LS

271011

CINCFE (CARPENTER LEGAL SECTION)

WAR (WDSCA WC) . . . . PRIORITY

PAREN C -53663 PAREN REURAD WAR EIGHT ZERO SIX SEVEN ONE CMA TWO TWO JUNE FOUR SEVEN CMA HELD ANOTHER CONFERENCE WITH T VENNER OF ITEM PETER SUGAR WHO REPORTS FOLLOWING CLN PARA ONE ON TWO SEVEN OCTOBER ONE NINE FOUR ZERO JAPANESE PLANES SCATTERED QUANTITIES OF WHEAT GRAIN OVER NINGPO PD EPIDEMIC OF BUBONIC PLAGUE BROKE OUT TWO NINE OCTOBER FOUR ZERO PD KARAZAWA AFFIDAVIT IN PARA THREE BELOW CONFIRMS THIS AS ISHII DETACHMENT EXPERIMENT PD NINE SEVEN PLAGUE FATALITIES PD PARA TWO STRONG CIRCUMSTANTIAL EVIDENCE EXISTS OF USE OF BACTERIA WARFARE AT CHUHSIEN CMA KINGHWA AND CHANGTEH PD AT CHUHSIEN JAPANESE PLANES SCATTERED RICE AND WHEAT GRAINS MIXED WITH FLEAS ON FOUR OCTOBER ONE NINE FOUR ZERO PD BUBONIC PLAGUE APPEARED IN SAME AREA ON ONE TWO NOVEMBER PD PLAGUE NEVER OCCURRED IN CHUHSIEN BEFORE OCCURRENCE PD FLEAS WERE NOT PROPERLY EXAMINED TO DETERMINE WHETHER PLAGUE INFECTED PD AT KINGHWA CMA LOCATED BETWEEN NINGPO AND CHUHSIEN CMA THREE JAPANESE PLANES DROPPED A LARGE QUANTITY OF SMALL GRANULES ON TWO EIGHT NOVEMBER ONE NINE FOUR ZERO PD MICROSCOPIC EXAMINATION REVEALED PRESENCE OF NUMEROUS GRAM DASH NEGATIVE BACILLI POSSESSING THE MORPHOLOGICAL CHARACTERISTICS OF PETER PESTIS PD INOCULATION TESTS WERE PERFORMED ON GUINEA PIGS IN JANUARY ONE NINE FOUR ONE

CONFIDENTIAL

A.G. FILE

Copy No 8

27 JUNE 1947 LS

PAGE 2

CINCFE

WAR (WDSCA WC) . . . . .PRIORITY

WITH NEGATIVE RESULTS PD NO EPIDEMIC OF PLAGUE OCCURRED IN KINGHWA PD AT CHANGTEH A JAPANESE PLANE DROPPED WHEAT AND RICE GRAINS CMA PIECES OF PAPER CMA COTTON WADDING AND UNIDENTIFIED PARTICLES ON FOUR NOVEMBER ONE NINE FOUR ONE PD BETWEEN NOVEMBER ONE ONE AND TWO THREE CMA FIVE CASES OF SUSPECTED PLAGUE OCCURRED AND ONE CASE DEFINITELY DIAGNOSED AS BUBONIC PLAGUE PD NO EVIDENCE OF PLAGUE FOUND AMONG RATS AND CHANGTEH NEVER BEFORE AFFLICTED BY PLAGUE PD PARA THREE AT TIME OF FORWARDING OURAD CHARLIE FIVE THREE ONE SIX NINE ONLY SOVIET SYNOPSES OF AFFIDAVITS WERE AVAILABLE PD SINCE RECEIPT URAD WAR EIGHT ZERO SIX SEVEN ONE FULL JAPANESE TEXTS OF AFFIDAVITS HAVE BEEN SECURED AND TRANSLATED PD FROM KARAZAWA AFFIDAVIT IT APPEARS AFFIANT WAS ENGAGED IN MANUFACTURE OF GERMS AT ISHII UNIT ONE NINE THREE NINE TO ONE NINE FOUR FOUR PD BETWEEN AUGUST AND DECEMBER ONE NINE FOUR ZERO ISHII CMA ACCOMPANIED BY ONE ZERO ZERO SUBORDINATES CMA LEFT FOR HANG DASH CHOW CMA CENTRAL CHINA CMA FOR AN EXPERIMENTAL TEST PD AFFIANT MANUFACTURED SEVEN ZERO KILOGRAMS OF TYPHUS AND FIVE KILOGRAMS OF CHOLERA BACILLI FOR THIS EXPERIMENT PD FIVE KILOGRAMS OF FLEAS INFECTED WITH PLAGUE WERE LIKEWISE PRODUCED PD THE SUBJECT OF EXPERIMENT WAS SPRAYING OF BACTERIA BY AIRCRAFT IN THE

~~CONFIDENTIAL~~

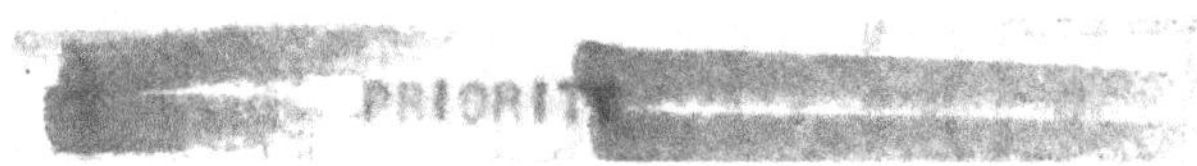

40

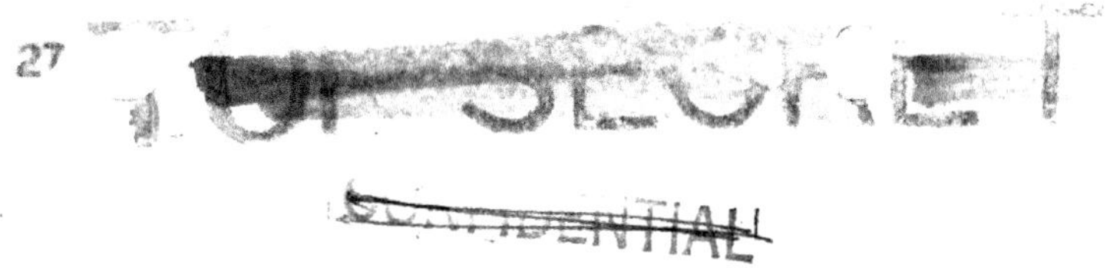

27 JUNE 1947 L

PAGE 3

CINCFE

WAR (WDSCA WD) . . . . .PRIORITY

ZONE OCCUPIED BY THE CHINESE ARMY PD AFTER THE EXPERIMENT A PLAGUE EPIDEMIC OCCURRED AT NINGPO PD AFFIANT WAS ADVISED OF THIS BY ENGINEER MINATO CMA MAJOR TAKAHASHI AND LIEUTENANT COLONEL IKARI WHO PARTICIPATED IN IT AND AFFIANT SAW CHINESE NEWSPAPERS DEPICTING INCIDENT CMA WHICH PAPERS WERE GATHERED BY PERSONS SENT TO CHINA TO INSPECT RESULTS PD IN WINTER CMA ONE NINE THREE NINE CMA ISHII TOLD AFFIANT THAT HE HAD EFFECTIVELY EXPERIMENTED WITH CHOLERA AND PLAGUE ON THE MOUNTAIN BANDITS OF MANCHURIA PD ABOUT JULY CMA ONE NINE FOUR TWO CMA ISHII WENT TO CENTRAL CHINA AGAIN WITH ABOUT SEVENTY SUBORDINATES CARRYING ONE THREE ZERO KILOGRAMS OF TYPHOID AND PLAGUE BACILLI AND NECESSARY FLEAS INFECTED WITH PLAGUE PD AT THAT TIME THE JAPANESE ARMY EXECUTED RETREAT OPERATION AND ISHII INFECTED THE VICINITY OF CHUHSIEN AND YUSHAN WITH TYPHOID AND PLAGUE BACILLI PD AT THE ANTA EXPERIMENTAL LABORATORY EXPERIMENTS WERE MADE SEVEN OR EIGHT TIMES DURING ONE NINE FOUR THREE AND ONE NINE FOUR FOUR WITH PLAGUE AND ANTHRAX BACILLI ON HUMAN BEINGS PD THE GENDARMES FURNISHED MANCHURIANS FOR THESE EXPERIMENTS WHO HAD BEEN SENTENCED TO DEATH PD DIRECTORS OF THIS EXPERIMENT WERE ISHII AND IKARI PD AFFIANT OBSERVED SOME OF THESE EXPERIMENTS AND WAS ADVISED REGARDING OTHERS BY IKARI CMA MAJOR

~~CONFIDENTIAL~~

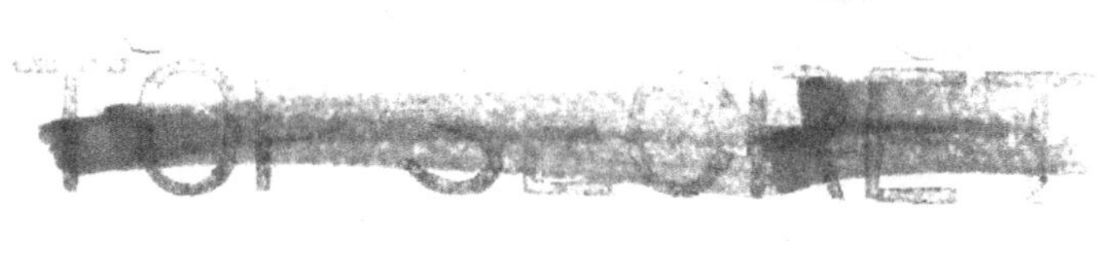

CONFIDENTIAL

27 JUNE 1947 LS

PAGE 4

CINCFE

WAR (WDSCA WC) . . . . .PRIORITY

HINOFUJI AND TAKAHASHI PD MANY TONS OF MATERIALS FOR CULTIVATION OF BACILLI WERE ACCUMULATED IN ONE NINE FOUR FOUR FOR PREPARATION OF MASS PRODUCTION OF BACTERIA PD PARA FOUR FROM KAWASHIMA AFFIDAVIT IT CLEARLY APPEARS THAT ISHII DETACHMENT HAD SECRET MISSION OF STUDYING USE OF BACILLI AS A WAR WEAPON PD EXTENSIVE EXPERIMENTS WERE CONDUCTED BY DROPPING PEST DASH BACILLI INFECTED FLEAS FROM AIRPLANES AND BY DROPPING BOMBS CONTAINING LIVE FLEAS PD THESE EXPERIMENTS WERE CONDUCTED UPON ANIMALS AND TWENTY MANCHURIANS UNDER DEATH SENTENCES PD KAWASHIMA AFFIDAVIT MAKES NO MENTION OF EXPERIMENTS AGAINST CHINESE TROOPS OR ON CHINESE CITIES PD ACCORDING TO THIS AFFIANT CMA MAJOR GENERAL KITANO SUCCEEDED ISHII AS COMMANDER OF THE UNIT IN AUGUST CMA ONE NINE FOUR TWO PD PARA FIVE ITEM PETER SUGAR OF THE OPINION THAT FOREGOING INFORMATION WARRANTS CONCLUSION THAT JAPANESE BAKER WILLIAM GROUP HEADED BY ISHII DID VIOLATE RULES OF LAND WARFARE CMA BUT THIS EXPRESSION OF OPINION IS NOT A RECOMMENDATION THAT GROUP BE CHARGED AND TRIED FOR SUCH PD KARAZAWA AFFIDAVIT WOULD NECESSARILY NEED CORROBORATION AND TESTING FOR TRUSTWORTHINESS BY A THOROUGH INVESTIGATION BEFORE PROSECUTIVE ACTION IS DECIDED UPON PD PARA SIX WITH REFERENCE TO FIVE FOX OURAD CHARLIE FIVE THREE ONE SIX NINE ITEM PETER SUGAR DID

53169-000.5 WC (TS-S)

CONFIDENTIAL

PRIORITY

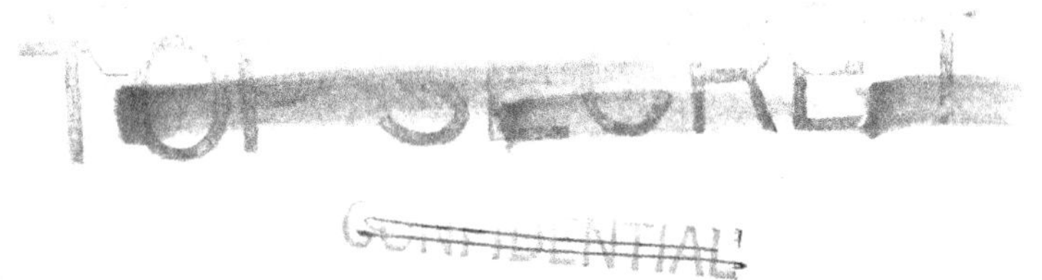

~~CONFIDENTIAL~~

27 JUNE 1947 LS

PAGE 5

CINCFE

WAR (WDSCA WC) . . . . .PRIORITY

NOT INCLUDE ANY EVIDENCE REFERENCE BAKER WILLIAM IN ITS CASE IN CHIEF BECAUSE AT TIME OF CLOSING CASE IT COULD NOT ASSURE THE TRIBUNAL UNDER ITS RULINGS THAT THE ACCUSED OR SOME OF THEM WOULD BE SHOWN TO HAVE BEEN ASSOCIATED WITH ACTS OF BAKER WILLIAM GROUP PD SINCE SEEING TRANSLATION OF KARAZAWA AFFIDAVIT ITEM PETER SUGAR MORE CERTAIN THAN BEFORE THAT SOVIET PROSECUTOR WILL ENDEAVOR IN CROSS DASH EXAMINATION OF ONE OR MORE OF THE ACCUSED TO LAY FOUNDATION FOR THE USE IN REBUTTAL OF SOME OF THE EVIDENCE ABOVE RECITED AND OTHER EVIDENCE ON THIS SUBJECT WHICH MAY HAVE RESULTED FROM THEIR INDEPENDENT INVESTIGATION IN MANCHURIA AND IN JAPAN PD PARA SEVEN COPIES OF PERTINENT AFFIDAVITS ARE BEING FORWARDED FOR YOUR INFORMATION PD

OFFICIAL: APPROVED BY:

R. M. LEVY
COLONEL, AGD
ADJUTANT GENERAL

ALVA C. CARPENTER
CHIEF
LEGAL SECTION

~~CONFIDENTIAL~~

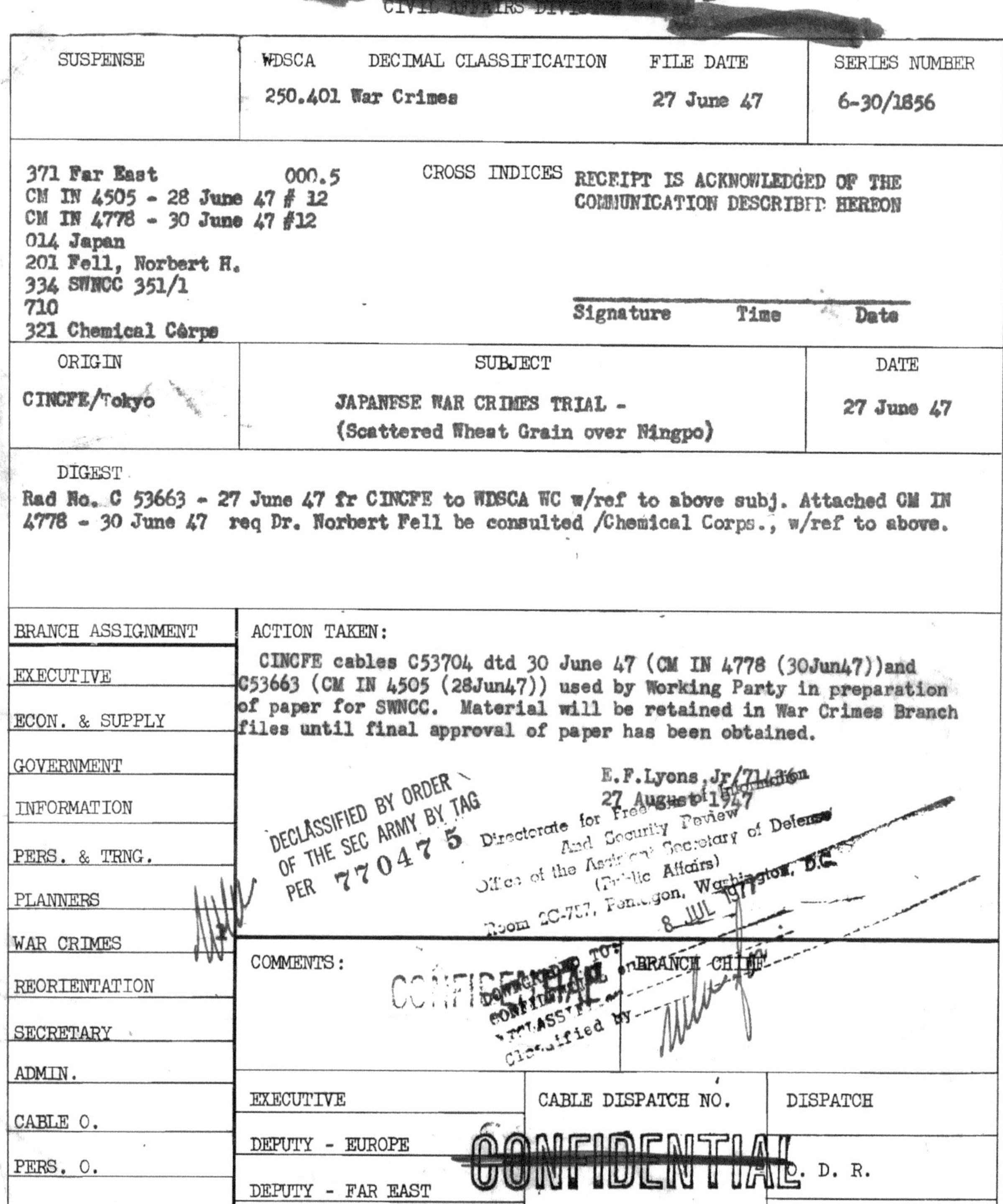

CIVIL AFFAIRS DIVISION

SUSPENSE	WDSCA DECIMAL CLASSIFICATION	FILE DATE	SERIES NUMBER
	250.401 War Crimes	27 June 47	6-30/1856

371 Far East 000.5
CM IN 4505 - 28 June 47 # 12
CM IN 4778 - 30 June 47 #12
014 Japan
201 Fell, Norbert H.
334 SWNCC 351/1
710
321 Chemical Corps

CROSS INDICES

RECEIPT IS ACKNOWLEDGED OF THE COMMUNICATION DESCRIBED HEREON

Signature Time Date

ORIGIN	SUBJECT	DATE
CINCFE/Tokyo	JAPANESE WAR CRIMES TRIAL - (Scattered Wheat Grain over Ningpo)	27 June 47

DIGEST

Rad No. C 53663 - 27 June 47 fr CINCFE to WDSCA WC w/ref to above subj. Attached CM IN 4778 - 30 June 47 req Dr. Norbert Fell be consulted /Chemical Corps., w/ref to above.

BRANCH ASSIGNMENT: EXECUTIVE; ECON. & SUPPLY; GOVERNMENT; INFORMATION; PERS. & TRNG.; PLANNERS; WAR CRIMES; REORIENTATION; SECRETARY; ADMIN.; CABLE O.; PERS. O.

ACTION TAKEN:

CINCFE cables C53704 dtd 30 June 47 (CM IN 4778 (30Jun47)) and C53663 (CM IN 4505 (28Jun47)) used by Working Party in preparation of paper for SWNCC. Material will be retained in War Crimes Branch files until final approval of paper has been obtained.

E.F.Lyons, Jr/71436
27 August 1947

DECLASSIFIED BY ORDER OF THE SEC ARMY BY TAG PER 770475

Directorate for Freedom of Information And Security Review
Office of the Assistant Secretary of Defense (Public Affairs)
Room 2C-757, Pentagon, Washington, D.C.
8 JUL 1977

COMMENTS:

CONFIDENTIAL

DOWNGRADED TO: CONFIDENTIAL
UNCLASSIFIED
Classified by

BRANCH CHIEF

EXECUTIVE	CABLE DISPATCH NO.	DISPATCH
DEPUTY - EUROPE		
DEPUTY - FAR EAST		D. D. R.
CHIEF CAD		FILE

CONFIDENTIAL

25-99383

READING COPY

27 June 1947

FROM: CINCFE (CARPENTER LEGAL SECTION)

TO : WAR (WDSCA WC). . . . . .PRIORITY

Reurad WAR 80671, 22 June 47, held another conference with Tavenner of IPS who reports following:

1. On 27 October 1940 Japanese planes scattered quanitities of wheat grain over Ningpo. Epidemic of bubonic plague broke out 29 October 40. Karazawa affidavit in paragraph 3 below confirms this as ISHII Detachment experiment. Ninety-seven plague fatalities.

2. Strong circumstantial evidence exists of use of bacteria warfare at Chuhsien, Kinghwa and Changteh. At Chuhsien Japanese planes scattered rice and wheat grains mixed with fleas on 4 October 1940. Bubonic plague appeared in same area on 12 November. Plague never occurred in Chuhsien before occurrence. Fleas were not properly examined to determine whether plague infected. At Kinghwa, located between Ningpo and Chuhsien, three Japanese planes dropped a large quantity of small granules on 28 November 1940. Microscopic examination revealed presence of numerous gram-negative bacilli possessing the morphological characteristics of P. pestis. Inoculation tests were performed on guinea pigs in January 1941, with negative results. No epidemic of plague occurred in Kinghwa. At Changteh a Japanese plane dropped wheat and rice grains, pieces of paper, cotton wadding and unidentified particles on 4 November 1941. Between November 11th and 23rd five cases of suspected plague occurred and one case definitely diagnosed as bubonic plague. No evidence of plague found among rats and Changteh never before afflicted by plague.

3. At time of forwarding ourad C 52169 only Soviet synopses of affidavits were available. Since receipt ourad WAR 80671 full Japanese texts of affidavits have been secured and translated. From KARAZAWA affidavit it appears affiant was engaged in manufacture of germs at ISHII Unit 1939 to 1944. Between August and December 1940 ISHII, accompanied by 100 subordinates, left for Hang-Chow, central China, for an experimental test. Affiant manufactured 70 kilograms of typhus and 5 kilograms of cholera bacilli for this experiment. Five kilograms of fleas infected with plague were likewise produced. The subject of experiment was spraying of bacteria by aircraft in the zone occupied by the Chinese Army. After the experiment a plague epidemic occurred at Ningpo. Affiant was advised of this by engineer MINATO, Major TAKAHASHI and Lt. Col. IKARI who participated in it and affiant saw Chinese newspapers depicting incident, which papers were gathered by persons sent to China to inspect results. In winter, 1939, ISHII told affiant that he had effectively experimented with cholera and plague on the mountain bandits of Manchuria. About July, 1942, ISHII went to central China again with about seventy subordinates carrying 130 kilograms of typhoid and plague bacilli and necessary fleas infected with plague. At that time the Japanese Army executed retreat operations and ISHII infected the vicinity of Chuhsien and Yushan with typhoid and plague bacilli. At the ANTA experimental Laboratory experiments were made seven or eight times during 1943 and 1944 with plague and anthrax bacilli on human beings. The gendarmes furnished Manchurians for these experiments who had been sentenced to death. Directors of this experiment were ISHII and IKARI. Affiant observed some of these experiments and was advised regarding others by IKARI, Major HINOFUJI and TAKAHASHI. Many tons of materials for cultivation of bacilli were accumulated in 1944 for preparation of mass production of bacteria.

4. From KAWASHIMA affidavit it clearly appears that ISHII Detachment had secret mission of studying use of bacilli as a war weapon. Extensive experiments

CONFIDENTIAL

Page 2

were conducted by dropping pest-bacilli infested fleas from airplanes and by dropping bombs containing live fleas. These experiments were conducted upon animals and twenty Manchurians under death sentences. KAWASHIMA affidavit makes no mention of experiments against Chinese troops or on Chinese cities. According to this affiant, Major General KITANO succeeded ISHII as commander of the unit in August, 1942.

5. IPS of the opinion that foregoing information warrants conclusion that Japanese BW group headed by ISHII did violate rules of land warfare, but this expression of opinion is not a recommendation that group be charged and tried for such. KARAZAWA affidavit would necessarily need corroboration and testing for trustworthiness by a thorough investigation before prosecutive actionmis decided upon.

6. With reference to 5f ourad C 53169 IPS did not include any evidence re BW in its case in chief because at time of closing case it could not assure the Tribunal under its rulings that the accused or some of them would be shown to have been associated with acts of BW group. Since seeing translation of KARAZAWA affidavit IPS more certain than before that Soviet prosecutor will endeavor in cross-examination of one or more of the accused to lay foundation for the use in rebuttal of some of the evidence above recited and other evidence on this subject which may have resulted from their independent investigation in Manchuria and in Japan.

7. Copies of pertinent affidavits are being forwarded for your information.

CONFIDENTIAL

Copies to: C in C
C of S
G-2
IPS
AG RECORDS-2
LS COMEBACK
LS FILE

000.5 WC (TS-S)

AG RECORD

MEMO FOR RECORD: 27 June 1947- Ourad C 53169, 6 June 47 to WDSCA WC in response to radio from them (WAR 99277, 3 June 47), states that LS does not possess sufficient War Crimes evidence against Ishii BW activities, that four possible superiors of Ishii now on trial before IMTFE, that Ishii not War Crime suspect. Tavenner of IPS reports gist of four affiants on subject of Japanese BW experiments, and that Soviet prosecutor of IPS may use evidence in rebuttal.

2. WAR 80671, 22 June 47 requests clarification and further details from IPS and whether in IPS opinion ISHII BW group violated rules of land warfare.

3. Subject radio supplies clarification and opinion requested.

ACC 26-6889.

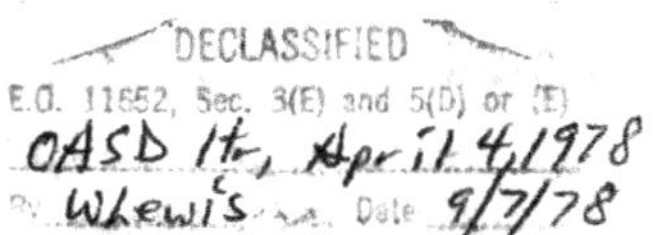

9.37 30 Jun. 1947: Frank S. Tavenner, Jr., Acting Chief of Council, IPS, GHQ, SCAP to Col. A. C. Carpenter, Chief, Legal Section, BW Group

资料出处： The University of Virginia Law Library, the Personal Papers of Frank S. Tavenner, Jr. and Official Records from the IMTFE, 1945-1948, Box 5, US.

内容点评： 本资料为 1947 年 6 月 30 日国际检察局代理长官 Frank S. Tavenner, Jr. 予法务局长官 A. C. Carpenter 上校电文：BW Group，附上川岛清（Kawashima Kiyoshi）少将证词两份、柄泽十三夫（Karasawa Tomio）少佐证词一份（此处略），建议将有关证人证词送交华盛顿。

Major General KAWASHIMA, Kiyoshi, and Major KARAZAWA, Tomio subordinates of ISHII, are held by the Soviets, presumably as war criminal suspects. No subordinates are charged or held here as war crimes suspects. Affidavits of above-mentioned subordinates and of Lieutenant-General HATA, Hikosaburo, Chief of Staff, Kwantung Army, and Dr. P. Z. King, are on file in IPS.

KAWASHIMA affidavit alleges detachment had secret duty of research of virus for the purpose of using them in war and experiments were conducted. ISHII called attention of his staff to instructions from General Staff in Tokyo to improve virus war researches.

KARAZAWA affidavit states that ISHII Detachment experimented as to most effective virus, germ cultivation, the way of infection, dispersing germs as means of attack, large-scale production of virus, preservation of virus, and discovery of preventive materials.

HATA affidavit states that ISHII was very anxiously controlling detachment under the instruction of General Staff in order to find out new virus and preventive materials, but it does not state that the General Staff intended to resort to bacteria warfare.

The affidavit of Dr. P. Z. King reflects that Japanese planes scattered wheat grains at Ningpo October 29, 1940, at Chuhsin October 4, 1940, at Kinghwa on November 28, 1940, and Changteh on November 4, 1940, and shortly after each occurrence bubonic plague appeared.

Since certain of ISHII's superiors are now on trial for major war crimes before IMTFE, use of this material was considered by IPS and decision was reached by IPS in December on the basis of information then available that these witnesses should not be produced as evidence was not sufficient to connect any of these accused with ISHII's Detachment's secret activities, the Tribunal having announced prior thereto that evidence relating to atrocities and prisoners of war would not be received in the absence of an assurance by the prosecution that the accused or some of them could be associated with the acts charged. The Soviet Prosecutor probably will endeavor in cross-examination of one or more accused to lay foundation for the use in rebuttal of the above-mentioned evidence and other evidence which may have resulted from their independent investigation.

BW Group

Frank S.Tavenner,Jr.
Acting Chief of Counsel
IPS, GHQ, SCAP

Col. A. C. Carpenter
Chief, Legal Section

30 June 1947

In the body of the proposed telegram I handed you Friday, June 27, regarding the above subject, I suggested that copies of the pertinent affidavits be forwarded Washington for their information. As the cable has been handled through your office probably this detail should likewise be handled by you. Accordingly, I am attaching an original and two copies of two statements by Major General Kiyoshi KAWASHIMA and one statement by Major Tomio KARASAWA. One copy is for your files.

Attachments (3)

- F. S. T. - - - - - - - - -

9.38 30 Jun. 1947: Transmittal of Affidavits, TO: Civil Affairs Division, War Crimes Branch, FROM: ALVA. C. CARPENTER, Chief, Legal Section

资料出处：National Archives of the United States, R331, B1434.

内容点评：本资料为 1947 年 6 月 30 日盟军总司令部法务局长官 Alva. C. Carpenter 发往华盛顿战争犯罪局内务科的文件：苏联在押日军战俘、731 部队第四部部长川岛清（Kiyoshi Kawashima）少将及其下属柄泽十三夫（Karasawa Tomio）少佐的证词。附：

1. 国际检察局文件编号 9305，1946 年 9 月 12 日伯力 Kawashima（川岛）；
2. 国际检察局文件编号 9309，1946 年 9 月 12~16 日伯力 Kawashima（川岛）；
3. 国际检察局文件编号 9306，Karasawa（柄泽）。

CONFIDENTIAL

LEGAL SECTION

APO 500
30 June 1947

SUBJECT: Transmittal of Affidavits

TO: Civil Affairs Division, War Crimes Branch, Washington 25, D.C.

1. Reference is made our radio C-53663 of 22 June 1947 concerning Ishii BW activities. Paragraph seven of this radio states that copies of pertinent affidavits will be forwarded.

2. Submitted as inclosures are two statements by Major General Kawashima, Kiyoshi and one by Major Karasawa, Tomio.

3 Incls
1. Kawashima Doc. 9305
2. Kawashima Doc. 9309
3. Karasawa Doc. 9306

ALVA C. CARPENTER
Chief, Legal Section

Interpreter, Puriachenko /phonetic/

Ogorodenikof /phonetic/

Stenographer, Timafeef /phonetic/

(This translation is correct but it has not been approved for reproduction without further checking.)

DOC. 9305

QUESTIONNAIRE

P.O.W. - THE FORMER CHIEF MEDICAL OFFICER OF THE 1ST ARMY GROUP OF THE KWANTUNG ARMY. MAJOR GENERAL (MED.) KIYOSHI KAWASHIMA. AT KHABAROVSK ON SEPTEMBER 12TH, 1946.

The witness was told beforehand that he would be held responsible under Art. 95 of the U.S.S.R. Criminal Code if he made any false statements.

Q. Was ISHII unit using any laboratory or patients' accommodations in other hospitals other than the facilities of the unit itself?

A. A detachment from the ISHII unit was stationed in the city of Harbin, which included sanitation, water supply and medical units. I know that these units were located adjoining to the Japanese Military Hospital near the Russian cemetery on Tai-tung Street of Harbin city.

Q. What were the duties of these units?

A. The function of the Medical Unit was practically the same as that of the other hospitals except that its main duties were directed to the research of contagious diseases.

Q. What sort of experiments were made upon the infectious cases? How many of these patients were there?

A. Most of the patients were Japanese. When I was on duty with the ISHII Unit, this department was making researches in medical treatment of bacillus carriers of typhoid and paratyphus.

Q. Who was the chief of this department when you were on duty with the unit?

A. It was Lt. Colonel NAGAYAMA. He is now a colonel.

Q. From when to when was Lt. Colonel NAGAYAMA on duty with the department?

A. I don't know from when he was on duty, but I think he served in the department until the termination of the war.

Q. Do you know Lt. General KAJITSUKA, Ryuji, ...?

A. Yes, I know him well.

CONFIDENTIAL

DECLASSIFIED BY ORDER OF THE SEC ARMY BY TAG PER 770175

Q. Did KAJITSUKA, Ryuji know of your duty with the unit?

A. I think, he knew.

Q. Did you make reports to him of your above-mentioned work when you were on duty as the Chief Medical Officer? I suppose, you reported it, when you were on the said duty?

A. No, I never reported it.

Q. Did you see KAJITSUKA while you were serving in the ISHII Unit, when he visited the unit?

A. No, while I was on duty with the ISHII Unit, I never saw him within the unit. I saw him at the New Harbin /Hotel/ while he was staying there on his supervising trip in autumn 1941.

Q. Did KAJITSUKA invite you?

A. I saw him when he dined with officers residing in Harbin. The dinner was held by KAJITSUKA for officers of troops in Harbin, at the time of his visit to the unit.

Q. Were you on duty with the ISHII Unit at that time?

A. Yes, I was.

Q. About what did you speak with KAJITSUKA at this dinner?

A. As it was an old account, I do not remember the particulars of the story. But they probably were not important.

Q. Who was the direct commander of the ISHII Unit in the Kwan-tung Army?

A. The Commander of the Kwan-tung Army.

Q. To what extent was this unit directly controlled by the Chief Medical Officer of the Kwan-tung Army, KAJITSUKA, Lieutenant General (Med.)?

A. KAJITSUKA, Ryuji had no authority to command this unit. He was only able to give instructions regarding the sanitation in the unit.

Q. Did KAJITSUKA, Ryuki ever visit this unit? If so, do you remember how many times did he make visits?

TOP SECRET

A. I do not remember how many times KAJITSUKA, Ryuji made visits to the ISHII Unit. But I am certain that he visited it.

Q. Can you tell me to what extent KAJITSUKA, Ryuji was interested in the research of the preparation for bacterial warfare of the unit?

A. I do not know to what extent KAJITSUKA, Ryuji was interested in the researches by this unit. But he should have known of the work the unit was doing.

Q. Is this your conjecture, or can you actually prove it?

A. It is impossible to prove the fact whether he was interested in the preparation for bacterial warfare or he was aware of the work being done, but, as he was the Chief Medical Officer, he ought to have been aware of it. We have never received instruction from him about the preparation of bacterial warfare.

Q. Was KAJITSUKA connected with the other duties of the unit, especially, on plan for the prevention of epidemics and the water supply of the Kwan-tung Army?

A. Regarding other duties in the unit, such as the manufacturing of vaccine and other preventative measures, we were given instructions by KAJITSUKA under his authority as the Chief Medical Officer of the Kwan-tung Army, and, for instance, in case of an outbreak of a contagion somewhere, we were notified by him.

Q. Who else had direct control over the ISHII Unit as an organ of the Kwan-tung Army Headquarters besides the commanding officer?

A. The Chief of the First Section of the Kwan-tung Army (Col. TAMURA) had something to do with the ISHII Unit. It was because he visited the ISHII Unit in the autumn or winter of 1941.

Q. Did the ISHII Unit receive any instruction from Tokyo or the Headquarters of the Kwan-tung Army, concerning the basic problems?

A. I do not know anything certain about it.

Q. How often did the representatives of the Army General Staff visit the ISHII Unit?

CONFIDENTIAL

A. I do not know. I think no one visited the unit during my service.

Q. Was the Quarantine and Water Supply Section of the Kwan-tung Army included in the general policy of the Kwan-tung Army Special Maneuvers?

A. Yes, it was included in the plan of the Kwan-tung Army. But it was limited only to organization of new quarantine and water supply units for the respective units. I don't remember how many quarantine and water supply units were formed at that time for the Special Maneuvers of the Kwan-tung Army, and I think these units were formed in each division and army, and needed a large number of personnel. I believe it was done about June of 1941.

Q. From what source and when did you learn that some personnel of your unit had been adopted for the Kwan-tung Army Special Maneuvers?

A. That was announced by the order we received. The order, to exercise the Kwan-tung Army Special Maneuvers and also dispatch a certain number of the personnel to join them, came to us in June of 1941.

Q. Did you read the order or did you hear about it from others?

A. I read it myself.

Q. Were personnel who were dispatched to the armies and divisions in charge of only quarantine and water supply in the ISHII Unit or were they engaged in the preparation for and study of bacterial warfare?

A. They were both.

Q. What problems were studied concerning the bacterial warfare preparation of the Kwan-tung Army Special Maneuvers?

A. As far as I know, the preparation for a bacterial warfare had nothing to do with the Kwan-tung Army's Special Maneuvers.

Q. What instructions were given, during this period, concerning the preparation for bacterial warfare?

A. Instructions were given for production and increase of vaccine as well as for more study in this field.

Q. You have testified that the Kwan-tung Army's special maneuvers had not been influenced by the preparation measures for bacterial warfare. But what were the instructions given to the ISHII Unit concerning increase of vaccine production and dispatch of men for service in the Army and the Division?

A. The instructions cannot be regarded as the preparation for bacterial warfare; these units having been organized for the purpose of prevention of epidemics and precaution against diseases, were mere Water Supply and Purification Units; they had no equipments whatever for bacterial warfare.

Q. But was it not that those who were dispatched from the ISHII Unit to newly organized units had knowledge of implements for bacterial warfare and could discharge, if necessary, the duty of the ISHII Unit? And was it not that for the above reason the ISHII Unit had in mind not only water supply and purification but also some other purpose when dispatching those men?

A. Of course, some of those who were dispatched from the ISHII Unit to newly organized Water Supply and Purification Units knew the preparation measures for bacterial warfare. If such an order came, they could use them. But, among the dispatched, there were also some who knew nothing about this matter.

KAWASHIMA, Kiyoshi
Major General, A.M.C.

Examiner: NIKITIN, Captain

Interpreter: PRIACHENKO
OGORODENIKOV

Stenographer: TIMOFEEVA

(This translation is correct but it has not been approved for reproduction without further checking.)

DOC. 9309

INTERROGATION REPORT

P.O.W. - KWANTUNG ARMY. MAJOR GENERAL KAWASHIMA, KIYOSHI. AT KHABAROVSK ON SEPTEMBER 12-16, 1946.

Q. We are questioning you as an important witness in regard to major Japanese war criminals by request of the Soviet representative of the IMTFE. We are warning you beforehand that false statements will not be accepted. Which language do you prefer in making the statement.

A. I prefer to make the testimony in Japanese, my mother tongue. And I will bear the responsibilities of telling only the truth. So I will offer a sworn statement.

Q. When you were ordered to serve in the laboratory under the direction of Maj. Gen. ISHII, what kind of work did you do?

A. I received orders to serve in the ISHII Unit in March 1941. I was assigned as Chief of Production Section and concurrently as Chief of the General Affairs Section. The ISHII Unit was stationed in Harbin and was assigned to work concerned with epidemic prevention. In the Japanese language it is called the Kwantung Army Water Supply and Purification Department.

Q. What was the nature of the duties assigned to the ISHII Unit?

A. The Kwantung Army Water Supply and Purification Department was in charge of the prevention of contagious diseases, research and investigation of the methods of prevention, training in connection with it, and the manufacture, supply and repair of materials for the prevention of contagious diseases. However, this was only the official duties of the ISHII Unit. Besides the above-mentioned duties, the ISHII Unit was also in charge of secret work on a special mission concerned with the study and use of bacilla as a war weapon. The important duties of the ISHII Unit were not made public, being secret. Only persons specially in charge of this work knew about it.

Q. What work did the Production Section, of which you were the Chief, do, and what did it manufacture?

A. This section was carrying out bacterial culture, and producing preventive vaccine and serum. This was the important part of our work.

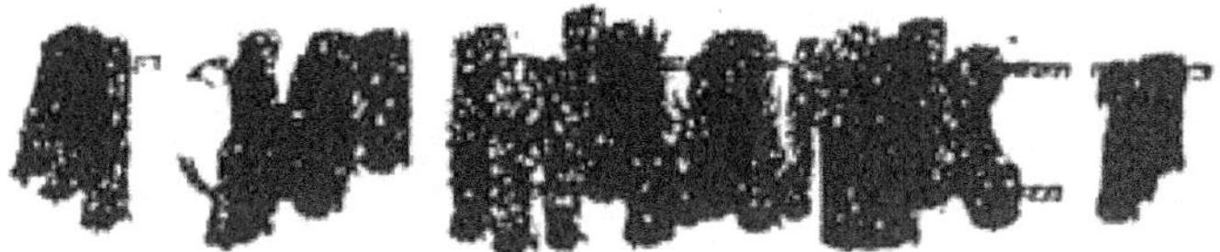

Q. Who and what sections were in charge of manufacturing bacilli material for experiments for military use?

A. There was no special section in charge of preparing material for the purpose of research regarding military use or bacterial warfare. The materials for these researches and experiments were supplied by various sections depending on the nature of the research. For instance, the Production Section which was in charge of bacterial culture was in charge of preparing bacilli. They also supplied experimental culture media. The section having extremely close connections with these experiments were Section One (research) which was in charge of fundamental experiments, Section Two (epidemic prevention) which was in charge of breeding fleas and practical experiments, and Section Four (Production) which was in charge of preparing bacilli and culture media, as mentioned above.

Q. To which supreme organization did the ISHII Unit come under?

A. The ISHII Unit was directly under the control of the Commander of the Kwantung Army.

Q. Who in the Kwantung Army directed and supervised the work of the ISHII Unit.

A. The sanitation duties of the ISHII Unit were supervised by the Chief of the Medical Department of the Kwantung Army. Major General ISHII reported directly to the Tokyo Medical Affairs Bureau and the Section in Charge in the General Staff AO on matters concerned with research and experiments. The budget and materials were supplied by the Kwantung Army.

Q. State accurately as to who prepared the bacterial materials for the ISHII laboratory.

A. The ISHII Unit prepared necessary materials such as insects by itself. However, pest-bacilli colonies were probably received from other laboratories and hospitals carrying out pest-treatments. There are cases when Typhoid-bacilli colonies were received from all the Army hospitals for the purpose of studying Typhoid Fever. However, there were no such cases while I was on duty.

Q. You have testified that the ISHII Unit settled in a positive manner the problem of the practical application of bacterial warfare. But we are interested in what scope and with what method the preparation of bacterial materials were made.

-2-

A. There was a store of bacterial materials for a small scale research. But it was difficult to use bacterial material as a weapon in military operations. It was practically impossible to have a large supply and the ISHII laboratory was conducting a research in that field.

Q. During your tour of duty, what results were attained by the research of the ISHII Unit?

A. Considering the research facilities of the Unit, quite satisfactory results were obtained in germiculture. I do not know whether or not research were being made, during my term of duty, on large stores of bacilli.

Q. Tell about the practical solution of the problem of preparing bacterial materials for military use.

A. This was a big problem for the Unit. Actually, it is not enough to only have a great supply of bacilli or to simply produce and store them. The method of practical uses had to be figured out. This was the objective of the ISHII Unit.

Q. Were good results obtained by the Unit in its study and actual application of the method of bacterial warfare?

A. I believe quite good results were obtained in the use of pest-bacilli. I heard from Colonel KITAGAWA, former Chief of the Research Section of the ISHII Unit that good results were obtained in the study of the uses of pest-bacilli.

Q. Have you heard anything about this matter, or did you participate in these studies?

A. No, I only heard about it.

Q. State what you heard, and give the circumstances, dates, and from whom you heard it.

A. Soon after I arrived at the Unit in 1941, Colonel KITAGAWA, then the Chief of the Research Section, told me that good results were obtained in the research which was carried out previously on the use of pest-bacilli as aggressive military purpose. As I learned later, these studies were made before I arrived at the unit.

Q. Can you explain the method of using pest-bacilli as a weapon?

A. Among the researches made by the ISHII Unit, the following three methods were being planned:

1. <u>The method to drop from aircrafts infected insect, mainly pest-bacilli infected fleas</u>. This method obtained extremely effective results and is easy to apply in a military operation. Furthermore, it is a technically easy method.

2. <u>Method of dropping bombs containing live fleas from airplanes</u>. I can declare that research work was being conducted in regard to this method, but I am not acquainted with the results. I was told that this was rather difficult.

3. <u>Method of directly spreading fleas on the ground</u>. This method is difficult. This is due namely to the fact that the best way of spreading fleas has not been discovered. There are here two possibilities, namely to use schemers (plotters) in order to spread same either in the rear of the enemy or within the enemy's lines, or to infest the entire land area at time of withdrawal.

Q. What kind of experiments were carried out by the ISHII Detachment regarding the use of the pest-bacilli-infested fleas? State also when and where.

A. I myself remember having once seen the methods as per Nos. 1 and 2, viz. the spreading of fleas from an airplane and the dropping of bombs containing fleas. These were carried out in around May or June. I participated in the experiments for one day. The experiments were conducted near ADACHI Station (100 kms. distant from Harbin along the Chinese Eastern Railway) on a testing ground about 10 kms. north of ADACHI Station. I do not recollect how close it was to the residental zone. However, the entire residential area lay to the South, and there were no buildings whatsoever to the North of the testing ground. Experiments were carried out on animals and human beings.

Q. Under whose leadership were the experiments conducted, and what did you observe at the testing ground?

A. The experiments were conducted under the leadership of Colonel OHTA, who was the Chief of the Epidemic Prevention Section at the time. Senior Civilian Technician YAMAGUCHI, Captain YAMADA and Lieut. KOIKE also took part in the experiments. There were also a few scores of other people -- I do not remember who they were -- comprising officers, NCOs and civilian employees.

~~CONFIDENTIAL~~

The testing ground was divided into numerous sections depending upon the method of experiment. The following methods were experimented:

1. Spreading of bacilli-infested fleas from an airplane.

2. Dropping bombs containing bacilli-infested fleas from an airplane.

3. Bombs containing bacilli were also dropped from an airplane.

4. Spraying of bacilli.

The testing ground was encircled by proper watchmen. This was for the sake of preserving secrets as well as to prevent others from coming inside the ground. The observers stayed in a safe and sheltered zone. The testing lots were indicated by means of flags (I do not remember exactly but there were also cases where same were indicated by raising smoke) and made so that they could be clearly distinguished from the airplanes. Upon the said preparations being completed, the Harbin Airfield was contacted, following which airplanes started out carrying virus materials.

After a short while after the dropping of the virus materials, the test participants examined how the virus materials were dropped into the testing areas, how many fleas assembled themselves on the animals or human beings, the state in which the experimented animals are, and, for the purpose of ascertaining whether the bacilli were properly sprayed onto the object(s) of experiment, inspect beforehand ~~the test-sheets~~ (paper) that are spread out beforehand, and also inspect the culture media and the state (condition) of the animal(s). The last two inspections were made in a laboratory manner. The culture media were examined in order to determine whether the dropped bacilli were still alive or not. Animals were utilized for determining the poisonous strength of the bacilli. As regards appliances, the above-mentioned culture media and testing-paper were used. The experiments were made on rats and human beings, the latter comprised about 20 Manchurian capital punishment convicts. I do not remember anyone else who was there merely as an observer. I believe that I was the only one.

As regards the results of the tests, I can remark as follows:

The testing ability was excellent, there not having been a single instance of the virus materials not dropping on the

~~CONFIDENTIAL~~

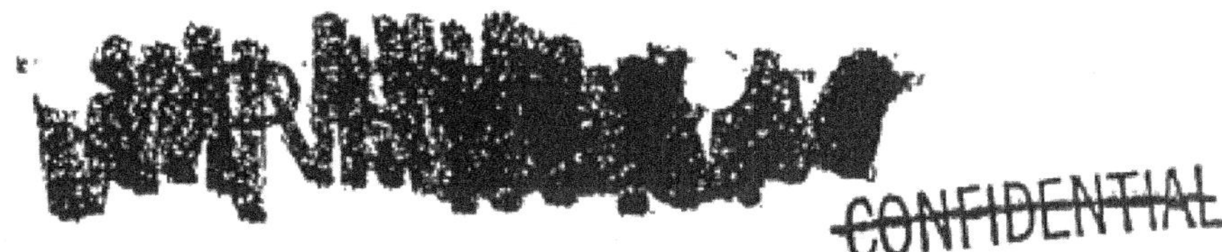

right spot. However, the degree of contagion of the virus materials was unsatisfactory. I was told by KITAGAWA that the rate of contagion was low in view of the fact that the fleas dropped were not in the right state. I recollect from this remark that the rate of infection was extremely low. I am unable to state the exact percentage. In regard to these tests no official announcement was made by the laboratory nor was any research meeting held on this subject.

The foregoing represent what I saw myself, and I learned of the results in part from what KITAGAWA told me.

Q. Did someone from the Kwantung Army attend the tests?

A. Nobody from the Kwantung Army was present at these tests. There was also nobody present from the Japanese General Staff Office.

Q. Were any tests other than the afore-mentioned tests made at the testing ground?

A. Before replying to this question, I would state that I was present at one more test during the Winter of 1941. This was carried out on some frozen ground near Harbin. I do not remember the name of the spot. On this occasion shrapnel bombs were dropped from a plane in order to determine the effective power of the bombs. The characteristics of the bombs were as follows:

Sometimes the metal bomb case would explode in the air, and sometimes it would explode when contacting the ground, and as a result of the explosion fragments are dispersed from the shrapnel bomb. In actual usage these shrapnel bombs can be infested with [illegible] materials and can attain their offensive purpose by exploding. These tests were also held under the leadership of Colonel OHTA, and Senior Civilian Technician YAMAGUCHI was also present. I observed these tests from an airplane.

Within the scope of my knowledge there were no other tests regarding the practical use of bacilli in the event of a war. There were scholastic /T.N. scientific?/ tests, but these were, at the same time, preparations for war purposes.

Q. Can it be considered that, as a result of research work and experiments, the ISHII Detachment solved the problem of use of the pest-bacilli-weapon as a means of offensive warfare?

CONFIDENTIAL

A. According to a chat which I had with Major-General ISHII while serving with his Detachment, the said General was of the opinion that the methods of dropping fleas from airplanes or spreading fleas on the ground can be used in the case of bacterial warfare; the former as an offensive weapon and the latter as a defensive measure and for purpose of stratagem /T.N. possibly implies "nerve warfare"/.

Q. Were the Japanese General Staff Office and the Kwantung Army Headquarters aware of the results of these undertakings?

A. I do not know for certain, but their Staff Officers must presumably have known about them. I do not know when and how these matters were reported. But I presume that reports must have been made. Otherwise the tests would lose their meaning.

Q. Can you tell whether or not the ISHII Unit ever made reports to the General Staff HQ, and the Kwantung Army, based upon work reports of your Production Section?

A. My reports were all submitted to Major General ISHII, but I do not know whether or not they were submitted to other offices.

Q. As preparations for bacterial warfare methods, did the ISHII Unit receive any directive from any HQ in Japan, or from the Kwantung Army, or the War Ministry?

A. I do not know if there were any directives from the War Ministry or the General Staff HQ during my tour of duty. Even if directives had been received, I believe they would have been extremely secret, and only special persons would receive them, and would not have been shown to me. Had there been any directive on the preparations for a bacterial warfare, it would probably have been before I was assigned (April 1941). I make this presumption because of its secret nature and because the experiments were carried out before I took the post. During my tour of duty, I believe this experiment was being carried out as a result of some directive.

Q. That is your own conclusion, but I want you to state what you heard from personnel connected with military organs of the ISHII Unit, on directives issued by those organs.

A. I have not heard anything on these matters from the personnel of the ISHII Unit.

Q. While you were serving in the ISHII Unit, who was the Commanding Officer of the Kwantung Army?

A. General UMEZU was the Commanding Officer of the Kwantung Army when I was serving in the ISHII Unit, but I have never seen him at the unit.

Q. Was the reason you did not see UMEZU because of the fact that he never visited the unit, or don't you know?

A. I know for a certainty that he did not visit the ISHII Unit.

Q. Who made the report to the Commander of Kwantung Army UMETSU about the condition of services of ISHII Unit?

A. I don't know about it.

Q. Which is the officer who came from Kwantung Army Headquarters to ISHII Unit?

A. Colonel TAMURA visited the unit, but I don't know whether he had any connection with the unit or not. I knew him to be on the staff of the Kwantung Army. Before I had been working with him in the North China Expeditionary Forces.

Q. For what purpose and how many times did Colonel TAMURA visit ISHII Unit?

A. I know TAMURA visited the unit once, but I don't know for what purpose.

Q. You met TAMURA at the unit and what did you report to him about your service?

A. At that time Colonel TAMURA was inspecting the experiments and the laboratory work at the ISHII Unit. I saw him but did not report anything to him. I do not clearly remember the details of my meeting with Colonel TAMURA now. /T.N. Japanese text is very ambiguous./

Q. Did Colonel TAMURA, the delegate from Kwantung Army, visit ISHII Unit before the Great Asia War or after the 8th of December, 1941?

A. I think it was before the war, because it was in the autumn (when he visited) and the war with America began in December of 1941.

Q. What do you know about the military plan of Kwantung Army--Secret name KWAN TOKU EN (Special Maneuvers of Kwantung Army)?

CONFIDENTIAL

CONFIDENTIAL

A. This is to realize a plan for deploying the mobilization of the Kwantung Army. I remember putting into force the KWAN TOKU EN (Special Maneuvers of Kwantung Army) which was closely related with the ISHII Unit. It was with the deployment of the Kwantung Army it became necessary to extend the work of epidemic prevention and epidemic prevention corps. Besides this our unit had to detail a number of officers, non-commissioned officers and other ranks. Two-thirds of our officers were detailed to make the cadre of epidemic prevention and water supplying and purification corps in newly organized military forces. I think this is to supply with bacteriological specialists the corps of the Kwantung Army. Also I remember receiving an order for the product of a large quantity of vaccine for epidemic prevention, but it was difficult to accomplish this order, because so far we have had no experience of making such a large quantity of vaccine.

Q. Would you mind telling me when and at what period these plans were worked out by ISHII Unit?

A. I have no precise memory when these were put into operation. But I think they began to work with KANTOKUEN (Special Maneuvers of Kwantung Army). It may have been in June 1941.

Q. Was it at the beginning of June 1941 or at the end of the same month namely after Germany began on her treacherous attack on Soviet Russia?

A. The whole scheme of KANTOKUEN (Special Maneuvers of Kwantung Army) was put in force after the outbreak of the Ruso-German war.

Q. Was the experiment to make the bacterial warfare as a weapon of war strengthened with the outbreak of the Ruso-German war?

A. As I have said before, by putting into operation of KANTOEN (Maneuvers of Kwantung Army), several men were offered from ISHII Unit. For this reason the work of our unit was somewhat delayed. Added to this there was a demand for increasing production of vaccine and preventive serum. This also affected our experiment.

Q. How many officers and specialists were serving with the ISHII Unit on June 1st, 1941?

A. I don't remember exactly but I think there were about 130 officers and specialists forming the cadre of the unit and about 2,000 non-commissioned officers and employees.

Q. About how many persons were sent from the ISHII Unit to serve in the KWAN-TOKU-EN /T.N. Special Maneuvers of the Kwantung Army/?

A. When the Kwantung Army plans were carried out, fifty officers and engineers and about one thousand non-commissioned officers and employees were left behind. But the unit was in difficulty in losing technicians.

Q. Then, when the Kwantung Army Special Maneuvers was being organized, were the technicians from the ISHII Unit used to strengthen the old unit and a new unit organized?

A. Originally there were no water supply and purification departments in the Army. This department was organized in order to carry out the Kwantung Army Special Maneuvers in various corps by Kwantung Army, and it was filled by technicians from the ISHII Unit.

Q. Were the previously established and newly organized units serving on some method of bacterial warfare? Did the leaders of these units receive instructions in this field?

A. At that time, since the unit was newly organized, it was not strictly a water supply and purification unit. There was no preparation for bacterial warfare, and preparations were not made, and no study was made on bacilli materials, for the purpose of carrying out bacterial warfare. There were no instructions and orders for the purpose of carrying out bacterial warfare.

Q. Besides the Production Department that you commanded, was there any supply depot or supply base where the manufacture and preparation of a large quantity of materials was conducted for the purpose of bacterial warfare as a means for waging war?

A. No supply base for supplying virus materials existed excepting the Vaccine Manufacture Research Institute. This institute was located in Dairen city, and directed by Dr. ANDŌ, M.D.. Although this institute was independent, it used to manufacture vaccine for the ISHII Unit at the request of the Kwantung Army.

Q. When did you visit the ANDŌ Institute?

A. I visited it in 1941. I do not remember well the month, but sometime around June, I presume.

Q. Did you have any acquaintances there? CONFIDENTIAL

A. I did not have any. Because of the close connection of my unit with the institute in manufacturing vaccines, I called on it for the settlement of some business matters.

Q. Had ANDŌ Unit been carrying out any secret business as a military organ?

A. This unit was by no means charged with any secret business in relation to the execution of bacterial warfare. This I know for certain.

Q. On what authority are you sure that the ANDŌ Unit was not charged with business in relation to the measures of bacterial warfare?

A. That firm belief of mine was brought about from my visit to and observation of this institute. Moreover, there had been no special requisitions from the ISHII Unit.

Q. Was any military bacteriologist in service in the ANDŌ Unit?

A. In order to maintain liaison between the ISHII Unit, ANDŌ Institute and Headquarters of Kwantung Army, an Army surgeon was in service. However, I do not remember his name.

Q. What other requisitions were made by the ISHII Unit to the ANTUNG Laboratory?

A. There was no requisition besides those for vaccine and serum.

Q. Then, if the ANTUNG Laboratory was not studying military problems, why was this liaison officer necessary?

A. I cannot completely answer this question. I presume that the liaison officer was placed there to requisition vaccine and serum.

Q. Did the ISHII Unit have any outlying station in Manchuria? If so, where was it and what was its function?

A. There were four detachments besides the ISHII Unit.

1. The chief of the LINKOW branch was Lieutenant Colonel YAMAGUCHI.

2. The chief of HAILAR branch was Major FUJII.

CONFIDENTIAL

CONFIDENTIAL

3. I do not remember the name of the HAILIN branch chief.

4. The chief of SUNWU branch was Major SASAKI.

These units had duties of water supply and purification, for the Kwantung Army forces stationed in their respective districts and did not make any study of bacteriological methods. Their activities were limited to the duties I have stated.

Q. In December, 1941, when Japan first entered into a state of war with the United States and Britain, did the ISHII Unit receive any special directive in concerning the preparations for bacterial materials necessary for military problems?

A. I have not heard anything about this matter.

Q. While you were serving as the head of Production Section, did you receive any directive concerning the preparation of bacterial materials necessary for military purposes, or detailed orders for the unit based on this?

A. I did not directly receive any orders on bacterial warfare from the Supreme Headquarters.

Q. Do you know whether Major General ISHII received similar instructions?

A. I don't know whether he received due instructions or orders from a military organ concerning preparations for bacterial warfare, but I remember a chat by him when he told me that he had received instructions from the Japanese General Staff Office about encouraging the study of fleas infested with pest bacilli which could be actually utilized for bacterial warfare.

Q. When did Major General ISHII make the talk?

A. The conversation with Major General ISHII was made at the time of my arrival at the unit.

Q. Was anyone present at the time of the conversation?

A. I remember that the chiefs of other sections were present, but I am not certain whether all of them were present or not.

Q. Had the conversation between Major General ISHII and you or other men under his command the nature of instructions or was it a mere private conversation?

CONFIDENTIAL

A. This conversation had the nature of suggestive instructions to decide the principle of the unit's research work for militaristic purposes. This meeting had the general nature of the unit's general business and there was some mention about pest bacilli infected fleas. I should like to make a correction here. That is, Major General ISHII who was present at this meeting called the attention of those present to the encouragement of the study of pest infected bodies. Concerning this, he told us about the instructions from the Japanese General Staff Office telling him to deal with the matter adequately. He had visited the General Staff Office before the meeting.

Q. Didn't ISHII say when he was summoned by the General Staff Headquarters of Japan, and with whom he had an interview?

A. Major General ISHII did not say when he went to the General Staff Headquarters and with whom he had a talk.

Q. Did Major General ISHII go to the General Staff Headquarters in Tokyo either before or after you were assigned to the unit?

A. I think this was before my assignment, that is, before March 1941.

Q. Was the order concerning the strengthening of the work of research on bacterial warfare by the General Staff Headquarters included in the immediately necessary work plan as the result of this meeting? Or, was this Major General ISHII's personal instruction made at his discretion?

A. No work plan for this policy was made, as the result of this meeting. This order only concerned units in charge of these researches.

Q. Then, by order of the Japanese General Staff Headquarters, what was done to strengthen the research work on bacterial warfare method, as a result of this meeting?

A. I don't know what was done for this purpose. I did not see anything such as the increase of workers or equipments, which would enable me to judge this.

Q. But you can state about the fact that the research work and experiments were strengthened after the meeting, can't you?

A. I cannot definitely say that they were especially strengthened.

CONFIDENTIAL

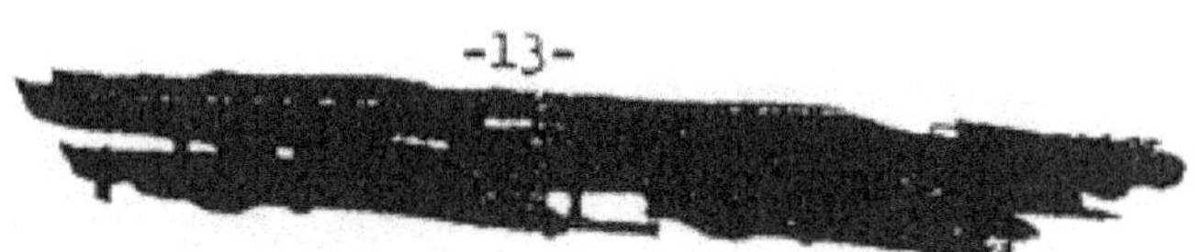

Q. From what date to what date was Major General ISHII the commander of the unit?

A. I don't know when he was appointed the unit commander, but he was the commander till August, 1942, and after which Major General KITANO took his place.

CONFIDENTIAL

Q. By what reason was this shift made?

A. I don't know the reason why.

Q. Was there any conversation about this among your men?

A. I don't remember what kind of conversation went on among my men about the shift of Major General ISHII with the new Unit Commander.

Q. Did the work of the unit become improved since it was placed under Major General KITANO?

A. With regard to the research regarding Sunwu (?) fever, special attention was paid to the research of the manner of its infection. The work regarding eruptive typhus did not undergo any fundamental change. Only the method of manufacturing the eruptive typhus vaccine invented by Major General KITANO was adopted. Generally speaking, the work was not improved so much, but in the days of ISHII we felt a shortage of personnel because of the enforcement of the "KANTOKUEN." /T.N. Special Maneuvers of the Kwantung Army/ In the days of KITANO, the replenishment of specialists made the work more active.

Q. What experiments were made in the days of KITANO?

A. I repeat that no practical experiment was made in connection with the preparation for bacterial warfare and attention was mainly directed toward the prevention of epidemics. The new Unit Commander encouraged work regarding prevention.

Major General, A.M.G. Kiyoshi KAWASHIMA

Investigator, Colonel Kudoriafutsuef /phonetic/

Captain Nikichin /phonetic/

CONFIDENTIAL

-14-

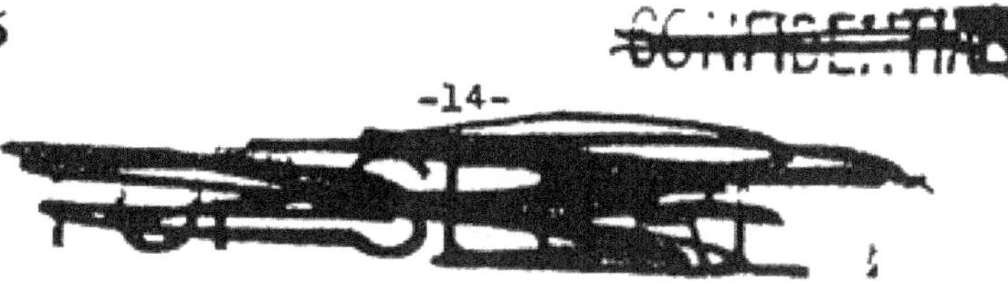

DOC. 9306

STATEMENT

of

Major KARASAWA Tomio CONFIDENTIAL

Q. You are being questioned as a witness. Therefore, if you make any false statement, you will be charged with strict responsibility. You are requested to understand this point well. In what language do you wish to make your statement?

A. I will promise to make correct statements, recognize the responsibility for false statements, and sign the attached certificate. I wish to make my statement in Japanese.

Q. Tell me about yourself briefly.

A. I am KARASAWA Tomio born at Toyosato-Mura, Ogata-Gun, Nagano Prefecture, on July 18, 1911. Besides Japanese, I can read German a little. My father is KARASAWA Shōtarō, a commoner, and was a schoolmaster of a village primary school. I am married and have two children.

Q. What is your educational standard?

A. I was graduated from the primary school in 1924, and from the UEDA Middle School in 1929. I entered the Tokyo Medical College the same year. Then, the next year, I became a student commissioned to the army medical department to become a medical officer of the Army; and in 1933, I graduated from the school and was appointed a surgeon 2d lieutenant. In August of the same year, I was sent to the Military Medical College as a second class student. In July of the next year, I returned and served as a unit surgeon till March, 1936. In April of that year, I was ordered to enter the Military Medical College as a company officer student and made a special study on the prevention of epidemics. While in school, in July, 1937, I was assigned to a mobilized force for the China Incident and went to North China. In April, 1939, I re-entered the school. At that time I was a captain. I graduated in September of the same year.

Q. When you were a unit surgeon did you serve as a bacteriologist?

A. From 1934 to March, 1936, I served as an ordinary unit surgeon. It was after April 1936 that I served as a bacteria specialist.

Q. Tell me about your work in the Army as a bacteria special ist.

A. As I have stated before, I started working as a bacteria specialist from April 1936. For twelve years since 1936 I studied the generals and particulars of bacteriology as a student in the classroom for science of epidemic prevention of the Military Medical School. The nature of the research work of that time was as a student. In July, 1937, I was assigned as a member of the First Field Quarantine Unit Epidemic Prevention organized in Tokyo. The Force commander was Lieutenant Colonel KIKUCHI (later major general) and after organization we went to Tentsin where we were put under the control of the expeditionary force in China. The aim of this sanitation force was the investigation of epidemics and the supervision of their prevention. In December 1937 we returned to the Headquarters in Peiping and there we engaged in the prevention and inspection of typhus, cholera and dysentery which broke out among troops in the various areas. From April 1938 to March of the next year I was engaged in the quarantine business in Tsingtao as the chief of the Tsingtao Branch of the North China Water Supply and Purification Department. From April 1939 to September I was ordered to re-enter the Army Medical College and studied. I graduated in September of the same year.

Q. Testify in detail whatever you know on the matter of preparation for bacteriological warfare in the Japanese Army.

A. I heard about preparations for bacteriological warfare in Japanese Army for the first time after assuming my post on December in 1939 as a member of the Quarantine Unit of the Kwan-tung Army. During my service with the North China Expeditionary Force I knew nothing about this matter. I had thought the duty of the quarantine organs of Japan and the Army was merely prevention of epidemics. Since the residences and villages in North China were in a very unsanitary condition and very suitable for the spreading of epidemics, the prevention of epidemics was a very important problem for the Japanese troops in China. After I was ordered to serve with the Quarantine Unit of the Kwan-tung Army, namely the ISHII Unit, by the War Ministry and assumed my post, I engaged in the culture of bacteria. Consequently I was reluctantly a witness for the preparation activities for bacteriological warfare. I definitely believed that Lieutenant General ISHII had done a great scientific experiment there regarding preparation for bacteriological warfare under the name of the Kwan-tung Army Quarantine and Water Supply Unit. This work was intensified year by year. Strict secrecy was maintained on all works in this field. Special instructions were

CONFIDENTIAL

-2-

given members of the unit to keep the secret, and the civilian army employees were compelled to hand in special written oaths. All the members of the unit were strictly forbidden from disclosing anything concerning their own work and special gendarmeries were assigned in order to prevent spying. Lieutenant General ISHII had attached special importance to the maintenance of secrecy. Accordingly, the ordinary scientific research society of the corps took charge of general subjects only,--especially those concerning epidemic prevention. The study of bacteriological warfare methods was conducted by individual students. As I had made a specialty of the cultivation of bacteria, I naturally acquired knowledge of the fundamental bacteriological warfare methods which had been studied by the corps.

Q. To what was the fundamental study of powerful bacteriological warfare methods directed?

A. From 1939 to 1944, the fundamental study of powerful bacteriological warfare methods was directed to the following:

1. Selection of proper, effective bacilli.
2. Methods of cultivation.
3. Carrier of bacilli.
4. Methods of large-scale bacillus scattering as one of the bacillus attack measures.
5. Problems in the mass production of bacilli.
6. Problems in preserving parent bacilli.
7. Preparation of materials for epidemic prevention.

The above-mentioned items are connected with one another, and, if perfected, will constitute all the preparatory measures for bacteriological warfare. On the basis of the facts and the work carried on in the corps under the leadership of Lieutenant General ISHII, with which I was well acquainted, I hereby certify on my responsibility that experiments were conducted in the ISHII Corps in which living human bodies were sacrificed in testing the above-mentioned items. However, I think this action, completely contrary to the most exceptional and super-human medical civility in the world, proves that the Army Central Headquarters and Lieutenant General ISHII were not satisfied with the usual bacteriological method of study although they had shown fanatical speed in this work. I participated in this work so I hate to say anything about it, but I will explain it because it will be a burden on my mind if I don't. I had thought at that time that the execution of this work would be explained as a duty of a Japanese officer, but now I shall explain it as a doctor who engages in the benevolent art. At the same time I wish to say that as a result of the entire research work of

our force (I had served till July 1944), it was decided that the execution of the above problems would be possible. This was proven by the outdoor experiments carried out a number of times under natural conditions. As mankind has no experience in bacteriological warfare, it cannot be definitely said that the settlement of these various problems would completely satisfy the demand of such warfare. However, the problem of culturing and spreading of great quantities of bacteria was, of course, decided.

Q. Before giving examples of your testimony tell us about the organization and the number of personnel of the ISHII Unit.

A. As far as I know, there were approximately 2,000 men in the unit including research workers and guards. The guards were picked from the loyal and efficient men among those being discharged from the Army. The organization of the unit was made up of eight departments, four subdepartments and one branch office.

(a) General Affairs Department - General affairs of the entire force.

Major General KAWASHIMA was first the chief of the department, then it was Major General NAKATOME. According to what I have heard he was killed in action in the south in about the spring of 1945. A guard unit and a military police unit were attached to the force.

(b) 1st Department (Research Department).

This department carried on bacteriological researches and it was divided into the respective sections to study the various kinds of bacteria. The chief of the department first was Major General KITAGAWA, Masataka, then it was Major General KIKUCHI, Hitoshi.

(c) 2d Department - Mainly engaged in outdoor experiments.

This Department consists of four Sections:

1) 1st Section re Aviation Section Chief Major MASUDA, Yoshio.

2) 2d Section, re Maintenance, Section Chief Major HIRAZAWA, Masanori.

3) 3d Section, re Culture of Fleas, Section Chief Eng. TANAKA, Hideo.

4) 4th Section, re Bombs, Section Chief Eng. YAMAGUCHI.

The Chief of the Department at first was Col. MURAKAMI, Takashi and later from 1943 Col. IKARI, Tsuneshige became the Chief.

(d) 3d Department. This Department alone as Water Supply and Purification Department did all the works as enumerated by the ISHII Unit. This Department consisted of four Sections:

1) 1st Section, re Water Examination, Section Chief--held additionally by the Department Chief.

2) 2d Section, re Manufacture of Water Filtering Pipes, Section Chief, Capt. SUZUKI.

3) 3d Section, re Construction and Repair, Section Chief, unknown.

4) 4th Section, re Transportation and Water Supply, Section Chief, Capt. NAKATA.

The Department Chief was Lieutenant Colonel EGUCHI, Toyokiyo.

(e) 4th Department. This Department consisted of two Sections and manufactured a large quantity of vaccine, serum and bacteria.

1) 1st Section engaged in the manufacturing vaccine and bacteria which was under my leadership. Capt. MITANI took charge of preservation. This Section was well equipped for the work.

2) 2d Section - Manufactured serum. This Section consisted of three Sub-Sections: 1st Sub-Section manufactured vaccine for eruptive typhus under Sub-Section Chief Major ARITA; 2d Sub-Section manufactured vaccine for tetanus and gas-gangrene under

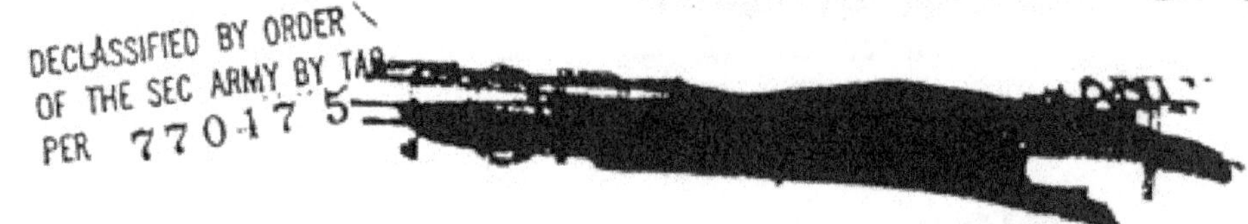

Sub-Section Chief Major UEMURA and 3d Sub-Section manufactured B.C.G. vaccine for tuberculosis under Sub-Section Chief FUTAGI, engineer.

The Department Chief was at first Colonel OHTA, Tohru. From about 1942 Major General KAWASHIMA took the post but was transferred to another post in March of 1943 and Colonel OHTA became the Department Chief again.

(f) Supply Department. This Department engaged in supplying units with necessary materials under Department Chief Major General OHTANI.

(g) Education Department. The duty of this department was to instruct officers, non-commissioned officers and soldiers of the medical corps Kwantung Army about popularizing sanitation and water supply, and it distributed the necessary printed matters. The Chief at first was Colonel SONODA, Tarō but later Lieutenant Colonel NISHI, Toshihide succeeded to him.

(h) Medical Department: Took charge of medical treatment for cases of special infectious diseases that broke out in the Army, and also for cases of typhoid fever and those who excreted paratyphoid bacteria. The capacity of the hospital was about one hundred patients. The Chief was Colonel NAGAYAMA, Tarō.

(i) Beside the aforesaid departments, there were four sub-departments attached to the headquarters.

(a) The First Sub-Department was at Linkow. The first chief was Lieutenant Colonel YAMAGUCHI, and later Major ARASE, Seiichi became the chief.

(b) The Second Sub-Department was at Mutanchiang, and the first chief was Lieutenant Colonel IKEI, and later Major ONOUE became the chief.

(c) The Third Sub-Department was at Sunwoo, and the first chief was Lieutenant Colonel SASAKI, and later Lieutenant Colonel NISHI, Toshihide became the chief.

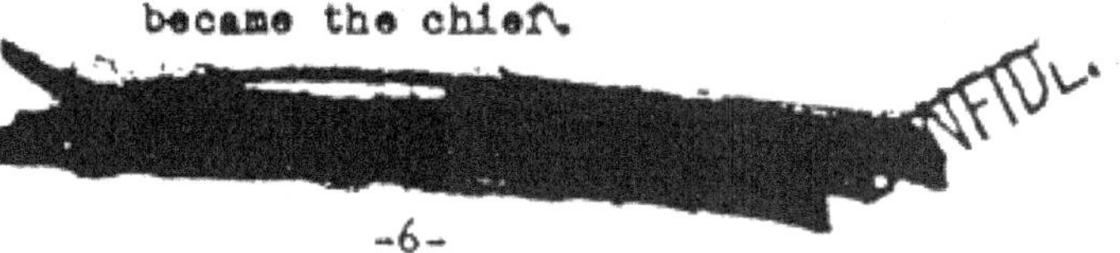

-6-

(d) The Fourth Sub-Department was at Hailar, and the first chief was Major FUJII, and later Major SHIMIDZU, Fujio became the chief.

The duty of these Sub-Departments was sanitation and water supply.

(j) The ANTA Examination Laboratory: Near the ANTA Station there was a well equipped examination laboratory which belonged to the Headquarters. The laboratory belonged directly to the Second Department, but I do not remember the names of the leaders of the laboratory.

(k) The Dairen Branch Office: This was formerly the Dairen Sanitation Research Laboratory belonging to the Manchurian Railway Co. When this building was taken over, several persons were dispatched from the headquarters to this laboratory. Dr. ANDŌ, Kōji was the chief of the Sanitation Research Laboratory. In order to manufacture vaccines and serums, the ISHII Unit received the laboratory from the Manchurian Railway Co. in 1938. The headquarters sent about ten persons here, whose leader was Major NAKAGURO.

Q. Please tell me in detail about the relations in being attached to the ISHII Unit.

A. The ISHII Unit was directly attached to the Commander of the Kwantung Army, and the Medical Department of the Kwantung Army had little relation with the ISHII Unit. The ISHII Unit made a report of the prevention of epidemics and water supply to the Commander of the Kwantung Army. Lieutenant General ISHII made a report of scientific researches, especially of the items relating to a bacteriological warfare directly to the section concerned of the General Staff and the Medical Bureau and at the same time to the Kwantung Army Headquarters. I have never heard personally whether the report was made or not of the items in regard to a bacteriological warfare by Lieutenant General ISHII to the Commander of the Kwantung Army nor whether the Kwantung Army Headquarters interferred in the special work pursued by the ISHII Unit. General UMEZU, Commander of the Kwantung Army (1943), and Lieutenant General KASAHARA, Chief of the Staff of the Kwantung Army, visited our unit once each, but I have no other knowledge of a similar kind. Concerning the prevention of epidemics and water supply, Colonel YAMAMOTO of the

Staff of the Kwantung Army was dispatched to the Section of Epidemics Prevention and Water Supply in the Kwantung Army to form a connection with them, but he was transferred to Inner Mongolia as military councillor about 1944.

Q. How can you prove your affirmation that the means of a bacteriological warfare was actually completed?

A. As I mentioned above, I had been engaged in the business of germ manufacturing at the ISHII Unit from 1939 to 1944. During that period I was convinced that the fundamental question in regard to a bacteriological warfare had been actually completed. As I promise in the above, I will tell what I think certain and I am ready to shoulder the whole responsibility for the testimony.

Q. We have no ground not to believe you. Please understand that we need the fact that will materially prove the affirmation made by you who assumes such responsibility.

A. Of course it is true. I will endeavour to state the whole fact which is in my memory. First of all, I'll tell you about the selection of powerful disease germs. The research in that line had been continuously conducted for a few years. As a result of the research it was found that the most powerful germs were disease germs, plague bacilli and anthrax germs. It goes without saying that the prevalence of eruptive typhus and bleeding fever is effective, but the voluminous culture of lice which carry germs of eruptive typhus was very difficult; we can expect it only in an insanitary life. The carriers of bleeding fever are wood-lice (?), and their artificial culture being very difficult, it naturally follows that it is difficult to cause the prevalence of the disease. Bacteria or lice could be infected with plague germs and the cleanliness of a body cannot prevent infection, so is it especially when at the front or marching. Anthrax bacteria could be sprinkled over domestic animals so as to destroy the whole store of animal food and the effect could also be influenced over a human body. On Bacterial Culture. The decision of this duty did not raise a question. We had only to follow what had been decided by bacteriologists. But there was one thing to be called in question: that is, the question of how to prevent miscellaneous bacteria (?) /T.N. One Chinese character is illegible/ from being generated, though we did succeed, to a certain extent, in preventing them. We added vitamin and some special elements to the culture base to strengthen the power of bacteria, but in vain, therefore we adopted a usual method in cultivating them. A research was conducted in the unit to decide the

reaction of an immunizing serum inoculation according to races. To accomplish this purpose, a small party from the 1st Section headed by Mr. UTSUMI, a technical expert, was dispatched to Inner Mongolia at the beginning of 1943 and Mr. MINATO, a technical expert, examined the blood of American prisoners of war who were near Mukden about the summer of 1943. About this MINATO told me that as a result of the study of blood which was started simultaneously with the experimental research of strengthening the power of bacteria, no distinction had been found in serum immunity between races. The result caused us to adopt a usual cultural method. Regarding the Process of Infection: The process of infection which aroused the special interest of the unit was the one that related to the active use of anthrax bacteria and gland pest germs; in other words the question of finding out with ease the process of infection in a human body evoked our interest. Man is less susceptible to anthrax than domestic animals. The experiment of infection through incised wounds was conducted in order to apply actively anthrax bacteria to human bodies as a fatal weapon. Major HINOFUJI (?) /T.N. phonetic/ of the 1st Section told me about the results of the experiment. He was the officer who had conducted the experiment. Major TAKAHASHI had similar practice with pest bacillus. Major TAKAHASHI told me that these experiments were confirmed by means of infection in wounds. The process of infection by plague bacillus and an anthrax bacillus which had a positive result made possible a decision on the problem of spraying these bacteria. Regarding methods of large-scale spraying as a means of bacteria attack: This is an important and decisive problem among troops, and at the same time is a problem to confirm a degree of preparation for the means of bacteria war. I certainly know that in this connection, experiments have, in succession, been made and anticipated results have been obtained. These experiments were commenced in about 1940. The first of them was a tentative and field experiment to test the resistance of bacteria to climate. The resistance of these bacteria was examined under various climatic conditions such as hot season, cold season, rainy season, etc., and also upon adherence to paper, cotton, gauze, dried weed, (anthrax bacillus), fodder, water, (typhoid bacillus, paratyphoid bacillus, cholera bacillus, and dysentery bacillus), etc. Later, the experiment of spraying of bacteria by airplanes was made. I know the following test: Between August and December 1940 Lieutenant General ISHII, accompanied by about 100 subordinates, left for HANG-CHOW, Central China, for a test. For experimental use, I manufactured 70 kilograms of typhoid bacilli and 50 kilograms of cholera bacilli, and 5 kilograms of fleas infested with plague bacilli were produced in the Second Section. The subject of the experiment was carrying out the spraying of bacteria by aircraft

in the zone occupied by the Chinese Army. After the experiment, a plague epidemic occurred and prevailed in NINGPO. Cholera bacilli and typhoid bacilli were not successful, but it showed that pest bacilli were efficacious.

Q. Where did you hear the above and by what means can you prove it?

A. Engineer MINATO, Major TAKAHASHI and Lieutenant Colonel IKARI who took part in the work told about the above. Besides this, I saw Chinese newspapers regarding the prevalence of plague gathered by the persons who went to China to inspect the results of the experiment. Those papers say that an epidemic of plague prevailed in the vicinity of NINGPO and its responsibility lies with the Japanese Army, because, prior to its outbreak, Japanese aircraft made low flights and sprayed something like fog which the papers called bacteria spray.

Q. Can you read Chinese?

A. As China and Japan both use the same characters, I can understand the meaning. Besides, I more or less studied Chinese characters while I was residing in China.

Q. Please continue with your testimony on the experiments.

A. Until June 1941 we conducted experiments on the resistance power of bacteria. Those experiments were mainly conducted in our research laboratory. In about 1940, experiments were made in the neighborhood of TAOLAICHAO with shells. By this experiment, it was confirmed that the anthrax bacilli can resist the heat generated at the time of the explosion of the shell and survive. In the winter of 1939, Lieutenant General ISHII told me that he had experimented on cholera and plague on the mounted bandits of Manchuria during 1933-1934 and discovered that plague was effective. He told me that we must proceed with our research along this line, but in regard to this, he did not give me any details of the result. In July, 1941, in conformity with the KWAN-TOKU-EN, /T.N. Abbreviation for "Special Activities Organization of the Kwantung Army"/ many specialists were transferred from the unit, and in the Kwantung Army, about new water supply and purification units were formed. In spite of that, the work of the unit did not lessen, but on the contrary, it increased. About July of 1942, Lieutenant General ISHII went to Central China again with about seventy subordinates with 130 kilograms of typhoid and plague bacilli cultivated by our section and necessary fleas infected with plague

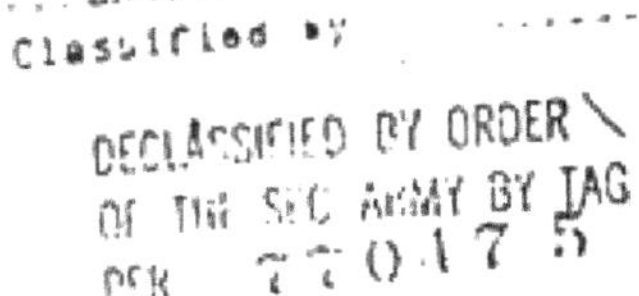

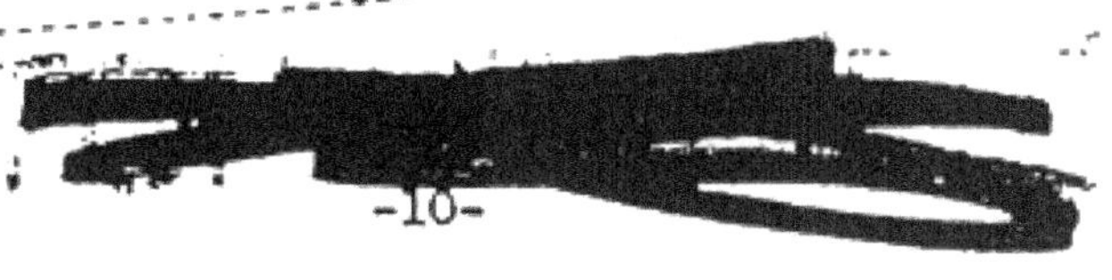

cultivated by the 2d Section. At that time the Japanese Army executed retreat operations and on the occasion of that retreat, Lieutenant General ISHII infected the vicinities of CHUHSIEN and YUSHAN with plague and typhoid bacilli. I do not know the details of that experiment. I must state that prior to this, in about 1940, experiments were conducted with cholera bacilli for the infection of reservoirs (wells) in the neighborhood of the unit. After the experiment, water was taken and tested. However, since the results was unsatisfactory it was decided to use typhoid and para-typhoid bacilli to infect well water. During 1943 and 1944, extensive experiments were conducted in the spreading of germs. The order in which those experiments were conducted is as follows. At first experiments were made with shells and bombs, and later, with human beings. To study the effective area of the bomb we made a test using pigment in winter and summer; and through this test the sphere of the effective area was decided. The shrapnel exploded in the air scattering fragments of glass over the sphere of the effective area. By this experiment the bomb proved its effectiveness. A bomb which exploded automatically was used to scatter fleas infected with plague. Then, in connection with this, an experiment to examine the effectiveness of bacilli was made on /by using/ living men at the ANTA Experimental Laboratory. In achieving this purpose, the headquarters of the gendarmerie sent to the laboratory Manchurians who had been sentenced to death. As far as I know, such experiments were made seven or eight times. Sometimes I witnessed these experiments and on other occasions I heard of them from Colonel IKARI, the director of the experiment, and Major HINOFUJI and Major TAKAHASHI, both of them in charge of the experiment. Aside from these I have had oral reports from other participants in the experiment. Several experiments particularly important regarding the infection of wounds were conducted at the ANTA Experimental Laboratory during the period from 1943 to 1944. The plague bacilli and anthrax bacilli were used for these experiments. The experiment on the human body at ANTA Experimental Laboratory was conducted in the following way: a bomb filled with bacteria was placed on the ground and about twenty Manchurians were tied to poles or made to sit down on the ground at a proper distance (that is, enough distance to prevent men's death) from the bomb, which were electrically exploded. By the bomb blast, which was caused by the explosion of the bomb, and its fragments, the plague bacilli and anthrax bacilli penetrated through the wound into human bodies. The wounded were kept in the laboratory until the sumptoms of the disease appeared and when they were taken ill, they were given medical treatment and their cases were studied, but most of them died in

agony. The experiment obtained results just as expected. The directors of this experiment were Lieutenant General ISHII and Colonel IKARI. Similar experiment was also made on animals. From the results of these researches the best method of scattering bacteria was decided. At the same time, continuously, study of the means with which bacteria could be scattered strategically over the areas behind the enemy front were also made. Thermoses and ampules were provided as the container of bacilli, but after various practices it was decided to use common bottles such as: cider, beer and medicine bottles. These containers attracted little attention and were also suitable for the preservation of bacilli. On mass production of bacteria materials: This matter was decided positively as in the above stated problem. When I was a student of the Army Medical College, I had a slight acquaintance with Lieutenant General ISHII's work in that field. At that time Lieutenant General ISHII had made an experimental installation, by which mass production of bacteria had been easily pushed on. But the defect of this installation was the growing of various germs. Afterward, about 1939, an instructor of the Army Medical College, Major FUJITA, succeeded to this installation and mechanized it. By this improvement the defect was eliminated to some degree. This fact has experimental significance. I saw myself the cultivation apparatus. Its capacity of producing bacteria was about 5 tons. The capacity of apparatus in our unit is above 30 tons. After I was transferred (1944), a new apparatus (its capacity was unknown to me) was due to arrive at the ISHII Unit from the homeland. I did not know about it, but I was informed about the arrival of the apparatus by Colonel ŌTA, Chief of the Department. In spring, 1944, Lieutenant General ISHII issued an order to each branch,

(Chief of the LINKOW Branch, Major ARASE,
Chief of the MUTANCHIANG Branch, Major OGAMI,
Chief of the SUNWU Branch, Lieutenant Colonel NISHI)

to establish an installation of bacteria mass production. So apparatuses, which were taken in charge by our unit, were sent to each branch, and I participated in this sending. I don't know whether the apparatus was installed at each branch. Until 1944 in our unit were piled up in large quantity necessary materials for cultivating bacteria, that is, vegetable gelatin, peptone and meat extracts, amounting to many tons. Of course, such stores of material for cultivation were not for experimentation, but for preparation for mass production of bacteria. On preservation of bacteria materials: Anthrax bacteria are able to be preserved for several years. It is difficult to conserve plague bacteria

for a long period. In the Japanese Army mass production of bacteria had been decided, and so it is of no particular significance to preserve bacteria for a long period. On securing the supply of materials for Prevention of Epidemics: According to orders from Kwantung Army Headquarters (at the end of July 1941), the KWAN-TOKU-EN was required to hasten the production of the anti-bubonic plague vaccine as well as other anti-epidemic injections in great quantities. Although I don't remember with certainty there were mentioned vaccine doses for one million men as well as a great quantity of serum. This request was fulfilled during a two months period. The whole army, freshly sent to Manchuria for strengthening the Kwantung Army, received all of those inoculations. To attain this purpose, the former South Manchurian Railway Research Laboratory, which was assigned under the ISHII Unit was used. (The chief Doctor of Medicine ANDO) This laboratory during a short period of time fulfilled the duties entrusted to it, and after that continued its functions in preparation of anti-epidemic materials. In the year 1942 or 1943, in order to attain knowledge of the efficacy of the inoculations prepared, Chinese prisoners of war stationed at TA-YUAN were inoculated with the preparations allotted for use by the Japanese Army. I heard this from the elder brother of Lieutenant General ISHII, Mr. ISHII, Takeo (The officer in charge of production). That is all I know about the fundamentals in the preparations for bacteriological warfare ever made by the Japanese Army.

Q. Do you know something of the German assistance in the preparations for bacteriological warfare by Japan?

A. I don't know the concrete facts about that. Although I know positively that from Germany there arrived all kinds of materials used, as sugars of various kinds, dyestuffs and microscopes. And I know, too, about exchange between Japan and Germany of scientific literature concerning bacteriology. It seems that, in view of the difficulty in getting the finished products from Germany, there were given orders to restrict the purchase to the smallest minimum needed.

Q. When and where were you made a prisoner of war?

A. I became a captive of the Soviet Army at Mukden 1st September 1945.

Q. Did you become a prisoner of war with the ISHII Unit, as a member of it?

A. No; this time, i.e. from 1944 by orders from the War Ministry I served in the 44th Army of the Kwantung Army. Major HITATARI took my place.

Q. Why did you, a member of Water Supply Unit, become a member of the 44th Army?

A. Although I do not know the true cause, in regard to this appointment, I have the following views. The War Ministry previously had a plan to distribute bacteriologists to each unit in the Kwantung Army. As far as I know, the ISHII Unit, prior to the surrender of the Kwantung Army, left Harbin on a special train in the direction of Korea. Where they withdrew, I do not know.

The above is correctly recorded. The Russian text was translated into Japanese for me by an interpreter.

KARASAWA, Tomio

Military Investigator	Peters /s/
Interpreter	Priachenko /s/
Secretary	Timofeeva /s/

Acknowledgment

I, Major KARASAWA, Tomio of the Japanese Army and presently a prisoner of war, knowing beforehand that I will be punished under the criminal code for false representations, do swear to tell the truth to the investigating organ of the U.S.S.R.

Major KARASAWA, Tomio /s/

Recipient of the Acknowledgment: Captain Peters /s/

(This translation is correct but it has not been approved for reproduction without further checking.)

-14-

9.39 17 Jul. 1947: Investigation Division Case 330, Motoji YAMAGUCHI, et al., MEMORANDUM TO: Chief, Investigation Division, Legal Section, GHQ, SCAP, FROM: Neal R. SMITH, 1st Lt. Inf, Investigating Officer, Legal Section, GHQ, SCAP

资料出处： National Archives of the United States, R331, B1434.

内容点评： 本资料为1947年7月17日盟军总司令部法务局调查科 Neal R. Smith 中尉提交法务局调查科主任编号330#细菌战有关调查备忘录，题目：调查科案件330，Motoji YAMAGUCHI, et al.。说明了调查的经过，从技术角度进行了调查，直到G–2接手。此案法律追究被中止，处于停滞状态，有待G–2授权方能完成调查；石井等被指控战争犯罪，违反陆战法规用俘虏做实验。

17 July 1947

MEMORANDUM TO: Chief, Investigation Division, Legal Section, GHQ, SCAP.

SUBJECT : Investigation Division Case 330, Motoji YAMAGUCHI, et al.

Investigation Division Case No. 330, Motoji YAMAGUCHI, et al, was originally predicated upon communications directed to General MacARTHUR in which individuals giving their names as Takeshi KINO and Takeshi NISHIMURA, respectively, made allegations stating human guinea pigs had been used for experimental purposes at Mokotan, Hsinking, China, and requested that certain individuals, former General Yujiro WAKAMATSU, former Captain Yasataro YOSAKA, former Captain Shiro YAMASHITA and former Major Motoji YAMAGUCHI, be arrested as War Criminalsuspects for their participation in said experiments.

KINO and NISHIMURA were interviewed and it was learned that the allegations directed at the men in the communication were of hearsay nature and that no definite evidence was in the possession of either of the two accusers.

The accused were summoned to the Tokyo office of the Legal Section, and interviewed in connection with the allegations set out by KINO and NISHIMURA. It was learned through the interview that the persons accused were former veterinarians connected with the KWANTUNG Army Quarantine Stables and the KWANTUNG Army Water Purification and Supply Unit of the KWANTUNG Army. It was further revealed that a General Shiro ISHII was the Commanding Officer of the Army Quarantine Stables. All witnesses categorically denied any or all participation in experimenting on human beings, but each stated that General ISHII had operated a secret laboratory in connection with the Water Purification and Supply Unit and was conducting research in Bacterial Warfare. Witnesses stated that they had heard of humans having been used for experimental purposes but they did not have firsthand evidence to warrant a direct accusation.

It was brought out in the interview that General Shiro ISHII was the person who had initiated Bacterial Warfare to the Japanese Military after returhingfrom Europe in 1936, and that he had received unlimited help from high ranking personages in Japan to carry on his research in Bacterial Warfare.

LEGAL SECTION
INV. DIV.
FILE NO. 330 SERIAL NO
INITIALS Rem

Several anonymous communications alleged that members of the Imperial Household, Prince CHICHIBU and Prince HIGASHIKUNI, were also connected with and financing ISHII's project in Bacterial Warfare. Also connected with the ISHII Unit and doing research in Bacterial Warfare were; the Tokyo Army Medical College in Tokyo, Tokyo Imperial University, Kyoto Imperial University, Nagoya Imperial University, Infectious Diseases Reserach Laboratory (Outline laboratory of the Tokyo Imperial University), Niigata Medical College, and unlimited private bacteriologists and bio-chemists throughout the Japanese Empire.

Records reveal that General Shiro ISHII was in charge of the Tokyo Army Medical College, on the faculty of the Tokyo Imperial University and in charge of the KWANTUNG Water Purification and Supply in Harbin, thus, giving him access to numerous laboratories for the pursuit of his work along with his laboratory in Harbin in which experimental work was conducted in comparative secrecy.

Investigation Division Case 330 was developed to the extent that G-2 took over the case to investigate from a technical standpoint on Bacterial Warfare and progress made at Bacterial Warfare by the Japanese Military. Legal action on the case was suspended. The case is now on a pending inactive status until such time that legal action will be authorized by G-2 and the investigation on atrocities can be completed, and the accused arraigned as war criminals for using Prisoners of War for experimental purposes in violation of the Rules of Land Warfare.

Neal R. Smith

Neal R. SMITH, 1st Lt. Inf.
Investigating Officer
Legal Section, GHQ, SCAP

9.40 30 Aug. 1947: FROM: WAR (WDGID), TO: CINCFE, NR: W 85347; 15 Sep. 1947: FROM: CINCEF, TO: WDGID, C-55493

资料出处：MacArthur Archives, US.

内容点评：本资料包括两份电文，第一份电文是1947年8月30日美国陆军部发送美远东军司令部电文No.W85347，提及已全面分析增田（知贞）提交的“A Compilation of BW Agents”，要求有关安达野外实验地的进一步情报，详细的地图、炭疽实验地点等。

第二份电文为1947年9月15日G-2执行长官上校C.S.Myers发送美国陆军部的电文No.C-55493：有关安达实验地的进一步情报，9月16日航空信函送往美国。

以上电文中提及的增田（知贞）的“A Compilation of BW Agents”及“有关安达实验地的进一步情报”航空信函，目前尚未发现。

GENERAL HEADQUARTERS, ~~U. S. ARMY FORCES~~, PACIFIC FAR EAST COMMAND
ADJUTANT GENERAL'S OFFICE
RADIO AND CABLE CENTER

JRS
rcv

INCOMING MESSAGE

~~TOP SECRET~~
~~Top Secret~~
PRIORITY

30 Aug 47

FROM : WAR (WDGID)

TO : CINCFE

NR : W 85347

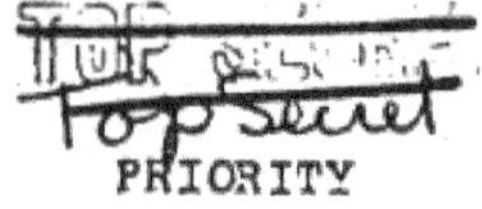

On Masuda report entitled "A Compilation of BW Agents," following additional information required for complete analysis:

1. Pin point location of Anda Station Experimental Field. Largest scale Japanese maps available keyed to Army Map Service L 541 desired.

2. Detailed sketch or sketches of Anda Station Experimental Field to include: (a) Natural and man-made land marks, (b) vegetation, (c) location of precise areas where all experiments with anthrax took place with relation to land marks. Areas contaminated with anthrax should be indicated. (d) Additional data, explanatory notes and descriptions which will aid in visualizing exact experimental setup. Forward report if possible prior to 17 Sept by air mail.

NO SIG

DECLASSIFIED PER Joslty of 20 Aug 75

ACTION: G-2

INFORMATION: COMMANDER IN CHIEF, CHIEF OF STAFF

MACARTHUR ARCHIVES

46576

PRIORITY
~~Top Secret~~

TOO: 292247/Z
MCN: 60520

"Paraphrase not required. Handle as TOP SECRET correspondence per para 51 i and 60 a (4) AR 380-5."

~~TOP SECRET~~

Handling and transmission of literal plain text of this message as correspondence of the same classification has been authorized by the War Department in accordance with the provisions of paragraphs 16-C, 18-E, 53-A, 53-D (1) (2) (3), and 60-A (1) (2) (3) (4), AR 380-5, 6 March 1946.

COPY NO. 2

"WC" 157

INDEXED BY MacARTHUR ARCHIVES

C-55493 replies

~~TOP SECRET~~ 00985

GB GAN/ WDD/ mjd
15 Sept 1947

CINCFE

151009

WDGSA (FOR WDGID)..................ROUTINE

PARKN C-55493 PAREN REURAD WILLIAM EIGHT FIVE THREE FOUR SEVEN REQUESTING ADDITIONAL INFORMATION ON ABLE NAN DOG ABLE STATION EXPERIMENTAL FIELD PD REPORT BEING DISPATCHED BY AIR MAIL ONE SIX SEPTEMBER FOUR SEVEN PD

OFFICIAL:

APPROVED BY:

R. M. LEVY
Colonel, AGD
Adjutant General

C. S. MYERS
Colonel G.S.C.
Executive Officer G-2

C-in-C copy
WDD/ mjd

COPIES TO:
AG
G-2 Return
C-in-C
C/S

MEMO FOR RECORD:
Radio W 85347 requested additional information on Anda Station Experimental Field to allow complete analysis of a previously submitted report "A Compilation of BW Agents". Instant radio advises WDGID that information requested is being forwarded.

WDD ( ) 26-4165

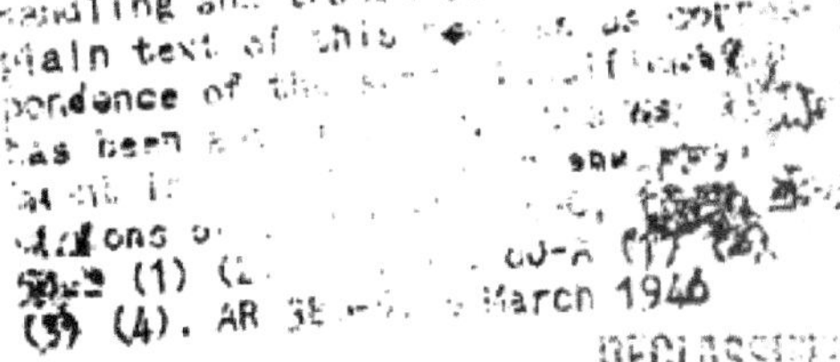

DECLASSIFIED PER JES ltr of 20 Aug 75

Reference Radio W 85347

Reference Radio W 85347

INFORMATION COPY

5

~~TOP SECRET~~

"WC" 158

9.41 5 Dec. 1947: Report by: Neal R. Smith, 1st Lt., Infantry: Harbin Experimental Laboratory

资料出处：National Archives of the United States, R331, B1434.

内容点评：本资料为 1947 年 12 月 5 日盟军总司令部法务局调查科 Neal R. Smith 中尉提交的报告，题目：哈尔滨实验室。Motoji YAMAGUCHI et al. 一案有关调查由盟军总司令部 G-2 实行，法务局调查科不再进行该案的调查。

Date: 5 December 1947

Report of Investigation Division, Legal Section, GHQ. SCAP.

Inv. Div. No. 2239

CRD No.

Report by: Neal R. Smith
1st Lt., Infantry

Title: Harbin Experimental Laboratory

Synopsis of facts:
Case being investigated by G-2 in connection with Motoji YAMAGUCHI, et al.

- C -

DETAILS:

At Tokyo:

No investigation is being conducted at the present time on the Harbin Experimental Laboratory due to the fact that it is being investigated by G-2, SCAP in connection with the case Motoji YAMAGUCHI, et al.

CLOSED

Distribution:
1 Prosecution
1 CRD
1 Inv Div (File #2239)
1 Inv Div (File #2238)

Do not write in this space.

LEGAL SECTION
INV. DIV.
FILE NO. 2239 SERIAL NO.
INITIALS Ach

10　苏联的追究与美国的对策

10.1 9 Jan. 1947: From: IPS, GHQ, SCAP, Inv. Div. To: G-2 Inv. Div. : Request for Interrogations,Memorandum for Major-Genderal Willoughby, Chief of G-2, GHQ SCAP, THROUGH: Investigation Division of the I.P.S., FROM: Major-General Vasiliev, Associate Procecutor for the USSR at the IMTFE; 17 Jan. 1947: To: Assistant Chief of Staff, G-2: Bacteriological Warfare Experiments by Japanese, From: Robert P.McQuail, Lt. Col. Inf.

资料出处：National Archives of the United States, RG331.

内容点评：本资料为为两份文件。1947 年 1 月 9 日，盟军占领军司令部 McQuail 中校提交苏联助理检察官 Vasiliev 少将通过国际检察局调查部门转交的予 G-2 长官 Willoughby 少将备忘录：要求讯问关东军 731 部队人员石井、菊池、大田，有证据证明关东军有实施细菌战的准备；讯问目的是向法庭提交有关关东军细菌战的证据材料。1947 年 1 月 15 日，Robert P. McQuail 中校提交 G-2 副长官报告，题目：日本人的细菌战实验。有关 1 月 15 日，G-2 安排 McQuail 中校于苏联检察官一行，就 1 月 7 日苏联检方通过国际检察局向 G-2 提出的要求对细菌战，讯问石井等人的会谈内容。

GENERAL HEADQUARTERS
SUPREME COMMANDER FOR THE ALLIED POWERS

C O P Y

CHECK SHEET TG/EPM/hk

(Do not remove from attached sheets)

CONFIDENTIAL

File No.: Subject: Request for Interrogations

Note No.:	
	From: IPS, GHQ, SCAP To: G-2 Date: 9 Jan 47 Inv. Div.
1	1. Pursuant to conversation with Colonel McQuail, attached herewith is memorandum from Russian Division, IPS to G-2 through Investigation Division, which is self-explanatory. Request this Section be advised of appropriate action regarding memorandum. 1 Incl. (Memo fr USSR, IMTFE) T. G. Ex.O.
	CERTIFIED TRUE COPY: Robert P. McQuail Robert P. McQuail Lt. Col. Inf.

DECLASSIFIED
E.O. 11652, Sec. 3(E) and 5(D) or (E)
OASD Ltr, April 4, 1978
By WLewis Date 9/8/78

GENERAL HEADQUARTERS
SUPREME COMMANDER FOR THE ALLIED POWERS

CHECK SHEET TO/EPM/hk

(Do not remove from attached sheets)

File No.: Subject: Request for Interrogations

Note No.:	From: IPS, GHQ, SCAP Inv. Div. To: G-2 Date: 9 Jan 47
1.	1. Pursuant to conversation with Colonel McQuail, attached herewith is memorandum from Russian Division, IPS to G-2 through Investigation Division, which is self-explanatory. Request this Section be advised of appropriate action regarding memorandum. 1 Incl. (Memo fr USSR, IMTFE) T. G. Ex.O.
	CERTIFIED TRUE COPY: Robert P. McQuail Robert P. McQuail Lt. Col. Inf.

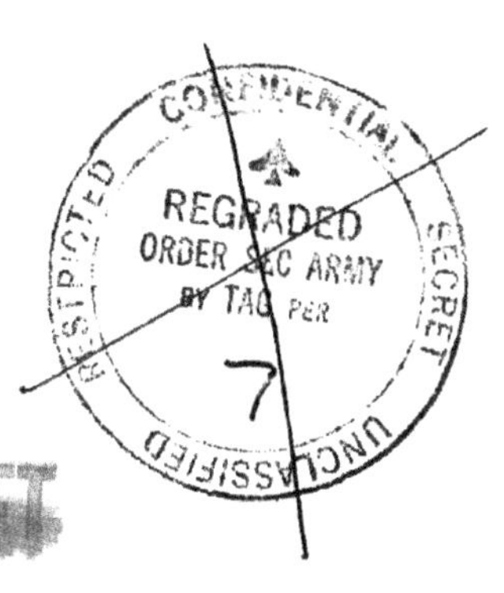

DECLASSIFIED
E.O. 11652, Sec. 3(E) and 5(D) or (E)
OASD Hr, April 4,1978
By WLewis Date 9/8/78

TOP SECRET

CONFIDENTIAL

MEMORANDUM

Major-General Willoughby,
Chief of G-2,
GHQ SCAP

~~CONFIDENTIAL~~

THROUGH: Investigation Division of the I.P.S.

FROM : Major-General Vasiliev,
Associate Prosecutor for the USSR at the International
Military Tribunal for the Far East.

At the disposal of the Soviet Division of the International Prosecution Section there are materials showing the preparations of the Kwantung Army for bacteriological warfare.

To present these materials as evidence to the Military Tribunal it is necessary to conduct a number of supplementary interrogations of persons who worked previously in the Anti-epidemic group (Manshu) N 731 of the Kwantung Army.

These persons are:

1. Major-General of Medical Corps Ishii, commander of the Anti-epidemic group N 731.

2. Colonel Kikuchi, Hitoshi, Chief of the 1st Section of the Anti-epidemic group N 731.

3. Colonel Ota, Chief of the 4th Section (and prior to the chief of the 2nd Section) of the Anti-epidemic group N 731.

These persons are to testify about research work on bacterias carried out by them for the purpose of using bacteria in warfare and also about the cases of mass murders of people as the result of those experiments. I believe that it would be expedient to take preliminary measures preventing the spreading of information concerning this investigation before the investigation is completed and the materials are presented

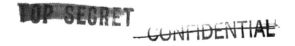

DECLASSIFIED
E.O. 11652, Sec. 3(E) and 5(D) or (E)
OASD Ltr, April 4, 1978
By W. Lewis Date 9/8/78

TOP SECRET ~~CONFIDENTIAL~~

TOP SECRET

to the Tribunal, i.e., to take from these witnesses certificates to the effect that they promise not to tell anybody about the investigation of this matter and to conduct the preliminary interrogations not in the premises of the War Ministry Building.

In connection with the above-said I ask you to render us assistance through the I.P.S. in conducting the interrogation of the said persons on January 13, 1947 in premises specially assigned for this purpose and after taking from them certificates containing promise not to speak about the investigation.

Besides that I request you to provide, the Soviet Division of the I.P.S. with certificates of the whereabouts of Lt. Colonel Murakami, Takashi, former Chief of the 2nd Section of the Anti-epidemic group N731, and Nakatome, Kinzo, former Chief of the General Affairs Section of the same group. These certificates are needed for the purpose of submitting them to the Tribunal.

Major-General V Vasiliev,
Associate Prosecutor for
the USSR,
At the IMTFE.

CERTIFIED TRUE COPY:

Robert P. McQuail
Robert P. McQuail
Lt. Col. Inf.

TOP SECRET

CONFIDENTIAL

GENERAL HEADQUARTERS
FAR EAST COMMAND
Military Intelligence Section, General Staff

17 January 1947

SUBJECT: Bacteriological Warfare Experiments by Japanese

TO: Assistant Chief of Staff, G-2
Far East Command

1. Following statement, obtained from Col. SMIRNOV, USSR, member of Russian Prosecution Section, Tokyo, is reported. It is recommended that this information be forwarded by Targets Branch, War Department Intelligence Division, to War Department as supplementary report on Biological Warfare.

2. Russian interest in above subject came to attention of G-2 Section, 7 Jan 1947, when Mr. WAIDORF of International Prosecution Section stated that he was approached by Russians with request to provide Japanese for interrogation on BW. IPS was advised by G-2 to have Russians submit written memorandum setting forth reason for request, which resulted in attached memorandum (Incl. 1). Russians were then advised that Lt. Col. McQUAIL would confer with them on subject, and meeting was arranged for 0900, 15 Jan 47, in War Ministry Building, Tokyo.

3. Following were present:

Lt. Col. R. P. McQUAIL	G-2, FEC
Major O. V. KELLER	OC Chem O
Mr. A. J. JAVROTSKY	G-2, FEC, Interpreter
Mr. D. L. WALDORF	IPS, SCAP
Col. LEON N. SMIRNOV	USSR Officer
Major NIKALOI A. BAZENKO	USSR Officer
Mr. ALEX. N. KUNIV	USSR Interpreter

4. Lt. Col. MCQUAIL requested Col. SMIRNOV to explain what material or information he had which led USSR to want to interrogate on subject. Col. SMIRNOV replied through Mr. KUNIV as follows:

"Shortly after cessation of hostilities, General KAWASHIMA, 4th Section, Manchu 731, and his assistant, Major KURASABA were interrogated. (Spelling of these names is by sound. It was thought best not to request exact spelling or indicate interest in these officers. KAWASHIMA is possibly KOYOSHI KAWASHIMA, Col., Medical, who was in charge of 4th Section during early years of war. KURASABA cannot be identified.) They testified as follows. The Japanese carried out

CONFIDENTIAL

TOP SECRET

20

Memo to AC of S, G-2 15 Jan 47

extensive experiments in Biological Warfare at PINGFAN Laboratory and field experiments at ANOA, using Manchurians and Chinese bandits as material. Total of 2,000 died as result of experiments. Facilities for producing typhus-carrying fleas in quantity, and a two-conveyor system of producing cholera and typhus cultures in quantity existed at PINGFAN. Forty-five kilograms of fleas were produced in three months. The one conveyor in operation produced 140 kilograms of cholera culture or 200 kilograms of typhus culture in a single month.

"Typhus-carrying fleas were produced in following manner. White (?) rats infected with typhus were placed in 4,500 special cans and infested with fleas. After short time, special light in can was turned on and infected fleas were thereby stimulated to leave rat and enter a detachable flea trap. Fleas were then collected in quantity. Flea bites were infectious for seven hours after fleas bit infected rats.

"At PINGFAN, humans were kept in cells and infected in various ways to provide data as to effectiveness of various cultures produced in laboratory. Humans were also transported to ANOA in closed vans, tied to stakes, and exposed to various methods of spreading bacteria in the field, principally aerial bombs and sprays. Victims were returned to PINGFAN for observation.

"Above information was so preposterous to Russians that Russian BW experts were called in. They reinterrogated, checked ruins of PINGFAN and confirmed information. (PINGFAN was destroyed by Japanese. Lt. Col. McQUAIL asked following question to determine how well job was done. Q. The Colonel said "ruins of PINGFAN". Was it bombed or destroyed as a result of fighting?)

"PINGFAN was completely destroyed by Japanese who attempted to cover up all evidence. All documents were also destroyed, and our experts did not even bother to photograph ruins, so thorough was damage.

"Japanese committed a horrible crime killing 2,000 Manchurians and Chinese, and General ISHII, Col. KIKUCHI, and Col. OTA are involved. (Names of Japanese Russians want to interrogate). Also quantity production of fleas and bacteria is very important. At Nuerenberg trials, a German expert witness said spreading typhus by fleas was considered best method of BW. Japanese seem to have this technique. It would be of value to USA as well as USSR to get this information. It is requested that these three Japanese be interrogated without being told they are liable to be war criminals, and that they be made to swear not to tell anyone about interrogation."

5. The information obtained above corresponds with knowledge previously in possession of United States, or suspected by previous

~~TOP SECRET~~

Memo to AC of S, G-2 15 Jan 47

investigators. Figures on production are new. Experiments on humans was suspected. Information that PINGFAN was completely destroyed with documents confirms previous information. See SECRET Reports:

a. Volume V, Biological Warfare, Report on Scientific Intelligence in Japan, September and October 1945

b. Report on Japanese Biological Warfare (BW) Activities, 31 May 1946, ASF, Camp Detnick, Maryland

/s/ Robert P. McQuail
ROBERT P. McQUAIL
Lt Col Inf

1 Incl:
Memo, Gen Yasiliev

DISTRIBUTION:
1 - WDID, Targets Branch
1 - Chief Chemical Officer
1 - Chief Surgeon
1 - ~~Chief-of-Staff~~ AG
1 - G-2 file
3 - WDI Div file

CERTIFIED TRUE COPY:

Robert P. McQuail
ROBERT P. McQUAIL
Lt Col Inf

10.2 7 Feb. 1947: MEMORANDUM FOR RECORD: Russian Request to Interrogate Japanese on Bacteriological Warfare, TO: Chief of Staff, FROM: C. A. W.

资料出处： National Archives of the United States, R153, E154.

内容点评： 本资料为 1947 年 2 月 7 日盟军总司令部 G-2 长官 C.A.W.（Charles A. Willoughby）提交总参谋长的备忘录，题目：关于苏联要求讯问日本人有关细菌战。

TOP SECRET

CONFIDENTIAL

GENERAL HEADQUARTERS
UNITED STATES ARMY FORCES, PACIFIC
MILITARY INTELLIGENCE SECTION, GENERAL STAFF

APO 500
7 Feb 1947

MEMORANDUM FOR RECORD

SUBJECT : Russian Request to Interrogate Japanese on Bacteriological Warfare
TO : Chief of Staff

1. Prosecutor, USSR, IMTFE, requested permission to interrogate former Japanese Officers on Bacteriological Warfare (Tab A).

2. Two of the Japanese whom the Soviet prosecutor wishes to interrogate have been interrogated thoroughly by U.S. Authorities. Records of the interrogations have been classified as Secret and Top Secret and copies dispatched to the War Department.

3. Russians stated that information is needed to substantiate charges of War Criminals they wish to initiate in supplementary trials at IMTFE which they anticipate are sure to be approved by US authorities, but they also indicate interest in suspected Japanese mass productions of typhus, cholera, and typhus-bearing fleas (Tab B). Based on information obtained from Russians it is not likely that they will obtain information not already known to United States nor that they will confirm information they say is in their possession.

4. If granted permission for United States monitored and arranged interrogations, United States may learn some additional information concerning Japanese B.W. activities and gain some information from analysis of Russian line of questioning.

5. WD Radio WX 95147 (Tab C) establishes policy for international coordination and exchange of intelligence with allied nations. The USSR request falls under par 3E which provides that intelligence which "might jeopardize the security of the US; —— or derogate from US advantage in the field —— should not be provided without specific reference to and authorization of the Joint Chiefs of Staff ——" and par 5 which states that "intelligence relating to research and development in field of science and war material should not be disclosed to nations other than British Commonwealth (less Eire) without specific reference to and authorization of the Joint Chiefs of Staff."

DECLASSIFIED BY ORDER OF THE SEC ARMY BY TAG PER 770175

CONFIDENTIAL
TOP SECRET

TOP SECRET

CONFIDENTIAL

6. Recommend dispatch of radio to War Department to comply with par 2E and 5 of WD radio WC 95147.

C. A. W.

3 Incl:
1 - Tab A, Memo, USSR,
2 - Tab B, Rpt, 17 Jan 47, USSR interest in BW
3 - Tab C, WD Radio WX 95147

Concurrences:
Cml O
CS ______
SJTA
OCS ______
IPS ______

DECLASSIFIED BY ORDER
OF THE SEC ARMY BY TAG
PER 770475

CONFIDENTIAL

TOP SECRET

C O P Y

GENERAL HEADQUARTERS
UNITED STATES ARMY FORCES, PACIFIC

OUTGOING MESSAGE

00376
GB/CAW/RPM/arc
Date: 7 Feb 1947

TOP SECRET

TOP SECRET

CONFIDENTIAL

FROM: CINCFE

TO : WDCSA

Prosecutor for USSR at IMTFE requests permission to interrogate former Japanese General ISHII, Colonel KIKUCHI, and Colonel OTA, all formerly connected with Bacteriological Warfare research and experiments at PINGFAN Laboratory near HARBIN, MANCHURIA. Request based on information alleged to have been obtained from unidentified prisoners of war who stated that experiments authorized and conducted by above three Japanese resulted in deaths of 2000 Chinese and Manchurians. Russians present request on their assumption that supplementary war crimes trials will be authorized by United States, but also admit interest in mass production of typhus and cholera bacteria and typhus bearing fleas at PINGFAN said to have been described by prisoners of war to them. Opinion here that Russians not likely to obtain information from Japanese not already known to United States and that United States might get some additional information from Russian line of questioning in monitored interrogations. In compliance with paragraphs 3E and 5 of URAD WX 95147, 24 July 1946 request decision as to whether to permit USSR to conduct these interrogations.

Handling and transmission of literal plain text of this message as correspondence of the same classification has been authorized by the War Department in accordance with the provisions of paragraphs 16-C, 18-E, 53-A, 53-D (1) (2) (3), and 60-A (1) (2) (3) (4), AR 380-5, 6 March 1946

APPROVED
DEPUTY C/S, SCAP
/s/ 8 Feb 1947
INITIALS /s/

TOP SECRET

TOP SECRET

AFPAC AGO FORM No. 36
(23 July 1945)

THE MAKING OF AN EXACT
COPY OF THIS MESSAGE IS FORBIDDEN

CONFIDENTIAL

10.3 11 Feb. 1947: SWNCC 351/D: STATE-WAR-NAVY COORDINATING COMMITTEE DIRECTIVE: REQUEST OF RUSSIAN PROSECUTOR FOR PERMISSION TO INTERROGATE CERTAIN JAPANPESE, Reference: SWNCC 216/1

资料出处：National Archives of the United States, R165, E468, B428.

内容点评：本资料为1947年2月11日美国国务院—陆军部—海军部三部协调委员会（SWNCC）秘书处发布的三部协调委员会指示，题目：关于苏联检察官要求准许讯问某些日本人；附东京美远东军司令部发送美军总参谋长电文C-69946号。

12 FEB 1947

014 Japan (13 Apr 44) Sec II B

TOP SECRET

TOP SECRET

COPY NO. 20

SWNCC 351/D

11 February 1947

Pages 1 - 2, incl.

STATE-WAR-NAVY COORDINATING COMMITTEE

DIRECTIVE

REQUEST OF RUSSIAN PROSECUTOR FOR PERMISSION TO INTERROGATE CERTAIN JAPANESE

Reference: SWNCC 216/1

Note by the Secretaries

The enclosure, a message from the Commander-in-Chief, Far East, forwarded by the Joint Chiefs of Staff with a request for the basis of a reply, is referred to the State-War-Navy Coordinating Subcommittee for the Far East for preparation of a draft reply.

H. W. MOSELEY

W. A. SCHULGEN

V. L. LOWRANCE

Secretariat

Carded
Indexed

TOP SECRET

SWNCC 351/D

TOP SECRET

TOP SECRET

ENCLOSURE

From: CINCFE Tokyo Japan

To: War Department for WDCSA

Nr: C-69946 10 February 1947

Prosecutor for USSR at IMTFE requests permission to interrogate former Japanese General Ishii, Colonel Kikughi, and Colonel Ota, all formerly connected with bacteriological warfare research and experiments at Pingfan laboratory near Harbin, Manchuria. Request based on information alleged to have been obtained from unidentified prisoners of war who stated that experiments authorized and conducted by above 3 Japanese resulted in deaths of 2,000 Chinese and Manchurians. Russians present request on their assumption that supplementary war crimes trials will be authorized by United States, but also admit interest in mass production of typhus and cholera bacteria and typhus bearing fleas at Pingfan said to have been described by prisoners of war to them.

Opinion here that Russians not likely to obtain information from Japanese not already known to United States and that United States might get some additional information from Russian line of questioning in monitored interrogations. In compliance with paragraphs 3 E and 5 of urad WX 95147, 24 July 1946 (Appendix) request decision as to whether to permit USSR to conduct these interrogations.

End.

CM-IN 1604 (10 Feb 47)

S E C R E T

A P P E N D I X

EXCERPTS FROM WARX 95147 (July 1946)

. . . .

3. . . . .

"e. Intelligence which, in the opinion of the American commander responsible for action on and coordination of requests, might jeopardize the security of the United States; prejudice United States relations with a foreign government with which the United States maintains friendly relations; or derogate from United States advantages in the field of scientific research and development, should not be provided without specific reference to and authorization of the Joint Chiefs of Staff and, where appropriate, by the State-War-Navy Coordinating Committee."

. . . .

"Par 5, Regarding paragraph 3e above, under present circumstances, Intelligence relating to research and development in field of science and war material should not be disclosed to nations other than the British Commonwealth (omitting Eire) without specific reference to and authorization of the Joint Chiefs of Staff."

. . . .

10.4　21 Feb. 1947: C-50333, Urgent, TO: WDSCA, FROM: CINCFE, C.S. Myers, Col., GSC, Executive Officer G-2

资料出处： National Archives of the United States, R153, E154.

内容点评： 本资料为 1947 年 2 月 21 日美远东军司令部 G-2 执行长官 C. S. Myers 上校发送美陆军部 WDSCA 紧急电文，要求尽快回复电文 C-69946，就苏联方面提出的讯问原日军细菌战部队人员的要求迅速给予答复。苏联每天提出要求答复。

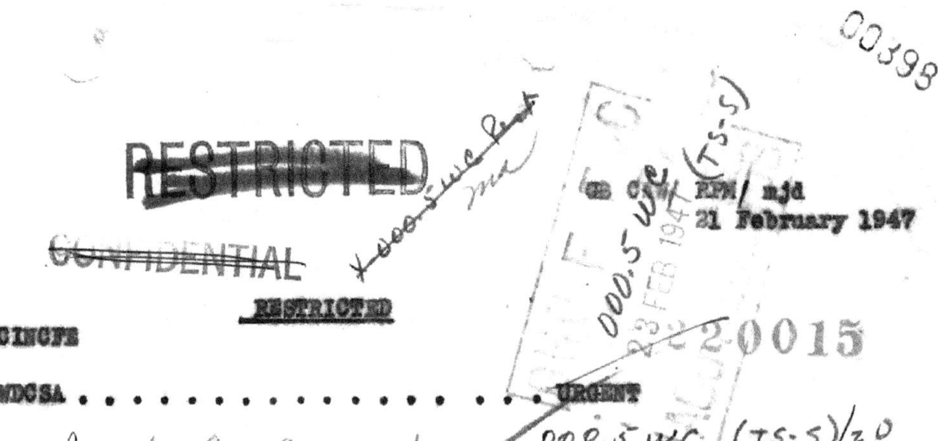

RESTRICTED

~~CONFIDENTIAL~~

GB C... RPM/ mjd
21 February 1947

RESTRICTED

CINCFE

WDCSA . . . . URGENT

REOURAD CHARLIE SIX NINE NINE FOUR SIX CMA THIRTEEN FEBRUARY NINETEEN FORTY SEVEN REQUEST REPLY SOONEST PD

C-50333

OFFICIAL:

JOHN B. COOLEY
Colonel, AGD
Adjutant General

APPROVED BY:

C. S. MYERS,
Colonel, G S C
Deputy & Executive Officer G-2

A. G.
RPM/ mjd

COPIES TO:

5 - A.G.
1 - G-2 file
1 - G-2 return
1 - IPS

MEMO FOR RECORD:

1. C-69946, 13 Feb. 1947, requests decision from WD on allowing USSR Prosecution to interrogate certain Japanese. USSR is inquiring daily for decision. Instant radio is urgent tracer to WD. Immediate answer to USSR is considered desirable from an intelligence standpoint.

RPM 25038

Handling ... literal plain text of this message as correspondence of the same classification has been authorized by the War Department in accordance with the provisions of paragraphs 16-C, 18-E, 53-A, 53-D (1) (2) (3), and 60-A (1) (2) (3) (4), AR 380-5, 6 March 1946

DECLASSIFIED
E.O. 11652, Sec. 3(E) and 5(D) or (E)
OASD Ltr, April 4, 1978
By WLewis Date 9/8/78

Reference Radio C69946.

RESTRICTED

RESTRICTED

~~CONFIDENTIAL~~

A. G. FILE

10.5 26 Feb. 1947: SFE 188: STATE-WAR-NAVY COORDINATING SUBCOMMITTEE FOR THE FAR EAST, REQUEST OF RUSSIAN PROSECUTOR FOR PERMISSION TO INTERROGATE CERTAIN JAPANESE, Reference: a. SWNCC 351/D; b. CM-IN-1604 (22 Feb); SFE 188 BRIEF: REQUEST OF RUSSIAN PROSECUTOR FOR PERMISSION TO INTERROGATE CERTAIN JAPANESE

资料出处：National Archives of the United States, R165, E468, B428.

内容点评：本资料为1947年2月26日，美国国务院—陆军部—海军部三部协调远东小委员会秘书处美海军中校J.B.Cresap传送小委员会讨论提交三部协调委员会的报告提议，有关苏联检察官要求准许讯问日本人。附：简报SFE188。

TOP SECRET

COPY NO. 4

SFE 188

26 February 1947

Pages 1 to 3

ACTION ASSIGNED TO War Crimes Mr Hubbert Brief

STATE-WAR-NAVY COORDINATING SUBCOMMITTEE FOR THE FAR EAST

REQUEST OF RUSSIAN PROSECUTOR FOR PERMISSION TO INTERROGATE CERTAIN JAPANESE

References: a. SWNCC 351/D
b. CM-IN-1604 (22 Feb)

Note by the Secretary

1. The enclosure, a proposed report to the SWNCC by the Working Group, is circulated for consideration by the Subcommittee.

2. In view of reference b, the Joint Chiefs of Staff have requested the State-War-Navy Coordinating Committee to consider this paper as a matter of urgency.

J. B. Cresap
Commander, USN
Secretary

File SWNCC 351 Series
Looks OK.

TOP SECRET

SFE 188

CONFIDENTIAL

B R I E F

REQUEST OF RUSSIAN PROSECUTOR FOR PERMISSION TO INTERROGATE CERTAIN JAPANESE

PURPOSE OF PAPER:

1. To instruct SCAP as to the request of the Russian Prosecutor at Tokyo to interrogate certain Japanese concerning B. W.

BACKGROUND

2. In accordance with JCS WX 95147, 24 July 1946, SCAP has referred to JCS a request of the Soviet Prosecutor in Tokyo to interview General Ishi and Colonels Kikuchi and Ota re biological warfare. The request is based on the theory that there will be a second international trial at Tokyo in which the Russians will participate. The alleged offenses were committed against the Japanese by the Chinese in Manchuria.

DISCUSSION:

3. The War Department expert on B.W. states that General Ishi is the leading Japanese expert, and that we are fully informed as to his knowledge and experiments in the fields of B.W., and that he believes that the Russians cannot gain any information which they do not already possess in this field. On the other hand, it would be helpful to the United States to have the opportunity to learn from Russian questioning of Japanese the extent of Russian knowledge in this field. Since Colonels Kikuchi and Ota were never questioned by United States experts, there is a very remote chance they might have some technical knowledge not possessed by General Ishi. It appears advantageous to the United States to permit the interrogation, but in order to be sure that no surprises occur, we should first interrogate Kikuchi and Ota ourselves.

4. Apparently the request was made on the theory that there will be a second international military trial at Tokyo in which the Russians will participate. It is established War Department policy that there shall be no more international trials. For this reason it seems undesirable to permit the request to be granted as a War Crimes matter.

RECOMMENDATION:

5. It is recommended that SFE 188 be approved.

10.6 27 Feb. 1947: MEMORANDUM FOR RECORD: Conversation between Col. Bethune, Gen. Vassiliev and Col. Pash

资料出处： National Archives of the United States, R153, E154.

内容点评： 本资料为 1947 年 2 月 27 日美太平洋军司令部参谋部军事情报局备忘录，主题为 Bethune 上校与 Vas(s)iliev 将军、Pash 上校谈话。苏联检察官 Vas(s)iliev 将军向盟军总司令部 G-2 催促准许就细菌战讯问石井中将，打听石井四郎等人在日本的下落，并强调，苏联方面只是要得到与战争犯罪有关的情报。

GENERAL HEADQUARTERS
UNITED STATES ARMY FORCES, PACIFIC
MILITARY INTELLIGENCE SECTION, GENERAL STAFF

CONFIDENTIAL

APO 500
27 February 1947

MEMORANDUM FOR RECORD

SUBJECT : Conversation between Col. Bethune, Gen. Vassiliev and Colonel Pash

TO :

1. General Vassiliev, Prosecutor for the USSR at the Military Tribunal for the Far East, and Lt. Petrov, interpreter, discussed the question of interrogating former Lt. General Ishii, et al, on the subject of bacteriological warfare.

2. General Vassiliev requested information as to whether or not interrogations would be permitted, and Colonel Bethune, through Colonel Pash as interpreter, stated that no decision had been made as to whether or not interrogations would be permitted.

3. General Vassiliev asked if the locations of the subject Japanese were known. Colonel Bethune stated that if they were in Japan they could be found, presumably.

4. General Vassiliev insisted that the USSR merely wanted information pertaining to war crimes and agreed to make the documents which the USSR has available for use of American interrogators, if desired. He also stated that Russian bacteriological warfare experts were being held in readiness in Vladivostok.

5. Colonel Bethune stated that when the interrogations had been authorized by higher authority the International Prosecution Section would be notified.

Bethune

CONFIDENTIAL

TOP SECRET

20

10.7 28 Feb. 1947: 280803, C-50474, TO: WDSCA, FROM: CINCFE, TO: WDCSA, C.S. Myers, Col., GSC, Executive Officer G-2

资料出处： National Archives of the United States, R153, E154.

内容点评： 本资料为 1947 年 2 月 28 日美远东军司令部 G-2 执行长官 C.S. Myers 上校向美军总参谋长发送的电文，报告苏联检察官每天提出要求准许讯问日军有关细菌战人员。

00419

GB/CAW/RPM/mjd/arc
28 February 1947

280803

CONFIDENTIAL

CINCFE

WDCSA . . . . .URGENT

PAREN C-50474 PAREN REOURAD CHARLIE SIX NINE NINE FOUR SIX CMA ONE THREE FEBRUARY AND CHARLIE FIVE ZERO THREE THREE THREE CMA TWO ONE FEBRUARY ONE NINE FOUR SEVEN PD PARA ONE UNCLE SUGAR SUGAR ROGER PROSECUTOR MAKING DAILY REQUEST FOR DECISION ON INTERROGATION OF FORMER JAPANESE ARMY OFFICERS FORMERLY ENGAGED IN BACTERIOLOGICAL WARFARE AND STATED TWO SEVEN FEBRUARY CMA SUB PARA ABLE WAS EAGER TO SHARE INFORMATION GAINED WITH UNCLE SUGAR SUB PARA BAKER WOULD PRESENT FOR EXAMINATION DOCUMENTORY EVIDENCE AVAILABLE SUB PARA CHARLIE HAD TWO WITNESSES IN VLADIVOSTOCK WHOM HE WISHED TO BRING TO JAPAN TO PARTICIPATE IN INTERROGATION SUB PARA DOG WAS AGREEABLE TO ONE ZERO ZERO PERCENT INTERROGATION OF JAPANESE BY UNCLE SUGAR ARMY USING SOVIETS DOCUMENTS PD PARA TWO UNCLE SUGAR SUGAR ROGER PROSECUTOR IS APPARENTLY BEING PRESSED BY SUPERIORS FOR ANSWER ON MATTER CMA AND VOLUNTEERS STATEMENTS IN POSSIBLE EFFORT TO HASTEN OUR REPLY PD REQUEST REPLY SOONEST PD

OFFICIAL: APPROVED BY:

John B. Cooley
Colonel, AGD
Adjutant General

C. S. MYERS,
Colonel, G.S.C.
Executive Officer, G-2

Copies to:
5 - AG
1 - G-2 Admin
1 - G-2 Return
1 - IPS

Reference Radios C 69946 and C 50333
TOP SECRET

CONFIDENTIAL

10.8 28 Feb. 1947: WAR 92911, FROM: WAR (THE JOINT CHIEF OF STAFF), TO: CINCFE (TO MACARTHUR)

资料出处：National Archives of the United States, R153, E154.

内容点评：本资料为 1947 年 2 月 28 日美军总参谋部发送给美军远东司令部（MACARTHUR）电文：有关电文 C-69946，约 3 月 5 日决定。

FAR EAST COMMAND
GENERAL HEADQUARTERS, ~~U.S. ARMY FORCES PACIFIC~~
ADJUTANT GENERAL'S OFFICE
RADIO AND CABLE CENTER

JLR
rfc

INCOMING MESSAGE

CONFIDENTIAL

CORRECTED COPY

PRIORITY 28 Feb 47

FROM : WAR (THE JOINT CHIEFS OF STAFF)

TO : CINCFE (TO MACARTHUR)

NR : WAR 92911

Your C 69946 under study by State, War and Navy Departments. Decision expected about 5 March 47.

NO SIG

REGRADED
ORDER SEC ARMY
BY TAG

ACTION: G-2

INFORMATION: COMMANDER-IN-CHIEF, CHIEF OF STAFF, AG

NOTE: Corrected copy received in AG R/C office 222035/I.

DECLASSIFIED BY ORDER
OF THE SEC ARMY BY TAG
PER 7 5

PRIORITY

72763

TOO: 281729 Z
MCN: SA 119/27

"Paraphrase not required. Handle as RESTRICTED correspondence per paragraphs 51 d and 60 a (4) AR 380-5."

CONFIDENTIAL

AG FILE

Handling and transmission of literal plain text of this message as correspondence of the same classification has been authorized by the War Department in accordance with the provisions of paragraphs 16-C, 18-E, 53-A, 53-D (1) (2) (3), and 60-A (1) (2) (3) (4), AR 380-5, 6 March 1946.

COPY No.

00413

CONFIDENTIAL

MEMO FOR RECORD:

1. C-69946, 13 Feb 1947, approved by CS requests decision from WD on USSR Prosecutor's original request to G-2 for permission to interrogate certain Japanese on bacteriological warefare; WD radio WX 95147, 24 Jul 1946 requires that JCS permission is necessary on exchange of information pertaining to bacteriological warfare and certain other subjects. 350.09 Sans Secret

2. Since original request, USSR Prosecutor has been making frequent inquiries as to decision. Urgent C-50333, 21 Feb 1947, requests WD reply soonest.

3. USSR Prosecutor, 27 Feb 1947, made another request and volunteered two witnesses and US access to USSR documentary evidence. Instant radio acquaints WD with latest development.

RPM 28 Feb 1947 2-5180

CONFIDENTIAL

10.9 28 Feb. 1947: SFE 188/1: STATE-WAR-NAVY COORDINATING SUBCOMMITTEE FOR THE FAR EAST, REQUEST OF RUSSIAN PROSECUTOR FOR PERMISSION TO INTERROGATE CERTAIN JAPANESE, Note by the Secretary, Reference: a. SWNCC 351/D, b. CM-IN-1604 (22 Feb 47), c. SFE 188, d. CM-IN-4858 (28 Feb 47)

资料出处：National Archives of the United States, R165, E468, B428.

内容点评：本资料为 1947 年 2 月 28 日美国国务院—陆军部—海军部三部协调远东小委员会秘书处美国海军中校 J. B. Cresap 发布三部协调远东小委员会通告，题目：关于苏联检察官要求准许讯问某些日本人。附：空军人员意见。

TOP SECRET　　　　COPY NO. 4

SFE 188/1

28 February 1947

Pages 1 - 2, incl.

TOP SECRET

ACTION ASSIGNED TO War Crimes Office Mr. Hebbert

STATE-WAR-NAVY COORDINATING SUBCOMMITTEE FOR THE FAR EAST

REQUEST OF RUSSIAN PROSECUTOR FOR PERMISSION TO INTERROGATE CERTAIN JAPANESE

References: a. SWNCC 351/D
b. CM-IN-1604 (22 Feb 47)
c. SFE 188
d. CM-IN-4858 (28 Feb 47)

OK.

Note by the Secretary

1. The enclosure, a memorandum by the Air Forces Member, is circulated to the Subcommittee in connection with their consideration of reference c.

2. The attention of the Subcommittee is invited to the following message from SCAP dated 28 February 1947, which was forwarded to the State-War-Navy Coordinating Committee by the Joint Chiefs of Staff for information:

"1. USSR prosecutor making daily request for decision on interrogation of former Japanese Army Officers formerly engaged in Bacteriological Warfare and stated 27th February,

A. Was eager to share information gained with US.

B. Would present for examination documentory evidence available.

C. Had two witnesses in Vladivostock whom he wished to bring to Japan to participate in interrogation.

D. Was agreeable to 100 per cent interrogation of Japanese by US Army using Soviets documents.

"2. USSR prosecutor is apparently being pressed by superiors for answer on matter, and volunteered statements in possible effort to hasten our reply. Request soonest."

DECLASSIFIED NND790032 By [illegible] NARS, Date 10/8[illegible]

J. B. CRESAP,
Commander, USN
Secretary

TOP SECRET

SFE 188/1

TOP SECRET

E N C L O S U R E

REQUEST OF RUSSIAN PROSECUTOR FOR PERMISSION TO INTERROGATE CERTAIN JAPANESE
Reference: SFE 188

Memorandum by the Air Forces Member, State-War-Navy Coordinating Subcommittee for the Far East

27 February 1947

1. In view of the fact that there are available personnel especially trained in interrogating on BW matters, it is felt that such personnel should, with SCAP's concurrence, be immediately dispatched to Japan to conduct the preliminary interrogation and monitor the subsequent Soviet interrogation. This is especially desirable in as much as two of the individuals to be questioned have not been previously interrogated and the monitoring of the general trend of Soviet questioning may have special significance to such trained personnel. It is therefore recommended that the following changes to SFE 188 be considered by the Subcommittee:

a. Change paragraph 3 to read: "In as much as we do not know whether Colonel Kikuchi and Colonel Ota possess knowledge in the BW field which might be of military value to the Soviets, it is considered that they should be interviewed by ~~the most~~ competent U.S. personnel ~~available in Japan~~ before being interrogated by the Soviets. Prior to the interview by the Soviets, the three Japanese BW experts should be briefed that no mention be made of the U.S. interview on this subject. If any information is brought out by preliminary interrogation of Ota and Kikuchi, and this information is considered of such importance that its divulgence to the Soviets should not be permitted, they should be instructed not to reveal such information to the Soviets. ~~If it is felt by SCAP that no officer on his staff is a competent judge to determine whether any such vital BW information might be revealed by either Colonel Kikuchi or Colonel Ota, a transcript of the preliminary U.S. interrogation should be forwarded by air to the War Department.~~ It is felt that the

SFE 188/1 - 1 - Enclosure

TOP SECRET

TOP SECRET

interrogation should be conducted by personnel who have been especially trained in BW interrogation and, subject to SCAP's concurrence, competent personnel for this purpose should immediately be dispatched by the appropriate War Department agency."

b. Change Appendix, Part I, to read: "Re URAD 69946 of 10 February. Subject to following conditions permission granted for SCAP controlled Soviet interrogation General Ishii, Colonels Kikuchi and Ota topic Biological Warfare.

"a. Colonels Kikuchi and Ota to be interviewed by ~~the most~~ competent U.S. personnel. ~~available in Japan.~~ Subject your concurrence, War Department prepared to dispatch immediately especially trained representatives to conduct interrogation and monitor subsequent interrogation by Soviets.

"b. If any information brought out by preliminary interrogation considered of sufficient importance that divulgence to Soviets should not be permitted, Kikuchi and Ota are to be instructed not to reveal such information to Soviets.

"~~c. If in your opinion no officer on your staff competent to determine whether such vital BW info might be revealed, a transcript of the preliminary U.S. interrogation should be forwarded by air to War Department.~~

" c. Prior to interview by Soviets the Japanese BW experts should be instructed to make no mention of U.S. interview on this subject."

SFE 188/1 - 2 - Enclosure

TOP SECRET

10.10 3 Mar. 1947: SWNCC 351/1: STATE-WAR-NAVY COORDINATING COMMITTEE, REQUEST OF RUSSIAN PROSECUTOR FOR PERMISSION TO INTERROGATE CERTAIN JAPANESE, Reference: a. SWNCC 351/D, b. CM-IN-1604 (22 Feb 47), c. SFE 188, d. CM-IN-4858 (28 Feb 47) (Appendix "B"); Report by the State-War-Navy Coordinating Subcommittee for the Far East

资料出处：National Archives of the United States, R165, E468, B428.

内容点评：本资料为 1947 年 3 月 3 日美国国务院—陆军部—海军部三部协调委员会秘书处对三部协调委员会发布的通报，题目：关于苏联检察官要求准许讯问某些日本人。附：三部协调远东小委员会报告。

6 MAR 1947

014 Jap (13 Apr 44) Sec 11

TOP SECRET

SWNCC 351/1

3 March 1947

Pages 3 - 6, incl.

COPY NO. 20

TOP SECRET

STATE-WAR-NAVY COORDINATING COMMITTEE

REQUEST OF RUSSIAN PROSECUTOR FOR PERMISSION TO INTERROGATE CERTAIN JAPANESE

References: a. SWNCC 351/D
b. CM-IN-1604 (22 Feb 47)
c. SFE 188
d. CM-IN-4858 (28 Feb 47) (Appendix "B")

Note by the Secretaries

The enclosure, a report by the State-War-Navy Coordinating Subcommittee for the Far East in response to reference a, is circulated for consideration by the Committee as a matter of urgency.

H. W. MOSELEY

W. A. SCHULGEN

V. L. LOWRANCE

Secretariat

SWNCC 351/1

Carded
Indexed M.W.

TOP SECRET

TOP SECRET

TOP SECRET

E N C L O S U R E

REQUEST OF RUSSIAN PROSECUTOR FOR PERMISSION
TO INTERROGATE CERTAIN JAPANESE

Report by the
State-War-Navy Coordinating Subcommittee for the Far East

THE PROBLEM

1. To formulate a reply to SCAP's radio C-69946 regarding the request of the Soviet Prosecutor, International Military Tribunal for the Far East, to interview three Japanese formerly connected with biological warfare research in Manchuria.

DISCUSSION

2. U. S. investigators interviewed Lt. Gen. Ishii, leading Japanese BW expert, in Tokyo, January 22-29, 1946. On the basis of their interview it is believed that the Soviets will not gain any positive technical intelligence in the BW field if permission to hold this interrogation is granted. Colonel Kikuchi and Colonel Ota were not interviewed, nor is there any information concerning them. It is further believed that by permitting this interrogation, under controlled conditions, the general trend of Soviet questioning might serve as a key to Soviet knowledge and activity in the BW field.

3. In as much as we do not know whether Colonel Kikuchi and Colonel Ota possess knowledge in the BW field which might be of military value to the Soviets, it is considered that they should be interviewed by competent U.S. personnel before being interrogated by the Soviets. Prior to the interview by the Soviets, the three Japanese BW experts should be briefed that no mention be made of the U.S. interview on this subject. If any information is brought out by preliminary interrogation of Ota and Kikuchi, and this information is considered of such importance that its divulgence to the Soviets should not be permitted, they should be instructed not to reveal such information to the Soviets. It is felt that the interrogation should

SWNCC 351/1 - 3 - Enclosure

TOP SECRET

TOP SECRET

be conducted by personnel who have been especially trained in BW interrogation and, subject to SCAP's concurrence, competent personnel for this purpose should immediately be dispatched by the appropriate War Department agency.

4. Since there is no clear cut war crime interest by the Soviets in acts allegedly committed by the Japanese against the Chinese, permission for the interrogation should not be granted on that basis, but rather as an amiable gesture toward a friendly government. It should be made clear to the Soviets that the permission granted in this instance does not create a precedent for future requests, which shall be considered on their individual merits.

CONCLUSION

5. It is concluded that permis ion should be granted for Soviet interrogation of three Japanese formerly connected with biological warfare research in Manchuria subject to the conditions set forth in Appendix "A".

RECOMMENDATIONS

6. It is recommended that:

a. SWNCC approve the above conclusion.

b. After approval by SWNCC, the JCS be requested to transmit the message in Appendix "A" to SCAP providing they have no objection from a military point of view.

TOP SECRET

APPENDIX "A"

MESSAGE TO SCAP

Following Radio in two parts.

PART I

Re URAD 69946 of 10 February. Subject to following conditions permission granted for SCAP controlled Soviet interrogation General Ishii, Colonels Kikuchi and Ota topic Biological Warfare.

a. Colonels Kikuchi and Ota to be interviewed by competent U.S. personnel. Subject your concurrence, War Department prepared to dispatch immediately especially trained representatives to conduct interrogation and monitor subsequent interrogation by Soviets.

b. If any information brought out by preliminary interrogation considered of sufficient importance that divulgence to Soviets should not be permitted, Kikuchi and Ota areto be instructed not to reveal such information to Soviets.

c. Prior to interview by Soviets the Japanese BW experts should be instructed to make no mention of U.S. interview on this subject.

PART II

Since there is no clear cut war crime interest by the Soviets in acts allegedly committed by the Japanese against the Chinese, permission for the interrogation should not be granted on that basis, but rather as an amiable gesture toward a friendly government. It should be made clear to the Soviets that the permission granted in this instance does not create a precedent for future requests, which shall be considered on their individual merits.

TOP SECRET

APPENDIX "B"

MESSAGE FROM SCAP

1. USSR prosecutor making daily request for decision on interrogation of former Japanese Army Officers formerly engaged in Bacteriological Warfare and stated 27th February,

A. Was eager to share information gained with US.

B. Would present for examination documentory evidence available.

C. Had two witnesses in Vladivostock whom he wished to bring to Japan to participate in interrogation.

D. Was agreeable to 100 per cent interrogation of Japanese by US Army using Soviets documents.

2. USSR prosecutor is apparently being pressed by superiors for answer on matter, and volunteered statements in possible effort to hasten our reply. Request soonest.

10.11 4 Mar. 1947: MEMORANDUM FOR THE ASSISTANT SCRETARY OF WAR: Request of Russian Prosecutor for Permission to Interrogate Certain Japanese (SWNCC 351/1), G. A. L.

资料出处：National Archives of the United States, R165, E468, B428.

内容点评：本资料为 1947 年 3 月 4 日美国陆军部部长助理收到的备忘录，题目：关于苏联检察官要求准许讯问某些日本人。

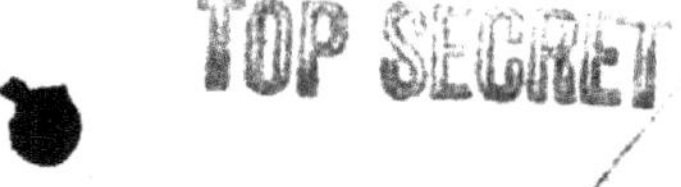

6 MAR 1947

P&O [illegible]icy/2273
Maj Liggett/mlb

4 March 1947

MEMORANDUM FOR THE ASSISTANT SECRETARY OF WAR:

SUBJECT: Request of Russian Prosecutor for Permission to Interrogate Certain Japanese (SWNCC 351/1)

1. General MacArthur has requested (Enclosure to SWNCC 351/D) a decision on a proposal that the USSR be permitted to interrogate three former Jap officers who were connected with bacteriological warfare (BW) activities in Manchuria. General MacArthur considers that the Soviets are not likely to obtain information from the Japanese not already known to the US and that we might obtain information from the Russian line of questioning.

2. The Subcommittee for the Far East in SWNCC 351/1 reports that two of the Jap officers concerned have not heretofore been interviewed by the US and that there is no information concerning them. The Subcommittee considers that these two officers should be interviewed by competent US personnel before being interrogated by the Soviets.

3. The Subcommittee recommends transmission of a message to General MacArthur authorizing the controlled Soviet interrogation of the three Jap officers subject to the following conditions:

a. The two Jap Colonels be interviewed by competent US personnel. The War Department is prepared to dispatch representatives to conduct the interrogation if General MacArthur desires.

b. If interrogation brings out information that should not be given to Soviets, the Jap officers are to be instructed not to reveal such information.

c. Jap officers should be instructed to make no mention of US interview on this subject.

4. P&O has been informed that General Waitt, Chief of the Chemical Corps concurred in the Subcommittee report and is prepared to dispatch an expert if General MacArthur so requests.

P&O RECOMMENDS:

Approval of the Far East Subcommittee's recommendations.

COORINDATION:

AAF concurs (Lt Col Forbes, ext 74355)
I/D concurs (Col Treacy, ext 74970)

PLANS & POLICY

TOP SECRET

G. A. L.

10.12 5 Mar. 1947: SWN-5199: MEMORADUM FOR THE SECRETARY, JOINT CHIEFS OF STAFF: SWNCC 351/1, Reference: a. SM-7570 (10 Feb 47), b. SM-7680 (24 Feb 47) c. SWNCC 351/D, d. SWNCC 351/1, H.W. MOSLEY, Secretary

资料出处：National Archives of the United States, R165, E468, B428.

内容点评：本资料为 1947 年 3 月 5 日美国国务院—陆军部—海军部三部协调委员会秘书处秘书 H.W.MOSLEY 提交美军总参谋部秘书处的备忘录，题目：SWNCC 351/1。

014 Japan (13 ... 44) Sec 11

THE STATE-WAR-NAVY COORDINATING COMMITTEE
WASHINGTON, D. C.

13 MAR 1947

SWN-5199
5 March 1947

MEMORANDUM FOR THE SECRETARY, JOINT CHIEFS OF STAFF:

Subject: SWNCC 351/1

References: a. SM-7570 (10 Feb 47)
b. SM-7680 (24 Feb 47)
c. SWNCC 351/D
d. SWNCC 351/1

By informal action on 5 March 1947 the State-War-Navy Coordinating Committee approved SWNCC 351/1, a copy of which is enclosed.

It is requested that the Joint Chiefs of Staff transmit the message in Appendix "A" to the Supreme Commander for the Allied Powers, provided they have no objection from a military point of view.

For the State-War-Navy Coordinating Committee:

H. W. MOSELEY,
Secretary

OK
Hold for JCS
X-J-1753

Enclosure:
Copy No. 49, SWNCC 351/1

COPY FOR OPD

10.13 6 Mar. 1947: STATE-WAR-NAVY COORDINATING COMMITTEE, DECISION ON SWNCC 351/1: REQUEST OF RUSSIAN PROSECUTOR FOR PERMISSION TO INTERROGATE CERTAIN JAPANESE, Note by the Secretaries

资料出处：National Archives of the United States, R165, E468, B428.

内容点评：本资料为 1946 年 3 月 6 日美国国务院—陆军部—海军部三部协调委员会秘书处通告三部协调委员会：核准 SWNCC 351/1。

OK WKA

TOP SECRET

2 MAR 1947

TOP SECRET

6 March 1947

014 Japan (13 Apr 44) Sec 11

COPY NO. 20

STATE-WAR-NAVY COORDINATING COMMITTEE 8

DECISION ON SWNCC 351/1

REQUEST OF RUSSIAN PROSECUTOR FOR PERMISSION TO INTERROGATE CERTAIN JAPANESE

Note by the Secretaries

By informal action on 5 March 1947 the State-War-Navy Coordinating Committee approved SWNCC 351/1.

H. W. MOSELEY

W. A. SCHULGEN

V. L. LOWRANCE

Secretariat

TOP SECRET

TOP SECRET

10.14 6 Mar. 1947: J. C. S. 1753: JOINT CHIEFS OF STAFF, REQUEST OF RUSSIAN PROSECUTOR FOR PERMISSION TO INTERROGATE CERTAIN JAPANESE

资料出处： National Archives of the United States, R153, E145, B73.

内容点评： 本资料为 1947 年 3 月 6 日美军总参谋部秘书处通告总参谋部的绝密文件，题目：关于苏联检察官要求准许讯问某些日本人。三部协调委员会要求将附件（SWNCC 351/1 附录“A”）尽快发送盟军总司令部。

TOP-SECRET

TOP SECRET
J.C.S. 1753
6 March 1947
Page 1

COPY NO. 15
(SPECIAL DISTRIBUTION)

JOINT CHIEFS OF STAFF

REQUEST OF RUSSIAN PROSECUTOR FOR PERMISSION TO INTERROGATE CERTAIN JAPANESE

Note by the Secretaries

The State-War-Navy Coordinating Committee has requested that the enclosed message (Appendix "A" to SWNCC 351/1) be transmitted to the Supreme Commander for the Allied Powers (SCAP) provided the Joint Chiefs of Staff have no objection from a military point of view.

A. J. McFARLAND,
W. G. LALOR,
Joint Secretariat.

DISTRIBUTION

Adm. Leahy
Adm. Nimitz
Gen. Eisenhower
Gen. Spaatz
Gen. Handy
Adm. Ramsey
Adm. Sherman
Gen. Norstad
Gen. Weyland
Adm. Glover
Gen. Kissner
Gen. Lincoln
Capt. Carter
Secy, JCS
Secy, JSSC
Secy, JPS

JCS 1753

TOP SECRET

E N C L O S U R E

D R A F T

MESSAGE TO THE SUPREME COMMANDER FOR THE ALLIED POWERS

Following radio in two parts.

PART I

Re URAD 69946 of 10 February. Subject to following conditions permission granted for SCAP controlled Soviet interrogation General Ishii, Colonels Kikuchi and Ota topic biological warfare.

a. Colonels Kikuchi and Ota to be interviewed by competent U. S. personnel. Subject your concurrence, War Department prepared to dispatch immediately especially trained representatives to conduct interrogation and monitor subsequent interrogation by Soviets.

b. If any information brought out by preliminary interrogation considered of sufficient importance that divulgence to Soviets should not be permitted, Kikuchi and Ota are to be instructed not to reveal such information to Soviets.

c. Prior to interview by Soviets the Japanese biological warfare experts should be instructed to make no mention of U. S. interview on this subject.

PART II

Since there is no clear cut war crime interest by the Soviets in acts allegedly committed by the Japanese against the Chinese, permission for the interrogation should not be granted on that basis, but rather as an amiable gesture toward a friendly government. It should be made clear to the Soviets that the permission granted in this instance does not create a precedent for future requests, which shall be considered on their individual merits.

JCS 1753 - 1 - Enclosure

10.15 20 Mar. 1947: TOPSEC TO MacARTHUR, SUPREME COMMANDER FOR THE ALLIED POWERS TOKYO JAPAN, FROM THE JOINT CHIEFS OF STAFF PD., M. M. STEPHENS, Captain, U. S. Navy, Asst. Exec. Secretary

资料出处：National Archives of the United States, R153, E145, B73.

内容点评：本资料为1947年3月20日美军总参谋部助理执行秘书M. M. Stephens海军上校发送日本东京盟军最高司令官MacARTHUR电文：允许苏联人在盟军最高司令部掌控下讯问石井四郎等，讯问前，必须告知日本细菌战专家不得提及美国的相关讯问。

21 MAR 1947

014 Japan (13 apr 49)
Sec II-B

PHP

Priority

Joint Chiefs of Staff

W.D. Ext. 77500

20 March 1947

TOP SECRET

Capt.M.M.Stephens,USN.

X

SUPREME COMMANDER FOR THE ALLIED POWERS TOKYO JAPAN.

TOPSEC TO MacARTHUR FROM THE JOINT CHIEFS OF STAFF PD.

THE FOLLOWING CMA RECEIVED FROM THE STATE CMA WAR AND NAVY DEPARTMENTS CMA IS IN REPLY TO YOUR C SIX NINE NINE FOUR SIX PD MESSAGE IS IN TWO PARTS PD PARA PART I PARA SUBJECT TO FOLLOWING CONDITIONS PERMISSION GRANTED FOR SCAP CONTROLLED SOVIET INTERROGATION GENERAL ISHII CMA COLONELS KIKUCHI AND OTA TOPIC BIOLOGICAL WARFARE PD BRACKET INDENT SUBPARAGRAPHS USING LOWER CASE UNDERSCORED LETTERS BRACKET SUBPARA A PD COLONELS KIKUCHI AND OTA TO BE INTERVIEWED BY COMPETENT U PD S PD PERSONNEL PD SUBJECT YOUR CONCURRENCE CMA WAR DEPARTMENT PREPARED TO DISPATCH IMMEDIATELY ESPECIALLY TRAINED REPRESENTATIVES TO CONDUCT INTERROGATION AND MONITOR SUBSEQUENT INTERROGATION BY SOVIETS PD SUBPARA B PD IF ANY INFORMATION BROUGHT OUT BY PRELIMINARY INTERROGATION CONSIDERED OF SUFFICIENT IMPORTANCE THAT DIVULGENCE TO SOVIETS SHOULD NOT RPT NOT BE PERMITTED CMA KIKUCHI AND OTA ARE TO BE INSTRUCTED NOT RPT NOT TO REVEAL SUCH INFORMATION TO SOVIETS

WAR 94446/20 Mar

TOP SECRET

SCAP - Page 2

Priority　　Joint Chiefs of Staff　　W.D. Ext. 77500

20 March 1947　　TOP SECRET　　Capt.M.M.Stephens,USN

X

PD SUBPARA C PD PRIOR TO INTERVIEW BY SOVIETS THE JAPANESE BIOLOGICAL WARFARE EXPERTS SHOULD BE INSTRUCTED TO MAKE NO RPT NO MENTION OF U PD S PD INTERVIEW ON THIS SUBJECT PD PARA PART II PARA SINCE THERE IS NO RPT NO CLEAR CUT WAR CRIME INTEREST BY THE SOVIETS IN ACTS ALLEGEDLY COMMITTED BY THE JAPANESE AGAINST THE CHINESE CMA PERMISSION FOR THE INTERROGATION SHOULD NOT RPT NOT BE GRANTED ON THAT BASIS CMA BUT RATHER AS AN AMIABLE GESTURE TOWARD A FRIENDLY GOVERNMENT PD IT SHOULD BE MADE CLEAR TO THE SOVIETS THAT THE PERMISSION GRANTED IN THIS INSTANCE DOES NOT RPT NOT CREATE A PRECEDENT FOR FUTURE REQUESTS CMA WHICH SHALL BE CONSIDERED ON THEIR INDIVIDUAL MERITS

C 69946 is CM-IN-1604 (10 Feb 47).

(SIGNED)
M. M. STEPHENS,
Captain, U.S. Navy, Asst.Exec. Secretary.

C54394

(JCS 1753)　　TOP SECRET

10.16 20 Mar. 1947: J.C.S. 1753: REQUEST OF RUSSIAN PROSECUTOR FOR PERMISSION TO INTERROGATE CERTAIN JAPANESE, PRESENT STATUS: COMPLETED

资料出处：National Archives of the United States, R153, E145, B73.

内容点评：本资料为1947年3月20日美军总参谋部JSC1753文件提要，题目：有关苏联检察官要求准许讯问某些日本人；目前状况：完成。1947年3月20日总参谋部JSC1753文件中批准以上要求（于3月20日以电文WAR94446发送盟军最高司令官）。

EXTRACT OF STATUS OF PAPERS

	COMBINED CHIEFS OF STAFF ________ SPECIAL DISTRIBUTION
✓	JOINT CHIEFS OF STAFF ________ REGULAR DISTRIBUTION
✓	STATE-WAR-COORDINATING COMMITTEE COMPLETED MATTERS.

DATE 20 March 47

014 Japan (13 Apr 44) Sec 11-B

Request of Russian Prosecutor for Permission to Interrogate Certain Japanese

PRESENT STATUS

JCS 1753 COMPLETED. On 20 March 1947 the JCS approved the request in JCS 1753. (Message dispatched to SCAP as WAR 94446, 20 Mar.)

10.17 21 Mar. 1947: JOINT CHIEFS OF STAFF, DECISION ON J.C.S. 1753: REQUEST OF RUSSIAN PROSECUTOR FOR PERMISSION TO INTERROGATE CERTAIN JAPANESE

资料出处：National Archives of the United States, R153, E145, B73.

内容点评：本资料为 1947 年 3 月 21 日美军总参谋部秘书处发布的总参谋部有关“苏联检察官要求准许讯问某些日本人”的决定：从军事角度无异义。

TOP-SECRET

TOP SECRET
21 March 1947

COPY NO. 15
(SPECIAL DISTRIBUTION)

JOINT CHIEFS OF STAFF

DECISION ON J.C.S. 1753

REQUEST OF RUSSIAN PROSECUTOR FOR PERMISSION TO INTERROGATE CERTAIN JAPANESE

Note by the Secretaries

wK9 On 20 March 1947 the Joint Chiefs of Staff, perceiving no objection from a military point of view, dispatched the message in the Enclosure to J.C.S. 1753 to the Supreme Commander for the Allied Powers.

A. J. McFARLAND,
W. G. LALOR,
Joint Secretariat.

DISTRIBUTION

Adm. Leahy	Adm. Sherman	Capt. Carter
Adm. Nimitz	Gen. Norstad	Secy, JCS
Gen. Eisenhower	Gen. Weyland	Secy, JSSC
Gen. Spaatz	Adm. Glover	Secy, JPS
Gen. Handy	Gen. Kissner	
Adm. Ramsey	Gen. Lincoln	

10.18　25 Mar. 1947: CHECK SHEET File No: TS 52: Availability of Bacteriological Warfare Expert in FEC, CAW/RPM/mk

资料出处：National Archives of the United States, R153, E145.

内容点评：本资料为 1947 年 3 月 25 日盟军总司令部 C. A. W.（G-2 长官 C. A. Willoughby）发给各部门的指令：征募远东军内细菌战专家，将再次讯问某些牵涉细菌战的日军人员。

GENERAL HEADQUARTERS
SUPREME COMMANDER FOR THE ALLIED POWERS CONFIDENTIAL

CHECK SHEET

(Do not remove from attached sheets)

File No.: TS 52 Subject: Availability of Bacteriological Warfare Expert in FEC CAW/RPM/mk

Note No.: From: G-2 To: Surg PH Cml G-4 ESS IPS Date: 25 Mar 1947

1 1. It is contemplated that, in the near future, certain former Japanese officers who were engaged in Bacteriological Warfare during and before World War II will be re-interrogated on the basis of new information available.

2. The War Department offers especially trained representatives. However, if qualified personnel is available in the theater, their services are desired.

3. In the event that it is your opinion that especially trained War Department representatives are desirable, request initials opposite section designation above.

4. If qualified personnel are available, request such information by check note below.

for Bethune
C.A.W.

10.19 27 Mar. 1947: MEMORANDUM FOR RECORD, PRESENTED BY: A. C. OF S., G-2, GHQ, FEC: REQUEST OF RUSSIANS TO ARREST AND INTERROGATE JAPANPESE BACTERIOLOGICAL WARFARE EXPERTS IN WHOM U.S. HAS PRIOR INTEREST

资料出处：National Archives of the United States, R153, E145.

内容点评：本资料为 1947 年 3 月 27 日美远东军司令部 A. C. OF S.，G-2 提交美军总参谋长的备忘录，题目：苏联要求讯问并逮捕日本细菌战专家，对这些人美国有优先权利。

MEMORANDUM FOR RECORD

SUBJECT: REQUEST OF RUSSIANS TO ARREST AND INTERROGATE JAPANESE BACTERIOLOGICAL WARFARE EXPERTS IN WHOM U.S. HAS PRIOR INTEREST

PRESENTED BY:
A C OF S G-2, GHQ, FEC
27 MARCH 1947

DECLASSIFIED BY ORDER OF THE SEC ARMY BY TAG PER 770475

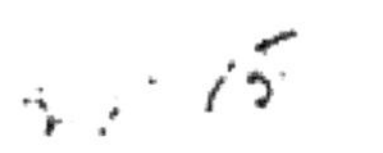

CONFIDENTIAL

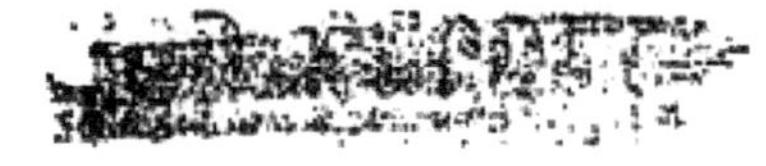

GENERAL HEADQUARTERS
~~UNITED STATES ARMY FORCES, PACIFIC~~
MILITARY INTELLIGENCE SECTION, GENERAL STAFF
FAR EAST COMMAND

APO 500
27 Mar 1947

MEMORANDUM FOR RECORD

SUBJECT : USSR Request to Interrogate and Arrest Japanese Bacteriological Warfare Experts.

TO : Chief of Staff

1. The International Prosecution Section notified A C of S, G-2 by telephone, 7 Jan 1947, that the USSR representative to the IMTFE requested permission to interrogate former Japanese officers on bacteriological warfare. IPS was requested to have USSR submit written request. Written request, consisting of a memorandum to the A C of S, G-2 signed by A. Visiliev, Associate Prosecutor for the USSR, was forwarded by CN from IPS, 9 Jan 1947 (Tab A). Meeting with USSR was held on 15 January which indicated Soviet interest in intelligence side of the problem. (Tab B)

2. The written request from the Soviets resulted in a Memorandum for Record to the Chief of Staff (Tab C) and dispatch of Radio C 69946, 10 Feb 1947, which was approved by DCS, 8 Feb 1947. (Tab D) Such matters must be referred to Joint Chiefs of Staff for decision.

3. No definite reply to the Soviets was made, other than oral reply through IPS that the request was being considered. The Russians were persistant in almost daily inquiries which became so unpleasant that a simple tracer radio was dispatched 21 Feb 1947.

4. Soviet General Vasiliev, who signed original request, requested interview with A C of S, G-2, and on 27 Feb 1947, stated that USSR wanted evidence only for war crimes, and that Soviet documents would be made available to the United States. (Tab E) He announced that he would bring Russian experts to assist if wanted. The Soviet General was notified that when a decision was reached, he would be notified through IPS. Radio C 50474, 28 Feb 1947, was dispatched to the War Department (Tab F).

5. Radio from War Department received 1 Mar 1947 stated: "Your C-69946 under study by State, War and Navy Departments. Decision expected about 5 Mar 1947".

6. On 7 Mar 1947, the USSR Member of Allied Council for Japan, General DEREVYANKO, submitted a memorandum. (Tab G) This memorandum

CONFIDENTIAL

stated:

a. Certain Japanese desired by Legal Section for war crimes were prisoners of USSR.

b. USSR requested charges against Japanese by Legal Section.

c. USSR requested United States turn over two Japanese to USSR for trial as war criminals. These two Japanese were two of those mentioned in memorandum from USSR Associate Prosecutor in January 1947.

d. Implied that there was a connection between the Japanese wanted by the United States and those wanted by USSR.

7. No reply was made to USSR pending the decision of the War Department. As reply from War Department was delayed, another radio, C-51008, 19 Mar 1947 was dispatched. (Tab E)

8. WD Radio, W-94446, 21 Mar 47, (Basic Radio), submitted JCS decision through War Department on original radio request (see par 2 above), and stated as follows:

a. SCAP-controlled Soviet interrogations approved.

b. War Department ready to send qualified assistants.

c. On preliminary interrogation, if Japanese have important information, Japanese will be told not to reveal it to USSR.

d. USSR will be told that interrogations are on basis of United States goodwill and not for war crimes, and that this instance does not set a precedent.

9. It is apparent that the Soviets are cloaking their interest in the intelligence aspects of Bacteriological Warfare by simulated concern over alleged use of bacteria against Chinese and Manchurians. The evidence which the Soviets say they possess may be of importance, and for that reason it is considered desirable from an intelligence standpoint to attempt coordinated action with USSR.

10. A C of S, G-2 proposes to concur in basic radio and to request two qualified War Department representatives as qualified personnel are not available here. (Tab I) There is the possibility that the Soviets may withdraw their offer at any time, but this chance cannot be predicted.

11. A C of S, G-2 proposes to make a reply to the Soviet Member of the Allied Council which will separate the Japanese personnel wanted by the United States from the Japanese concerned with Bacteriological Warfare . The plan is to deal with the Soviet Associate Prosecutor for the IMTFE, through the normal channel of the International Prosecution Section. Reply will be based on Part II of Basic Radio.

12. The reply to the USSR Associate Prosecutor will go through IPS and will be based on Part II of Basic Radio, but will attempt to gain

- 2 -

MEMORANDUM S E C R E T

CONFIDENTIAL

access to Soviet evidence in preparation for the arrival of War Department representatives.

13. Recommend approval of:

a. Radio to War Department.
b. Letter of reply to Soviet Member of Allied Council.
c. Reply to Soviet Associate Prosecutor by CN through IPS.

C. A. W.

CONCURRENCES:

G-1 Concurs ([signature])

11 Incls:
1- Basic WD Radio W 94446
2-11 -inclusive Tabs A through I
(listed in Table of Contents)

CONFIDENTIAL

3

T O P S E C R E T

10.20 27 Mar. 1947: BRIEF FOR THE CHIEF OF STAFF, C. A. W.

资料出处： National Archives of the United States, R153, E145, B73.

内容点评： 本资料为 1947 年 3 月 27 日 C. A. W.（G–2 长官 C. A. Willoughby）提交参谋长的概要：要求陆军部派两名专家等。

GENERAL HEADQUARTERS
SUPREME COMMANDER FOR THE ALLIED POWERS
Military Intelligence Section, General Staff

APO 500
27 Mar 47

BRIEF FOR THE CHIEF OF STAFF

1. This has to do with Russian requests for transfer of the former Japanese expert in Bacteriological Warfare.

2. The United States has primary interest, has already interrogated this man and his information is held by the U.S. Chemical Corps classified as TOP SECRET.

3. The Russian has made several attempts to get at this man. We have stalled. He now hopes to make his point by suddenly claiming the Japanese expert as a war criminal.

4. Joint Chiefs of Staff direct that this not be done but concur in a SCAP controlled interrogation requiring expert assistance not available in FEC.

5. This memorandum recommends:

a. Radio to WD for two experts.

b. Letter to USSR refusing to turn over Japanese expert.

c. Check Note to International Prosecution Section initiating action on the JCS approved interrogations.

C. A. W.

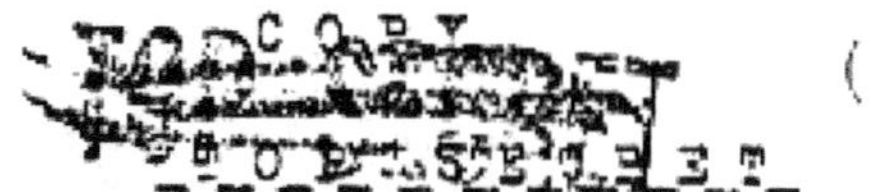

MEMO FOR RECORD:

1. C-69946, 13 Feb 1947, approved by CS requests decision from WD on USSR Prosecutor's original request to G-2 for permission to interrogate certain Japanese on bacteriological warfare; WD radio WX 95147, 24 Jul 1946 requires that JCS permission is necessary on exchange of information pertaining to bacteriological warfare and certain other subjects.

2. Since original request, USSR Prosecutor has been making frequent inquiries as to decision. Urgent C-50333, 21 Feb 1947, requests WD reply soonest.

3. USSR Prosecutor, 27 Feb 1947, made another request and volunteered two witnesses and US access to USSR documentory evidence. Instant radio acquaints WD with latest development.

RPM 8 Feb 1947 2-5180

10.21 30 Mar. 1947: A. C. of S., G-2, GHQ SCAP, C. A. W., TO: Col. Sackton: Russ Interrogation Bacteriology on War Crime Basis

资料出处：National Archives of the United States, R153, E145.

内容点评：本资料为 1947 年 3 月 30 日美远东军司令部 G-2 长官 C.A.W.（C.A. Willoughby）予 Sackton 上校的函件，题目：苏联以战争犯罪为由的细菌战有关讯问。提请参谋长注意有关要点。

A. C. of S., G-2
GHQ SCAP

March 30, 1947

SUBJECT : Russ Interrogation
Bacteriology on War Crimes Basis

TO : Col Sackton

I feel that I must advise the C/S on this matter and reiterate certain points :

1 W D interrogated the Japs, last year
2 Their product is "Top Secret" and now in hands of U S ChmnicalCorsp.
3 We were warned not to let the Russians in on th
4 They have been at us for months.
5 We stalled : Failing in this, the Russ now approaches this via the War Crimes Theory
6 This is a clear-cut fake ; a trumped-up method to get their hands on these people and take them away. They were in the War five Days.
7 This is quite clear to the War Dept.
8 They specifically prohibit this method : See Sec II Basic Radio 94446.
9 This is a Joint Chief of Staff Direction.
10 I deliberately used and quoted their own language thruout.
11 The same position must be taken in letter to Derevyanko

CAWilly
C.A.W

10.22 10 Apr. 1947: MEMORANDUN TO: Lt. Gen. K. Derevyanko, Member for U.S.S.R., Allied Council for Japan: Memorandum No. 1087, 7 Mar. 1947, FROM: JOHN B. COOLEY, Col.; 1 Apr. 1947: Col. P.H. Bethune Revised MEMORANDUN TO: Lt. Gen. K. Derevyanko, Member for U.S.S.R., Allied Council for Japan: Memorandum No. 1087, 7 Mar. 1947

资料出处：National Archives of the United States, R153, E145.

内容点评：本资料为1947年4月10日盟军总司令部John B. Cooley上校予盟军日本委员会苏联代表K. Derevyanko少将的备忘录，题目：1947年3月7日备忘录1087号。内容为对该备忘录的回复：石井四郎将军和大田澄大佐不能移交苏方；对作为战争犯罪调查的讯问要求不予准许。

附1947年4月1日P.H. Bethune上校提交的对上述发给K.Derevyanko备忘录3月27日稿件的手写修订，提及将于3月30日送交Sackton上校，确认经参谋长过目。

APO 500
10 April 1947

AGCCO.5(Soviet)(10 Apr 47) GB

MEMORANDUM TO: Lieutenant General K. Derevyanko, Member for U.S.S.R., Allied Council for Japan.

SUBJECT : Memorandum No. 1087, 7 March 1947 10/21

1. Reference paragraphs 1 and 2 of your Memorandum No. 1087, 7 March 1947, separate communication on the persons mentioned will be forthcoming at an early date.

2. Reference paragraph 3 of your Memorandum No. 1087, former Japanese General Ishii and Colonel Ota cannot be turned over to U.S.S.R. as there appears to be no clear cut war-crimes interest by the Soviets in acts allegedly committed by the Japanese on Chinese or Manchurians.

3. Personnel referred to in your paragraph 3 are already under consideration for interrogation in conjunction with International Prosecution Section, SCAP in cooperation with the Associate Prosecution for the U.S.S.R., I.M.T.F.E. It should be noted, however, that joint interrogation is not granted on a basis of a war-crimes investigation nor does permission granted create a precedent for future requests.

FOR THE SUPREME COMMANDER:

JOHN B. COOLEY,
Colonel, AGD,
Adjutant General.

MAILED 1 7 0 0 APR 10 47 AG. - GHQ.

pfd/m

GENERAL HEADQUARTERS
SUPREME COMMANDER FOR THE ALLIED POWERS
Military Intelligence Section, General Staff x

APO 500
27 March 1947

AG 091 (Soviet) (27 Mar 47)GB

MEMORANDUM TO : Lieutenant General K. Derevyanko, Member for USSR,
Allied Council for Japan

SUBJECT : Memorandum No. 1037, 7 March 1947

1. Reference paragraphs 1 and 2 of your Memorandum No. 1037, 7 March 1947, separate communication on the persons mentioned will be forthcoming at an early date.

2. Reference paragraph 3 of your Memorandum No. 1037, former Japanese General Ishii and Colonel Ota cannot be turned over to USSR as there appears to be no clear cut war-crimes interest by the Soviets in acts allegedly committed by the Japanese on Chinese or Manchurians.

3. Personnel referred to in your paragraph 3 are already under consideration for interrogation in conjunction with International Prosecution Section, SCAP in cooperation with the Associate Prosecution for the USSR, IMTFE. It should be noted, however, that joint interrogation is granted ~~[illegible]~~ not on a basis of a war-crimes investigation nor does ~~[illegible]~~ permission granted ~~does not~~ create a precedent for future requests.

FOR THE SUPREME COMMANDER:

30 Mar - This was given to Lt Col Sackton SGS to see whether deletion was intended to change meaning from WD Radio 94446 especially in view of approved draft of ... to IPS which contains ...

CHIEF OF STAFF
APPROVED
31.4.47
INIT AND

out to Lt Col Sackton. Col Sackton called me by phone and stated that the Chief of Staff had been shown the paper, and that he had commented that while it might appear to a discrepancy, it was an intentional change.

P. H. Bethune
Col GSC
Asst Ex O. G-2

Changes made in ink par 3 by C/S made 1 Apr 47
PHB.

10.23　6 May 1947: MEMORANDUM FOR RECORD, RPM ( ) 26-6166

资料出处：National Archives of the United States, R153, E145.

内容点评：本资料为 1947 年 5 月 6 日美方有关无线电通讯备忘录。

TOP SECRET

6 May 1947

MEMORANDUM FOR RECORD:

1. War Department Radio W-94446 and SWNCC 351/1 authorized joint interrogations of certain Japanese on BW with USSR, but not on basis of "war crimes". BW information of type described below follows your JCS directive and requires reference to War Department.

2. USSR interest arises from interrogations of two captured Japanese formerly associated with BW. Copies of these interrogations were given to US. Preliminary investigation confirm authenticity of USSR interrogations and indicate Japanese activity in

a. Human experiments.
b. Field trials against Chinese
c. Large scale program.
d. Research on BW by crop destruction.
e. Possible that Japanese General Staff knew and authorized program.
f. Thought and research devoted to strategic and tactical use of BW.

3. Data in detail on above topics are of great intelligence value to US. Dr. Fell, War Department representative, states that this new evidence was not known by US.

4. Certain low echelon Japanese are now working to assemble most of the necessary BW technical data. Nothing except indications of high echelon information have, so far, been obtained.

5. Information to the present have been obtained by persuasion, exploitation of Japanese fear of USSR and Japanese desire to cooperate with US.

6. Additional information including some material on theoretical, strategic and tactical employment probably can be obtained by informing Japanese involved that information will be kept in intelligence channels and not employed for "war crimes" evidence.

7. Documentary immunity from "war crimes" given to higher echelon personnel involved will result in exploiting the twenty years experience of the director, former General ISHII, who can assure complete cooperation of his former subordinates, indicate the connection of the Japanese General Staff

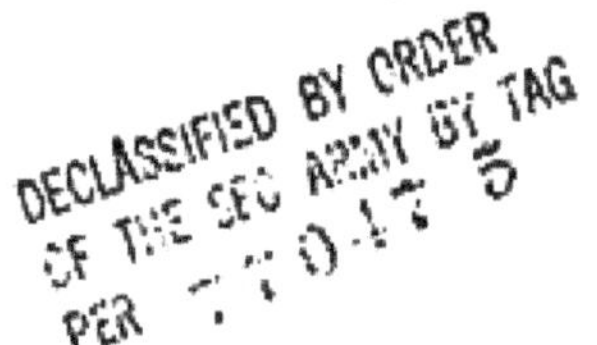

CONFIDENTIAL

TOP SECRET

TOP SECRET — CONFIDENTIAL

6 May 1947

MEMO FOR RECORD: (continued)

and provide the tactical and strategic information.

8. Method described in paragraph 6 will best guard against possibility of publicity and will safeguard valuable intelligence information. This method is recommended in suggested radio.

RPM ( ) 26-6166

DECLASSIFIED BY ORDER OF THE SEC ARMY BY TAG PER

TOP SECRET

2 TIAL

10.24 6 May 1947: C-52423, FROM: CINCFE, TO: WDGID (PASS TO CCMLC), C. S. MYERS, Col. G. S. C. Executive Off. G-2

资料出处：National Archives of the United States, R153, E145.

内容点评：本资料为 1947 年 5 月 6 日美军远东司令部 G-2 执行长官 C. S. Myers 上校发送美陆军部电文 C-52423，Fell 博士予将军 Waitt 的信函 4 月 29 日、5 月 3 日由航空信使送达。本电文共 5 部分，内容参考 1947 年 5 月 13 日 SWNCC 351/2/D 文件（资料 10.25）。

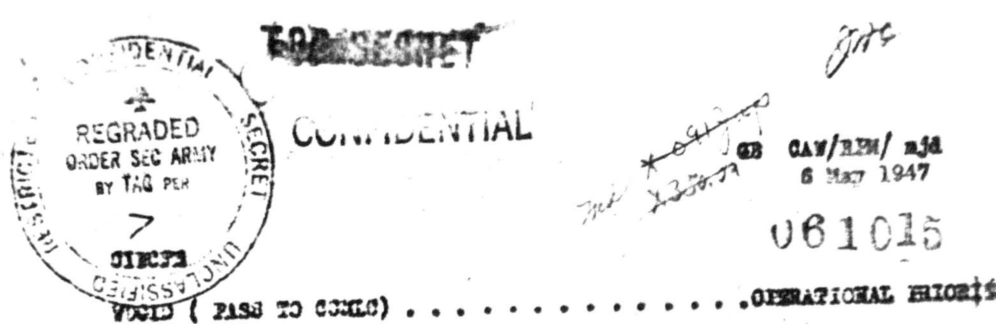

TOP SECRET

CONFIDENTIAL

REGRADED ORDER SEC ARMY BY TAG PER

CINCFE

WCSD (PASS TO CGCMLC) . . . . .OPERATIONAL PRIORITY

GB CAW/RBM/ mjd
6 May 1947

061015

PARTY C-52423 PAREN REQUEST MIKE ITEM DOG PASS TO MAJOR GENERAL ALDEN WAITT PD RE JIG CHARLIE SUGAR RADIO WILLIAM NINE FOUR FOUR FOUR SIX CMA SUGAR WILLIAM NAN CHARLIE CHARLIE THREE FIVE ONE LINE ONE AND DOCTOR FELLS LETTERS VIA AIR COURIER TO GENERAL WAITT TWENTY NINE APRIL AND THREE MAY NINETEEN FORTY SEVEN PD THIS RADIO IS IN FIVE PARTS PD PARA PART ONE DASH STATEMENTS OBTAINED FROM JAPANESE HERE CONFIRM STATEMENTS OF UNCLE SUGAR SUGAR ROGER PRISONERS KAWASHIMA AND KARASAWA CONTAINED IN COPIES OF INTERROGATIONS GIVEN UNCLE SUGAR BY UNCLE SUGAR SUGAR ROGER PD PARA PART TWO DASH EXPERIMENTS ON HUMANS WERE KNOWN TO AND DESCRIBED BY THREE JAPANESE AND CONFIRMED TACITLY BY ISHII SMCLN FIELD TRIALS AGAINST CHINESE ARMY TOOK PLACE ON AT LEAST THREE OCCASIONS SMCLN SCOPE OF PROGRAM INDICATED BY REPORT OF RELIABLE INFORMANT MATSUDA THAT FOUR HUNDRED KILOGRAMS OF DRIED ANTHRAX ORGANISMS DESTROYED AT PINGFAN IN AUGUST NINETEEN FORTY FIVE SEMICLN AND RESEARCH ON USE OF BAKER WILLIAM AGAINST PLANT LIFE WAS CARRIED OUT PD RELUCTANT STATEMENTS BY ISHII INDICATE HE HAD SUPERIORS PAREN POSSIBLY GENERAL STAFF PAREN WHO KNEW AND AUTHORIZED THE PROGRAM PD ISHII STATES THAT IF GUARANTEED IMMUNITY FROM QUOTE WAR CRIMES UNQUOTE IN DOCUMENTARY FORM FOR HIMSELF CMA SUPERIORS AND SUBORDINATES CMA HE CAN DESCRIBE PROGRAM IN DETAIL PD ISHII CLAIMS TO HAVE EXTENSIVE THEORETICAL HIGH DASH LEVEL KNOWLEDGE INCLUDING STRATEGIC AND TACTICAL USE OF BAKER WILLIAM ON DEFENSE AND OFFENSE CMA BACKED BY SOME RESEARCH ON BEST BAKER WILLIAM AGENTS TO EMPLOY BY GEOGRAPHICAL AREAS OF FAR EAST CMA AND THE USE OF BAKER WILLIAM IN COLD CLIMATES

44446-000.5 W.C. (TS-S)
SWNCC 351/1 - Current files

A G RECORDS RBM/ mjd

DECLASSIFIED BY ORDER OF THE SEC ARMY BY TAG PER

TOP SECRET

CONFIDENTIAL

TOP SECRET

GB CAW/RPM/ mjd
6 May 1947

CONFIDENTIAL

CINCFE

WDGID (PASS TO CCMLC) . . . . .OPERATIONAL PRIORITY
(PAGE 2 continued)

PD PARA PART THREE DASH ABLE PD STATEMENTS SO FAR HAVE BEEN OBTAINED BY PERSUASION CMA EXPLOITATION OF JAPANESE FEAR OF UNCLE SUGAR SUGAR ROGER CMA AND DESIRE TO COOPERATE WITH UNCLE SUGAR PD LARGE PART OF DATA INCLUDING MOST OF THE VALUABLE TECHNICAL BAKER WILLIAM INFORMATION AS TO RESULTS OF HUMAN EXPERIMENTS AND RESEARCH IN BAKER WILLIAM FOR CROP DESTRUCTION PROBABLY CAN BE OBTAINED IN THIS MANNER FROM LOW ECHELON JAPANESE PERSONNEL NOT RELIEVED LIABLE TO QUOTE WAR CRIMES UNQUOTE TRIALS PD PARA BAKER PD ADDITIONAL DATA CMA POSSIBLY INCLUDING SOME STATEMENTS FROM ISHII PROBABLY CAN BE OBTAINED BY INFORMING JAPANESE INVOLVED THAT INFORMATION WILL BE RETAINED IN INTELLIGENCE CHANNELS AND WILL NOT CMA REPEAT NOT CMA BE EMPLOYED AS QUOTE WAR CRIMES UNQUOTE EVIDENCE PD PARA CHARLIE PD COMPLETE STORY CMA TO INCLUDE PLANS AND THEORIES OF ISHII AND SUPERIORS CMA PROBABLY CAN BE OBTAINED BY DOCUMENTARY IMMUNITY TO ISHII AND ASSOCIATES PD ISHII ALSO CAN ASSIST IN SECURING COMPLETE COOPERATION OF HIS FORMER SUBORDINATES PD PARA PART FOUR DASH NONE OF ABOVE INFLUENCES JOINT INTERROGATIONS TO BE HELD SHORTLY WITH UNCLE SUGAR SUGAR/ ROGER UNDER PROVISIONS OF YOUR RADIO WILLIAM DASH NINE FOUR FOUR FOUR SIX PD PARA PART FIVE DASH ADOPTION OF METHOD IN PART THREE BAKER ABOVE RECOMMENDED BY CHARLIE ITEM NAN CHARLIE FOX EASY PERIOD REQUEST REPLY SOONEST PD

DECLASSIFIED BY ORDER OF THE SEC ARMY BY TAG PER 770475

OFFICIAL

APPROVED BY:

TOP SECRET

R. M. LEVY
Colonel, AGD
Adjutant General

REFERENCE RADIO W-94446

C. S. MYERS
Colonel, G.S.C.
Executive Off. G-2

Dist: 5-AG, 1-G-2 File, 1-G-2 Return

- 2 -

10.25 13 May 1947: SWNCC 351/2/D: STATE-WAR-NAVY COORDINATING COMMITTEE, DIRECTIVE, INTERROGATION OF CERTAIN JAPANESE BY RUSSIAN PROSECUTOR, References: a. SWNCC 351/D, b. SWNCC 351/1

资料出处：National Archives of the United States, R153,E145,B73.

内容点评：本资料为 1947 年 5 月 13 日美国国务院—陆军部—海军部三部协调委员会秘书处通告三部协调委员会（SWNCC 351/2/D），题目：苏联检察官讯问某些日本人。附：总参谋部转来电文 C-52423，请远东小委员会准备答复草案。C-52423 第 2 部分提及：对中国军队至少实施了三次试验性实战攻击；1945 年 8 月，在平房销毁了 400 公斤干燥炭疽菌。

20 MAY 1947

014 Japan (13 Apr 44)
Sec 11-B

TOP SECRET COPY NO 20

SWNCC 351/2/D

13 May 1947

TOP SECRET

TOP SECRET COPY NO. 20

SWNCC 351/2/D

13 May 1947

Pages 7 and 8

STATE-WAR-NAVY COORDINATING COMMITTEE

DIRECTIVE

INTERROGATION OF CERTAIN JAPANESE
BY RUSSIAN PROSECUTOR

References: a. SWNCC 351/D
b. SWNCC 351/1

Note by the Secretaries

The enclosure, a message from the Commander-in-Chief, Far East, forwarded by the Joint Chiefs of Staff for the basis of a reply, is referred to the State-War-Navy Coordinating Subcommittee for the Far East for preparation of a draft reply.

H. W. MOSELEY

W. A. SCHULGEN

V. L. LOWRANCE

Secretariat

SWNCC 351/2/D

TOP SECRET

TOP SECRET

E N C L O S U R E

From: CINCFE Tokyo Japan

To: War Department for WDGID (pass to CCMLC) MID pass to Major General Alden Waitt

Nr: C-52423 6 May 1947

JCS radio W 94446 (Appendix "A" to SWNCC 351/1) SWNCC 351/1 and Doctor Fell's letters via air courier to General Waitt 29 April and 3 May 1947. This radio is in 5 parts.

Part 1-Statements obtained from Japanese here confirm statements of USSR prisoners Kawashima and Karasawa contained in copies of interrogations given US by USSR.

Part 2-Experiments on humans were known to and described by 3 Japanese and confirmed tacitly by Ishii; field trials against Chinese Army took place on at least 3 occasions; scope of program indicated by report of reliable informant Matsuda that 400 kilograms of dried anthrax organisms destroyed at Pingfan in August 1945; and research on use of BW against plant life was carried out. Reluctant statements by Ishii indicate he had superiors (possibly General Staff) who knew and authorized the program. Ishii states that if guaranteed immunity from "war crimes" in documentary form for himself, superiors and subordinates, he can describe program in detail. Ishii claims to have extensive theoretical high-level knowledge including strategic and tactical use of BW on defense and offense, backed by some research on best BW agents to employ by geographical areas of Far East, and the use of BW in cold climates.

Part 3-A. Statements so far have been obtained by persuasion, exploitation of Japanese fear of USSR, and desire to cooperate with US. Large part of data including most of the valuable technical BW information as to results of human experiments and research in BW for crop destruction probably can be obtained in this manner from low echelon Japanese personnel not

TOP SECRET

believed liable to "war crimes" trials.

B. Additional data, possibly including some statements from Ishii probably can be obtained by informing Japanese involved that information will be retained in intelligence channels and will not be employed as "war crimes" evidence.

C. Complete story, to include plans and theories of Ishii and superiors, probably can be obtained by documentary immunity to Ishii and associates. Ishii also can assist in securing complete cooperation of his former subordinates.

4. None of above influences joint interrogations to be held shortly with USSR under provisions of your radio W-94446.

5-Adoption of method in Part 3B above recommended by CINCFE. Request reply soonest.

End

CM IN 912　　(May 47)

10.26　13 May 1947: Interrogation of MURAKAMI, Takashi, Interrogator: Col. SMIRNOV, Monitors: Dr. Fell & Lt. Col. McQUAIL; 16 May 1947: Interrogation of OTA Kiyoshi, Interrogator: Col. SMIRNOV, Monitors: Dr. Fell & Lt. Col. McQUAIL; 13 Jun. 1947: Interrogation of ISHII, Shiro, Interrogator: Col. SMIRNOV, Sponsor: Lt. Col. McQUAIL

资料出处： The University of Virginia Law Library, the Paper of Tavenner, Box 5.

内容点评： 本资料包括三份文件，远东国际法庭苏联检察官 SMIRNOV 上校 1947 年 5 月 13 日对村上隆（MURAKAMI，Takashi）讯问记录，监督：Dr. Fell 调查官、McQuail 中校；5 月 16 日对大田澄（OTA，Kiyoshi）讯问记录，监督：Dr. Fell 调查官、McQuail 中校；6 月 13 日对石井四郎（ISHII，Shiro）讯问记录；主办：McQuail 中校。

GENERAL HEADQUARTERS
FAR EAST COMMAND
ALLIED TRANSLATOR & INTERPRETER SECTION
CENTRAL INTERROGATION CENTER

APO 500
10 Jun 47

Interrogation: 13 May 1947

Interrogee: MURAKAMI, Takashi

Interrogator: Col SMIRNOV

Interpreter: W/O YOSHIHASHI & Capt SHVEITZER

Stenographer: NODA, Ichiro

Monitors: Dr. FELL & Lt Col McQUAIL

Q. First, do you have anything to say?

A. I thought it over last night quietly and I would like to make a statement.

Q. Please tell us about it.

A. There was a research sub-section of Technician YAMAGUCHI among the sub-sections, such as a Navigation, General Affairs, Air, and Material which I mentioned yesterday. In addition to the 2nd Section there was the Insect sub-section which belonged to the 4th Section and others from time to time.

Q. And what else?

A. I only recalled that much. I will tell you if I recall some more.

Q. Was the laboratory building in which the insects were cultivated a two story structure?

A. Yes, it was.

Q. Was the sub-section chief TANAKA, Hideo?

A. Yes.

Q. Was he in that position before you were appointed as a section chief?

A. He was in that position before I was appointed.

Q. Was TANAKA receiving material directly from you or from some other party?

A. He used to ask me on the matters concerning routine office work and personnel affairs problems but I never directed him on other matters since I was unable to instruct him in his work.

Q. From whom did TANAKA receive orders for his experiments?

A. In formality there was a 2nd Section chief, and superficially he was under my command and he used to receive orders directly in many cases.

Q. What was the main duty of Technician TANAKA? Was he studying the breeding of insects?

A. I believe he was an entomologist well informed in that field. I was informed as such and he probably was.

Q. He was experimenting with various insects but wasn't he especially interested in lice, fleas and ticks? Lice are related with typhoid, fleas with plague, and ticks with hemorrhagic fever (Songo fever) aren't they?

A. Yes, that is right.

Q. Among them on which insect did he study most enthusiastically?

A. With fleas.

Q. For what reasons? Who was most interested in fleas?

A. Plague epidemics broke out frequently in the CHANGCHUNG and NUNG-AN Areas. Since these areas are the plague infected zones and because we were located near that zone, from the standpoint of anti-epidemic, more research was pursued in that line.

Q. Is it true that there was a Materials sub-section in your section?

A. Yes.

Q. What sort of machine and installation and how many did the Materials sub-section have and distribute to the Insect Sub-section which was carrying out laboratory experiments with insects and parasites?

A. In YAMAGUCHI's sub-section isn't it? There were shells which they manufactured for experimental purposes and which I more or less referred to previously as a Material sub-section. The materials were for manufacturing experimental shells.

Q. What I want to know is through what channels were the materials supplied to the flea sub-section.

A. The 2nd Section was not engaged in distribution of materials for the flea sub-section.

Q. What installations did the insect sub-section have?

A. There were no special things to be mentioned except the fact that it had some cans and glass containers.

Q. How many empty cans were there?

A. I don't remember the number. I don't remember it because I was not interested in it.

Q. I will read a statement made by a high ranking officer. He belonged to the same unit as yours and he was working with you. "There were about 4,500 empty cans to be used as cultivators in the section. We could breed approximately 45 kilograms of fleas within three or four months." Was it true?

A. I don't remember that the number of the cans was 4,500, however I believe that it was a considerable number. That general officer probably knew in detail about mass production of vaccines. I believe he knew about such matters because he was well acquainted with the mass production method. I believe he was more professional than I.

Q. Not only this general officer knew about the mass cultivation of fleas but also other persons who held important positions did too. Of course you don't know the exact number because you had no direct connection with the flea cultivation. However, can you agree that it was a considerable number?

A. Although they cultivated them, the amount of production was much less than anticipated. The large quantity stated was merely a plan, and I think I have heard that it was actually unable to produce them in large quantities.

Q. Do you mean fleas?

A. Yes.

Q. Was it rather easy to obtain 45 kilograms of fleas when needed?

A. I don't know exactly because I was not a specialist and was not interested in that line, but I believe that the numerical figure given was exaggerated. I believe that they were far short of that figure in actual production.

Q. Then don't you know how much it was?

A. I can't say exactly. I believe it has been the traits of the research workers to exaggerate their results and boast about their achievement, and it was a prevalent trend for them to speak about things as successful even when the results were far short of their original plans. I believe it was a common practice to announce the results, though only one-fifth or one-tenth of the original estimate, as if succeeding in producing ten or twenty times more than they planned and boasting about their achievement.

Q. Because probably you, yourself, had seen the experimental reports submitted by the flea sub-section, I would think you knew the approximate quantities of fleas cultivated.

A. The flea cultivation was a failure and certainly not as much as it was stated. The section failed to produce even one-tenth of the contemplated amount.

Q. In that case, whom were they trying to deceive by submitting false reports? Were they trying to deceive you or the unit commander?

A. I don't know the psychological factors involved, but I believe that in those days that tendency was quite prevalent, and they tend to give exaggerated reports.

Q. Were exaggerated false reports for the unit commander? Were they submitting false experimental reports to deceive the unit commander?

A. By exaggerating their reports, the result was that they were deceiving him. But I don't know whether they purposely tried to deceive him or not.

Q. I am going to ask you once more about the cultivators. Approximately how many empty cans were being used? Were they using about 100, 200, or several thousands?

A. It depends upon the season, but as far as I know I believe it was around a thousand

Q. Why is it that the unit had empty cans as much as a thousand then they were using them only for flea experiments?

A. I believe the surplus cans owned by the 4th Section were given to them. They were given because there was no space to store them in the 4th Section. I don't think that they used all of them at one time. They were just stocked there. I don't think they were all used at one time.

Q. Are you saying that they did not use all of the empty cans at the same time?

A. They did not use all of them for cultivation of fleas.

Q. I'll ask you more about this later. I'll ask you after I know more about your position and duty. Your responsibility as a chief of the 2nd Section must have been especially great. I agree with you that you performed your duties as ordered from above and then, these various orders were carried out by others. So, I think you should be able to inform us who issued the orders and who was most interested in flea cultivation. Who was that person? It is inconceivable that you were totally ignorant of these matters.

A. I may be impolite but may I leave that to your imagination? I am unable to answer any more than what I've said already.

Q. You stated that to leave it to our imagination. Does that mean you are unable to answer any more or merely you don't want to tell us any more?

A. In regards to the source of orders for flea cultivation, there are points which we are not too aware of.

Q. The flea sub-section was already in existence when you were appointed as the chief of the 2nd Section, wasn't it?

A. The sub-section was attached here and there depending upon the period, and sometimes it was with the 2nd Section. It was already in existence before I assumed my position with the unit.

Q. No matter how we look at it, the number of empty cans was more than sufficient for cultivating fleas needed for carrying out the anti-epidemic research. Why was it necessary to have so many empty cans to cultivate fleas for the typhus experiments?

A. The unit possessed many empty cans to be used as cultivators but the surplus was given to the aviation sub-section, etc., and the insect sub-section did not use all of them.

Q. Weren't these numerous empty cans stored with the thought that they were to be used in case of emergency?

A. I don't know about that.

Q. Then do you remember that you went to Central CHINA in summer of 1942?

A. I don't remember it.

Q. I appreciate that it is difficult for you to recall on account of your malaria, but it is difficult to conceive that your almost total forgetfulness can be attributed solely to malaria. Recall as much as you can.

A. I understand.

Q. By whose order was this expeditionary unit sent?

A. I don't know.

Q. Three conferences were held in relation to this expeditionary unit. Where and who convened these conferences?

A. Many conferences were held irregularly so I don't remember the time, place and the nature of these conferences.

Q. As for yourself, under whose order were you fulfilling your duty?

A. I received order directly from the unit commander. Not only the chief of the 2nd Section but all the section chiefs were under the control of unit commander. Everybody was in a subordinate position to the unit commander.

Q. Who was he?

A. The unit commander from March 1939 to August 1942 was Maj Gen ISHII.

Q. Well then, do you remember yourself the whereabouts of Maj Gen ISHII during the spring or summer of 1942?

A. I am not sure.

Q. Do you know, at least, that Maj Gen ISHII did go somewhere during that time?

A. Since Maj Gen ISHII was also an instructor at the military medical school, he often went away from the unit on airplane or train. I don't remember definitely, however.

Q. If that is the case, did he go to TOKYO?

A. I don't know about then. He was instructing a course on anti-epidemic measures at the military medical school. It doesn't necessarily mean that he went to TOKYO only then. Sometimes he went to instruct after being called by the school. I don't mean to say that he came to school under such circumstances. He went out now and then so I don't remember clearly where he had gone at any certain time.

Q. Where was this military medical school?

A. In USHIGOME, TOKYO.

Q. Now lets go back to the previous question. Was he at the military medical school at that time?

A. I don't remember clearly the places of his assignments during that year.

Q. Do you remember that Maj Gen ISHII returned from TOKYO, and convened a special conference in July 1942, and that chief of General Affairs Col NAKATOMI, chief of the 1st, and Lt Col MURAKAMI, the chief of the 2nd Section attended the conference?

A. Since conferences were held often with section chiefs, I don't remember what conference was held at any certain time. Furthermore, when section chiefs were to attend the conferences, the chief of all the sections attended the conferences also. It was never limited to such that only the chief of the General Affairs and chiefs of the 1st and the 2nd Sections attended the conference.

Q. I forgot to mention just now, but was Maj Gen KANASHIMA, chief of the 4th Section, present at that conference?

A. When a conference was held the chiefs of all the sections assembled. It was customary to have a long conference with all the section chiefs even on those matters for which a conference seemed unnecessary.

Q. Then do you remember who were present at the conference which was held with the purpose of formulating a plan to send a special expeditionary unit to JAGAW in CENTRAL CHINA?

A. I don't recall any such conference.

Q. Please recall as much as possible. It was a very important conference. Do you recall exactly what Maj Gen ISHII said at this conference?

A. Since I don't recall any such conference being held, then naturally, I don't know its nature.

Q. Then under whose order was the expeditionary unit sent in 1942?

A. I don't know anything about the chain of commands. I don't even remember of any expeditionary unit being sent.

Q. You were the one who was sent as the commander of the expeditionary unit. Why don't you remember such a thing?

A. I was never an expeditionary unit commander.

Q. Then, who was its commander?

A. I don't know.

Q. What was your duty with the expeditionary unit?

A. Other than being the 2nd Section chief I was never appointed as commander of any unit and sent out. I have never gone out as a commander in charge of any unit.

Q. But, in regards to being sent to Central CHINA, you promised us that you'll recall it.

A. It is customary for the highest ranking person to become the unit commander. Heretofore there has been no case in which the junior officer becoming a unit commander when there was a higher ranking person within the unit.

Q. If that is the case, for the first question, were you or were you not sent to Central CHINA in 1942 with the expeditionary unit?

A. I did not go with the unit as a member of an expeditionary unit.

Q. Then on what mission did you go to Central CHINA?

A. During the CHEKUAN ( ) operation I went to Central CHINA on a plane in order to make arrangements for anti-epidemic work and inspection of nucleus unit.

Q. Was your mission to assist the Water Purification Unit in NANKING?

A. It was not so, since anti-epidemic materials for NANKING were to be sent from HARBIN as ordered. I went there to make necessary arrangements.

Q. Did Col NAKATOME go with you?

A. He did not go with me.

Q. If that is the case, Col NAKATOME did not go there, did he?

A. He did not go with us.

Q. Col NAKATOME did go, but he did not go with you, isn't that right?

A. I don't quite remember.

Q. Do you mean he did go but you were not with him, is that it?

A. I am not clear.

Q. According to quite a reliable testimony we know that you and Col NAKATOME went to NANKING. Maj Gen ISHII did not go and the dispatch unit that was sent to Central CHINA was under the command of Lt Col MURAKAMI. Later, Col NAKATOME, the chief of the General Affairs, proceeded to the same place. Is it true that Maj Gen ISHII joined this dispatch unit and later went to Central CHINA?

A. I don't remember.

Q. Who was the commander of the expeditionary unit? Were you the commander? Or Maj Gen ISHII himself the commander?

A. This may not concern the question but I wish to make an explanation on military customs in general. It is not permissable for me to become a unit commander when there are other higher ranking officers. When, however, a transportation commander is required while moving the unit, as for instance from TOKYO to OSAKA, one might be appointed as the transportation commander. In any other case there is no such thing as a subordinate who just happens to be there on a certain mission, taking over the entire command, superseding his superiors.

Q. If that is the case, the highest ranking person that time was Maj Gen ISHII, so Maj Gen ISHII himself must have been the commander, wasn't he?

A. My memory is poor.

Q. The only thing that stands to reason, according to your statement, is that Maj Gen ISHII, Col NAKATOME, and Lt Col MURAKAMI were in the expeditionary unit. Among these, since Maj Gen ISHII was the highest ranking officer, in the final analysis, he must have been the commander.

A. What I said was that was the general custom that was being done. I don't recall anything concerning Central CHINA.

Q. We want you to try harder in recalling the past events. Especially what we want you to recall is why was this expeditionary unit sent and where was it sent?

A. I don't remember.

Q. Why don't you remember? Is it because such an expeditionary unit was sent out frequently and therefore you don't recall?

A. When there were only few soldiers in a unit when a severe epidemic broke out, members of the water purification unit of KWANTUNG Army were dispatched frequently to assist in controlling the epidemic. Consequently, even within the KWANTUNG Army if plague and typhus broke out a part of the unit was sent out to control the epidemic.

Q. You stated that it was sent when an epidemic broke out. If you remember such a dispatch, you must remember when you yourself were sent.

A. I once went to CHANG-CHUN in 1940 when plague broke out.

Q. Then what about when plague broke out at NING PO, located south of SHANGHAI? Do you remember that?

A. I don't remember.

Q. When plague broke out in 1941, in what area were you sent to?

A. Where did I go in 1941? I'm talking about 1940. It was CHANG-CHUN.

Q. When the pest eqidemic broke out in CHANG-CHUN in 1940, why were you sent there? What was your mission?

A. When the plague epidemic broke out in CHANG-CHUN the KWANTUNG Army asked for assistance from the water purification unit. Many specialists were sent then. I was called to take care of the administrative matters.

Q. It was in MANCHURIA, wasn't it?

A. That's right.

Q. Was it a city in MANCHURIA?

A. It is the capital.

Q. Was any expeditionary unit sent from your unit besides this? That is in 1940?

A. I don't know.

Q. Weren't you the chief of the 2nd Section in 1941? Who was your predecessor?

A. He was Col OTA.

Q. Where was an expeditionary unit sent in 1941?

A. I don't remember.

Q. Where was Col OTA sent in 1941?

A. Col OTA was transferred to the Water Purification Unit in NANKING.

Q. Wasn't Col OTA sent to CHENGTE near TUNGTINGHU then?

A. I don't know.

Q. Now, will you recall why you were sent to Central CHINA in ~~1943~~ 1942?

A. I was sent then to carry on the anti-epidemic work inspecting men returning from the operational area, disinfecting them and examining their stools, etc.

Q. Then you have just recollected that you were sent to Central China in 1942.

A. That is as I have already stated before, I went by plane separately from the unit.

Q. If you say that you went by an airplane, then you went separately from the expeditionary unit.

A. I went separately.

Q. At the time you went to NANKING, in what region was the expeditionary unit located?

A. It was at HANGCHOU (KOSHU).

Q. Please recall various activities which the unit performed along the JUGAN RR.

A. I don't know what JUGAN means.

Q. Any way, it was in the vicinity of railroad tracks.

A. At the time there were some military operations taking place in Central China and because the troops were evacuating to this area, a quarantine station was organized in HANGCHOU for the purpose of quarantine, analysis of stool, disinfections, and segregation of patients.

Q. Was it you who organised it?

A. I did not organize it, but it was formed.

Q. Was that the time the Japanese Army was carrying out its strategical retreat?

A. Whether it was a strategical retreat or not I don't know. I don't know know anything about the tactical aspects.

Q. Anyway it was during the period when they were retreating, wasn't it?

A. Of course it was during the time when the army was retreating. A medical inpection station was organized there and peformed its duties.

Q. At the time they were evacuating what were you doing? What was your responsibility.

A. I didn't have any responsibility. I performed the administrative and liaison work.

Q. Well, what were the duties of the unit?

A. Anti-epidemic work.

Q. Well, then for an anti-epidemic work, did you place plague and dysentery bacilli in capsules and took them with you?

A. I don't know any truth to that.

Q. Didn't you personally take those bacteria with you?

A. No, I did not.

Q. Then who took them?

A. I don't know.

Q. What did you personally take with you on the airplane?

A. Just myself.

Q. Well, what about your previous statement that you took some bacteria to NANKING.

A. I did not say that. What I stated was that I took vaccines and various other items with me and went there to discuss about the anti-epidemic measures to be taken.

Q. With whom did you discuss about vaccines?

A. I talked with the people connected with the anti-epidemic work. I don't remember their names.

Q. What sort of specialists did you talk with? Were they members of the Water Purification Unit?

A. I talked with the members of the Water Purification Unit too, but I don't remmber precisely who they were.

Q. What was theresult of this negotiation?

A. As a result of this negotiation, it was decided by the Army to establish a medical inspection station in HANGCHOU, and it was organized there.

Q. Of course, we understand well that you were dispatched there for the purpose of carrying out the anti-epidemic work, butwhydid you go so far as to take several kilograms of fleas with you?

A. I don't know a thing about that statement that I took several kilograms of fleas with me and consequently, I don't know the reason for it.

Q. It is strange that you don't know about it since in 1942 you were the CO of the 2nd Section and one of the duties of your section was cultivation of fleas.

A. A thing like that cannot be carried out with my command. I don't know whether a thing like that occurred or not.

Q. Well, then what sort of an establishment did the Nanking Water Purification Unit have?

A. I don't know about the detail matters.

Q. However, you discussed with the members of the Nanking Water Purification Unit concerning anti-epidemic work while you were in NANKING.

A. Of course, I discussed about the number of personnel required to be sent to HANGCHOU Medical Inspection Station, but they were merely administrative matters, and I don't know anything about the detail aspects.

Q. Well, what did the Nanking Water Purification Unit do?

A. Carrying out anti-epidemic and water purification were its duties.

Q. In 1942, by whose orders were you performing the cultivation of fleas? Were you doing it on your own or was there an order from some one else?

A. I don't know about it; I don't know.

Q. Don't you know or don't you remember?

A. I don't know about the orders.

Q. Well, I'll question you again later about the expeditionary unit. Now I'll question you about some of the experiments performed with bombs. What type of bombs was engineer YAMAGUCHI experimenting with?

A. Experimental models were being made. They were porcelain bombs with double walls and were filled with steel fragments. He was carrying out trial experiments with these bombs.

Q. Were there some small steel fragments in these bombs or were there some small steel shots in them?

A. They were steel fragments.

Q. How were the steel fragments contaminated with bacteria?

A. I don't know of any such methods. From the standpoint of anti-epidemic measure, the experiments were done to determine the area of contamination and dispersion of iron fragments should we be attacked with bombs in a BW and also the trajectory of the bombs.

Q. Please draw the shape of the bombs.

A. (Drawings)

Q. There were bacteria in these porcelain bombs, weren't they?

A. It was not filled with bacteria.

Q. If it were to be filled with bacteria, where would they be placed?

A. I don't know how to fill it. We filled it with dyed liquid, and carried out simulated experiments for determination of the area of dispersion.

Q. Well, from where was the dyed liquid filled?

A. I don't know about it.

Q. At where were the trials performed?

A. They were done with in the airfield around the runway since the results were more noticeable.

Q. Was it a pace called ANDA?

A. I don't know.

Q. Why is it that you don't know of the experimental station called ANDA? The experimental station was under your direction.

A. I wish you would check the period. It was not there at the time I was in Manchuria.

Q. Well, we, ourselves, will investigate about that. Then, at where were the experiments on livestock carried out?

A. In our work we never experimented with livestock.

Q. Considering from the standpoint of anti-epidemic, it is odd that no experiments with livestock were done.

A. At that time while I was the section chief mostly, it could even be said all, the tests were concerned with dispersion of bomb fragments and dyed liquid and trajectory. We found no necessity in performing experiments on animals. What we were seeking was the physical data of these bombs.

Q. Do you remember KITAGAWA?

A. KITAGAWA and I were together for only a brief period so we didn't have much time to be acquainted.

Q. However, weren't you one of KITAGAWA's subordinates?

A. I was never a subordinate of KITAGAWA.

Q. Was KITAGAWA, at any time, one of your subordinates?

A. KITAGAWA was about two or three years senior to me.

Q. Wasn't he a colonel and a chief of the research section?

A. I don't know about it exactly. KITAGAWA was transferred from some other unit to ours, and I had known him for a very brief period. Since I, myself, did not always remain with the unit, being dispatched to other places, our stay together was, indeed short.

Q. Well, then, when was KITAGAWA the chief of the 1st section?

A. I think it was around 1941.

Q. At the time of experiments with bombs containing bacteria, especially plague, didn't Col KITAGAWA confer with you.

A. I had never discussed with KITAGAWA on that matter.

Q. Isn't it quite impossible for the 1st section to be performing experiments without discussing with your section since the 2nd section had the planes and bombs?

A. KITAGAWA was with the unit from 1941. From the time I became the section chief in July 1941 to the time I departed from the unit during that short period, we didn't peform any experiments. He was transferred to the unit in 1941 and left it in the spring of 1942.

Q. When did KITAGAWA become the chief of the 1st section.

A. I think it was about August 1941.

Q. And when did he join the unit.

A. I believe it was about spring of 41.

Q. When did you become the chief of the 2nd Section?

A. It was in July 1941.

Q. According to your testimony, from summer of 1941 to spring of 1942 you worked together with KITAGAWA?

A. During that time KITAGAWA was on temporary duty to Formosa and the Army Medical School, and I think our acquaintance was of very short period. I don't remember exactly.

Q. This time I am going to read an accurate testimony given by a person so will you please listen.

In the vicinity of ANDA Station there was an experiment station. I personally witnessed a test, and in this test two methods of disseminating bacteria were performed. One method was to drop fleas from an airplane, the other was dropping of bombs filled with fleas. I witnessed both of these tests, but I don't exactly remember the date. I think it was about in June of 1941. I stayed at the place all day and witnessed the trials. The trials were held in the vicinity of ANDA Station. That station was one of the stations located in the western end of the Eastern Chinese RR. It was about one hundred kilometers from HARBIN. The experimental station was about ten kilometers away from the station. There were many houses in that vicinity. I don't exactly remember as to the number. The houses were located on the south side and none were in the north. Furthermore, these tests were on animals and human beings.

A. I don't know a thing about them. At that time I couldn't have been the section chief. You just stated as being around May, and I became the section chief in June. I don't know such an experiment at all. While I was the section chief, such a maneuver was never held aside from one or two basic physical tests and a maneuver in air communication between the ground unit and a plane.

Q. If the test had been conducted at ANDA before you became the chief of the section, weren't there any other tests performed after you became the chief of the 2nd Section?

A. It seems to me that there wasn't any regular practice field possessed by the unit. Elementary maneuvers were frequently held near the airfield of the unit.

- NOON RECESS -

Q. Have you anything to say after thinking the matters over?

A. I don't have any just now.

Q. Who was the first one who thought about the BW?

A. I do not know.

Q. Why don't you know that such things were carried out? Please listen to me because I have considerable reliable proof. The experimental field itself was divided in sections and the following different trials were being experimented:

The first method was dropping of infected fleas, the second method, dropping of bombs filled with infected fleas; the third, dropping of bombs filled with bacteria from an airplane; and the fourth, the bacterial rain. I don't think you can state that you have never seen these trials?

A. I have never seen any experiments with loaded bombs, however, I have seen, near the airfield, simulated trials which were to promote defense measures and the tests were to determine the area of dispersion of bomb fragments.

Q. Does loaded shell mean that which is filled with bacteria?

A. Yes, that's what I meant.

Q. Then, you have not seen any actual tests with loaded bombs, however, you have seen bomb trials filled with dyed liquid.

A. Yes, that is right.

Q. Then, please listen to another testimony.

After the bombs were dropped the laboratory workers investigated the dispersion area of the bacteria, the conditions of the animals and approximately how many fleas were on each animal. These tests were conducted not only on animals but also on human beings and checked the degrees of infection. Papers were placed on the ground of the experimental field to check whether the bacteria rain dropped in that particular area or not. They also checked the condition of the cultured media. The last two tests were checked within the laboratory. The contaminated culture media were analysed within the laboratory to determine whether they were really infected or not. The degrees of infection on the animals were checked. What do you think about this testimony? Haven't you seen any of these tests?

A. Actually I have never seen any of them, but I have seen the tests which were to determine the area dispersion of the dyed liquid by checking our clothes, papers placed on the ground and the runway within the airfield. I have never seen any experiments with animals as stated in the latter part of the testimony. I've never seen it while I was there.

Q. What kind of tests were the ones you saw being conducted near the airfield?

A. I saw tests in which dyed liquid representing bacteria sprinkled from an airplane to determine the condition of dispersion. It was also done with porcelain bombs to determine the area of dispersion of the dyed liquid and fragments and ascertain the area of "contamination". As to the papers, number of droplets per unit square was checked.

Q. If such a bomb were to be used in the war, were the fleas to be placed in these porcelain bombs?

A. I don't know. I believe it is very difficult to say whether it would be successful or not.

Q. We are interested in the experiments.

A. I am not a bacteriologist and have never studied about bombs and airplanes. I might be able to answer you if I had studied about them even a little. In that respect, I'm an amateur and can not answer your question. With my average doctor's knowledge I don't think it is possible to keep bacteria alive for any appreciable time. With my common sense, I think it is impossible to keep living things alive after they are placed in bombs and heated to a certain temperature.

Q. We know that the two methods were used for the tests. One method was to drop the infected fleas directly from an airplane; the other was to drop bombs filled with infected fleas. What do you know about these two methods?

A. I don't think there are any methods of using them. I don't think they could be used.

Q. We are not concerned with your own ideas, what we want to know is whether such tests were conducted and whether you have witnessed these tests or not.

A. I can not answer it.

Q. Have you ever heard about it?

A. I have not heard that it was actually done.

Q. Didn't they conduct any similar experiments?

A. As I stated before, simulated experiments with dyed liquid were conducted on a small scale near the airfield.

Q. What I am interested in is not such experiments but the one which actually used fleas.

A. While I was there such shell was never used.

Q. Then I am going to read about the test which you must have seen or heard. The following can be said as a result of the test:

The result of the experiment was very successful and the bacteria did hit the target, however, the degree of infection was not very good. According to KITAGAWA, this was caused by the poor condition of the fleas used. The percentage of infection was very poor and I don't know how many percent was infected.

Did KITAGAWA himself tell you about the result of the experiment?

A. KITAGAWA was assigned to our unit in August 1941 and the following spring he was transferred to another unit. During the time we were together, Colonel KITAGAWA and I never discussed about such subject since both of us were away on trips frequently. Col KITAGAWA was with the unit previously, but I was not there at that time.

Q. Did Colonel OTA speak to you about these experiments?

A. No, he did not.

Q. It is regrettable that you are ignorant of these experiments. You were chief of the 2nd Section, and since you had an important position surely you must have heard aboutthem.

A. Although I was the section chief, I was not an authority in that field and I always had a doubt as to my command and its limitations. Superficially I was the section chief but I was never definite as to the limit of my responsibility.

Q. Was Technician YAMAGUCHI working under you?

A. Yes, he was.

Q. From whom was Capt. YAMADA receiving instructions to carry out his duties?

A. Major HIRAZAWA.

Q. In another word, Captain YAMADA was one of your subordinates, wasn't he?

A. Yes, he was.

Q. Whose subordinate was 1st Lt. KOIKE?

A. He was in the 1st Section.

Q. Didn't your men speak to you about various experiments?

A. The experiments conducted by my men were as I've mentioned before, elementary experiments using planes of the aviation sub-section under Major HIRAZAWA, and I had no control over things connected with bacteriology. I was not connected with it.

Q. Of course, we know that the bacteriology is connected with machinery, however we know that 2nd section was related with bacteria from the technical standpoint too. What sort of experiments did you conduct within your section?

A. I didn't do any. I never handled animals or bacteria. I want to make it clear that aside from my regular duty I tested the blood which I extracted from the ears of the patient who had SONGO fever in SUNWU Hospital. The test was requested by SUNWU Hospital.

Q. I don't want to know what you did. Isn't it true that nobody in the world would overlook experiments on animals in studying bacteriology?

A. No, no one does.

Q. Do you mean to say that you never conducted experiments with animals or you never knew about them?

A. I said that in the fundamental experiments with which I was connected, we never conducted any experiments on animals.

Q. Then were there some experiments on animals conducted within the unit?

A. Animals were used in manufacturing vaccines and for the bacterial tests.

Q. What type of animals were used?

A. They were guinea pigs, rabbits, horses and white mice.

Q. Then did you use some cows at the field experimental station?

A. No cows were used. I do not know about it.

Q. Did you use any other large animals?

A. I do not know, I have never been to the place.

Q. Other interrogees told us that they used large animals for their experiments.

A. It might be true if they saw such trials, but I've never seen it. Such an experiment has never been conducted in my section.

Q. Then what section was conducting these field experiments?

A. The field experiments were never conducted in my section. The serum sub-section would use horses. It is inconceivable that the 4th Section would be using large animals in their laboratory.

Q. Do you know that they were experimenting on open-wound infection with plague and anthrax within your section?

A. While I was the section chief I have never done it or heard about it?

Q. Haven't you forgotten about it?

A. During my stay from July 1941 to July 1943 as theChief of the section, the outdoor experiments on infection through open wounds which you said wereconducted on horses and cows and small animals were never carried out. They were never done.

Q. Then what was the purpose of taking a large quantity of fleas to Central CHINA in 1942?

A. I did not take any.

Q. Who took them?

A. I do not know.

Q. Your attitude anddenials about all of these things are well understood by the investigators. What did your subordinate technician TANAKA, Hideo say about fleas? How were the fleas cultivated?

A. I do not know. I don't think they were bred in quantity.

Q. What was the purpose of flea cultivation?

A. I think it was carried out with the purpose of advancement of anti-epidemic measure.

Q. We know, too, that immunization methods can be studied by experimenting with fleas. With what immunization are fleas related?

A. I do not know, I think the immunization was studied by experimenting with fleas and flea-carrying animals.

Q. What was the object of these experiments?

A. As I have said before, it was for the purpose of developing a better anti-epidemic method.

Q. What were used in the experiments with fleas? What kind of animals were used by the 1st Section?

A. Rats and guinea pigs were used.

Q. Were the rats guarded by the manchurian guards?

A. I do not know.

Q. Why don't you know about these things? We know that there were special guards. Wouldn't it be better if you didn't say such nonsense? Of course we know that they had rats there. We know that they were kept, and that human experiments were done too. Can you recollect these things?

A. I do not know.

Q. Is this diagram correct?

A. I think it is generally correct.

Q. What were in these two buildings?

A. The laboratories of the 1st and 4th sections were located here. As I have already stated yesterday, I came near here on business, but it was large and far. This whole place was taken up by the laboratories of 1st and 4th sections.

Q. When experiments similar to the field experiments were carried out within the unit, what kind of people were brought and from where?

A. I do not know.

Q. Please recall it because we know about them anyway.

A. I have never used such a thing before. I don't know where they were brought over from or whether there were such people there or not.

Q. We are not asking you whether or not you yourself did such experiments. We want to know whether or not there were such experiments being done within the unit.

A. I don't know.

Q. What we cannot comprehend is why you don't say the truth.

A. I can't tell you what I don't know.

Q. Then I want you to explain in detail the kind of work you did when you were dispatched to Central CHINA.

A. I went to NANKING by plane during the early part of June, though I don't remember the day. I made preliminary arrangements on anti-epidemic work with NANKING Water Purification Unit and NANKING Army Hq. This was the preliminary arrangement for the establishment of a quarantine station in HANG CHOU and to serve the returning troops in disinfecting them, examining their stool, giving them baths and changing their clothing.

Q. What other thing did you do at the same time?

A. I performed administrative affairs relating to these.

Q. What kind of work did you do? By administrative affairs, do you mean that you did general affairs work?

A. Such things as sending workers to the HANG-CHOU quarantine station, and buying disinfectants and other necessary things through orderlies.

Q. Of course we recognize that as being a part of the work done by the expeditionary unit. But what other things did the unit do?

A. It assisted in carrying out the anti-epidemic work of the returning units.

Q. Then how long did you stay in Central CHINA?

A. In 1942, isn't it, about four months.

Q. Were you related solely with the anti-epidemic work during that four-month period?

A. Yes.

Q. Then by whose order did you go to CHINA in 1942?

A. By order of the unit commander.

Q. Do you mean Major General ISHII?

A. Yes.

Q. By whose order was the expeditionary unit sent to Central CHINA?

A. I do not know.

Q. Do you know from whom Major General ISHII received the order to send the expeditionary unit to CHINA?

A. That, I do not know.

Q. Then was the place in CHINA where it was sent under the supreme command of the KWANTUNG Army or was it a jurisdiction of another army?

A. I do not know such things pertaining to subordination.

Q. However, you knew whether the men under your direction was under the command of the KWANGTUNG Army or under some other army, when you practiced anti-epidemic work didn't you?

A. Since I wasn't a unit commander and although I was there, I was always unattached and I received no direct order from the KWANTUNG Army. I had Major General ISHII as my immediate unit commander.

Q. Ones more thing which we want to know is, was your anti-epidemic work performed on the men of the KWANGTUNG Army or on men of some other army?

A. Anti-epidemic measure was done on the men of the Central China Army.

Q. Do you mean then, that the expeditionary unit was sent to a place outside of the Kwangtung Army's jurisdiction?

A. A very few of them were in the Army in CHINA.

Q. Such a thing wasn't done by the Kwangtung Army on its own authority, was it?

A. It wasn't done by its own discretion.

Q. Then, did such orders come from some other headquarters?

A. I don't know too well aboutthose matters.

Q. Then what did Major General ISHII himself tell you about this expedition?

A. I don't remember.

Q. Then I'll read it again and hope that you will be able to recall these things. This is the scene on the day a certain general officer attended a conference called by Major General ISHII. Please listen to this. At this conference, Maj. Gen. ISHII himself said that an order had come specially from the General Staff Headquarter in TOKYO. This order said that a special expeditionary unit was to be sent to Central CHINA in the near future. Then he said that Chinese soldiers were to be attacked with bacteria. According to ISHII at that time, this attack was to be carried out at JAGAN, near a railway line. Maj. Gen. ISHII called a conference three times for the purpose of bacterialogical warfare against the Chinese forces and at this conference it was discussed as to the type of bacteria to be used and by what methods the bacteria are to be disseminated. It was decided at this conference to use plague, cholera, typhoid and paratyphoid. Can you recall now such a conference was held after listening to what I have just read?

A. Maj. Gen. ISHII was one who held conferences frequently, calling conferences for important and unimportant matters alike, so I don't remember definitely when and what he said.

Q. Bacterial attacks were not carried out so often: therefore there weren't very many conference relating to that.

A. I'll think it over.

Q. Please consider it well, so as not to put yourself into an unkward position because others have testified on this matter too. We are waiting for you to answer.

A. I still don't have any recollection.

Q. You shouldn't fail to recall the fact that there was such a conference. Of course we understand that the despatching of the expeditionary unit wasn't your responsibility, nor are we questioning whether you did this or that thing. They may have been your duty as the chief of 2nd Section. You may have had to obey orders against your will. Aren't you putting yourself into an awkward position by denying these things? We have many proofs, and know these to be facts from the testimonies given by others, so please think it over once more. If you can please recollect about the expeditionary unit.

A. I can not say right now more than what I have already said until I Quiet down a little more.

Q. Then I'll read one more statement to assist your memory. This is a testimony given by a former section member. The bacteriologists employed things like plague, typhoid and cholera when the Japanese army was on the retreat. These bacteria were scattered especially in the towns of JAGAN in the vicinity ofa railway line, ZUIKON and ZUIJO. Bacteria were also scattered in places like water-sheds and wells. By whose order was this carried out?

A. I don't know.

Q. I must remind you again that you are putting yourself in a very awkward position by denying these things. Why can't you testify on these things? Others have come out in detail to a certain extent. You were warned to tell all the facts that you know, even before this interrogation began.

A. I'm sorry I have to take so much time, but please give me enough time to think.

Q. Of course, we have considered the necessary time.

A. I have nothing more to add to what I have just said from my recollection.

Q. Where are you living now?

A. Demobilization Bureau.

Q. How far is it from here?

A. I think you can get there in 30 minutes.

Q. You have placed yourself in a serious position by your own testimony. We will call it a recess now, but please think it over and try to recollect by the time we meet again.

GENERAL HEADQUARTERS
FAR EAST COMMAND
ALLIED TRANSLATOR & INTERPRETER SECTION
CENTRAL INTERROGATION CENTER

APO 500
14 July 1947

Interrogation : 16 May 1947

Interrogee : OTA, Kiyoshi

Interrogator : Col SMIRNOV

Interpreters : Capt SHVEITZER & CWO YOSHIHASHI

Stenographer : NODA, Ichiro

Monitors : Dr FELL & Lt Col McQUAIL

Q. When were the branches established?

A. I don't remember precisely, but I believe it was in 1940.

Q. What was the object of establishing these branches?

A. I heard that these branches were established to supply purified water to those units located in the remote areas as well as to other units and also to repair the materials used in water purification because the divisions and the units in MANCHURIA did not have separate water purification units of their own.

Q. Then can you say that these branches were not connected at all with the BW activities even when the BW should ensue?

A. It was not a peculiar organization solely limited to MANCHURIA. A similar organization existed in North CHINA as well as in Central CHINA. The branches were not related with any of the BW activities.

Q. Then what were the activities of these units?

A. The activities of these branches were as follows:

1. To investigate the cause of the outbreak of the epidemic among the units.
2. Carry out bacterial analysis, disinfection, and segregation of the contaminated ones.
3. Disinfection of the clothings and beddings.
4. Instruct in the usage of the water purifiers.
5. Constant investigation of the epidemics within its sector and submit reports to the headquarters.

Q. In case of an outbreak of war what would have been the functions of these branches?

A. When there is a war, the field water purification units and divisional water purification units are organized. Since the main unit at HARBIN and these branches are responsible for organizing these water purification units, they initiate action in that line. Constant trainings in anti-epidemic work are given to the future cadre and in case of war, the main unit, though I am not too positive of the exact numbers, was to organize seven or eight and each branch four or five field water purification units with these cadre and by recalling former veterans, etc., divisional field water purification units are formed and they move to various localities with the divisions.

Q. Was it supervising even prior to the war?

A. Yes. Moreover, from 1941 on a considerable number of units were formed and because of this many water purification units were organized by the main unit as well as by the branches and they experienced difficulties on account of insufficient number of personnel.

Q. Then, many units were formed in 1941?

A. Many units were formed in 1941 but after that some new units continued to be organized. Since I was away, I am not too positive but I have heard that these newly formed units were sent to CHINA and from the fall of 1941, many were dispatched to the southern areas.

Q. Explain to me about the KANTOKU-EN plan and how did it affect the unit?

A. I don't know about the KANTOKU-EN plan. I heard that it was a large scale plan, but I was transferred to CHINA soon after the plan went into effect.

Q. Then, in 1943, when you returned to your original unit, what changes were recognized by you?

A. I noticed that there were many new personnel. The veterans of the unit left when many new water purification units were organized.

Q. Then all the experienced personnel were dispatched with the newly organized units, and many new people had joined the unit?

A. The experienced personnel were gone and many inexperienced people were there.

Q. I am told that a Japanese military mission was in HARBIN. What was the relation between this mission and the ISHII Unit?

A. I don't know a thing about it. That is the first time I've heard that there was a representative group sent from JAPAN.

Q. We heard that the unit had in its possession some special bags to be used by the saboteurs and that these bags were manufactured within the unit. By whose order were these bags manufactured? These bags were to be used by spies.

A. I have neither seen nor heard about them.

Q. The activities in this line were done by the 2nd Section and of course, in conjunction with the 1st Section.

A. The 2nd Section never did things like that.

Q. But, bacteria were placed in capsules, weren't they?

A. There was no one who inserted bacteria into capsules.

Q. But we have evidence that bacteria were inserted into capsules and that these bags were used because we captured a member of 731 Unit at NOBUSHIBIRISK in the Russian territory.

A. We never thought of engaging in any spylike activities and never experimented in that line. I heard about it now for the first time.

Q. Then, I want you to listen to a testimony given by one of your subordinates.

"As one of the researches in bacteriology, experiments in the line of disseminating the disease in the rear areas of the enemy were conducted and a small thermos bottle was invented. In this bottle capsules filled with bacteria were to be transported, and the best method of transportation was by use of wine, soda, and medicine bottles. The reason for this being that it was an effective way and not conspicious."

A. I don't think he was my subordinate.I don't remember ever giving such an order.

Q. But this testimony was given by one of your subordinates.

A. I don't recall it at all.

Q. Of course it was not your responsibility, but who issued the order?

A. I don't recollect at all of ever issuing such an order or saying anything about it. There were none among my subordinates who were conducting experiments in that field, Of course I am totally ignorant about the others.

Q. Then what other unit in MANCHURIA, aside from the 731 Unit, was conducting research work on bacteriological warfare?

A. I don't think there was any other unit.

Q. Was there any other unit in MANCHURIA conducting research work on BW besides the following units: The 731 Unit, the NI Unit, and the Scientific Research Laboratory of the Manchurian RR?

A. Shall I say the defense for BW - - - there were no other units aside from the 731 Unit which was engaged in experimenting with the basic BW defense measures. The NI Unit and the Scientific Research Laboratory of the Manchurian RR were not engaged in that line at all.

Q. In other words, only the 731 Unit was concerned with the BW defense?

A. That's right.

Q. If only the 731 Unit was concerned along that line, then why did some other unit send spies into the rear areas of the enemy?

A. We have never used spies and no other units have employed them either.

Q. Of course the Japanese mission which came to HARBIN could have given pistols, cameras, etc., to the spies and incendiary bombs were made at the ordnance plant. But these spies were captured at various places and the bacteria they possessed must have come from the 731 Unit.

A. No, I don't recall ever giving any bacteria. Not only don't I recall, but also there were no units which had spies and of course there were no spies within the divisions. I don't remember at all ever giving any bacteria to that type of people.

Q. But isn't it one of the BW tactics to disseminate bacteria by spies in the enemy's rear?

A. That is wrong. In BW, in regards to defense in BW, anyone who has done any research work in that line will readily see that any small scale BW attacks, such as placing bacteria in capsules, is useless and ineffective. Only the non-professional people think that it can be done. The lay-men place great fear in bacteria but it is not that dangerous. Any such tactics are merely to intimidate the masses and are not effective BW.

Q. Then by what reasoning were the anthrax bacilli mixed with hay and given to the horses?

A. That experiment was conducted to determine the effectiveness of the immunization of the Japanese horses if the bacilli were spread on a grand scale on pastures.

Q. You stated that the anthrax bacilli might be disseminated on pastures through enemy action. On what basis was your conjecture formed?

A. It was not a conjecture. There are many publications on BW. They are found in France, Germany, America, etc., and since there are these publications, by merely reading them, one can grasp the various possibilities of the BW attacks without using one's head; and by knowing them we conducted those experiments.

Q. You don't precisely understand the nature of my question. What I want to know is through what methods were the pastures to be contaminated?

A. I conducted no research work in that line. We merely experimented on the defensive aspect for the protection of the Japanese horses. Since we did not go as far as to determine the methods to be used for contamination, the quantities of bacteria to be used, etc., I am unable to answer your question.

Q. But the conjecture that the pastures might be contaminated with bacteria is related in what way with your yesterday's statement that in your experiments you mixed bacteria with hay and barley and fed it to the horses?

A. That concerned only one of the methods of feeding the horses. By mixing the bacteria with the hay, the horse swallowed the bacteria. It was merely one way of feeding the horses. In regards to the conjecture that the pastures might be contaminated, that was derived from reading the published articles. It was merely a method of feeding the horses and there was no other reasoning involved.

Q. In the final analysis, the experiments which you were conducting were to determine the methods of infecting a large number of livestock, weren't they?

A. That is not true. I conducted the experiments for only a short period to determine the effectiveness of the innoculations administered to the Japanese military horses.

Q. Through these experiments you were able to determine the symptoms of anthrax, weren't you? But these matters were already known, weren't they?

A. I don't think they were known. The Japanese military horses were innoculated by using the Pasteur method. We felt that this innoculation method was one hundred percent effective but through our experiments we discovered that the method was not perfect and that we had to strengthen the immunizing agent.

Q. What was the paramount objective underlying these experiments?

A. These experiments were conducted with the purpose of determining the effectiveness of Pasteur's innoculation against anthrax.

Q. But why did you mix anthrax with the forage and feed it to the horses?

A. It was merely a method of feeding the horses. If the horses will consume just the bacillus there is no need for this, but since they don't, as a method of compelling them to eat, we had to mix the bacillus with the forage.

Q. But there must be other means of infecting the horses?

A. No, there are no other methods.

Q. But wasn't the method of mixing the bacteria with the dry forage one of the ways of carrying out the sabotage activities in the enemy's rear areas?

A. No, it was not. It was merely a way of feeding the horses. I don't think it could actually be done.

Q. But aren't there any other easier methods of infecting the horses?

A. We conducted no other experiments. At that time we gave it no other thought.

Q. Then, did Pasteur himself use the method of mixing bacteria with the dry forage in feeding the horses?

A. I don't know about that.

Q. From the tactical standpoint, in bacteriological war, which bacteria, do you think, are most virulent?

A. I am not well informed on that.

Q. But you were the 2nd Section chief and that section conducted experiments along this line.

A. I conducted only few experiments during the initial period. Since the chief of 2nd Section was not concerned in that field, I don't know.

Q. Then I'll read you the testimony informing the unit's activities.

"Firstly, several years of experiments were conducted to select the most virulent bacteria and through these experiments it was discovered that plague and anthrax were most toxic. Of course when the symptoms of typhoid and the SONGO Fever were studied, they too were effective. But it is difficult to disseminate typhoid and the SONGO Fever because the vectors, which are lice, are difficult to cultivate on a mass production basis. Furthermore, lice can survive only in unsanitary places. The tick forests are the instrumental vectors of the SONGO Fever but they can be cultivated only artificially. Plague can be disseminated by using two methods: firstly, by using the bacilli, secondly, by scattering the plague infected fleas. It is almost impossible to prevent from being bitten by the fleas regardless of the sanitary conditions maintained and it is still more difficult to be free from flea bites under field conditions. Through the experiments conducted by the unit, it was found that not only the livestock but men can also be infected with anthrax."

A. I am not well acquainted with those academic problems. In the testimony, the SONGO Fever was mentioned but that occurred while I was away in CHINA. My personal feeling is that bacteria cultivation cannot be accomplished so easily. I feel that some imagination on the part of the testifir is included, and undoubtedly, the problem cannot be solved so easily. I don't know too well about these problems.

Q. In what ways do you feel that it was imagined?

A. The life span of bacteria is short and they die within four or five days. Different bacteria has different levels of toxicity and the degree of toxicity is decreased as the bacteria is transferred from one cultivator to another and once the toxicity is reduced it is difficult to increase the strength. These are the two reasons why I feel that it is very difficult to form any conclusions. Some imagination must be included in the statement. I have neither seen nor heard that a better method was discovered whereby the hindering factors mentioned have been successfully eliminated.

Q. Then you, yourself, have stated that many difficulties were experienced in the experiments. Why were the members of the unit conducting research work along that line?

A. I don't quite comprehend.

Q. When you already knew that such matter as an immediate reduction of toxicity of bacteria occurs, why was the unit engaging in experiments on the factors already known?

A. These experiments were performed to ascertain the methods by which the bacteria's life span could be prolonged and the reduction of toxicity could be eliminated.

Q. Then, it can be said that one of the interests of the unit was to increase the virulence of the bacteria and that the unit's efforts were stressed along that line?

A. I don't know the details of the experiments. I stated my viewpoints on bacteriology. Since the experiments were conducted by another section, I am ignorant of their true interest in conducting those experiments.

Q. Why was it necessary to increase the virulence of the bacteria?

A. In explaining from the standpoint of our 4th Section, in manufacturing vaccines, if the vaccines are made from weak bacteria, the degree of the immunity is also low. Good vaccines can be made by using bacteria high in toxicity. From this standpoint alone, it must be considered important.

Q. Why was an enormous amount of fleas kept within the unit?

A. I don't believe there was a large amount of fleas. I don't know anything about there being a large amount of fleas.

Q. Have you seen the activities of the flea sub-section?

A. No, I have not.

Q. What was the object of cultivating fleas?

A. I believe that the paramount reason was to conduct research work on prevention of plague; it is an inseparable problem.

Q. Then the fleas were used as vectors in the plague infection, weren't they?

A. Yes. Since I believe it is a known fact that fleas are the vectors of plague, they were used.

Q. On what objects were the plague bacilli infected?

A. I don't know that and I have never seen it. Ordinarily, mice are used in plague research, aren't they?

Q. Then, why did the Japanese KEMPEI TAI deliver Chinese and Manchurians, who were sentenced to death, to the unit?

A. No such people came to the unit.

Q. You have a very good memory but when it comes to these important problems you have memory lapses.

A. I remember most of the things which I have heard or seen, but I don't remember anything which I have neither seen nor heard.

Q. The question just asked was on things which you had seen and heard and in which you took an active part.

A. No, it is entirely untrue.

Q. According to this testimony, "the KEMPEI TAI delivered Chinese who were sentenced to death, to the unit. I personally know that seven or eight human experiments had taken place, and I, myself, have heard about these experiments and seen some of them. Col IKARI, Maj HINOFUJI, Maj TAKAHASHI, etc., participated in these experiments. I also heard about it from other sources. The experiments on anthrax were to determine whether the disease is contageous to man or not. For the experiment, approximately twenty criminals were tied to the stakes, sufficiently away from the bombs to avoid being killed instantly but only to be injured. The bombs were detonated electrically and these bombs contained plague and anthrax. The subjects were infected through the open wounds. The wounded people were kept at the experimental field until the first symptoms appeared and then they were removed to the hospital where their condition was observed. The subjects usually died within a few days in great agony." You must know something about these experiments.

A. I don't know anything about it. I have never heard about it, and I have never seen any.

Q. Then did you, yourself, scatter infected fleas from an airplane over CHANGTE located near the TUNGTING Lake?

A. I don't recall scattering any.

Q. Are you saying that you don't remember or don't know? Which is it?

A. I don't know.

Q. But we know about this through the testimonies given by your friends. The specialists in this field have stated that you had carried out the experiment in 1941. Moreover, the Chinese government has given us the intelligence information that you were connected with these activities. In NANKING, wasn't there just the EI Unit and you were the unit commander?

A. That is right.

Q. I will read a testimony given by your friend who has testified as to your activities.

"By order of ISHII, approximately fifty bacteriologists, who were in the 1st and 2nd Sections, were sent to Central CHINA under the direction of Col OTA. According to what Col OTA told me, the expeditionary unit dropped the plague infected fleas over the city of CHANGTE. Moreover, OTA informed me that the object of this expeditionary unit was to sever the line of communication of the Chinese Army and for this purpose the bacteria were scattered over CHANGTE. And as I have stated before, I was there when Col OTA made this report to Lt Gen ISHII and he reported that a plague epidemic occurred in CHANGTE and in its vicinity." It is not a pleasant feeling to recall today what you have committed in 1941?

A. There never was an occasion in which I took the HARBIN Unit with me. I was transferred either in June or July and went there alone. I have never taken men from the HARBIN Unit with me. I have gone there alone. I don't know a thing about the others. The commander of NANKING Unit is under the command of the army commander at NANKING and does not receive orders from ISHII. The chain of commands do not run that way.

Q. Of course, in conducting preventive measures, if the unit is in NANKING, the order is given by the NANKING Army Commander, but in matters concerning the BW, the order must come from a higher source. Why did you take three kilograms of fleas with you to NANKING in 1942?

A. I don't remember taking any with me, and I don't remember receiving any order from the above.

Q. Then in 1942, did a part of the ISHII Unit come to your unit?

A. I don't think it came -- did you say in 1942? A part did come in 1942.

Q. Then, do you know that the Japanese army was making a retreat in Central CHINA around that time?

A. I do.

Q. Then, do you know that around that time some bacteriologists were sent to the areas where the Japanese army was retreating?

A. A thing like that never occurred.

Q. Then, did you know that an eqidemic occurred among the Chinese troops which occupied the areas abandoned by the Japanese?

A. I didn't know about it.

Q. Were you, yourself, actively engaged in anti-epidemic work in the region where the epidemic occurred?

A. I remember that since the troops were retreating to HANGCHOU, our unit with the cooperation of the members from MANCHURIA, established a medical inspection station there and we disinfected the soldiers and changed their clothing there.

Q. I will read you the activities of the bacteriologists, so listen.

(The activities of the bacteriologists read)

Q. You must have known about it from the preventive standpoint because the Japanese troops had to be disinfected to protect themselves from being contaminated.

A. I don't know a thing about what you have just read. Preventive measures were taken whenever the Japanese army was engaged in any large scale operations. It was not unusual and was not limited to that place.

Q. That place refers to HANGCHOU?

A. Yes, and for that reason there were some mobile disinfecting trucks which disinfected the clothing and the men and moved to the locality where the operation occurred.

Q. Then, did you know that an epidemic occurred subsequent to the retreat of the Japanese army from that particular locality?

A. No, I don't. I did not hear about it.

Q. Anyway, you knew that an epidemic occurred in the vicinities of CHANGTE and TUNGTING HO in 1942, didn't you?

A. As to that, as I informed you yesterday, I knew that epidemics of plague and malaria occurred by reading the Chinese newspaper.

Q. What kind of Chinese newspaper was it?

A. I don't remember the name of the newspaper.

Q. Was that newspaper published in the Japanese sector or was it published in the Chinese territory?

A. We did not get any newspapers published in the Chinese territory. I believe it was published in the Japanese occupied zone.

Q. Do you know Chinese?

A. No, I don't.

Q. Then, how can you read it?

A. We have people who can read Chinese. We have Chinese interpreters with us whenever there is an operation in CHINA.

Q. Then, why were you so keenly interested in reading, in the Chinese newspapers, about the epidemics?

A. As an anti-epidemic unit, we had to read Chinese newspapers and periodicals constantly and an immediate action had to be taken in case of outbreaks of epidemics. It was necessary for us, from the standpoint of anti-epidemic, to constantly read the Chinese papers.

Q. In regards to checking the outbreaks of these experiments, weren't there more organized units whose function was to report solely on the outbreaks of epidemics?

A. There were none.

Q. Did you have to rely on newspapers, etc.?

A. Yes.

Q. Wasn't it the function of the army medical corps to perform such investigations?

A. The anti-epidemic measures are taken by the medical corps as well as by the water purification units. Exchange of information between the two organizations took place constantly to expedite in handling all epidemic problems.

Q. Anyway, was the Central CHINA area controlled by the EI Unit?

A. Yes, you mean on the anti-epidemic activities?

Q. Was the EI Unit a considerable unit?

A. Yes. With the main unit located in NANKING, it had ten branches and 15 detachments. It was located wherever there was a Japanese unit stationed.

Q. And was it under the direct command of the Central CHINA Army?

A. Yes.

Q. In regards to the above question, to which particular army did it belong, such as to the 1st, 4th, etc.?

A. It was under the NANKING Supreme Headquarters. Each branch was receiving various orders from the local army headquarters.

Q. Then, the EI Unit was quite a large unit and did have much authority, didn't it?

A. It was in charge of everything which concerns with the anti-epidemic work.

Q. Why was it necessary to have some members of the ISHII Unit to be sent to the unit when the EI Unit itself was a large unit?

A. Although you say it is large, since it is scattered the number of personnel at any one place is few. Where did you get that term the EI Unit? Are you referring that name to the Water Purification Unit of Central CHINA? Are you referring to the NANKING Water Purification Unit?

Q. Exactly.

A. The unit was never referred to as being the EI Unit.

Q. Whenever the EI Unit is mentioned, I want you to know that it refers to the NANKING Water Purification Unit. Wasn't the ISHII Unit under the direct control of the supreme commander, Central CHINA?

A. That is not correct. It was under the command of KWANTUNG Army.

Q. The usual orders were issued by the CG, KWANTUNG Army but were not the more important orders issued directly from the Imperial General Headquarters to the unit?

A. It was not under direct control of the Imperial General Headquarters. It was under the jurisdiction of the KWANTUNG Army and had no connection with the Imperial General Headquarters.

Q. Anyhow, then, it had no connection with the Central CHINA Army?

A. No.

Q. Then, why is it that Lt Gen ISHII suddenly went to Central CHINA in 1940 and 1941 taking with him an expeditionary unit?

A. In 1940 and 1941? I believe in 1940, since there was a plague epidemic in CHANG CHUN, he went there to direct the anti-epidemic work.

Q. Why did Lt Gen ISHII head the expeditionary units in 1941 and 1942 and go to NANKING?

A. I don't know anything about his being in NANKING. Although I don't remember the exact month in 1942, I know he became a chief army surgeon and went to TAIYUAN in North CHINA.

Q. I want you to give a direct answer this time. In 1941, under your command, an expeditionary unit was sent to Central CHINA and in 1942, Lt Gen ISHII dispatched a detachment of his unit to Central CHINA?

A. I don't know about either one of them.

Q. But you have already stated that in 1942 a part of the ISHII Unit came to HANGCHOU to assist your unit in performing anti-epidemic activities.

A. Yes, they did come. I made an error as to the year of the transfer of ISHII since I didn't remember exactly whether it was in 1941 or 1942.

Q. Then, why did members of the ISHII Unit come to Central CHINA, a region not under the jurisdiction of KWANTUNG Army?

A. As to that, as I have stated before, there were no disinfecting trucks and only KWANTUNG Army had them, and the personnel who could handle these trucks were in the KWANTUNG Army. In the Central CHINA SEKKAN operation railroad, signal, engineer units, etc., were sent from KWANTUNG Army to assist. I believe there was insufficient number of troops in Central CHINA because the members of KWANTUNG Army were dispatched to Central CHINA. The members of KWANTUNG Army were intermixed with the troops there in carrying out the operation. I believe these are the two reasons why the members of KWANTUNG Army were there.

Q. Under whose order?

A. I don't know about the order. It was from the above - - we just performed our assigned duties and were ignorant of the nature and the source of the orders.

Q. But the order of this nature could not be issued by the supreme commander in Central CHINA, could it? Didn't it come from the Imperial General Headquarters?

A. Since we were with a very insignificant unit, we are totally ignorant of the formalities involved in which these orders were issued from the above and we know nothing about the matters related to such problem.

Q. Then by whose orders were the key personnel of the Water Purification Unit selected?

A. One did not have to be an important person. All army officers were assigned according to the orders issued by the assignment section of the War Ministry, and the members of the Water Purification Units were assigned in a similar manner.

Q. It wasn't the War Minister was it?

A. All officers of every unit were assigned by the assignment section. The assignments of the non-commissioned officers and below, in the unit, were done in the army headquarters to which the unit was subordinated.

Q. Why was there a jail within the unit and why were Chinese and Manchurians confined in it?

A. There was absolutely no such thing.

Q. Then, what buildings were located in this big yard?

A. There were warehouses.

Q. What were in these warehouses?

A. Chemicals to be used in the laboratories, expendible items and machinery were stored in them.

Q. Were there people in these buildings?

A. No.

Q. You are not answering truthfully. It is strange that you should conceal the facts.

A. I am not trying to conceal.

Q. I have another question to ask. Did you meet Gen UMEZU at the unit?

A. I have never met him at the unit.

Q. Did you meet Col TAMURA at the unit?

A. I have never met him at the unit.

Q. Do you know who Col TAMURA was?

A. I believe he was a staff officer of the KWANTUNG Army.

Q. Was he the chief of the Operation Section?

A. I don't know the details of his duties. I simply know him as a person.

Q. Why was the Water Purification Unit under the direct command of CO, KWANTUNG Army and not under Chief of Medical Department, KWANTUNG Army?

A. In the Japanese Army the Chief of the Medical Department is an assistant to the Commanding General, and he has no direct control over any unit. The command of the unit of KWANTUNG Army belongs to the Commanding General of the KWANTUNG Army.

GENERAL HEADQUARTERS
FAR EAST COMMAND
ALLIED TRANSLATOR & INTERPRETER SECTION
CENTRAL INTERROGATION CENTER

APO 500
16 Jul 47

Interrogation : 13 June 1947

Interrogee : ISHII, Shiro

Interrogator : Col SMIRNOV

Sponsor : Lt Col McQUAIL

Interpreter : CWO YOSHIHASHI

Interpreter : Capt. SVEITZER

Stenographer : NODA, Ichiro

Q. Explain in more detail than what you have stated previously the duties and activities of the 4th Section.

A. Do you mean the duties of the 4th Section? While I was there, the square building was divided into north and south but I was transferred while the building was still in the process of construction. I don't know whether it was completed or not since my transfer occurred in 1942.

Q. Wasn't the installation completed in 1942?

A. It was not completed and was not in operation, therefore, when the production of the south side was insufficient the north side was used. They were within the same building.

Q. Were the facilities for production of the 1st system completed?

A. Yes, they were.

Q. By what method were the bacteria produced in the 1st system?

A. Suppose we are to cultivate some dysentery bacilli, the materials were drawn from the central warehouse, weighed in the preparation rooms, and heated in the steam kettles. After they had been steamed, according to the product desired, the materials were placed in glass tubes or cultivating tubes and then placed in autoclaves with 15 pounds of pressure to sterilize them thoroughly and then they were cooled in the water. In the longer process, they required 24 hours to be cooled by the normal surrounding temperature.

Q. What kind of containers did you use in cultivating the bacteria?

A. It differs, depending upon the objective. There are various cases. There are three kinds of glass containers which can be used, one is called a turtle schalle, that is a bottle shaped like a turtle and there are also long or slender bottles. Aside from these glass containers there is a cultivating can, a square box made of metal.

Q. Were the bacteria cultivated in a special room?

A. Yes, that's correct.

Q. Were these cultivating apparatus delivered into the room by means of special conveyor?

A. We had planned to employ that system to reduce the number of personnel needed, but since the conveyor did not operate efficiently, we were able to use it for only a short time. Most of the time it was in need of repair and thus we hardly used it.

Q. Anyway, the conveyor was installed to carry the cultivators to place the the bacteria in the thermostatically controlled room, wasn't it?

A. Yes, that's right.

Q. How many steam kettles were there in the 1st system?

A. I think there were two of them.

Q. How large were they? How many centimeters were they?

A. They were sixty centimeters. I believe there were two but there may have been as many as four.

Q. And the height?

A. Initially, it was large but since it was found that more time was necessary and a complete disinfection was impossible when they were large, the steam kettles were improved repeatedly and finally smaller ones were made because less time would be consumed and less danger of foreign bacteria being introduced.

Q. Was it finally about 60 centimeters?

A. Approximately that.

Q. And the height?

A. I believe it was approximately one meter.

Q. What was the amount of bacteria which could be cultivated by one of these steam kettles?

A. I don't know such detail matters.

Q. What was the volume of one of these steam kettles?

A. Since one cubic meter is one ton, does it amount to about a fifth of that? It will have to be calculated.

Q. What was the production capacity of the 1st system?

A. I don't know the production capacity since there was no need of knowing about it. We were once thinking of operating a full 24 hours to determine its efficiency but since there was no need for that it was never done.

Q. Who invented the cultivating apparatus?

A. Is the cultivating apparatus which you refer to an apparatus in which agar-agar are inserted?

Q. The cultivating apparatus refers to the container. Who invented it?

A. I invented it.

Q. Explain in detail about this cultivating apparatus.

A. It was a square box with ten separate compartments to be seen when looked at from the above. Into these sections another divider was inserted in each section thus forming a space. Melted agar-agar solution was poured into these spaces.

Q. Were the dividers removed after the solution solidified?

A. That is correct. But this apparatus had too many defects necessitating more material and expenditure to be used and therefore better and more simplified ones were made, but the unit had only the inefficient old model.

Q. Where was this improved model being used?

A. The improved ones were being used at the Army Medical School. The motive for this improvement was that the internal medicine necessary for dysentery required a large amount of bacteria but frequent breakage of the test tubes prevented from obtaining the desired volume and confronted with this difficulty the improved model was made.

Q. Were only the dysentery bacilli cultivated in these cultivators?

A. Anything could be cultivated.

Q. It is correct to say that in 24 hours, from one of these cultivators, it was possible to produce 30 grams of plague bacilli and 80 grams of typhus bacilli?

A. Plague can be, but not typhus.

Q. Is it correct to say about 30 grams of plague?

A. In some cases it was 20 grams and in other cases it was 40 grams. Moreover, plague bacilli cannot be cultivated in 24 hours. It required 48 hours. The maximum production was approximately 40 grams with a minimum of 15 to 20 grams. Since there were many errors involved in the process of the making, no definite amount was known. There were cases in which the solidified agar-agar would crumble or some foreign bacteria would be introduced necessitating removal of the process, therefore, unless definite statistics were taken, it is difficult to assert how much could have been produced. It was about 40 grams for the typhoid. If everything went well, sometimes it was possible to produce 50 grams. It required 24 hours for the typhoid and 48 hours for the plague.

Q. It is said that it was possible to produce as much as 60 grams of cholera bacilli from one cultivator in 18 to 20 hours. Is that correct?

A. As to the cholera, several different factors such as presence or absence of sugar in the agar-agar, the PH concentration, the specie of cholera bacilli - - there are three types - - affected the production volume and therefore it cannot be stated definitely as being 50 or 60, etc. In some cases the amount was as great as 60 or 70 but on the other hand when the condition was unfavorable, the amount was as low as 30. Three factors which influenced the amount of production were: The type of cultivators used, the temperature, and the type of bacilli.

Q. And was it possible to produce the said amount in 18 to 20 hours?

A. No, that is not correct, it took anywhere from one and a half day to two days, since after being placed in the cultivator 24 hours, they were removed and formalin etc., were added.

Q. I'll read you the production capacity of the 4th Section. "At a full capacity within a months period, it was possible to produce 180 kilograms of plague bacilli, 300 kilograms of cholera, and anthrax, and 300 grams of the paratyphoid and furthermore it was possible to produce the above listed quantities without any undue strain." Is the statement correct?

A. If there were sufficient personnel and material, it was possible to produce the stated amount but the whole production system would have been taxed. The amount which could have been produced without unnecessary strain would have been a half of those figures given.

Q. But the original plan was to produce the stated amount, wasn't it?

A. The need for plague vaccines was 30 to 50 times more than what was being produced normally. We had to make more. We were short on the vaccines and so in 1940 we experienced some difficulties and we had to work on full capacity on 24 hour basis.

Q. Then, according to your ways of thinking, actually three to five tons of vaccines were necessary each month, wasn't it so?

A. As I stated previously, from September to December 1940, a plague epidemic occurred in the CHAN-CHUNG and NUNGAN Area and we were ordered to prepare a sufficient amount of vaccines for 500,000 people - - no, for 1,000,000. 50,000 were engaged in the anti-epidemic work and 1,000,000 people were to be administered, and we were ordered to produce a sufficient amount of vaccines for 1,000,000 people on 30 milligrams per person basis. The plague vaccine which we discovered required ten times more doses than the ones ordinarily used. Though we were ordered to produce such vast amount of vaccines, we were never able to fulfill the required amount, and I believe we were able to send an amount sufficient for only half a million. The facility was too small to produce the required amount.

Q. And what about the previous question in which it was asked that three to five tons were necessary?

A. It was not necessary to produce as much as five tons. In case of an outbreak of epidemic, it was necessary, but otherwise, it was not.

Q. Then, could you say that the facilities possessed by the 4th Section were merely for producing vaccines?

A. That is right.

Q. And were the bacteria to be used in BW also produced?

A. As I stated previously, I believe non-virulent bacteria were spread from an aircraft. No one in the unit thought of it as an offensive experiment for an offensive purpose. I heard a report that non-pathogenic bacteria were used in our own unit merely for furthering our own defensive measure and no more.

Q. What about the bacteria for the purpose of bacteriological warfare prepared by the 4th Section?

A. If it were done secretly on their own, I do not know but it did not have such duties.

Q. Did the 4th Section have the facilities to produce bacteria for a BW in the event of such war?

A. Nonsense! It is beyond question. It should have been about a hundred times more fully equipped to perform such a task. Even the equipment for the production of the vaccines was small and even if we were ordered to develop plague, cholera, and typhoid it could not have been done as we wished. Furthermore, the bacteria to be used in BW, even if we were ordered to develop such things,while developing immunization vaccines, we could not have accomplished this task. We were not able to produce even a sufficient amount of vaccines, so we extended to the northern side but even at that we were not able to produce enough vaccines. It was impossible to carry out a BW work while producing vaccine, that had to be sent to KOREA and CHINA, when the KWANTUNG Army expanded. It is like a fable.

Q. However, if the production of bacteria for a BW was desired, you could have done it with the method of producing the vaccines and with the equipment, weren't you? Also, you were able to produce virulent bacteria using the same cultivators, conveyors, autoclaves, and steam kettles, weren't you?

A. The method of producing is entirely different. Since vaccine is to be injected into human body, if any other bacteria is found in the vaccine, it has to be thrown away. Therefore, it must be worked with extreme care. But the method of production for bacteria to be used in BW needs no care and therefore, it is simple. Vaccines are to be injected into the human body so anthrax must not get into it, nothing must get into it, everything must be done with great care and a thorough disinfection must be done. However, I never engaged in any BW and do not know anything but, in the field, if bacteria were to be used, I think it does not matter what gets into it. I never did work on it, so I do not know anything but that is the way I think.

Q. Your answer is slightly off. What I said is that the method of producing vaccine is done with the same equipment and machines as that of producing virulent bacteria. Naturally, in the method of production, one side needs more care but in producing vaccines similar equipment and machines are employed; and also, if bacteria are needed to be produced they could have been produced, couldn't they?

A. I never produced them so I do not know but in producing different types of bacteria, different cultivators must be used. In order to strengthen the virulence of bacteria, such cultivator, that will cause the strengthening, must be employed. The temperature must be changed too. If they are to be used for the BW purpose, these changes must take place.

Q. Is it not with the same equipment?

A. It is not just trifle - - - I think there is a great difference.

Q. However, in regards to the two questions I just asked, bacteria can be produced by utilizing similar methods and similar culture media, isn't it so? Therefore, it can be said that, whether producing vaccines or bacteria, similar equipment and machines can be employed to produce them, couldn't it?

A. I do not know about that. I can not say it in few words. In the first place, I can not make any statement without conducting a research on whether the various elements of the vaccines are similar to that of the BW conditions or not. In case of the vaccines that does not matter so long as they have the immunization value. Therefore, since it is different with the condition of the bacteria I can not state that it can be done. I think nobody will assert that the bacteria for BW can be produced in the same manner as the vaccines.

Q. Were there any other units aside from the 731 Unit which were concerned with the BW work?

A. I think there were none aside from the 731 Unit. I do not know.

Q. Do you mean the 731 was the only unit?

A. I do not know anything about other units.

Q. However, as far as I know, the unit commanded by Lt Gen ISHII was the only unit in the Japanese Army that was concerned with BW and conducted researches.

A. I do not know where and what others did but we never thought of BW. I shall make it clear that our work was on the defensive measure. Our thoughts were concentrated on the defense, to protect our unit, our army. We never thought the offensive aspects. We have been disturbed greatly because of the misunderstanding caused from unnecessary propaganda.

Q. As I understand it, you have been much concerned with the BW work ever since 1933 and were actively connected with the problem.

A. Para-typhoid epidemic occurred toward the end of 1933; in 1932 cholera epidemic rose in MANCHURIA and it was also brought into JAPAN. There was a plague epidemic in MANCHURIA in 1933 and 1934; in 1934, 3,000 head of horses died of anthrax, and, about 10,000 people were stricken with GAERTNER bacilli in 1936 in HAMAMATSU. These epidemics, which occurred almost annually, caused much fear among the Japanese. The fear was further heightened when we heard about BW in 1934 or so. A party returning from the GENEVA Conference informed us about the possible BW attacks. Although we were not fully convinced of the possibilities, nevertheless, we launched upon conducting a research work on the defense since we were already alarmed by the yearly occurrences of the natural epidemics. We were frightened.

Q. You did think about it ever since 1934, haven't you?

A. We medical officers had no cannon, tank or airplane to take any offensive BW action. Realizing that it was our responsibility to establish defensive measures against BW attacks, I was concerned with the BW work.

Q. Anyway, only the 731 Unit, in the Japanese army, was concerned with BW and there wasn't any other unit that was concerned with it, was there?

A. Everyone was concerned with the defense problem and for that reason Water Purification Units were established. On the assumption that some nation might employ such tactics, the Water Purification Units were established. Furthermore, I believe that the men were oriented with the possibilities that enemy might employ such tactics. We never envisioned of launching any attacks with BW. That function belongs to the tactical officers and medical officers can not do it even if they wanted to because we have no weapons - - -

Q. You mentioned Water Purification Unit, are you referring to the 731 Unit?

A. Anywhere, where the division or the army went, the Water Purification Unit, the divisional or the army, went along for the purpose of protecting the unit against any natural epidemic. It was there to keep any outbreak of the cases to the minimum in that particular locality. With such view in mind, the Water Purification Unit accompanied each division and army.

Q. Your answer is somewhat deviated from the question. What I am asking is, was the 731 Unit the only unit concerned with BW?

A. I don't know about that. I don't know about others. I understand only about our function which was a defensive research work. I don't know about other units.

Q. If your unit was solely concerned with the defensive problems of BW, then why did the unit have Technician YAMAGUCHI who conducted experiments with bombs?

A. Of course, we knew definitely that unless we know something about the bombs, we could not formulate any protective measures. Even in the elementary defense, by being hit by a person one knows how to defend himself. Unless there is someone who could do the attacking how can we devise the defensive measures? We couldn't ask our enemy to take an offensive step. By conducting the trials within the unit, we learned something about the defense and various defensive measures were devised. Without any control, as physicians would say, there is no criterion. By encountering the offensive acts, the defensive steps are formulated. Defensive and offensive acts are synonymous in the primary stage, but I am ignorant of any large scale operations. To formulate defensive measures for BW we have to know something about the areas of dispersion, means of escape, and defense. It pertained to basic experiments and without them no plans could have been formulated.

Q. In other words one could still state that one of the unit's activities was concerned with the offensive aspect, wasn't it?

A. That is not so. The defensive aspect was the paramount interest and its scope was sought. If one considers the bombing attacks, one has to consider the effect of one-ton bombs, ten-ton bombs, etc., but we are not concerned with them. Since ours was a basic research, it was unnecessary for us to think that far. Our scope was limited to conducting basic defensive experiments. It was not necessary for us to think about attacks by ten-ton, five-ton, 100-ton bombs.

Q. Is it true that the YAMAGUCHI Sub-section performed experiments with bombs and shells?

A. We procured some old gas bombs which were discarded by some other units and by taking the gas out, the bombs were filled with green or red dyed liquids and by detonating them the area of dispersion and contamination was calculated. I know that much about the experiment but I don't know about others. We never thought of constructing any new type bombs. We used whatever was to be had and the basic experiments expefiments were conducted by using them.

Q. You stated that you experimented with whatever shells that were obtainable. What is the meaning of that? What other shells besides the gas shells were used?

A. I don't exactly know what they were. We got hold of any surplus materials.

Q. Didn't you experiment with some special porcelain bombs?

A. I don't know much about the porcelain bombs. I believe they were imitations of something else.

Q. I want you to recall the porcelain bombs. When and what did you use in them for the experiments?

A. I don't know because I did not conduct the experiments myself. They made many porcelain bombs which were called the practice bombs. They had been in production for some time to economize in using iron. I believe they used such bombs for their experiments.

Q. In 1940, did you not personally experiment at TAIRANCHI of the effect on anthrax when it was inserted into a shell and fired?

A. I don't know, I don't even know the place.

Q. Forget about the time and the place, have you not experimented on how long the anthrax bacilli will sustain when inserted into bombs or shells and also the stability of the anthrax bacilli?

A. I don't know.

Q. Why don't you, the unit commander, know about the experiment which was conducted by the section under you?

A. I don't know how many of the hundreds of experiments which the research workers did were reported to the commander. They don't report to the commander unless the results were successful because of their personal pride. That's why I don't know about their detail experiments.

Q. What bacteria were found to be most virulent and effective as a result of the experiments conducted within the unit?

A. I believe that we could have determined that, if the experiments were conducted under an identical condition, but since that was never done, I don't think anyone will be qualified to state which is most virulent and which is next, etc. I, too, don't know.

Q. It is inconceivable that you did not hear about the experiments of Maj Gen KITAGAWA who worked on various bacteria under varied climatic conditions.

A. I don't know. KITAGAWA is dead. I don't remember a thing about such experiments.

Q. I am not interested in whether Maj Gen KITAKAWA is dead or not. I just want to know about the experiments which he conducted. You said that you were interested in BW from the defensive point of view. I believe you had to be interested in the qualities of virulence and stability of the bacteria.

A. I was not concerned with them. If they were effective against us, we would have protected ourselves, and if ineffective they would have been ignored. It was unnecessary to be concerned with them if the bacteria was unstable, but on the other hand if they were stable the means of defense had to be perfected. No matter what you say, defense was our paramount objective. It was not our duty and we had no funds to be concerned with the offensive aspect of BW.

Q. But, why was Maj Gen KITAGAWA so concerned with the effect of weather on bacteria and conducted experiments in 1940?

A. I didn't know that KITAGAWA was conducting the experiments. I stated that previously.

Q. What was the duty of Maj Gen KITAGAWA in 1940?

A. I believe he was Chief of the 1st Section.

Q. If that is so, wasn't Maj Gen KITAGAWA the chief of the research section?

A. Yes.

Q. If such experiments were conducted, it must have been done by the 1st Section.

A. I don't know anything about the experiments conducted in 1940. Such experiment was not performed. Which experiment? You mean the experiments conducted in the field?

Q. Your answer is slightly incorrect. If such experiments were carried out, they must have been performed by the 1st Section which was commanded by Maj Gen KITAGAWA.

A. I don't know a thing.

Q. If they were experimenting, it was the 1st Section which conducted them, wasn't it?

A. Probably so, but I don't know.

Q. Even when the organization of 731 Unit and the duties of each section are considered, the 1st Section had to engage in that type of experiments, don't you think?

A. Since the 1st Section was engaged in conducting the basic experiments, when analyzed it could be thought as such, but I don't know about those experiments. I simply don't know.

Q. But, isn't the study of determining the degree of virulence of different bacteria considered as being a part of the fundamental experiments?

A. Yes, it is a basic experiment .

Q. But, I know for a fact that Maj Gen KITAGAWA was experimenting with the effect of climatical variations on different bacteria. I know that Maj Gen KITAGAWA experimented on the effects of the climatical changes on anthrax by contaminating paper, cotton, wool, straw, food and water with anthrax bacilli. He did not confine his experiments merely on anthrax but similar experiments were conducted on typhoid, para-typhoid, cholera, dysentery, etc.

A. Neither have I heard about it nor have I received any reports to that effect. I did not hear about it even informally. Those facts must be already published in some of the books.

Q. Then do you think that the stability of bacteria and the bacteria which can be employed in BW are all known without conducting any experiments and that those facts are already written in books?

A. I think it is unnecessary to conduct an individual detail experiment since it has been known for ages that anthrax is very virulent and that plague is comparatively non-virulent.

Q. Are you referring to the stability of the virulence of the bacteria?

A. All could be understood by reading books. Since young people don't read enough, they like to conduct various experiments on matters of which they are unfamiliar. Many facts are found to be well presented by reading the books. After all, the research work has been carried on for countless years now.

Q. There is a difference between the stability of the virulence and the stability which refers to the life-span of the bacteria, isn't there?

A. Yes, there is a difference.

Q. Then, the stability of the bacteria was already known in 1940, wasn't it?

A. Although there are various species of bacteria, the general concept on them was already known,probably there are some variations between the typhus bacillus found in DAIREN and the typhus bacilli found in AMERICA, but the major similarities were already known. One might discover some slight differences between the ones found in JAPAN and AMERICA.

Q. Changing the question, what methods were used in conducting the experiments on bacterial rain, and which method was found to be most effective?

A. I do not know about such detailed matters. I don't know since the experiments conducted were not extensive and only dyed liquids were sprayed.

Q. You previously stated that you yourself used bacteria in the bacterial rain, didn't you?

A. They were red colored, non-virulent bacteria.

Q. Didn't you go to the place named NANCHO in Central CHINA in 1940, taking with you quite a few personnel of your unit?

A. I did not.

Q. I want you to recall that event. Many of your subordinates went there and you went there, too, with them.

A. I stated that before, that it was not correct. The plague epidemic was prevalent in CHAN-CHUNG from September to the end of that year, and I was commanding a large unit of 80,000 men. I took my unit with me and also the people of MANCHURIA as well as those from JAPAN and KOREA and remained in that area until the beginning of the snow season. I was in the area of CHAN-CHUNG - NUNGAN.

Q. Do you know Lt Col IKARI? He was one of your subordinates.

A. I know him.

Q. And Maj TAKAHASHI?

A. There were three persons by name of TAKAHASHI. I know the names, but I don't remember their faces.

Q. I mean Maj TAKAHASHI.

A. I know the name, but I can't recall his face.

Q. Try and recall him as much as possible. Maj TAKAHASHI was interested in the same field as you were and that was on plague.

A. Maj TAKAHASHI was with the unit for quite some time. He was a member of the 1st Section, but I can't recall his face.

Q. Perhaps you can recall Technician MIHATA?

A. A man with a pale face. Yes, I remember him.

Q. Can you recall Maj KARASAWA? He was a member of the 4th Section.

A. I feel as if I have heard his name before but I don't remember him too well.

Q. IKARI, TAKAHASHI, and MIHATA, which I just mentioned, were the participants of the expeditional unit which was sent to CHINA, and Maj KARASAWA, which was mentioned the last, was responsible in manufacturing the bacteria.

A. I believe the man, TAKAHASHI, was connected with the anti-epidemic work on plague.

Q. In that year the expeditional unit conducted field experiments on bacterial rain in Central CHINA, and this was an experiment on plague.

A. I don't know.

Q. Then, we will continue with what we have discussed this morning on questions concerning the expeditionary unit. It was said that IKARI, TAKAHASHI, MIHATA, these three were the members of this expeditionary unit, and Maj KARASAWA cultivated the bacteria which were taken by this expeditionary unit.

A. I don't know about that. TAKAHASHI went to CHAN-CHUNG with me to participate in controlling the plague epidemic there.

Q. How is the bacterial rain which could be used in BW be employed and how is the effect determined? We are not interested in the area of dispersion but on the effect of bacterial rain.

A. I did not carry out any extensive research in that line. I think when they are dropped from a high altitude, the droplets will be scattered and blown away. I did not conduct such experiment so I don't know.

Q. Then, through the experiments conducted on bacterial rain, were cholera and typhus bacilli found to be ineffective?

A. I don't know since cholera and typhus bacilli were never used. What I mentioned previously refers to the dyed liquids. I don't know because we never experimented with them. I would think they will be ineffective.

Q. Then, when the bacterial rain was used against the Chinese troops in the vicinity of NINGPO, what bacteria were used?

A. I don't know anything about that.

Q. I have, in my possession, some testimonies given by those who participated in the expedition, and these people have stated about the field trial, but why are you ignorant of it?

A. I don't know since I didn't go. I don't think it is true.

Q. I am not interested in knowing the result of this particular experiment; the reason for this being that I know that it was not effective. But I know that cholera and typhus bacilli were used. Why do you deny this fact?

A. I do not know at all because I did not do it.

Q. Did you make an official trip in 1941?

A. As I said before, I came to TOKYO.

Q. How was the unit reorganized as a result of the KAN-TOKU-EN Plan? What changes were made?

A. Water Purification Units for four (4) armies and twelve (12) divisions were organized and sent out, therefore 90% of the original unit was gone.

Q. Anyway, you were compelled to organize 10 water purification units for the KWANTUNG Army, were you not?

A. I do not remember the exact number, but all were gone south, to CHINA as a result of the KAN-TOKU-EN Plan and none remained in the KWANTUNG Army. They all left by boat from DAIREN to CHINA.

Q. What tactics were used in causing an outbreak of plague epidemic in the NING-PO Area in the operation commanded by you?

A. There was no such thing. As I said before, I was in CHAN-CHUNG performing anti-epidemic work on plague, and then in the latter part of the year I was at the Army Medical School in TOKYO. I always returned to TOKYO in the fall to conduct the unit's business affairs such as submitting budget for the following year and requisitioning for materials, and aside from them, I was also connected with the Army Medical School.

Q. According to the testimonies given by the epidemiologists, who participated in that experiment, we know that the experiment was conducted in the vicinity of TUNG-T'ING-HU.

A. I do not know about that at all.

Q. In regards to the epidemic outbreak in Central CHINA, we have in our possession, the testimonies given by the Chinese Army personnel, Chinese doctors, and scientists. There is even a testimony given by a Czechoslovakian scientist who was with the Chinese Army, and even the scientists in RUSSIA know about it. At the time of the outbreak of that epidemic, these scientists did not know that the epidemic outbreak was caused by the Japanese Army and that a unit under the command of Maj Gen ISHII initiated the outbreak. Although the epidemiologists were able to investigate the cause of the epidemic after conducting autopsies of the victims, the method used for causing the epidemic outbreak was subsequently known through the testimonies given by the people who participated in that expedition.

A. We did not do such things. I do not know what sort of imagination that is but we did not do such things at all. I don't understand it.

Q. In regards to this operation conducted in Central CHINA, if it had been confined only to the testimonies made by the men who participated in that operation, then, naturally, there is a reason for one to deny or conceal this sort of information, but, today, aside from the testimonies given by the participants, the scientists, who investigated when that epidemic broke out, know the cause of this epidemic outbreak, therefore, isn't it futile to deny or conceal it at this time?

A. If a person does not know, no matter what you say it cannot be helped. However, plague broke out all over in that year, in CHAN-CHUNG and even in JAVA. Plague broke out spontaneously in various places because of the high humidity and temperature. I don't think an immediate outbreak of plague is possible by merely scattering plague bacilli.

Q. In the activities taken by the unit, did these expeditionary units use only plague bacilli or did they use some other bacteria?

A. I don't know anything about that. No bacteria were used.

Q. Well then, I shall alter my questions and ask you about the fleas. Why were the fleas bred within your unit, and what was the object of TANAKA breeding the fleas so religiously?

A. As I stated before, it was for the purpose of plague prevention as plague broke out yearly in NUNG-AN. There are several hundred different species of rats in MANCHURIA and about 40 different species of fleas are infested on these rats. Out of these fleas, 17 different species were found to be infected with plague. This was discovered as the result of the devoted study on the part of TANAKA. Extermination of insects and rats was the work of TANAKA and it was for the prevention of plague.

Q. Well then, was that the reason why Technician TANAKA bred several kilograms of fleas?

A. I don't know whether it had several kilograms or not, and I do not know who and how they were weighed, but I think it was not as much as that. I do not know what kind of scale was used or how it was weighed to determine the weight of such small objects, but it was not as much as that.

Q. What method was used to breed the fleas?

A. I have said it before. There are various species of fleas, therefore, the breeding varies according to the specie. Dog fleas were bred on dogs, and cat fleas on cats. Rat fleas were bred in the coops where rats were kept and fleas commonly found on human bodies were bred on dogs. Each specie of flea was bred differently. There were 17 species of fleas that carry plague bacillus such as dog fleas, cat fleas, and fleas on human bodies. All had to be bred accordingly.

Q. I want to know what sort of apparatus was used in the breeding of fleas.

A. I only heard that the fleas were placed in gasoline cans. Actually, I did not like to go and did not go near such a place. Therefore, I am not well acquainted but I believe heat and moisture were provided and the fleas were placed in some boxes.

Q. Didn't you personally conduct experiments on plague?

A. As I have said before, I was never in the laboratory at that time. I was too busy with the administrative work and making official trips, therefore, I personally was never engaged in the plague research. I believe the misunderstanding as to my activity was caused by the praises I received through newspapers, radio, and magazines of the work on plague at CHAN-CHUN.

Q. Now I will ask you some different questions. Didn't you personally think of using fleas in BW? You must have thought of it and because of that you were interested in that field, and consequently, you must have received detailed reports as to the activities in that field.

A. It is stated, firstly, in any text books that fleas carry plague. It is common sense. I am not the only one that knows it. Secondly, it is stated that the essence of plague prevention is immunization and extermination of fleas. These are well known facts stated in books. They are not my discovery.

Q. The things that I want to know about plague are not concerned with its prevention. Using fleas as a weapon to conduct a bacteriological warfare to cause possibly an outbreak of plague epidemic was your personal idea, wasn't it?

A. No, I think it is futile to do such a thing.

Q. Did you not stress the use of fleas as a weapon for offensive bacteriological warfare?

A. Does BW mean bacteriological warfare?

Q. Yes, for both defensive and offensive.

A. I understand. I think that sort of thing is absolutely necessary for the defense in preventing an outbreak of plague epidemic but was ascertained through the research work that it was worthless as an offensive weapon. The reason being that plague bacillus is comparatively non-virulent and fleas are not stable. Plague bacillus dies within several hours and fleas within four weeks. They are the reasons why I decided it is unsuitable, and that is why I felt only the defensive aspect needed to be considered. Because fleas are not stable, I reached the conclusion that extermination of rats will solve the problem. I don't think fleas could be used profitably.

Q. What sort of experiments did you carry out to determine that, using fleas as one of the weapons for bacteriological warfare is worthless?

A. In the epidemic prevention, fleas die immediately when potassium cyanide is used for rat extermination. Rats are susceptible to disinfectant and die easily, therefore, I think it is not suitable for use because it can not be kept for years. I found this out in the plague prevention work in CHAN-CHUN. Fleas are also easily exterminated by using DDT, pyrethrum (insecticide powder), and white birch oil.

Q. What I know is that your unit had a keen interest in the mass production of fleas. When it is considered that on each occasion when an expeditionary unit was dispatched to CHINA, it took with it five kilograms of fleas, then it is inconceivable that the fleas were cultivated solely for the defensive purpose.

A. No, it was strictly for the defensive purpose. I do not know whose imagination or how he said it but as far as the unit was concerned, it was strictly a defensive measure and no other measure aside from the defensive one was ever taken.

Q. Why did the expeditionary unit take approximately five kilograms of fleas when sent to Central CHINA?

A. I do not know who weighed the fleas and who saw them being weighed, but they were not sent. I think it is just an imagination. I do not know.

Q. Do you insist that it is a rumor even though men like Lt Col IKARI and Maj TAKAHASHI, who participated in the expedition, have testified to that fact?

A. Such things never happened. I do not know how Lt Col IKARI weighed them. I can't believe it. I believe it is untrue.

Q. Lt Col IKARI did not say that they took five kilograms of fleas with them. However, he said that they took a considerable amount of fleas with them. But Maj TAKAHASHI and Maj KARASAWA have stated that expeditional units took five kilograms of fleas with them whenever they were dispatched.

A. It is a lie. I can't possibly believe it. If TAKAHASHI stated what you have said, will you bring him to me? The question can be clarified if I ask him about the method by which the fleas were weighed or in what sort of container they carried the fleas. I believe that this trouble started when the original version of "Isn't it so?" was gradually altered to "It may be so" and then to "It must have been so," etc., as the matter was passed on from one party to the next. Anyway, aren't their statements based on their imagination? I can't believe it.

Q. Then, are you inferring that the testimonies of the Chinese doctors who stated that they saw a reconnaissance plane flying in a low altitude dropping fleas and rice contaminated with bacteria as also being false?

A. I can't believe it being true at all.

Q. What I think is that your former subordinates testified these matters to purposely degrade your character.

A. As a scholar, I can't believe it. The reason for my disbelief is that if such things have happened, and if such things were dropped it has to be investigated to determine whether they are infected with plague or not. If we were attacked by an enemy force we would investigate that. If TOKYO were attacked, the presence of plague bacilli would be checked. If none is present, it offers no problem. And to determine whether the bacilli are active or inactive, they will be injected into guinea pigs. By taking this procedure, for the first time the presence or the absence of the plague bacili is determined. But to assert that plague bacilli were scattered simply because a plague epidemic ensued soon after a low flying airplane passed over that locality sounds too fantastic and can not be accepted as facts. I can't rationalize it. I feel that it is based upon imagination.

Q. What I am referring to is not about the plague bacilli but about the plague infested fleas.

A. But the bacteria is there internally and that is to be cultivated. The plague bacilli are in the intestines of the fleas.

Q. Then why was it that you read the Chinese papers and held a keen interest concerning the epidemic which occurred in NINGPO?

A. That is not true at all. In regards to that, as I have stated before, the plague prevention in CHAN-CHUNG was very successful and everyone was grateful for that and words of appreciation were either published in newspapers or something. I believe what you have mentioned is a misunderstanding of the anti-plague work done at CHAN-CHUNG. In regards to the incident that occurred at NINGPO, I already stated last time that I don't know. Questioned as to where I heard about it, I stated I saw it in the newspapers at CHAN-CHUNG Army Hall. I don't know about NINGPO. I do know about the CHAN-CHUNG anti-plague work. It appeared in newspapers. I don't know about the newspaper article on NINGPO. I have stated this once before.

Q. My question neither concerns the plague epidemic which occurred in CHAN-CHUNG nor the newspaper article, but about the article you read in the newspaper concerning NINGPO and which your subordinates also read.

A. There was definitely no such thing.

Q. Many of your subordinates have testified this and they said that it was carried out under the command of Lt Gen ISHII and they said a result was obtained.

A. We cannot go out to such place as we please and assume such commands. We cannot go beyond the territory of MANCHURIA.

Q. Anyway, wasn't an expeditionary unit sent to Central CHINA from your unit?

A. I don't know.

Q. How can you deny these things? Your subordinates who were interrogated in TOKYO have confirmed as to the expeditionary unit. Even Col MURAKAMI and Col OTA have made a similar statement.

A. They are telling lies.

Q. Furthermore, you, yourself have stated previously that a unit composed of sterilising trucks - - disinfecting trucks - - were dispatched to Central CHINA.

A. You mean in 1942.

Q. Then tell us about the expeditionary unit of 1942.

A. The unit was composed of two trucks. One truck was a boiler truck which generated the steam, and the other truck was the disinfecting truck which was built so the clothes could be hung and disinfected. The unit was made up of these two types of trucks. I believe two units of these trucks were sent to Central CHINA as ordered, and some technicians to operate these trucks were sent with them. I don't know how many people were sent. Another unit was sent from the army medical school and that was all. I don't remember who went there.

Q. Do you think it is possible to contaminate rice with plague bacilli?

A. That is a meaningless conjecture and on the contrary. I believe plague bacillus will die if lyophilised while rice must be dry and therefore it is meaningless to use two factors which are not in harmony.

Q. Then, what was the reason of dropping contaminated rice and infected fleas in the vicinity of NINGPO and the lake?

A. I know nothing about it. I don't think that ever happened. I can't even bother to think about it - - seems so foolish.

Q. Then, why was there a special guard unit under your command?

A. They were just ordinary guards watching the surrounding area.

Q. You stated that around the unit's area. What area are you referring to?

A. HARBIN, you are asking about HARBIN, aren't you?

Q. What I am referring is that there was a special guard unit within the unit.

A. No, that is not true.

Q. Then, was anyone permitted to enter the unit's area? Was anyone allowed to enter the unit's area when the unit possessed virulent bacteria?

A. No, there was a guard at the gate and unless the person had a permit he was not allowed to go in.

Q. And who were guarding the people who were to be used for the experiments?

A. There were no such people held within the unit.

Q. But according to the testimonies given by the Manchurian police officials, the unit was receiving some condemned criminals.

A. I know nothing about that.

Q. Were the condemned criminals confined in the unit's largest building?

A. That is not so. Probably that is an error for the warehouse.

Q. But that is not an error. Maj Gen KAWASHIMA, who was one of your subordinates, has testified that there was such a place of confinement. He was a Maj Gen in the Japanese Army and possessed quite an extensive knowledge of everything.

A. I have neither seen nor heard of a place like that. I know that a warehouse was there, and I don't know what KANASHIMA saw there. There were no condemned criminals within the unit while I was in charge but of course I don't know anything about the condition while I was away. During my stay there absolutely no condemned criminals were kept within the unit. I think it is a false statement.

Q. How was the strength of vaccines determined? What sort of experiments were performed within the unit to determine that?

A. Various animals such as mice, guinea pigs, rabbits, goats were first experimented with the vaccine. Whatever our unit made, after experimenting with the animals and proven successful, then the soldiers of the KWANTUNG Army were vaccinated with it, but in some instances the members of our unit were initially vaccinated before giving it to the entire KWANTUNG Army personnel. Unless tried on numerous animals and men, the effectiveness cannot be determined.

Q. Do you think that these criminals were former members of your unit?

A. No, I don't.

Q. I want you to listen to what Maj Gen KANASHIMA has testified.

"From 150 to 200 criminals were confined in two guard houses, and the number of criminals which was delivered annually to the unit amounted to 500 to 600, and therefore, while I was with the unit, approximately 1,000 to 1,200 criminals were received by the unit. The experiments on them were performed before they were executed. Should an experimental subject survive, then he was used for some other experiment. The virulence of cholera, typhoid, typhus, plague was experimented on these criminals. I, personally, have seen the guardhouses and the condition within, and I have personally witnessed some of the human experiments which were conducted at the ANTA Experimental Field. Since I have seen these facts, I testify as these being the truth."

A. That is not true.

Q. Why do a man like Maj Gen KANASHIMA, who was occupying rather an important position in the Japanese Army should testify these things? First of all, he holds no animosity towards you, does he? Maj Gen KANASHIMA had quite an extensive knowledge of bacteriology and was well informed with the experiments which were conducted within the unit.

A. Since I have no recollection of them, I don't know. Later, when I was appointed for the second time as the unit commander, I found out that he harbored a feeling of animosity towards me.

Q. What sort of resentments did he have toward you?

A. I don't quite understand, I can't comprehend it at all. Even to this date, I have been thinking about it, but I am lost as to the cause. I don't understand it, but anyway, he was senior to me once but later I superseded him.

Q. Was he in the army for a long time?

A. Yes, very long. He was senior to me - - several years senior to me. Of course my reasoning is purely my conjecture, and I hesitate in making such an accusation and I don't know what KANASHIMA is thinking but I feel badly because I superseded him. I don't think badly of KANASHIMA. He was my former instructor while I was at the Army Hospital and then I assumed the command of the unit, and became several years senior to him in rank and I feel very badly about it. But I don't believe that this is the cause. I don't know what thoughts he had. Since I was feeling badly about it, I can't believe this could be the reason.

Q. Anyway, in regards to Maj Gen KANASHIMA, you grant that he was a good bacteriologis

A. Yes, a good bacteriologist.

Q. And was he serving for along time as one of your subordinates?

A. I believe it was for a year or two.

Q. Maj Gen KAWASHIMA was serving as your subordinate while he was with the unit for two years, wasn't he?

A. Yes, I believe for about a year and a half.

Q. Maj Gen KAWASHIMA was chief of General Affairs Section in 1941, wasn't he?

A. In 1941? I believe OTA came and replaced him. I remember OTA or KAWASHIMA replaced each other but I don't remember who replaced whom.

Q. And then Maj Gen KAWASHIMA became Chief of the 4th Section?

A. Yes. When he became Chief of the 4th Section it was more of a demotion since Chief of General Affairs Section is considered a more important assignment.

Q. Anyway, didn't Maj Gen KAWASHIMA possess quite a thorough knowledge concerning the unit's activities?

A. Since his time with the unit was rather short, I don't think so. The reason being that even I didn't know everything about that large unit. It was really large so even if one desires to know everything about it, it was rather difficult to do. By merely staying for a year or two would not have permitted KAWASHIMA to know everything.

Q. Anyway, as a bacteriologist, Maj Gen KAWASHIMA has given us quite an extensive intelligence concerning the unit's activities.

A. I can't think the same. I don't know. I believe in the contrary. I feel that he heard hearsay without actually conducting his own research. Those who actually did the work will not say so much because things did not work out so smoothly. By listening the hearsay and rumors of others, what originally stated as "probably so" changed to "It is so" and finally emerged as being "positively so". I feel that probably the statements were based on the final status.

Q. But if Maj Gen KAWASHIMA testifies that he has personally seen the guard houses and its interior and has witnessed the experiments, then certainly you can't dismiss his statement as being merely based on hearsay, can you?

A. I don't know its validity. It is strange that KAWASHIMA should know something which I don't know. I don't think the officers and the members of the unit know about it. If perchance some condemned criminals were received, then, of course, I wouldn't know. It is strange that he should say it when we don't know.

Q. But other members are also familiar with it. Only Lt Gen ISHII doesn't know.

A. I don't think so.

Q. Perhaps to help your recollection it might do some good to have some of these witnesses brought over here and interrogate jointly. This will be all for today.

10.27 1 Jul. 1947: Serial No. 000542, JBC/glh: MEMORANDUM, Interrogation of Certain Japanese by Russian Prosecutor, J. B. CHESAP, Comdr. USN, Secretary

资料出处： National Archives of the United States, R153, E145, B73.

内容点评： 本资料为 1947 年 7 月 1 日美国国务院—陆军部—海军部三部协调远东小委员会秘书处海军中校 J. B. Chesap 提交的备忘录，题目：有关苏联检察官讯问某些日本人。附：根据远东小委员会工作组讨论意见起草的美军远东司令部电文 C-52423 的回复意见，征求各部门反馈。

TOP SECRET

~~TOP SECRET~~
Serial No. 000542
JBC/glh

1 July 1947

MEMORANDUM FOR:

Mr. R. A. Fearey, Rm. 3258, New State Bldg., (S-3763)
Mr. C. F. Hubbert, Rm. 4B914, Pentagon, (W-73110)
Col. E. C. Wallington, Rm. 4E592, Pentagon, (W-3541) ← Returned herewith
Lt. Col. A. F. Metze, Rm. 3618, Navy Dept., (N-61293)
Capt. F. R. Duberg, Rm. 1828, Navy Dept., (N-2341)

Subject: Interrogation of Certain Japanese by Russian Prosecutor

Reference: SWNCC 351/2/D

Enclosure: Draft on subject.

1. The enclosure, drafted by Dr. Edw. Wetter and Mr. H. I. Stubblefield in light of the discussion at the Working Group meeting on 26 June 1947, is circulated herewith for approval.

For the State-War-Navy Coordinating Committee
For the Far East

J. B. Cresap
J. B. CRESAP
Comdr. USN
Secretary

cc: Lt. Col. Babcock
Col. C.C. Dusenbury

TOP SECRET

4. The only information concerning Japanese BW experiments on humans admitted by the Soviets to be in

TOP SECRET　　Enclosure

TOP SECRET

~~TOP SECRET~~

E N C L O S U R E

INTERROGATION OF CERTAIN JAPANESE
BY RUSSIAN PROSECUTOR

THE PROBLEM

1. To formulate a reply to CINCFE's radio C-52423, date 2 May 1947, (Appendix "A") recommending the retention of Japanese BW Information in Intelligence channels and that such material not be employed as "war crimes" evidence.

FACTS BEARING ON THE PROBLEM

2. Part 2 of cable cited in paragraph 1 above states that General Ishii and associates would supply technical BW information if guaranteed immunity from "war crimes" in documentary form. Ishii and associates have to date, voluntarily supplies and are continuing to supply such information without a documentary guarantee of immunity.

3. Nineteen Japanese BW experts have written a 60 page report concerning BW research using human subjects. A twenty page report covering 9 years of research on crop destruction has been prepared. A report by 10 Japanese scientists on research in the veterinary field is being written. A Japanese pathologist is engaged in recovering and making photomicrographs of selected examples of 8,000 slides of tissues from autopsies of humans and animals subjected to BW experiments. General Ishii is writing a treatise embracing his 20 years experience in all phases of BW.

4. The only information concerning Japanese BW experiments on humans admitted by the Soviets to be in

- 1 - Enclosure

TOP SECRET

their possession they state was obtained by them from two Japanese prisoners of war. These prisoners of war admitted to the Soviets that such experiments had been carried out. They stated, however, that their knowledge of the experiments was gained from observation only and that they could offer no technical details.

DISCUSSION

5. The value of Japanese BW information.

a. Data already obtained from Ishii and his colleagues have proven to be of great value in confirming, supplementing and complementing several phases of U.S. research in BW, and may suggest new fields for future research.

b. This Japanese information is the only known source of data from scientifically controlled experiments showing the direct effect of BW agents on man. In the past it has been necessary to evaluate the effects of BW agents on man from data obtained through animal experimentation. Such evaluation is inconclusive and far less complete than results obtained from certain types of human experimentation.

c. In addition to the results of human experimentation much valuable data is available from the Japanese experiments on animals and food crops. The voluntary imparting of this BW information may serve as a forerunner for obtaining much additional information in other fields of research.

6. Desirability of avoiding "war crimes" involvement.

a. Since it is believed that the USSR possesses only a small portion of this technical information, and

Enclosure

TOP SECRET

since any "war crimes" trial would completely reveal such data to all nations, it is felt that such publicity must be avoided in interests of defense and security of the U.S. It is believed also that "war crimes" prosecution of Ishii and his associates would serve to stop the flow of much additional information of a technical and scientific nature.

b. It is felt that the use of this information as a basis for "war crimes" evidence would be a grave detriment to Japanese cooperation with the United States occupation forces in Japan.

CONCLUSIONS

7. It is concluded that:

a. Information of Japanese BW experiments will be of great value to the U.S. BW research program.

b. In the interests of national security it would not be advisable to make this information available to other nations as would be the case in the event of a "war crimes" trial of Jap BW experts.

c. The value to U.S. of Japanese BW data is of such importance to national security as to far outweigh the value accruing from "war crimes" prosecution.

d. The BW information obtained from Japanese sources should be retained in Intelligence channels and should not be employed as "war crimes" evidence.

RECOMMENDATIONS

8. It is recommended that:

a. SWNCC approve the above Conclusions.

b. After approval by SWNCC, the JCS be requested to transmit the message in Appendix "B" to CINCFE providing they have no objection from the military point of view.

c. All subsequent communications dealing with this phase of the subject be classified Top Secret.

TOP SECRET

~~TOP SECRET~~

APPENDIX "A"

From: CINCFE Tokyo Japan

To: War Department for WDGID (pass to CGMLC) MID pass to Major General Alden Waitt

Nr: C-52423 6 May 1947

JCS radio W 94446 (Appendix "A" to SWNCC 351/1) SWNCC 351/1 and Doctor Fell's letters via air courier to General Waitt 29 April and 3 May 1947. This radio is in 5 parts.

Part 1-Statements obtained from Japanese here confirm statements of USSR prisoners Kawashima and Karasawa contained in copies of interrogations given US by USSR.

Part 2-Experiments on humans were known to and described by 3 Japanese and confirmed tacitly by Ishii; field trials against Chinese Army took place on at least 3 occasions; scope of program indicated by report of reliable informant Matsuda that 400 Kilograms of dried anthrax organisms destroyed at Pingfan in August 1945; and research on use of BW against plant life was carried out. Reluctant statements by Ishii indicate he had superiors (possibly General Staff) who knew and authorized the program. Ishii states that if guaranteed immunity from "war crimes" in documentary form for himself, superiors and subordinates, he can describe program in detail. Ishii claims to have extensive theoretical high-level knowledge including strategic and tactical use of BW on defense and offense, backed by some research on best BW agents to employ by geographical areas of Far East, and the use of BW in cold climates.

Part 3-A. Statements so far have been obtained by persuasion, exploitation of Japanese fear of USSR, and desire to cooperate with US. Large part of data including most of the

~~TOP SECRET~~ 4 Appendix "A"

TOP SECRET

valuable technical BW information as to results of human experiments and research in BW for crop destruction probably can be obtained in this manner from low echelon Japanese personnel not believed liable to "war crimes" trials.

B. Additional data, possibly including some statements from Ishii probably can be obtained by informing Japanese involved that information will be retained in intelligence channels and will not be employed as "war crimes" evidence.

C. Complete story, to include plans and theories of Ishii and superiors, probably can be obtained by documentary immunity to Ishii and associates. Ishii also can assist in securing complete cooperation of his former subordinates.

4. None of above influences joint interrogations to be held shortly with USSR under provisions of your radio W-94446.

5-Adoption of method in part 3B above recommended by CINCFE. Request reply soonest.

End

CM IN 912 (May 47)

Appendix "A"

~~TOP SECRET~~

~~TOP SECRET~~

APPENDIX "B"

MESSAGE TO CINCFE

Following Radio in 2 parts.

Part 1. Re URAD C-52423 of 6 May 1947. Recommendation in part 3B and 5 approved. Information obtained from Ishii and associates on BW will be retained in Intelligence channels and will not be employed as "war crimes" evidence.

Part 2. All communications above subject will be classified Top Secret.

10.28　3 Jul. 1947: Letter to Mr. F. S. Tavenner, Jr., International Prosecution Section, from Charles A. Willoughby, Brigadier General, GSC, Assistant Chief of Staff, G-2

资料出处： The University of Virginia Law Library, the Personal Papers of Frank S. Tavenner, Jr. and Official Records from the IMTFE, 1945-1948, Box 5.

内容点评： 本资料为 1947 年 7 月 3 日 G-2 副长官、准将 Charles A. Willoughby 致国际检察局 F. S. Tavenner, Jr. 信函：感谢对部属 McQuail 中校困难敏感工作提供的帮助和信息，相信会对本人对于任何公开均将造成对美国国家来说极为重要的情报泄露的警惕予以理解。

GENERAL HEADQUARTERS
SUPREME COMMANDER FOR THE ALLIED POWERS
Military Intelligence Section, General Staff

APO 500
3 July 1947

Mr F. S. Tavenner, Jr
International Prosecution Section, SCAP
APO 500

Dear Mr Tavenner:

I want to express my thanks to you for your past cooperation and the assistance and information on the difficult and sensitive matter which you recently gave to Lt Col McQuail of my section.

Having seen the instructions from Washington to me on the subject, I am sure you can appreciate my concern over any change of publicity which may result in endangering intelligence information of extreme importance to the United States.

Your kind offer to keep me informed of new developments and to provide copies of your documents for intelligence purposes is appreciated.

Sincerely yours,

C A Willoughby

Charles A. Willoughby
Brigadier General, GSC
Assistant Chief of Staff, G-2

10.29　10 Jul. 1947: Op-32-F2, (SC) AL7-1/EF37, Serial 04338P32: MEMORANDUM for the State-War-Navy Coordinating Committee for the Far East: SWNCC 351/2/D, Reference: (a) SWNCCTS Serial No. 000542 of 1 July 1947, THOS. B. INGLIS, Rear Admiral, U.S. Navy, Chief of Naval Intelligence

资料出处：National Archives of the United States, R153, E145, B73.

内容点评：本资料为 1947 年 7 月 10 日美国海军情报长官、海军上将 Thos. B. Inglis 提交美国国务院—陆军部—海军部三部协调远东委员会的备忘录，题目：SWNCC 351/2/D，海军部同意。

SFE 188 F,/c

~~CONFIDENTIAL~~

In reply refer to Initials and No.

Op-32-F2
(SC)A17-1/EF37
~~CONFIDENTIAL~~
Serial 04338P32

NAVY DEPARTMENT
OFFICE OF THE CHIEF OF NAVAL OPERATIONS
WASHINGTON 25, D. C.

10 JUL 1947

MEMORANDUM for the State-War-Navy Coordinating Committee For the Far East.

Subject: SWNCC 351/2/D

Reference: (a) SWNCC TS Serial No.000542 of 1 July 1947.

1. The Navy Department approves the enclosure to Reference (a).

Thos. B. Inglis

THOS. B. INGLIS
Rear Admiral, U.S. Navy
Chief of Naval Intelligence

~~CONFIDENTIAL~~

10.30 29 Jul. 1947: Letter to Mr. F. S. Tavenner, Jr., International Prosecution Section, from Charles A. Willoughby, Brigadier General, GSC, Assistant Chief of Staff, G-2

资料出处：The University of Virginia Law Library, the Personal Papers of Frank S. Tavenner, Jr. and Official Records from the IMTFE, 1945-1948, Box 5.

内容点评：本资料为1947年7月29日G-2副长官、准将Charles A. Willoughby致国际检察局F. S. Tavenner，Jr.的信函：再次感谢大力协助，递交部属McQuail中校文件及报告，其内容与美国国家利益密切相关。

24299

GENERAL HEADQUARTERS
FAR EAST COMMAND
MILITARY INTELLIGENCE SECTION, GENERAL STAFF

APO 500
29 July 1947

Mr. F. S. Tavenner, Jr.
International Prosecution Section, SCAP
APO 500

Dear Mr. Tavenner:

Again I wish to express my appreciation for your courtesy and consideration. I refer to your forwarding two copies of documents to Lt Col McQuail of my Section, completing a report in which the United States is intensely interested.

Your cooperation will assist greatly in the successful carrying out of a very profitable project.

Sincerely yours,

CHARLES A. WILLOUGHBY
Brigadier General G.S.C.,
Ass't Chief of Staff, G-2

10.31 1 Aug. 1947: SFE 188/2: STATE-WAR-NAVY COORDINATING SUB COMMITTEE FOR THE FAR EAST, INTERROGATION OF CERTAIN JAPANESE BY RUSSIAN RPOSECUTOR, Reference: SWNCC 351/2/D, APPENDIX "A": FACTS BEARING ON THE PROBLEM; APPENDIX "B": DISCUSSION; APPENDIX "C": Nr: C-52423, 6 May 1947, From: CINCFE Tokyo Japan, To: War Department for WDGID (pass to CCMLC) MID pass to Major General Alder Waitt; APPENDIX "D": MESSAGE TO CINCFE

资料出处：National Archives of the United States, R165, E468, B628.

内容点评：本资料为 1947 年 8 月 1 日美国国务院—陆军部—海军部三部协调远东小委员会秘书处海军中校 J.B.Cresap 对远东小委员会的通报：征求各部门对工作小组“有关苏联检察官讯问某些日本人”意见 SFE188/2 的反馈。附：A. 问题关联事实；B. 讨论意见；C. 1947 年 5 月 6 日东京远东军司令部发送陆军部电文 C-52423; D. 发送远东军司令部电文：回复 1947 年 5 月 6 日 C-52423 电文。SFE188/2 明确：石井等提供的细菌战资料保留于情报渠道，不作为“战争犯罪”的证据。

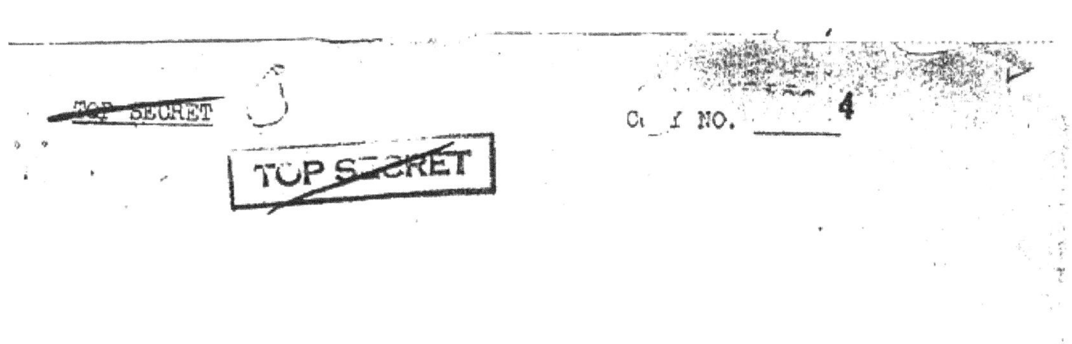

SFE 188/2

(1 August 1947)

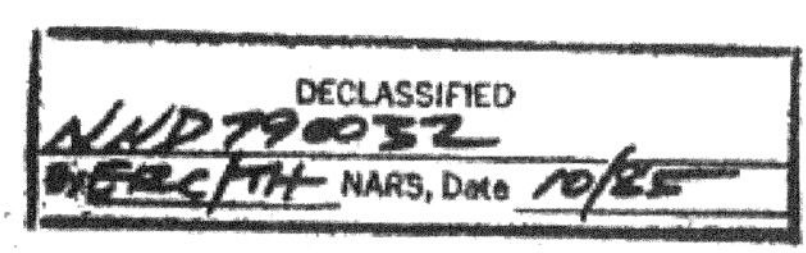

~~TOP SECRET~~ COPY NO. 4

SFE 188/2

1 August 1947

Pages 1 - 11, incl.

STATE-WAR-NAVY COORDINATING SUBCOMMITTEE FOR THE FAR EAST

INTERROGATION OF CERTAIN JAPANESE BY RUSSIAN PROSECUTOR

Reference: SWNCC 351/2/D

Note by the Secretary

1. The enclosure, a proposed report to the State-War-Navy Coordinating Committee by the working group, in response to the reference, is circulated for consideration by the Subcommittee.

2. In addition to the regular offices, representatives of the following activities were consulted in the preparation of this report:

War Crimes Branch (CAD)	-- War Department
Intelligence Division	-- War Department
Chemical Corps	-- War Department
Office of Naval Intelligence	-- Navy Department
Headquarters AAF, Air Chemical Office	-- U.S. Air Forces

J.B. CRESAP
Commander, USN
Secretary

SFE 188/2

~~TOP SECRET~~

E N C L O S U R E

INTERROGATION OF CERTAIN JAPANESE
BY RUSSIAN PROSECUTOR

THE PROBLEM

1. To formulate a reply to CINCFE's radio C-52423, dated 2 May 1947, (Appendix "C") which recommends that Japanese BW Information be retained in Intelligence channels and that such material not be employed as "war crimes" evidence.

FACTS BEARING ON THE PROBLEM

2. See Appendix "A".

DISCUSSION

3. See Appendix "B".

CONCLUSIONS

4. It is concluded that:

a. Information of Japanese BW experiments will be of great value to the U.S. BW research program.

b. The data on hand as substantially outlined in paragraph 3 of Appendix "A" does not appear sufficient at this time to constitute a basis for sustaining a war crimes charge against Ishii and/or his associates.

c. The value to the U.S. of Japanese BW data is of such importance to national security as to far outweigh the value accruing from "war crimes" prosecution.

d. In the interests of national security it would not be advisable to make this information available to other nations as would be the case in the event of a "war crimes" trial of Jap BW experts.

e. The BW information obtained from Japanese sources should be retained in Intelligence channels and should not be employed as "war crimes" evidence.

SFE 188/2 -1- Enclosure

~~TOP SECRET~~

RECOMMENDATIONS

5. It is recommended that:

a. SWNCC approve the above Conclusions.

b. After approval by SWNCC, the JCS be requested to transmit the message in Appendix "D" to CINCFE providing they have no objection from the military point of view.

c. All subsequent communications dealing with this phase of the subject be classified Top Secret.

TOP SECRET

APPENDIX "A"

FACTS BEARING ON THE PROBLEM

1. Part 2 of the cable cited in paragraph 1 (Enclosure) states that General Ishii, Japanese authority on BW, will describe Japanese BW program in detail if guaranteed immunity from "war crimes" in documentary form for himself, superiors and subordinates. Ishii and associates have to date, voluntarily supplied and are continuing to supply such information without a documentary guarantee of immunity.

2. Nineteen Japanese BW experts have written a 60 page report concerning BW research using human subjects. A twenty page report covering 9 years of research on crop destruction has been prepared. A report by 10 Japanese scientists on research in the veterinary field is being written. A Japanese pathologist is engaged in recovering and making photomicrographs of selected examples of 8,000 slides of tissues from autopsies of humans and animals subjected to BW experiments. General Ishii is writing a treatise embracing his 20 years experience in all phases of BW.

3. The only information concerning possible Japanese BW involvement in alleged war crimes may be summarized as follows:

a. Legal Section, SCAP, stated in cable No. C 53169, dated 7 June 1947, that the Japanese Communist Party alleges that the Ishii BW group conducted experiments on captured Americans in Mukden and that simultaneously research on similar lines was conducted in Tokyo and Kyoto. However, Legal Section, SCAP, also states that its investigation to date of the Japanese involved in BW in China does not reveal sufficient evidence to support war crimes charges such evidence consisting of anonymous letters, hearsay affidavits and rumors. In addition, SCAP says that none of Ishii's subordinates are charged or held as war crimes suspects, nor is there sufficient evidence on file against the

TOP SECRET

TOP SECRET

nor have any of our Allies to date filed war crimes charges against Ishii or any of his associates in the BW group, nor is Ishii nor any of his associates included among major Japanese war criminals awaiting trial.

b. The International Prosecution Section at Tokyo states in cable No. C 53663, dated 27 June 1947, that strong circumstantial evidence exists on use of BW in China in that Japanese planes scattered rice and wheat grains in area held by Chinese Army after which bubonic plague appeared, and also that it is of the opinion that, based on affidavits in its possession, Japanese BW group, headed by Ishii, did violate the rules of land warfare, but states that such expression of opinion is not a recommendation that the charges be brought because affidavits would need collaboration in testing their trustworthiness by an exhaustive investigation. One of these affidavits given by a Japanese prisoner of war, who was a member of the Ishii BW group, to Soviet interrogators, makes the following reference to use of human beings for experimental purposes:

> "During 1943 and 1944, extensive experiments were conducted in the spreading of germs. The order in which those experiments were conducted is as follows: At first experiments were made with shells and bombs, and later, with human beings. To study the effective area of the bomb we made a test using pigment in winter and summer; and through this test the sphere of the effective area was decided. The shrapnel exploded in the air scattering fragments of glass over the sphere of the effective area. By this experiment the bomb proved its effectiveness. A bomb which exploded automatically was used to scatter fleas infected with plague. Then, in connection with this, an experiment to examine the effectiveness of bacilli was made on /by using/ living men at the ANTA Experimental Laboratory. In achieving this purpose, the headquarters of the gendarmerie sent to the laboratory, Manchurians who had been sentenced to death. As far as I know, such experiments were made seven or eight times. Sometimes I witnessed these experiments and on other occasions I heard of them from Colonel IKARI, the director of the experiment, and Major HINOFUJI and Major TAKAHASHI, both of them in charge of the experiment. Aside from these I have had oral reports from other participants in the experiment. Several experiments particularly important regarding the infection of wounds were conducted at the ANTA Experimental Laboratory during the period from 1943 to 1944. The plague bacilli and anthrax bacilli were used for these experiments. The experiment on the human body at ANTA

SFE 188/2 -4- Appendix "A"

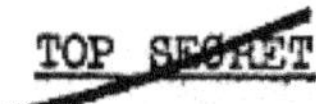
TOP SECRET

TOP SECRET

Experimental Laboratory was conducted in the following way: a bomb filled with bacteria was placed on the ground and about twenty Manchurians were tied to poles or made to sit down on the ground at a proper distance (that is, enough distance to prevent men's death) from the bomb, which were electrically exploded. By the bomb blast, which was caused by the explosion of the bomb, and its fragments, the plague bacilli and anthrax bacilli penetrated through the wound into human bodies. The wounded were kept in the laboratory until the symptoms of the disease appeared and when they were taken ill, they were given medical treatment and their cases were studied, but most of them died in agony. The experiment obtained results just as expected."

c. In discussing the use of evidence in its possession relating to war crimes committee by the Ishii BW group and its possible use in the International Military Trial now pending at Tokyo in cable No. C 53169, dated 7 June 1947, IPS states as follows:

"Since certain of Ishii superiors are now on trial for major war crimes before IMTFE, use of this material was considered by IPS and decision was reached by IPS in December 1946 on the basis of information then available that these witnesses should not be produced, as evidence was not sufficient to connect any of these accused with Ishii's detachments secret activities, the tribunal having announced prior thereto that evidence relating to atrocities and prisoners of war would not be received in the absence of an assurance by the prosecution that the accused or some of them could be associated with the acts charged. The Soviet prosecutor probably will endeavor in cross-examination of one or more accused to lay foundation for the use in rebuttal of the above-mentioned evidence and other evidence which may have resulted from their independent investigation."

d. In a later report, cable No. C 53663, dated 27 June 1947, with more evidence in its possession, IPS states that it is more certain than before that Soviet prosecutor will endeavor in cross-examination of one or more of the accused to lay foundation for the use in rebuttal of some of the evidence above cited and other evidence on this subject which may have resulted from their independent investigation in Manchuria and Japan.

e. Ishii's possible superiors, who are now on trial before IMTFE, include Umezu, Commander, Kwantung Army, 1939-44, Minami, Commander, Kwantung Army, 1934-36, Koiso, Chief of Staff, Kwantung Army, 1932-34, Tojo, Chief of Staff, Kwantung Army, 1937-38.

SFE 188/2 -5- Appendix "A"

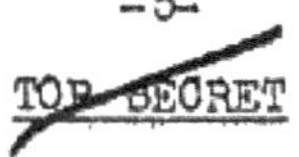

TOP SECRET

f. Experiments on human beings similar to those conducted by the Ishii BW group have been condemned as war crimes by the International Military Tribunal for the trial of major Nazi war criminals in its decision handed down at Nuremberg on 30 September 1946. This Government is at present prosecuting leading German scientists and medical doctors at Nuremberg for offenses which included experiments on human beings which resulted in the suffering and death of most of those experimented on.

TOP SECRET

APPENDIX "B"

DISCUSSION

1. The value of Japanese BW information.

a. Data already obtained from Ishii and his colleagues have proven to be of great value in confirming, supplementing and complementing several phases of U.S. research in BW, and may suggest new fields for future research.

b. This Japanese information is the only known source of data from scientifically controlled experiments showing the direct effect of BW agents on man. In the past it has been necessary to evaluate the effects of BW agents on man from data obtained through animal experimentation. Such evaluation is inconclusive and far less complete than results obtained from certain types of human experimentation.

c. In addition to the results of human experimentation much valuable data is available from the Japanese experiments on animals and food crops. The voluntary imparting of this BW information may serve as a forerunner for obtaining much additional information in other fields of research.

2. Desirability of avoiding "war crimes" involvement.

a. Since it is believed that the USSR possesses only a small portion of this technical information, and since any "war crimes" trial would completely reveal such data to all nations, it is felt that such publicity must be avoided in interests of defense and security of the U.S. It is believed also that "war crimes" prosecution of Ishii and his associates would serve to stop the flow of much additional information of a technical and scientific nature.

b. It is felt that the use of this information as a basis for "war crimes" evidence would be a grave detriment to Japanese cooperation with the United States occupation forces in Japan.

TOP SECRET

c. For all practical purposes an agreement with Ishii and his associates that information given by them on the Japanese BW program will be retained in intelligence channels is equivalent to an agreement that this Government will not prosecute any of those involved in BW activities in which war crimes were committed. Such an understanding would be of great value to the security of the American people because of the information which Ishii and his associates have already furnished and will continue to furnish. However, it should be kept in mind that there is a remote possibility that independent investigation conducted by the Soviets in the Mukden Area may have disclosed evidence that American prisoners of war were used for experimental purposes of a BW nature and that they lost their lives as a result of these experiments, and further, that such evidence may be introduced by the Soviet prosecutors in the course of cross-examination of certain of the major Japanese war criminals now on trial at Tokyo, particularly during the cross-examination of Umezu, Commander of the Kwantung Army from 1939 to 1944 of which army the Ishii BW group was a part. In addition, there is a strong possibility that the Soviet prosecutors will, in the course of cross-examination of Umezu, introduce evidence of experiments conducted on human beings by the Ishii BW group, which experiments do not differ greatly from those for which this Government is now prosecuting German scientists and medical doctors at Nuremberg.

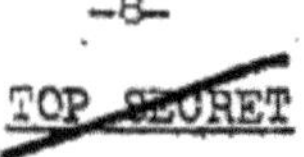

TOP SECRET

APPENDIX "C"

From: CINCFE Tokyo Japan

To: War Department for WDGID (pass to CCMLC) MID pass to Major General Alden Waitt

Nr: C-52423 6 May 1947

JCS radio W 94446 (Appendix "A" to SWNCC 351/1) SWNCC 351/1 and Doctor Fell's letters via air courier to General Waitt 29 April and 3 May 1947. This radio is in 5 parts.

Part 1-Statements obtained from Japanese here confirm statements of USSR prisoners Kawashima and Karasawa contained in copies of interrogations given US by USSR.

Part 2-Experiments on humans were known to and described by 3 Japanese and confirmed tacitly by Ishii; field trials against Chinese Army took place on at least 3 occasions; scope of program indicated by report of reliable informant Matsuda that 400 kilograms of dried anthrax organisms destroyed at Pengfan in August 1945; and research on use of BW against plant life was carried out. Reluctant statements by Ishii indicate he had superiors (possibly General Staff) who knew and authorized the program. Ishii states that if guaranteed immunity from "war crimes" in documentary form for himself, superiors and subordinates, he can describe program in detail. Ishii claims to have extensive theoretical high-level knowledge including strategic and tactical use of BW on defense and offense, backed by some research on best BW agents to employ by geographical areas of Far East, and the use of BW in cold climates.

Part 3-A. Statements so far have been obtained by persuasion, exploitation of Japanese fear of USSR, and desire to cooperate with US. Large part of data including most of the valuable technical BW information as to results of human experiments and research in BW for crop destruction probably can be obtained in this manner from low echelon Japanese personnel not believed liable to "war crimes" trials.

SFE 188/2 -9- Appendix "C"

TOP SECRET

TOP SECRET

B. Additional data, possibly including some statements from Ishii probably can be obtained by informing Japanese involved that information will be retained in intelligence channels and will not be employed as "war crimes" evidence.

C. Complete story, to include plans and theories of Ishii and superiors, probably can be obtained by documentary immunity to Ishii and associates. Ishii also can assist in securing complete cooperation of his former subordinates.

4. None of above influences joint interrogations to be held shortly with USSR under provisions of your radio W-94446.

5. Adoption of method in part 3 B above recommended by CINCFE. Request reply soonest.

End

CM IN 912 (May 47)

APPENDIX "D"

MESSAGE TO CINCFE

Following Radio in 2 parts.

Part 1. Re URAD C-52423 of 6 May 1947. Recommendation in part 3B and 5 approved. Information obtained from Ishii and associates on BW will be retained in Intelligence channels and will not be employed as "war crimes" evidence.

Part 2. All communications above subject will be classified Top Secret.

SFE 188/2 -11- Appendix "D"

TOP SECRET

10.32　8 Sep. 1947: SFE 188/3: STATE-WAR-NAVY COORDINATING COMMITTEE FOR THE FAR EAST, INTERROGATION OF CERTAIN JAPANESE BY RUSSIAN RPOSECUTOR, Reference: SFE 188/2, Note by the Acting Secretary E. L. TURNER, Captain, FA, Acting Secretary

资料出处： National Archives of the United States, R165, E468, B628.

内容点评： 本资料为 1947 年 9 月 8 日美国国务院—陆军部—海军部三部协调远东小委员会执行秘书 E.L.Turner 海军上校向远东小委员会通报的远东小委员会国务院成员提交的备忘录 SFE 188/3 “有关苏联检察官讯问某些日本人”：国务院不能同意 SFE188/2 的提议，即向石井中将等承诺，其提供的细菌战资料保留于情报渠道，不会作为“战争犯罪”的证据；不向其做出承诺，这些资料也有可能从其获取。如此承诺，则今后有可能使美国陷入严重的窘境。

COPY NO. 4

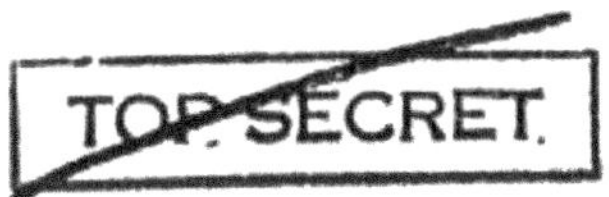

ACTION ASSIGNED TO War Crimes
Mr Lyons
Brict

SFE 188/3

8 September 1947

~~TOP SECRET~~

COPY NO. 4

SFE 188/3

8 September 1947

Pages 1 - 3, incl.

STATE-WAR-NAVY COORDINATING SUBCOMMITTEE FOR THE FAR EAST

INTERROGATION OF CERTAIN JAPANESE BY RUSSIAN PROSECUTOR

Reference: SFE 188/2

Note by the Acting Secretary

The enclosure, a memorandum by the State Member, SFE, is circulated to the Subcommittee in connection with their consideration of the above reference.

E. L. TURNER
Captain, FA
Acting Secretary

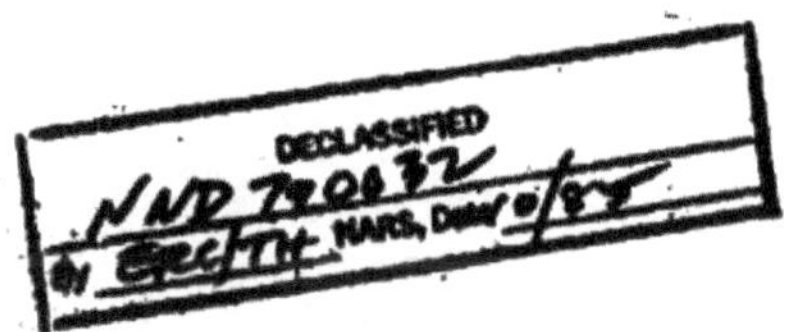

SFE 188/3

~~TOP SECRET~~

~~TOP SECRET~~

ENCLOSURE

INTERROGATION OF CERTAIN JAPANESE BY RUSSIAN PROSECUTOR

Memorandum by the State Member, SFE

The Department of State cannot approve the proposal in SFE 188/2 that Colonel Ishii and his associates should be promised that BW information given by them will be retained in intelligence channels and will not be employed as "war crimes" evidence. It is believed on the basis of facts brought out in the subject paper that is is possible that the desired information can be obtained from Colonel Ishii and his assistants without these asssurances, and that it might later be a source of serious embarrassment to the United States if the assurances were given. At the same time, every practicable precaution should be taken to prevent the BW information possessed by Colonel Ishii from being made generally known in a public trial. It is therefore recommended that (1) that CINCFE, without making any commitment to Ishii and the other Japanese involved, continue to obtain all possible information in the manner heretofore followed; (2) that information thus obtained be retained in fact in intelligence channels unless evidence developed at the International Military Trial presents overwhelming reasons why this procedure can no longer be followed; and (3) that, even though no commitment is made, the United States authorities for security reasons not prosecute war crimes charges against Ishii and his associates.

It is proposed that paragraph "c" of the "Conclusions" of SFE 188/2 be amended as in Appendix "A" hereof, and that Appendix "D" of SFE 188/2 be amended as in Appendix "B" hereof, to accord with the above recommendations.

SFE 188/3 - 1 - Enclosure

~~TOP SECRET~~

TOP SECRET

APPENDIX "A"

CONCLUSIONS

4. It is concluded that:

a. Information of Japanese BW experiments will be of great value to the U.S. BW research program.

b. The data on hand as substantially outlined in paragraph 3 of Appendix "A" does not appear sufficient at this time to constitute a basis for sustaining a war crimes charge against Ishii and/or his associates.

c. The value to the U.S. of Japanese BW data is of such importance to national security as to far outweigh the value accruing from "war crimes" prosecution.

d. In the interests of national security it would not be advisable to make this information available to other nations as would be the case in the event of a "war crimes" trial of Jap BW experts.

e. The BW information obtained from Japanese sources should be retained in Intelligence channels and should not be employed as "war crimes" evidence, unless evidence developed at the International Military Trial presents overwhelming reasons which this procedure can no longer be followed.

TOP SECRET

10.33 29 Sep. 1947: SFE188/4: STATE-WAR-NAVY COORDINATING SUB COMMITTEE FOR THE FAR EAST, INTERROGATION OF CERTAIN JAPANESE BY RUSSIAN RPOSECUTOR, References: a. SFE 188/2, b. SFE 188/3 (3), Note by J.B. CRESAP, Comdr., USN, Secretary

资料出处：National Archives of the United States, R165, E468, B628.

内容点评：本资料为 1947 年 9 月 29 日美国国务院—陆军部—海军部三部协调远东小委员会秘书处海军中校 J.B. Cresap 对远东小委员会的通报：有关苏联检察官讯问某些日本人。附：远东小委员会美总参谋部民政部门交替成员提交的有关意见备忘录。

TOP SECRET

SFE 188/4

29 September 1947

Pages 1 & 2

STATE-WAR-NAVY COORDINATING SUBCOMMITTEE
FOR THE FAR EAST

INTERROGATION OF CERTAIN JAPANESE BY RUSSIAN PROSECUTOR

References: a. SFE 188/2
b. SFE 188/3

Note by the Secretary

The enclosure, a memorandum by the Alternate CAD Member, SFE, is circulated to the Subcommittee in connection with their consideration of the above references.

J. B. CRESAP
Comdr., USN
Secretary

SFE 188/4

TOP SECRET

TOP SECRET

ENCLOSURE

Memorandum by the Alternate CAD Member, SFE

Subject: Interrogation of Certain Japanese by Russian Prosecutor

References: SWNCC 351/2/D, SFE 188/2 and SFE 188/3

1. The alternate CAD Member cannot agree with the statement by the State Member in the enclosure to SFE 188/3 that "on the basis of facts brought out in the subject paper (SFE 188/2) that it is possible that the desired information can be obtained from Colonel (General) Ishii and his assistants without these assurances." Appendix "C" SFE 188/2 (cable C-52423 dtd 6 May 1947 from CINCFE which message originally presented the problem for a decision) says in part, "Ishii states that if guaranteed immunity from 'war crimes' in documentary form for himself, superiors and subordinates, he can describe the program in detail." Paragraph 3 B of that message further states: "Additional data, possibly including some statements from Ishii probably can be obtained by informing Japanese involved that information will be retained in intelligence channels and will not be employed as 'war crimes' evidence." The message concludes by recommending the adoption of the method set forth in 3 B. It is apparent from a reading of the entire message that it is the wish of CINCFE to make the most expeditious arrangements possible with the Japanese BW group, headed by Ishii, for the desired information and that in his opinion this is the least possible offer than can be successfully made.

2. It is recognized that by informing Ishii and his associates that the information to be obtained re BW will be retained in intelligence channels and will not be employed as war crimes evidence, this government may at a later date be seriously embarrassed. However, the Army Department and Air Force Members strongly believe that this information, particularly

SFE 188/4 - 1 - Enclosure

TOP SECRET

that which will finally be obtained from the Japanese with respect to the effect of BW on humans, is of such importance to the security of this country that the risk of subsequent embarrassment should be taken.

3. Further, it is the considered opinion of responsible American officials, both military and civil, who have had close personal contact with General Ishii and other members of the BW group that all the desired information in the detailed form which will give it the greatest value cannot be obtained unless this Japanese group is informed that the information will not be employed as war crimes evidence.

4. Therefore it is believed that, in the final analysis, the security of the United States is of primary importance.

5. It is recommended that:

a. The message in Appendix "D", SFE 188/2, be transmitted without change and

b. If after further consideration, the differences of opinion between the departments cannot be reconciled, this paper be sent to the SWNCC as a split report setting forth the conflicting views of the respective departments.

6. The P&O Army Department and Air Force Members concur in the above.

10.34 11 Mar. 1948: SANACC 351/3: STATE-WAR-NAVY-AIR COORDINATING COMMITTEE, INTERROGATION OF CERTAIN JAPANESE BY RUSSIAN POSECUTOR, Reference: SWNCC 351/2/D, Note by the Secretaries; 13 Mar. 1948: Nr: WAR 97605, To MacArthur, SCAP Tokyo Japan, from the Joint Chief of Staff, Col John H. Ives, 72700

资料出处：National Archives of the United States, R165, E468, B628.

内容点评：本资料包括两份文件：1948 年 3 月 11 日美国国务院—陆军部—海军部—空军部四部协调委员会秘书处对四部协调委员会的通报：关于苏联检察官讯问某些日本人；1948 年 3 月 13 日美军总参谋部上校 John H. Ives 发送东京盟军占领军司令部 MacArthur 电文：回复 1947 年 5 月 6 日 C-52423 电文，据归国技术专家报告，所要的情报和科学数据已经到手。

COPY NO. ~~26~~

PRIMARY INTEREST War Crimes

SANACC 351/3

11 March 1948

OK
F 12/Mar

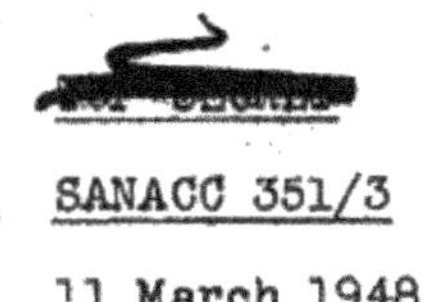

COPY NO. 2E

SANACC 351/3

11 March 1948

STATE-ARMY-NAVY-AIR FORCE COORDINATING COMMITTEE

INTERROGATION OF CERTAIN JAPANESE BY RUSSIAN PROSECUTOR
Reference: SWNCC 351/2/D

Note by the Secretaries

1. In response to the above reference, the following cable has been forwarded to the Joint Chiefs of Staff for transmittal to the Commander-in-Chief, Far East:

"Reurad C-52423 of 6 May 1947. Reports by technical experts who have returned from your theatre indicate that to date necessary information and scientific data have been obtained to your satisfaction. Suggest your recommendation Parts 3 B and 5 be resubmitted for further consideration if and when you consider necessary."

2. In view of the above, no further action is required on the directive contained in the above reference at this time,

H. W. MOSELEY
W. A, SCHULGEN
V, L, LOWRANCE
V, F. FIELD
Secretariat

SANACC 351/3

CONFIDENTIAL

PARAPHRASE NOT REQUIRED. HANDLE AS TOP SECRET CORRESP PER PARAS 511 and (4), AR 380-5.

Joint Chiefs of Staff
Col John H. Ives, 72700

13 March 1948

SCAP Tokyo Japan

Nr: WAR 97605

To MacArthur from the Joint Chiefs of Staff.

The following, received from the State, Army, Navy, and Air Force Departments, is in reply to your C 52423 of 6 May 1947: "Reports by technical experts who have returned from your theater indicate that to date necessary information and scientific data have been obtained to your satisfaction. Suggest your recommendation Parts 3 B and 5 be resubmitted for further consideration if and when you consider necessary."

End.

C 52423 is CM IN 912, 6 May 47

(33)

SANA 5974
11 Mar 48

ORIGINATOR: JCS

DISTRIBUTION: Adm Leahy, Gen Spaatz, Gen Noce, Gen Chamberlin, Adm Denfeld, Mr Draper, Gen Wedemeyer, CSA

CM OUT 97605 (Mar 48) DTG 131738Z hab

~~TOP SECRET~~

COPY NO.

THE MAKING OF AN EXACT COPY OF THIS MESSAGE IS FORBIDDEN

3-25-48

CONFIDENTIAL

SWNCC 351/3

DECLASSIFIED BY ORDER OF THE SEC ARMY BY TAG PER 770475

Directorate for Freedom of Information
And Security Review
Office of the Assistant Secretary of Defense
(Public Affairs)
Room 2C-757, Pentagon, Washington, D.C.

DOWNGRADED TO:
CONFIDENTIAL on 8 JUL 1977
DECLASSIFY on
Classified by

10.35 TELEGTAM, DEPARTMENT OF STATE-DIVISION OF COMMUNICATIONS AND RECORDS, TELEGRAPH BRANCH: 8 Feb. 1950: FROM: Tokyo, TO: Secretary of State, NO: 125, Control 3450; 9 Feb. 1950: FROM: Tokyo, TO: Secretary of State, NO: 129, Control 4133; 10 Feb. 1950: FROM: Tokyo, TO: Secretary of State, NO: 137, Control 4745; 10 Feb. 1950: FROM: Peiping, TO: Secretary of State, NO: 337, Control 4796; 10 Feb. 1950: FROM: London, TO: Secretary of State, NO: 762, Control 4833; 13 Feb. 1950: FROM: Moscow, TO: Secretary of State, NO: 495, Control 5850

资料出处：National Archives of the United States, R165, E468, B628.

内容点评：本资料为美国国务院通信记录局电报科的6份电文，分别为：

1950年2月8日东京Huston发送美国国务卿电文No.125：日本外务省次长Ohta要求提供媒体所报道的设立军事法庭审判昭和天皇及数位战争犯罪人的有关倡议。

1950年2月9日东京Huston发送美国国务卿电文No.129：日本外务省次长Ohta提出，澳大利亚政府要求拘押日本战争犯罪人以在澳大利亚法庭审判，苏联政府可能以此为例，要求引渡昭和天皇与四位将领到苏联予以审判。

1950年2月10日东京Huston发送美国国务卿电文No.137：2月10日《赤旗报》提出强烈要求惩处所有战犯；苏联揭露细菌战之前，东京审判时，天皇的战争责任已经清楚。

1950年2月10日北京Clubb发送美国国务卿电文No.337：中国外交部副部长李克农1950年2月8日予北京苏联大使馆照会：完全赞同苏联政府根据远东委员会决议提出的设立特别国际军事法庭，审判以日本昭和天皇为首的日本五名主要细菌战战犯的倡议。

1950年2月10日伦敦Holmes发送美国国务卿电文No.762：收到苏联大使馆发来的长文，指控日本天皇与四位日本军官准备并实施细菌战，提议根据远东委员会决议，尽早设立特别国际军事法庭予以审判。

1950年2月13日莫斯科Kirk发送美国国务卿电文No.495: 2月12日《真理报》刊登塔斯社北京通讯，据新华社报道，前远东国际军事法庭成员梅汝璈声明：支持苏联立场，1946年2月法庭仅决定不立即审判裕仁，1949年2月决定，如果可能，所有日本战犯的审判于9月结束；任何人以任何借口反对苏联的正义倡议即是细菌战准备的帮凶。

JB
KB7

TELEGRAM

DEPARTMENT OF STATE—DIVISION OF COMMUNICATIONS AND RECORDS

TELEGRAPH BRANCH

15 R

CONFIDENTIAL

A

Action: FE
Info:
SS
G
EUR
L
OLI
CIA
AAN
DCR

Control 3450

Rec'd February 8, 1950
4:52 a.m.

FROM: Tokyo

TO: Secretary of State

NO: 125, February 8

Vice Foreign Minister Ohta has asked for any available information re note reported by press to have been handed by Secretary of State to Soviet Ambassador proposing establishment international tribunal for trial of Emperor Hirohito and several former Japanese military leaders as war criminals.

I have given him gist of DEPTEL 105, February 1 and copy of press release quoted DEPTEL 107 and informed him no other information so far available this mission.

Would appreciate being provided such summary by telegram for text by air pouch as Department considers appropriate to furnish Japanese Government.

HUSTON

DU:EC

CONFIDENTIAL

INFORMATION COPY

KB7

TELEGRAM

DEPARTMENT OF STATE—DIVISION OF COMMUNICATIONS AND RECORDS TELEGRAPH BRANCH

15

CONFIDENTIAL A

Action: FE
Info:
SS
G
EUR
L
OLI
CIA
AAN
DCR

Control 4133

PRIORITY

Rec'd February 9, 1950
6:46 a.m.

FROM: Tokyo

TO: Secretary of State

NO: 129, February 9

Referring to current request Australian Government for apprehension Japanese war criminals in addition to those already detained for trial in Australian courts Vice Foreign Minister Ogta states Japanese Foreign Office apprehensive lest favorable action on Australian request might be seized upon by Soviet Government as precedent on which to base request for transfer Emperor Hirohito and four generals to USSR for trial upon rejection of Soviet proposal for international trial (MISTEL 125, February 8).

Australian request for apprehension additional war crimes suspects has been approved by GHQ. Majority of suspects already apprehended and anticipated they will depart Japan for Manus Island about February 20.

Headquarters has on number of occasions requested repatriation war crimes suspects from USSR for trial here, but no action ever taken by Soviet Government on requests.

HUSTON

BB:JAN

CONFIDENTIAL

INFORMATION COPY

Grr prm KB7

TELEGRAM

DEPARTMENT OF STATE—DIVISION OF COMMUNICATIONS AND RECORDS TELEGRAPH BRANCH

15

PLAIN N

Action: FE
Info:
SS
G
EUR
L
OLI
CIA
AAN
EURX
DCR

PRIORITY

Control 4796

Rec'd February 10, 1950
8:32 a.m.

FROM: Peiping

TO: Secretary of State

NO: 337, February 10

Received 2300 yesterday under cover letter same day from Li Ke Nung copy (in Chinese only) of his note February 8 addressed by him to Embassy USSR Peking with request it be transmitted Secretary State in transliteration as follows:

"Fa Pu Su No. 5 Peking February 8, 1950

F A Shibaev Esquire

Charge d"Affaires of the Soviet Embassy in China.

Mr. Charge d'Affaires:

I have the honor to acknowledge receipt of the note of February 1 of the USSR to the Central Peoples Government of the Peoples Republic of China. On behalf of the Central Peoples Government of the Peoples Republic of China, I declare full agreement with the proposal of the Government of the USSR to appoint in the nearest future a special international military court in accordance with article 5 (A) of the decision of the Far Eastern Commission of April 3, 1946 (Document FEC-007(3) to try the five major Japanese bacteriological warfare criminals of great crimes, extreme sins, destroyers of humanity namely Hirohito Emperor of Japan, Ishii Shiro and Kitano Masajo, Lieutenant Generals of the Medical Service, Wakamatsu Yujiro, Major General of Veterinary Service, Kasahara Yukio, Chief of Staff of the Kwantung Army.

The Central Peoples Government of the Peoples Republic of China considers that, when the special international

military

PLAIN

INFORMATION COPY

PLAIN

-2- #337, February 10, from Peiping

military court convenes, only the representatives of the Central Peoples Government of the Peoples Republic of China can attend, and definitely personnel of the Chiang Kai-shek reactionary bloc, which long ago lost all qualifications to represent China, cannot attend.

The Central Peoples Government of the Peoples Republic of China considers that the trial of the Japanese bacteriological warfare criminals held by the Military Tribunal of the Khabarovik maritime military area from December 25 to 29, 1949 fully shows that the Soviet Union has meted out due punishment to the Japanese war criminals who endanger humanity and has fulfilled its great responsibility with respect to the matter of protecting the interests of humanity and peace. The justice and the merit of the Soviet Government have won the acclamation and support of all peace-loving states and peoples in the world. The Chinese people who have suffered murder by bacteria by imperialist Japan, in particular feel greater indignation at the Fascist enemy, and deeper gratitude to their friend the great Soviet Union. The just call and proposal of the note of the USSR to appoint in the nearest future a special international military court to try the five major war criminals of bacteriologial warfare headed by Hirohito, Emperor of Japan, will meet with even greater ardent support from all peace-loving states and peoples in the world. Only imperialist governments, which still retain the desire to foster the resurgence of Japanese imperialism and are actively preparing for a new world war, will reject this just call and proposal of the government of the USSR and continue to shield the major war criminals Hirohito Emperor of Japan, of great crimes, extreme sins, killer of humanity.

Please accept, Mr. Charge d'Affaires, the assurance of my highest consideration.

Li Ke Nung"

Note office translation differs in several minor respects from NCNA version February 8.

CLUBB

DU:RA

NOTE: Advance copy to Mr. Efteland (CA)-10:30 a.m. 2/10 KW

PLAIN

RB7

TELEGRAM

DEPARTMENT OF STATE—DIVISION OF COMMUNICATIONS AND RECORDS TELEGRAPH BRANCH

4 RESTRICTED A

Action: FE
Info:
P
EUR
L
OLI
CIA
AAN
DCR

Control 4745

Rec'd February 10, 1950
7:12 a.m.

FROM: Tokyo

TO: Secretary of State

NO: 137, February 10

AKAHATA February 10 launched vigorous demand for punishment all criminals. Charged that even before Soviet revelations of bacteriological warfare, "Emperor's war crime guilt had been clarified at time of Tokyo trials". Failure to try Emperor "has endangered destiny of Japanese race, livelihood of masses, and peace of entire world". Article alleged plot afoot to resurrect Emperor politically as link in various intrigues of reactionaries to achieve separate peace and transform Japan into military base.

HUSTON

SMS:EC

RESTRICTED

INFORMATION COPY

KBK

TELEGRAM

DEPARTMENT OF STATE—DIVISION OF COMMUNICATIONS AND RECORDS TELEGRAPH BRANCH

SECRET N

Action: FE
Info:
SS
G

CORRECTED COPY
2/11/50 4 p.m.
CORRECTION UNDERSCORED

Control 4833

Rec'd February 10, 1950
9:39 a.m.

Miss Fite
Mr. Snow

To: ~~1/ Mr. Fisher~~ K. Fite

Classification: C

Attached for your information and use is a copy of a message brought to S/S-R by the special liaison officer from the Department of Defense. This may be retained in your files or returned to Room 5273 for destruction.

A copy has also been made available to __________

ate

0, noon

eived from Soviet Embassy long
Emperor and four Japanese Army
and executing bacteriological
early appointment special Inter-
t according with 5 (A) FEC 007/3.
ands similar note sent US and
ign Office considers Soviet note
e and does not plan reply for pre-
til after consultation US. Pre-
K might base reply on (A) fact
istent with directives already
evidence direct complicity persons

g Head FE Department Foreign Office,
ion Emperor in which Communist
ar rule out any likelihood subse-
e agreement discuss peace treaty
either jointly or separately with a Japan of which the
titular head is the Emperor.

Tomlinson states Foreign Office would appreciate receiving Department's views. Meanwhile Embassy making available Tomlinson text Department's press review February 3 this subject.

HOLMES

CSB:GMC

SECRET

INFORMATION COPY

☆ GPO : 1949—O—849241

KBX

TELEGRAM

DEPARTMENT OF STATE—DIVISION OF COMMUNICATIONS AND RECORDS **TELEGRAPH BRANCH**

7-R

SECRET N

Action: FE
Info:
SS
G
EUR
L
OLI
CIA
DCR
AAN

CORRECTED COPY
2/11/50 4 p.m.
CORRECTION UNDERSCORED

Control 4833

Rec'd February 10, 1950
9:39 a.m.

FROM: London

TO: Secretary of State

NO: 762, February 10, noon

Foreign Office has received from Soviet Embassy long note accusing Japanese Emperor and four Japanese Army officers of preparing and executing bacteriological warfare and proposing early appointment special International Military Court according with 5 (A) FEC 007/3. Foreign Office understands similar note sent US and Communist China. Foreign Office considers Soviet note obvious propaganda move and does not plan reply for present or in any case until after consultation US. Preliminary thinking is UK might base reply on (A) fact Soviet proposal inconsistent with directives already issued and (B) lack of evidence direct complicity persons accused.

Q. H. Tomlinson, Acting Head FE Department Foreign Office, remarks Soviet accusation Emperor in which Communist China joins would appear rule out any likelihood subsequent Soviet or Chinese agreement discuss peace treaty either jointly or separately with a Japan of which the titular head is the Emperor.

Tomlinson states Foreign Office would appreciate receiving Department's views. Meanwhile Embassy making available Tomlinson text Department's press review February 3 this subject.

HOLMES

CSB:GMC

SECRET

INFORMATION COPY

☆ GPO : 1949—O-849241

KB7

TELEGRAM

DEPARTMENT OF STATE—DIVISION OF COMMUNICATIONS AND RECORDS

TELEGRAPH BRANCH

4

PLAIN

Action: FE
Info:
P
EUR
OLI
CIA
AAN
IE
DCR

Air Request

Control 5850

Rec'd February 13, 1950
10:59 a.m.

FROM: Moscow

TO: Secretary of State

NO: 495, February 13

SENT DEPARTMENT 495, DEPARTMENT PASS TOKYO 21.

PRAVDA February 12 prints third column Peiping Tass dispatch based Hsinhua quoting statement Meechuao former member International Military Tribunal for Far East, supporting Soviet position on Jap war criminals, stating February 1946 only decided not try Hirohito immediately and February 1949 decided all trials Jap war criminals should be finished September that year "if possible", concluding "anyone who objects absolutely just Soviet proposition under any pretense whatsoever shows by that alone that he is helper in preparation bacteriological warfare"; Soviet press Soviet 12 prints brief Shanghai Tass dispatch following text "demanding trial Hirohito, newspaper AKAHATA writes: Not long after conclusion war Communist Party demanded trial Emperor **** now two Communist party, together with all honest patriots who desire create peace loving, independent Japan, will fight to bring to trial all military criminals, including Emperor.

KIRK

CSB:RT

NOTE: Relayed to Tokyo 2/13/50, 11:03 a.m. HEF.

PLAIN

INFORMATION COPY

10.36 27 Feb. 1950: CC 3, 4, 5, 6, USSR: OVERSEAS & FAR EAST, Moscow, TASS, Soviet Press Service, in English Morse to North America

资料出处： National Archives of the United States, R165, E468, B628.

内容点评： 本资料为1950年2月27日苏联的海外和远东媒体报道摘要，其中1950年2月23日塔斯社对北美英文报道摘要的题目为“Keenan Ignored Japanese Germ War Plans”，称1946年9月东京审判期间，苏联检察官将731部队主要干部川岛、柄泽的细菌战证据材料提交首席检察官Keenan，未予理睬。1946年1月3日，美国陆军部已经发布有关日军在细菌战方面成果的报告。

MCS —
Keenan Article

RESTRICTED

- CC 3 - USSR: OVERSEAS & FAR EAST
Feb. 27, 1950

KOREA TOPS PLANNED TRANSPORT NORMS

Moscow, TASS, Soviet Press Service, in English Morse to North America, Feb. 23, 1950, 2218 GMT -W

(Text)

"Pyongyang--A meeting of the railway workers' and transport workers' union held here has discussed the results of the work in 1949 measures for assuring the successful implementation of the 1950 plan and the progress of Labor competition. The report on the results of the execution of the 1949 plan and on tasks of transport workers in 1950 was made by (Pak I Won) Acting Minister of Railways, who pointed out that as a result of the selfless labor of the transport workers the plan for goods traffic by rail had been exceeded in 1949 by 8 percent, goods traffic by automobile by 20 percent, and by shipping 18.4 percent. As compared with 1948 the freight turn-over on railways in the northern part of the Korean People's Democratic Republic grew by 38.8 percent.

"A long speech about the tasks of the transport workers in the struggle for the overfulfillment of the Two Year Plan for the development of national economy was made by Prime Minister Kim Il Sung."

KEENAN IGNORED JAPANESE GERM WAR PLANS

Moscow, TASS, Soviet Press Service, in English Morse to North America, Feb. 23, 1950, 1600 GMT--W

(Text)

"An IZVESTIA commentator calls the American attorney Joseph Keenan, who dashed forth to defend the war criminal -- The Emperor of Japan Hirohito....

"The commentator writes: It seems that it would not befit the American chief prosecutor at the Tokyo trial of the Japanese war criminals to take under his protection militarists guilty of crimes against humanity. But it is not accidentially that the prosecutor now acts as counsel for the defense.

"Joseph Keenan has a longstanding weakness for renowed war criminals. Thus, for instance, in December 1947, with the help of Keenan, who at that time was head of the juridical department at MacArthur's Headquarters, 23 inveterate war criminals were set free, including Fujiwara, former Minister of the War Industry, one of the prominent representatives of the Zaibatsu, the former head of the Manchurian Industry Administration, big manufacturer of war materials Ayukawa, and others.

RESTRICTED

- CC 4 -

USSR: OVERSEAS & FAR EAST
Feb. 27, 1950

"Even during the Tokyo trial of the war criminals, materials...the Japanese ruling clique of applying inhuman bacteriological weapons were forwarded to Keenan as chief American prosecutor. But every time Joseph Keenan hushed up these atrocious plans of the Japanese military. At the Tokyo trial Joseph Keenan turned a deaf ear to the Soviet prosecution when the latter in September 1946 submitted to him as chief American prosecutor evidence (against) Kawashima and Karasawa, leading staff members of Brigade No. 731. This evidence convicted the Japanese militarists of preparing bacteriological war and conducting brutal experiments on live people.

1946 Report of War Department

"Even during Tokyo trial, the commentator writes further, the defender of the war criminals, wearing at that time a prosecutor's garb, knew that on Jan 3, 1946 the U.S. War Department published a report about 'the successes of Japan in the field of bacteriological warfare', which among other things stated:

"'The Japanese military conducted big work for the purpose of utilizing bacteriological means as a practical weapon of offensive war. Various kinds of weapons evolved as result of research in their laboratories were tested at Army experimental stations, where experiments on the use of bacteria for subversive purposes were also conducted.' But having published this material exposing Japanese militarists, American ruling circles became silent, since preparation of the bacteriological (warfare was envisaged) not only by plans of the Japanese but also of the American militarists, and the experience of Brigade No. 731 can certainly come useful for conducting equally insidious tests at experimental stations in Camp Detrick, Maryland.

Meaning of 'Impotent Rage'

"Now Joseph Keenan is again defending the Japanese war criminals and their leader--Emperor Hirohito, the article reads further. He is worried by the just demand contained in the Soviet note that Hirohito and his accomplices be arraigned for trial by an international military tribunal. He is dodging about and constantly gets entangled in his own ruses. Now he vaguely admits that during the Tokyo trial his investigators 'discovered a number of scrappy data' about the application of the bacteriological weapon by the Japanese--data 'which could arouse certain suspicions.' Now he cynically declares that 'the Japanese did not experiment (with the) bacteriological weapon on American war prisoners,' but passes in silence the brutal application of this weapon to the citizens of China and the USSR. Then he resorts to crude provocations and heinous anti-Soviet slander

"The impotent rage of Joseph Keenan and other warmongers of his ilk is comprehensible. Their base, futile attempts to vilify the Soviet Union expose them for what they really are.

RESTRICTED

- CC 5 - USSR: OVERSEAS & FAR EAST
Feb. 27, 1950

"With the help of the Keenans the American imperialists shelter..., the commentator concludes, whom they save for new, barbarous aggression. But the peoples of theworld are vigilant. They know how to halt the criminal hand of the genereals of the plague service and their dishonest protectors, including those who don prosecutor's garb."

U.S. CIRCULATES FAKE COMMUNIST PAPERS

Moscow, TASS, Soviet Press Service, in English Morse to North America, Feb. 24, 1950, 0125 GMT--W

(Text)

"New York--The progressive Brazilian newspaper VOZ OPERARIA has published an article denouncing the activities of United States agents in Brazil, Bolivia, and Chile who forge 'documents' which are then attributed to the Communists. VOZ OPERARIA declared that the State Department counselor Kennan 'is head of a spy chain operating in Latin America.'

"The newspaper accused Kennan of fabricating the 'document' which, as the Bolivian authorities recently asserted, allegedly proves the existence of a 'Communist conspiracy' in all Latin American countries. The newspaper urges Latin American democratic forces to staunchly resist the United States imperialist penetration and the machinations of United States spies and provocateurs."

CHINESE DELEGATES' TRIP HOME NOTED

Moscow, TASS, Soviet Press Service, in English Morse to North America, Feb. 24, 1950, 0145 GMT--W

(Text)

"Moscow--The chairman of the Central People's Government of the Chinese People's Republic, Mao Tse-tung, as well as the Premier of the State Administration Council and the Minister of Foreign Affairs of the Chinese People's Republic, Chou En-lai, and persons accompanying them, who on Feb. 17 left Moscow, on way to China visited Sverdlovsk, Omsk, Novosibirsk, and Kransoyarsk.

"On Feb. 20 the guests arrived in Sverdlovsk where they spent several hours visiting forge-press and mechanic shops and the combined electric power and heat generating plant of Uralmash works, as well as the Ural's Geological Museum.

"On the following day, Feb. 21, the guests arrived in Omsk where they also stopped for several hours, acquainting themselves with the city and visiting the machine tool building plant.

RESTRICTED

- CC 6 -

USSR: OVERSEAS & FAR EAST
Feb. 27, 1950

"In the evening of the same day the guests stopped in Novosibirsk where they visited plant named after Chkalov. Subsequently the guests attended the performance of 'Price Igor' at the State Theatre of Opera and Ballet.

"On Feb. 22, the guests stopped in Krasnoyarsk where they visited the plant which produces self-propelled combine harvesters. In the evening they attended concert of regional chorus of Russian songs. The sojourn of Mao Tse-tung, Chou En-lai, and persons accompanying them in Sverdlovsk, Omsk, Novosibirsk, and Krasnoyarsk found broad response among local public circles. The guests were welcomed in a friendly manner everywhere."

DUTCH SECRET SERVICE ATTACKS LIBERALS

Moscow, TASS, Soviet Press Service, in English Morse to North America, Feb 21, 1950, 1215 GMT--W

(Text)

"The Hague--Judging by press reports the Dutch ruling circles, who have bound themselves to the aggressive Atlantic Pact, seek to turn the country into a police state. Several million gulden have been additionally allocated for the upkeep of the secret police, which is now stepping up reprisals against democratic organizations. The Dutch authorities continue to persecute the Partisans of Peace.

"A representative of the French dockers, Porcheron, was recently sent out of Rotterdam only for wanting to convey greetings from his fellow workers to the Rotterdam dockers. Amsterdam police forbade a Belgian worker to address a meeting of Peace Partisans. The Dutch authorities have decided to refuse entry visas to all foreign organizations invited to attend the forthcoming congress of the Dutch Communist Party.

"Latest press reports indicate that, besides the Governmental secret service in Holland, there are various other secret intelligence services subordinated to Dutch (reaction) and American imperialists. It is pointed out in particular that the widely ramified espionage organization, the so-called 'Dutch Labor Reserves Training Institution' has been set up in the country.

"The newspapers HET PAROOL and DE WAARHEID say this organization is financed by various industrial and banking circles with the direct connivance and participation of the Dutch ruling circles. Thus for instance the management of Heineken's breweries has donated 100,000 gulden to the secret service.

10.37 31 May 1950: No. 93, Note from the Embassy of USSR to Mr. Dean G. Acheson, Secretary of State of the United States of America; 5 Jun. 1950: BBB 3, USSR RENEWS DEMAND FOR HIROHITO TRIAL, Peking, NCNA, in English Morse, to North America, June 3, 1950

资料出处： National Archives of the United States, R165, E468, B628.

内容点评： 本资料包括两件文件：1950 年 5 月 31 日苏联驻美大使予美国国务卿 Dean G. Acheson 的照会，提及 2 月 1 日苏联已照会，告知 1949 年 12 月伯力举行的对日本细菌战犯罪人的审判结果，证据证明日本天皇与四位原日军将领石井等负有责任；提议举行特别国际军事法庭予以审判，中国政府已表同意。请予答复。

附 1950 年 6 月 3 日中国新华社北京对北美的英文报道，题目：苏联再次提出审判昭和天皇，称 2 月 8 日中国政府已照会苏联表示完全赞同苏联的提议，但是美英政府至今尚未回应。

May 31, 1950 1

No. 93

Emperor

Sir:

On February 1, 1950 upon instruction of the Soviet Government, the Ambassador had the honor to send you a note regarding the results of the public court trial of the Japanese war criminals Yamada, Takahachi, Kajitsuka and others which took place in the Military Tribunal of the Primorski Military District at the City of Khabarovsk from December 25 to 30, 1949 where it was established that the Japanese ruling circles headed by Emperor Hirohito for a period of many years secretly prepared (against the USSR, China, USA and Great Britain) bacteriological warfare--one of the most inhumane weapons of aggression.

At this trial it was also established that the Japanese war criminals not only prepared but more than once employed the bacteriological weapon in the realization of their aggressive plans: In 1939 against the Mongolian Peoples Republic and the USSR in the region of the River Khalkin-Gol; in 1940-42 at the time of the war against China where bacteriological expeditions of the Japanese Army caused epidemics of the plague and typhus.

The reference note of February 1 pointed out the fact that it was proved by facts established at the court trial at Khabarovsk that a leading role in the preparation and realization of bacteriological warfare belonged not only to the already convicted Japanese war criminals but also to the Emperor of Japan, Hirohito, as well as to Generals of the Japanese Army Ishii Shiro (former Chief of Detachment

No. 731

-2-

No. 731), Kitano Masajo (also former Chief of Detachment No. 731), Wakamatsu Yujiro (former Chief of Detachment No. 100) and Kasahara Yukio (former Chief of Staff of the Kwantung Army).

Proceeding from the fact that the employment of the bacteriological weapon had already long ago been judged by civilized nations as a most serious crime contrary to the honor and conscience of peoples and as is known forbidden by the Geneva Protocol of June 17, 1925, the Soviet Government in its note of February 1, proposed the appointment in the near future of a special international military court and to transfer to the stated court as exposed war criminals the Emperor of Japan, Hirohito, and Generals Ishii Shiro, Kitano Masajo, Wakamatsu Yujiro and Kasahara Yukio.

The Embassy considers it necessary to point out that although more than three months have passed since the time of the delivery of the note referred to above, a reply to this note has not been received by the Embassy up to the present time. Drawing attention to this circumstance, upon instruction of the Soviet Government, the Embassy expects that reply to the note of the USSR of February 1 will be given by the Government of the USA with the least possible delay.

Accept, Sir, the assurances of my highest esteem.

(signature illegible)

Mr. Dean G. Acheson,

Secretary of State of the

United States of America.

cc - L
RA - Mr. Holder
UWY, FR
LET

TRANSLATED BY:
EUR:EBJMcSweeney:mt
5/31/50

"The Peking Government in a broadcast last month offered Tibet regional autonomy if she would join the Communist regime peacefully. It said Tibet was certain to be liberated in any case and that she could not count on Western help. It invited Tibet to send a delegation to meet Chinese Government leaders. A Chinese Nationalist mission was expelled from Tibet a year ago."

USSR RENEWS DEMAND FOR HIROHITO TRIAL

Peking, NCNA, in English Morse, to North America, June 3, 1950, 1400 GMT --R

(Text)

"Peking, June 2--The Government of the Soviet Union had, on Feb. 1 this year, forwarded notes to the Central People's Government of the People's Republic of China and the U.S. and British Governments with the proposal for the appointment of a special international military court at an earliest date to try the Japanese war criminal Emperor Hirohito and other Japanese war criminals of germ warfare, who had committed the most heinous of crimes.

"The Central People's Government expressed full agreement with the proposal in a note to the Soviet Government on Feb. 8. But the U.S. and British Governments have not made any reply up till now. The Soviet Government, through its embassies in the United States and Britain, again handed notes to the U.S. and British Governments on May 30, demanding a reply to the note of the Soviet Government of Feb. 1 at the earliest date. A copy of this note of the Soviet Government has been handed to the Foreign Ministry of the Central People's Government of the People's Republic of China by N. V. Roshchin, the Soviet Ambassador to China, on June 1. The full text of the Soviet Government's note to the U.S. and British Governments reads:

Text of Note

"'On Feb. 1, 1950, on instructions of the Soviet Government, the Ambassador had the honor of forwarding to you a note on the results of the public trial before a military tribunal of the Primorye Military Area in the city of Khabarovsk of Dec. 25-30, 1949, of Japanese war criminals Yamada, Takahashi, Kajitsuka, and others, where it was established that Japan's ruling circles headed by Emperor Hirohito had, over a period of many years, been secretly preparing to wage war (against the USSR, China, the United States, and Great Britain--NCNA) by bacteriological means--one of the most inhuman weapons of aggression.

- BBB 4 - CHINA
June 5, 1950

"'At that trial it was also established that not only did the Japanese aggressors prepare but on repeated occasions employed bacteriological weapons in furth erance of their aggressive plans: In 1939 against the Mongolian People's Republic and the USSR in the area of the River Khalkhin Gol; in 1940-42 in war against China, where Japanese Army bacteriological expeditionscaused epidemics of plague and typhoid.

"'In the aforementioned note of Feb. 1 it was pointed out that the facts established at the Khabarovsk trial proved that not only Japanese war criminals condemned earlier but also Emperor Hirohito of Japan as well as generals of the Japanese Army Shiro Ishii (former chief of Brigade 731--NCNA, Massazo Kitano (also former chief of Brigade 731--NCNA, Yujiro Wakamatsu (former chief of Brigade 100--NCNA, and Yukio Kasahara (former chief of staff of Kwantung Army--NCNA) played a leading role in preparing and waging bacteriological warfare.

Special Court

"'Bearing in mind that the bacteriological weapon has long ago been condemned by civilized nations as a severe crime contrary to the honor and conscience of peoples and is known to be prohibited by the Geneva Protocol of June 17, the Soviet Government in its note of Feb. 1 proposed the appointment at the earliest date of a special international military court and committment for trial before this international court of Emperor Hirohito and Generals Shiro Ishii, Massazo Kitano, Yujiro Wakamatsu and Yukio Kasahara as convincted war criminals.

"'The Embassy deems it necessary to recall the fact that although over three months have elapsed since the presentation of the aforementioned note, a reply to this note has not so far been received by the Embassy. Drawing attention to this circumstance on the instruction of the Soviet Government, the Embassy expects the United States Government to give a reply to the note of the USSR of Feb. 1 at the earliest date.'

"Copies of the aforegiven note were handed to the Governments represented in the Far Eastern Commission."

KIDNAPING OF CHUSHAN ISLANDERS CHARGED

Peking, Chinese International Service, in Cantonese, June 2, 1950, 1950 GMT--F

(Tinghai--More than 30,000 youths were reported to have been kidnaped by the Kuomintang remant bandits prior to the evacuation from Chushan Island. It was reported that on the night of May 15, the Kuomintang bandit troops in Chushan suddenly surrounded a number or villages, where they searched every nook and cranny and arrested persons on sight.

10.38 15 Dec. 1950: No. 182, Note from /s/ A. Panyushkin, To: Mr. Dean G. Acheson, Secretary of State of the United States of America

资料出处： National Archives of the United States, R165, E468, B628.

内容点评： 本资料为 1950 年 12 月 15 日苏联驻美大使 A. Panyushkin 予美国国务卿 Dean G. Acheson 的照会：1950 年 2 月 1 日、5 月 30 日苏联政府两次照会美国政府，提议同盟国设立特别国际军事法庭，追究日本细菌战战争犯罪，审判日本天皇与四位原日本将领石井等。请务必予以答复。

Washington, December 15, 1950

Em|p...

No. 182

Sir:

Ten months ago, on February 1, 1950, the Soviet Government sent the Government of the United States of America a note concerning the results of the public trial of the Japanese war criminals, Yamada, Kajitsuka, Kawashima and others, which took place in the Military Tribunal of the Maritime Military District at the City of Khabarovsk from December 25 to 30, 1949, where it was established that the Japanese ruling circles, headed by Emperor Hirohito, for a period of many years secretly prepared for bacteriological warfare---one of the most inhumane weapons of aggression--against the USSR, China, the USA and Great Britain.

In this note it was pointed out on the basis of facts established by the Court that the Emperor of Japan, Hirohito, was exposed by the testimony of Kajitsuka and Kawashima, who had taken part in the preparation for bacteriological warfare, as one of the main participants in the preparation for bacteriological warfare. In accordance with special secret instructions from Hirohito, a Japanese

army

Mr. Dean G. Acheson,

Secretary of State of the

United States of America.

army center for the preparation of bacteriological warfare against the USSR, China, the Mongolian Peoples Republic, the USA and other states was established on the territory of Manchuria, then occupied by Japan. The preparation for the accomplishment of these criminal plans of the Japanese militarists was accompanied by tests of the effect of deadly bacteria on thousands of people, mainly on citizens of China and the USSR.

It was also established at the above mentioned Khabarovsk trial that the Japanese war criminals not only prepared but also repeatedly used bacteriological weapons in carrying out their aggressive plans: in 1939--against the Mongolian Peoples Republic and the USSR in the region of the Khalkhin-Gol River; in 1940-1942--during the war against China where bacteriological expeditions of the Japanese army caused epidemics of the plague and typhus.

It was pointed out in the note of the Soviet Government that the crimes of the Japanese militarists and their chief organizer and inspirer, the Emperor of Japan, Hirohito, were a gross violation of the laws and customs of war and, in particular, of the Geneva Protocol of June 17, 1925, which forbids the use of bacteriological weapons, already long condemned by civilized nations, as a most serious crime contradictory to the honor and conscience of peoples.

Proceeding on the basis of the Potsdam Declaration of 1945, signed by the United States, Great Britain and China, and subscribed to by the USSR, which states that all war criminals must suffer severe punishment, and also in accordance with point A of Article 5 of the Far Eastern Commission's decision of April 3, 1946, which stipulated

that the

-3-

that the Supreme Commander of the Allied Powers should "appoint special international courts" for the examination of the cases of war criminals in the Far East, the Soviet Government in its note of February 1, 1950, proposed to the Government of the USA, as well as to the Government of Great Britain, that a special international military court be appointed and that the Emperor of Japan, Hirohito, and Generals of the former Japanese Army Ishii Shiro, Kitano Masajo, Wakamatsu Yujiro, and Kasahara Yukio, be brought to trial before this court as war criminals, exposed in the commission of the most serious crimes against humanity.

In spite of the long period of time which has passed since February 1, 1950, and in spite of the fact that the Soviet Government on May 30 of this year sent a new note concerning this question to the Government of the USA, the Government of the United States of America up to the present time has not replied to the Soviet Government's note of February 1, 1950, a fact which is causing natural bewilderment also among wide public circles, which cannot tolerate any indulgence or protection with regard to war criminals convicted of preparing and conducting inhumane bacteriological warfare.

The Soviet Government considers it necessary to state that the Peoples Government of the Chinese Peoples Republic already has replied with assent to the proposal made by the Soviet Government in its note of February 1 of this year.

The Soviet Government expects that the Government of the USA, in accordance with obligations undertaken by

it concerning

it concerning the arraignment before a special military court of Emperor Hirohito and the other above mentioned war criminals, who have been exposed in the preparation of bacteriological warfare and in the use of bacteriological weapons.

Accept, Sir, assurances of my highest consideration.

/s/ A. Panyushkin

cc - NA - Mrs. Dunning
FE/P - Mr. Kroll
L/FE - Miss Fite
EE - Mr. Holder
American Embassy, Moscow

TRANSLATED: EUR: EE: DEBoster: mt
CHECKED: EUR: EE: DHHenry
12/15/50

编 后 记

真诚感谢 Sheldon H. Harris 教授（故）、松村高夫教授、粟屋宪太郎教授、吉见义明教授、林博史教授、Dr. Micheal Franzblau、Dr. Martin Furmanski、青木富贵子女士、西里扶甬子女士、Daniel Barenblatt 先生、James H. Hong 先生与我们慷慨分享你们珍贵的研究资料，并予以指导。

由衷感谢北京大学历史学系对本课题研究的理解和支持，以及本项目首席专家徐勇、臧运祜教授对编者自始至终的信任，使我们感受到作为重大攻关项目研究团队成员的光荣。

最为真挚的感谢献给世界抗日战争史实维护会美国各地的华侨朋友们，在我们逗留美国进行课题研究期间，为我们团队提供的应有尽有的帮助。本课题组取得的所有成绩均有着你们的功劳。

特别感谢上海交通大学东京审判研究中心研究员赵玉蕙、交通大学出版社编辑张洁为我们提供了近年公开的远东国际军事法庭国际检察局美国检察官们个人所藏文献资料。

自 1997 年起，编者近藤昭二与王选开始了美国国家档案馆等美国官方机构所藏日本细菌战相关资料整理研究的合作。2003 年，近藤昭二与王选第一次共同赴美国国家档案馆查阅文献资料，王选检索发现《陆军军医学校防疫研究报告・第 2 部》的英文翻译。编者奈须重雄先生开始检索日本国会图书馆博士论文库，近 8 年后，首次发现本资料集收入的 731 部队核心研究人员金子顺一的博士论文集。

2010 年，北京大学历史学系项目组派遣三位北大历史学系年轻优秀的研究生陈卓、宋芳芳、张会芳，随同编者赴美国国家档案馆查档近一月，每日帮助我们带着两台扫描机、数台照相机、五台手提电脑，赶公共班车，开馆最早到，闭馆最迟离开。为节省经费，集体租用在美华人民宅，去廉价超市购买食品，自己做饭。为了完成检索，任劳任怨。

防化指挥工程学院研究生刘斌、李杰、王良勇分工美国国家档案馆扫描资料的分类整理。原宁波大学细菌战调查会会员骆洲分工信息处理，上海市工艺美术研究所赵以方、原山东大学鲁西细菌战历史真相调查会会员常晓龙担当了工作量极大的 3000 页文献的页面处理。

这些年轻人投入了种种旁人难以想象的努力。最后加入我们团队的是鼎力支持我们的编辑邵璐璐，本资料集得以问世，多亏了她的不辞辛劳。

我们叩首致敬所有这个课题领域里为探索这段历史，在迷雾中为揭开真相，与我们共同艰苦耕耘的无名的同仁们，是你们不懈的努力使我们最终攀登到了“巨人的肩上”，使本资料集在许许多多双手一起步步向前推进中，而“诞生”。

编者委员会成员（按姓名拼音排列）

主　编:〔日〕近藤昭二　王　选

副主编：骆　洲　〔日〕奈须重雄

编委：

检索：陈　卓　宋芳芳　张会芳
分类：刘　斌　李　杰　王良勇
整理：常晓龙　赵以方